THE ANATOMY OF CENSORSHIP

BOOKS IN
LIBRARY AND INFORMATION SCIENCE

A Series of Monographs and Textbooks

EDITOR

ALLEN KENT

Director, Office of Communications Programs
University of Pittsburgh
Pittsburgh, Pennsylvania

Volume 1. CLASSIFIED LIBRARY OF CONGRESS SUBJECT HEADINGS, Volume 1—CLASSIFIED LIST, edited by James G. Williams, Martha L. Manheimer, and Jay E. Daily.

Volume 2. CLASSIFIED LIBRARY OF CONGRESS SUBJECT HEADINGS, Volume 2 — ALPHABETIC LIST, edited by James G. Williams, Martha L. Manheimer, and Jay E. Daily.

Volume 3. ORGANIZING NONPRINT MATERIALS by Jay E. Daily.

Volume 4. COMPUTER-BASED CHEMICAL INFORMATION, edited by Edward McC. Arnett and Allen Kent.

Volume 5. STYLE MANUAL: A GUIDE FOR THE PREPARATION OF REPORTS AND DISSERTATIONS by Martha L. Manheimer.

Volume 6. THE ANATOMY OF CENSORSHIP by Jay E. Daily.

Volumes in Preparation

Volume 7. INFORMATION SCIENCE: RECENT DEVELOPMENTS AND CHALLENGES, edited by Anthony Debons.

Volume 8. RESOURCE SHARING IN LIBRARIES, edited by Allen Kent.

Volume 9. CATALOGING AND CLASSIFICATION: A WORKBOOK by Martha L. Manheimer.

Additional volumes in preparation

THE ANATOMY
OF CENSORSHIP

Jay E. Daily

Graduate School of Library
and Information Sciences
University of Pittsburgh
Pittsburgh, Pennsylvania

MARCEL DEKKER, INC., New York 1973

MARCEL DEKKER, INC.

95 Madison Avenue, New York, New York 10016

LIBRARY OF CONGRESS CATALOG CARD NUMBER 72-95841

ISBN 0-8247-6065-4

PRINTED IN THE UNITED STATES OF AMERICA

For Jennifer

in Honor of our Travels

That we can be together, Love,

Makes all this fair planet home;

Our pendent globe,

Hung on the reach of space;

Our tiny jewel

Glowing with time.

PREFACE

Authors customarily write prefaces after all else is finished. This is especially wise if the subject is censorship, which has usually been approached on a historical basis. This book, however, investigates the motivations of censors, governmental and voluntary, so that the conclusions should hold true whatever the changes in the field of study. Its scope is worldwide although necessarily centered in the United States. In the year spent in completing the manuscript, checking and rechecking the documentation, and preparing the final copy, the field of study has changed somewhat but not nearly so much as in the past few days. It is now evident that a new era of censorship has begun.

On June 21, 1973, the U.S. Supreme Court (the use of the abbreviation seems acceptable because of the number of references) as reported in the *New York Times* for the following day, announced new guidelines for state and local obscenity laws, and in *Miller vs. California*, Chief Justice Warren E. Burger, speaking for the majority of five with four justices opposed, also gave trial judges the following to consider when presiding in cases derived from those laws.

"The basic guidelines for the trier of fact must be:

"(A) Whether the average person, applying contemporary community standards, would find that the work taken as a whole appeals to the prurient interest.

"(B) Whether the work depicts or describes, in a patently offensive way, sexual conduct specifically defined by the applicable state law, and:

"(C) Whether the work, taken as a whole, lacks serious literary, artistic, political, or scientific value."

At first reading, especially if one is offended by aggressive promotion of sexually-oriented materials, the guidelines appear to be an improvement over those developed in 1957 and 1966. All depends on a point that formed the basis of the decision. The community standards to be used are local, not national, and certainly not international. Further, the intent is to provide state and local governments with an interpretation of the First Amendment to the U.S. Constitution so that criminal proceedings will not infringe upon a protected area of human rights. Justice William O. Douglas, in his dissent as quoted in the *New York Times* of June 22, 1973, observed: "The court has worked hard to define obscenity and concededly has failed." Nevertheless, the decisions specifically provide that states may regulate commercialized exploitation of sex as it appears in books, periodicals, motion pictures, and plays. Because those who publish or distribute "obscene" materials are liable to criminal proceedings and punishment, librarians are imperilled along with other professionals who work in mass communications in the United States.

At issue is a question that has not yet been resolved and only recently could even be stated. Is obscenity a characteristic of materials or a judgement formed by an individual as he uses the materials? Justice Douglas is of the opinion that obscene materials are protected by the First Amendment and that a law to impose censorship should be based on a constitutional amendment that would clarify the issue. A long succession of decisions has affirmed that obscene materials are not protected by the First Amendment, as clearly stated in *Roth vs. United States* and restated by Chief Justice Burger. But if obscenity is a personal conclusion then at least a legal definition would derive in a democracy from a vote of the people. This is what Chief Justice Burger intended when he addresses state and local law-makers. We must some time decide whether or not such a vote is very much like a vote to determine the only true religion.

Research for this book began, rather by accident, late in 1962 and was to be concluded by design in 1973. In that decade, obscenity ended in the world community when Denmark withdrew from agreements begun in the League of Nations and continued by the United

Nations. A proposition investigated was that if obscenity ends anywhere in the world community then it will tend to end everywhere.
The events of the decade seemed to support the statement. Further
events will not so much test the statement as elaborate evidence,
because a trip around the world will not be needed to determine
whether the obscenity laws and practices of one locality will become
the model for all. As the new guidelines are applied, it will be rather
easy to see whether the liberality of Las Vegas or New York City
becomes the standard or the highly restrictive, if not foolish, standard of what Justice Douglas called "some benighted place." The
hitherto unresolved question of the extent of community standards
has been fully and definitely answered. Librarians, book-dealers, publishers, and theatre owners will have to look to the local community
and decide whether to accede to censorship or fight it. On this
decision very much depends, despite Chief Justice Burger's assertion
that " 'there is no evidence, empirical or historical,' " as quoted in
the *New York Times* issue of June 22, 1973, (p. 1, col. 8, continued
on p. 42, col. 6), "that censorship of sexual subjects in the 19th century 'in any way limited or affected expression of serious literary,
artistic, political or scientific ideas.' " A purpose of this book was
to show that such limitation did occur and, indeed, was inevitable.
Although ideation may not have been affected everywhere, certainly
expression of ideas was limited, and in some cases made impossible.

This may be interpreted as bias on the part of the author, who
should, if purely motivated by academic custom, argue both sides
of the censorship question. But what may be bias elsewhere is the
foundation of professional ethics for a librarian. He has no choice
whatever. He must either be so dedicated to the cause of intellectual
freedom that he will fight unendingly to preserve it or accept the
status of the clerk who checks out books in a library or the page
who shelves them when they are returned. Intellectual freedom is an
absolute that a free society may restrict only at its peril. Censorship that is meant only to include the worst of the examples of

sex-exploitation will move from offensive details to unpopular ideas at a speed determined by the passivity of a given community as it faces the erosion of its freedom. Censorship is contagious and highly profitable.

Sex-exploitation had reached the point where saturation of the market would have reduced its appeal almost to the vanishing point. The U.S. Supreme Court decision could restore vigor to the sex-exploitation industry which had to rely on fraudulent practices to obtain the profits voluntary censors always imagined but dealers rarely if ever realized. Selective raids on uncooperative dealers and theatre owners assure a corrupt police organization of bribes by compliant persons and generally are effective in raising the going price for operating without restraint. Driving the sex-exploitation industry underground will save it by conferring the only value its products can have. As forbidden communication, the products of the industry need no longer compete with other material. A cheaply produced book or motion picture can be sold illicitly at very high prices, and even if some localities refuse to control sex-exploitation outlets, the dealers can raise prices and forget their worries over the quality of the material as the curious beat a track to their doors. Seen in this light, censorship may do much to popularize vacations in large cities where the products of the sex-exploitation industry are readily available.

There seemed to be no point in continuing research in the field until the adventitious decision of the U.S. Supreme Court made this preface necessary. The reader is asked to determine for himself whether the conclusions of this book hold true as the new era of censorship continues. Librarians are asked to use this book as it helps in their necessary battle for intellectual freedom, aided, it is hoped, by all who use libraries and agree. In a vote to determine what shall be considered obscene, it is possible to agree with Justice William J. Brennan, Jr., in his dissent in the Paris Theatre Case, as quoted in the *New York Times* cited above: "I would hold, therefore, that at least in the absence of distribution to juveniles or obtrusive exposure to unconsenting adults, the First and 14th Amendments prohibit the state and Federal governments from attempting wholly to suppress sexually-oriented materials on the basis of their allegedly 'obscene' contents." That is, obscenity is not cause for prosecution, although it may be regulated to prevent exposure to unconsenting adults and distribution to juveniles. This would seem to justify localities in making licensing laws that specify methods of advertisement and punish distribution to juveniles. It would leave police organizations free of the need to act as literary critics and with such obvious crimes as fraud to detect in addition to violations of the licensing laws. It would obviate the use of obscenity laws as a means of obtaining publicity while displaying civic virtue and personal morality for all to see.

In previous versions of this preface, a call to battle was issued in a weak, tinny fashion because it seemed unnecessary. That may still be the case, depending on the actions of those who believe that censorship is essential to assure public morality. If guided by the desires of corrupt law enforcement agencies, politicians who see no other means of finding the limelight, and voluntary censors motivated by an overwhelming fear that their own sex fantasies will be made public, then a repetition of history is inevitable. From increasing restriction of public communication will come, after much toil and trouble and vast expense, the so-called permissiveness that ended with the U.S. Supreme Court decision on June 21, 1973.

Just what character the continuing fight for intellectual freedom will take on remains at this point unknown, though it should be soon revealed. A librarian as he builds a collection has no morals, no politics, and no religion; he is bound solely to serve the interests of his community, hopefully in broadening them, but always in respecting them. The difference between selection and censorship is even more difficult, but a good guide is the collection as it now stands. Community standards are, after all, determined only by the free use of material representative of all in the communication process. Voluntary censors who invade the library to impose their point of view on the community may believe that the recent decision of the U.S. Supreme Court is a search warrant that gives them the right to confiscate and destroy everything to which they have an objection, as often political as allegedly obscene. It is clear, however, that the decision attempts to put in legal form the disapprobation that the sex-exploitation industry has gained in its pursuit of profits, especially among those citizens of middle age who have been exposed to sexually-oriented materials without full consent. Library schools must now include studies in the field of censorship in order to educate professionals who know how to fight for intellectual freedom.

The research dropped with much relief to myself and my wife will have to continue, because the key is once again how society will treat homosexuality. Will the Gay Synagogue in New York City be closed in a general wave of revulsion? What effect will the decision have on what are called here "raunchy romances?" How devastating will be decisions in "benighted places?" Can they truly reduce the whole communication process to the level that was attained by the Cockburn decision? Is the standard to be the most oblique discussion in pseudo-scientific terminology? Is the citizenry ready to abandon stereotypes? Will authors of homosexual novels be wanted for violating the obscenity laws in various places throughout the country? Will publishers of such fiction learn to distinguish quality from exploitation? Will the publishers face prosecution in a hit or miss fashion here and there throughout the land? Will the trial of *Therese and Isabelle* be repeated endlessly? (Diacritical marks are omitted intentionally because of the author's conviction that proper names in English translation acquire English spelling.)

The author of a preface generally concludes by explaining any deviant conventions of style, as indicated above, and by thanking those who aided him. It is only necessary to add that a dislike of footnotes is reflected in the documentation which has been put at the end of the text where my own method of citation would be less obtrusive.

Rather than listing all those with a major part in my research, whom I remember and to whom I am deeply indebted (friends, students, and colleagues) I limit my expressions of gratitude to those individuals who might possibly be blamed for my errors and to the officials of the University of Pittsburgh who awarded me sabbatical leave in 1971 so that I could travel around the world again collecting data at my own expense leaving me accountable to no one for my conclusions: Chancellor Wesley Posvar, Dr. Charles Peake, then Provost, and Dr. Harold Lancour, now Dean Emeritus. Mr. William Nasri and Professor Allen Kent encouraged me to expand into book form two articles "Censorship, Contemporary and Controversial Aspects of," and "Erotica," published in the *Encyclopedia of Library and Information Science* after a fellow editor, Dr. Lancour, inspired me in the first place. Mr. William Snyder assisted me in the documentation of those two articles and Ms. Marylin Smith in the documentation of this book. Mr. Frank Williams aided me in the indexing of the book by taking on all the proper names and leaving me only the nouns of substance. Ms. Darlene Fawcett typed earlier versions of the manuscript, but the heavy work of preparing the final copy was accomplished by Ms. Barbara Wonders, who is without peer as a typist. The publisher edited the manuscript thoroughly but flexibly so that any errors of fact or of statement are the result of my own inattention or aberrant preferences.

There are three necessary exceptions to the rule established. The proprietor of Jay's Book Stall offered friendly advice, guidance, and much encouragement, as well as research data, and is for me the ideal example of a reputable book dealer. Ms. Frances Kotler made my work much easier because of the help she gave my wife with unflagging interest and encouragement. A research topic as demanding as censorship imposes burdens that few can understand. Obviously I cannot thank my wife sufficiently, though I enjoy trying, for her wit, patience, encouragement, suggestions, and the endless love and patience that have made me a happy man. Hopefully, even with research renewed, we will not have to attend X-rated movies in first class theatres where we both fall asleep, bored out of consciousness.

The products of the sex-exploitation industry have very little to recommend them and would never be defended, except that thought control by an all-wise officialdom, however benevolent, is much worse. It is my firm conviction that those who believe they cannot be trusted with their moral future will find that they cannot be trusted with their political future either. The battle is now joined afresh, and hopefully it will be waged as a renewed interest in intellectual freedom and a demand that sexually explicit material be of literary, artistic, political, or scientific value, and of historical value if it applies. This will occur if the demand comes not from legislatures, city councils, policemen, voluntary censorship groups, juries, judges, and Supreme Court justices but from an informed public free to exercise choice in the marketplace of ideas.

Jay E. Daily

Graduate School of Library
  and Information Sciences
University of Pittsburgh
June 26, 1973

TABLE OF CONTENTS

THE ANATOMY OF CENSORSHIP

Part One

THE PATHETIC AGONY

I.

DON'T TOUCH MY DIRTY WORDS

The Irrational in the Communication Process

A young seminarian, when only five years old, was faced with the indignity of a bath at the hands of a jittery maiden aunt two dozen years his senior. His mother, who usually supervised ablutions and did much of the washing, was in the hospital giving birth to his sister. His grandmother, a nurse, was assisting her, and the maiden aunt was the only adult in the house who could take on the job. Her greatest worry was a detail of hygiene carefully explained by sister-in-law and grandmother. (None of the males in the family had been circumcised unless phimosis was evident.) The nephew protested and argued to no avail, until finally he proposed, rather grumpily, "You can give me a bath, but don't touch my dirty words." The agreement suited both the aunt and the nephew.

The story illustrates a central fact about what is meant here by the word 'censorship.' It is purposefully used as a higher order abstraction, in Hayakawa's sense, to mean the aversion we have for other people's dirty words and the protective attitude we assume for our own. This is a treatise on the irrational in the communication process, the wellspring from which we draw many of our attitudes and those prior assumptions that constitute the silent language of human communities everywhere. Censorship forbids knowledge of works already in the communication stream. Suppression would stop the stream itself. The Latin term *censura praevia*, always claimed as a privilege of the Roman Catholic Church, is roughly translated as 'suppression.' The First Amendment of the U.S. Constitution was specifically designed to prevent legal action of this kind, although open suppression prior to publication was secured in the Federal courts for the original *Valachi Papers*. Though unsuccessful, newspapers in the United States and abroad, were involved in the attempted suppression of what was later published as *The Pentagon Papers*.*

*Notes beginning p. 347.

3

From the study of censorship and suppression, an insight into the human condition is gained that no other research affords. One example is language itself, the curious fact that our words have many more meanings than any dictionary can list, and yet we do not have a sufficient supply. Semantic analysis is the process of establishing the meaning of words as found in context. It is the first step toward lexicology, the correct listing of words with their conventional meanings. Without considering what dirty words are and why they affect all human communication, we get only a limited view of our topic. We are like those psychologists who successfully avoided the mention of sex until Freud and Havelock Ellis demonstrated why this was ruinous if scientific objectivity were to prevail.

Returning to our seminarian in his childhood, the proper word for penis in the family was 'cuckoo.' The mother would tell the boy that he must wash his 'cuckoo' whenever he had a bath, precisely what the boy's father said. When he was younger and tended to fondle his penis, or grab onto it because it seemed so important to everyone, he was told not to handle his 'cuckoo.' Like most little boys he learned the slang word for penis and was told that it was a dirty word. Hence he had a choice of words to use when arguing with his aunt. "You can give me a bath but don't touch my cock," he could have said. "You can give me a bath but don't touch my cuckoo," would have had the same net effect with the advantage that it would not have shocked the aunt. He chose to say that his dirty words were to be inviolate because he had already made a distinction between the lexicology of his private language and that of the world around him.

The person telling this story has to be careful not to say that the maiden aunt had a distaste for dirty words. Suddenly, in the context of the story, the word distaste is armed with all its connotations of eating, and granting what 'dirty words' means in the context of the story, the reader will come to a false conclusion that is both quite true and highly inappropriate. In the jargon of communications, a message must have a sender and a receiver as well as a means of successful transmission from the one to the other. If the study of communication stopped there, it would simply be another division of an engineering or other applied physical science. The moment we begin investigating the purpose of the message and its effects, we have jumped into the social sciences. When we discuss interrupted messages, we are in the midst of applied social science as represented by library and information science.

Librarians have fought censorship vigorously for the past fifty years, and they have almost always won, especially if there was a public battle. When Senator Joseph McCarthy's travelling critics, Roy Cohn and G. David Schine, condemned the bookstock of United States Information Service libraries around the world, the American Library Association was the first to contradict the junior Senator from Wisconsin and his peripatetic assistants. It took nerve to challenge the Senator, who called any opponent a Communist. Librarians have fought censorship openly only since John Cotton Dana led the way in the period of the first World War. Today one of the important areas of the Association is in its Committee on Intellectual Freedom, which has funds and determination, so that no librarian has to accede passively to attempts at censorship.

Prior to Dana's courageous actions in Newark, New Jersey, the librarian was involved in concepts of public morality and his own role as missionary among those who needed conversion. Librarians worried over how to keep immoral novels off their shelves and at least away from the public. In fact, in many libraries at present, the worry is the same although the availability of literature has changed. The librarian has his dirty words too, and he may express his aversion by locking up books in a windowless wooden case shaped like a wardrobe but with shelves in place of hangers. One librarian of the author's acquaintance had no such convenient depository, but by pasting wrapping paper over the glass doors of an old bookcase, she achieved the desired result. The college students who served as pages were protected from items in the collection offending, it must be made clear, the librarian not the patrons.

The librarian was acting irrationally, and to the author's mind unethically, in forcing her aversions onto the public. But all censorship is irrational to the degree that conclusions about the effects of the message are drawn without basis in fact or science. We are all involved in the games of word magic that make the metonymy of one bird's name suitable and another crude, a dirty word, for an organ that every male mammal possesses. In fact, when the author learned the family euphemism, he was bound to observe that the word 'cuckoo' represented a high degree of metaphor because the bird lays its eggs in the nest of another species of bird. "Cock, cuckoo, prick, yard, member, piece, tool, organ, rod," one friend observed, "are only a few of the names used for a man's prize possession."

We must go to a foreign language to find a word for the male organ of generation that is not also the name of something else. We hold the penis in greatest respect, a kind of sacred object, deserving the highest form of worship in a verbal sense by having an unutterable name. We call it 'phallus' using the Greek word for an image or representation of the penis as the reproductive organ worshipped in the Dionysiac festivals. Psychoanalysts since Freud have explored the meaning of the penis in the silent language of each of us, and authors such as Philip Roth have used their lucubrations as the basis of their plots. The fact that in English all the names for the penis are derived from foreign sources or are extensions of meaning of native words gives rise to much verbal humor. The other taboo words used for the act of procreation and the female generative organ are of a different sort.

The derivation of the taboo word for the external female genitalia is readily traced. The Latin word, which Cicero avoided because he considered it obscene, is *cunnus*, interestingly a masculine noun of the second declension. It was used for animals as well as human beings, and by a transfer of meaning came to signify a lewd woman, as used by Horace, among other authors. The word 'cunny' is to be found in the suppressed works of the nineteenth century, especially *My Secret Life*. The common English vulgarism is 'cunt.' It is proper to the thing named, not in the sense that 'cunt' is the sort of word to employ while speaking with a maiden aunt, but in the sense of being precise in its meaning and conveying this idea even when used in extension by transfer of meaning or as the substance of metaphor. It is one of the rare taboo words that are not themselves the result of metaphor or metonym. The word is ancient and inescapably direct, traceable to the Greek and even to the Sanskrit, where it has been transliterated as *cushi* meaning ditch. The Greek word, *kusos* is rather far from *cunnus* but the relationship is there. It was not the most common word among the Romans who generally preferred the word 'pudenda,' the neuter plural of the gerund derived from *pudeo*, *pudere*, meaning to be ashamed. The choice word for the medical writers of the nineteenth century was 'pudenda,' which was accepted as the correct scientific term for a taboo topic, rather than a taboo word in its own right.

It might seem that a taboo word like 'cunt' would not lend itself to the word play associated with the variety of words that mean 'penis.' But the possible rhymes and puns are numberless, so that even Fletcher in *The Spanish Curate* has the witticism: "They spell *sunt* with a C." The Latin word is to be found among the taboo words of almost every Romance language transformed by much usage into the phonemic patterns of the common tongue, for instance the French *con*. Because the word 'cunt' is so taboo there are as many euphemisms and alternate expressions as there are words that mean 'penis.' Some of these are derived from the words of things that convey a visual image, like 'gash' or 'trench.'

English can boast of the most taboo word known to modern European languages, 'fuck,' of very doubtful origins but very old and not always taboo, at least among certain people at certain times.

In censorship trials, the number of times the word is used is some-times offered as evidence that a work is obscene. The censoring of Lillian Smith's novel *Strange Fruit* was ostensibly based not on its civil libertarian point of view but on the use of the word 'fuck.' The word is an essential element in the plot of J. D. Salinger's novel *The Catcher in the Rye*, and its use there is one of the reasons that the book has been the key issue in several censorship proceedings. An essay containing the word is likely to be censored even though the topic is the furthest from sexuality that one can imagine. It is the choice word of graffiti in the English-speaking countries because there is a connotation of defiance in simply writing or uttering the word. The Danish publisher who entitled his pornographic picture magazine *Fucking* could not have chosen a more apt but less accept-able name.

The words 'fuck,' 'cunt,' and 'prick' can, until the U.S. Supreme Court rules otherwise, get you arrested, especially if you utter them over the telephone. Until very recently, a Georgia law prevented the use of such words altogether, but the Supreme Court ruled that the law was vague. It is also unenforceable. The word 'prick' was mild enough so that Shakespeare could work a trope on it in one of his sonnets. "Since nature pricked thee out for women's pleasure . . ." Some critics of the Bowdler school of textual analysis have insisted that the word is 'tricked' in the mistaken belief that Shakespeare would never have written anything of which they would disapprove. In an era when the common people still wore codpieces, Shakespeare used the word 'prick' because it was rich with ambiguity and humor. The word 'prick;' possibly because it is also an epithet, has become virtually as taboo as the word 'cunt.'

Another taboo word that has only one meaning, derived from the French where it is not taboo, and perhaps losing its status rapidly in English is 'piss' from the Old French *pissier* allied to modern French *pisser*, probably of echoic origin. (The word has a sound that is appropriate for what it denotes.) Some dictionaries list the word as 'vulgar,' and others do not list it at all. At one point, saying 'pee' was about like saying 'what the h- - -' but now 'pee' has become as taboo as 'piss.' Its concomitant execretory word is now completely taboo, although used by some writers of Old English, for 'shit' or 'shite' was once the accepted word, the past tense, 'shitted,' indicating that it is grammatically a weak verb, not 'shat' as sometimes seen in modern fiction.

All these words indicate the censor in us. We hate to use them in proportion to the frequency with which we are confronted by them. If we see a word very rarely but are quite aware of its denotation and connotation, we will feel especially uncomfortable uttering it. As we use the words more appropriately and more often in situations calling for them, they lose their threat. They are taboo because of the restrictions placed upon them, and they gain these restrictions because the emotional charge they release is far stronger than that of other words. Language is a vehicle of emotion, refined by human beings to be capable of the subtlest feelings as well as the most intense. Taboo words become oaths because they release emotion. We can swear by uttering the unutterable names of a god or by uttering words that are obscene, vulgar, improper, as our mood strikes us. Everyone tends to establish certain words as beyond the pale and others as very mild. Furthermore, the various communities of people tend to set up their own standards of propriety. 'Damn' is so mild an oath that it is scarcely noticed and the television networks allow its use on certain occasions. When Clark Gable uttered this word in a technicolor scene at the end of a long movie, the epoch of utter propriety came to an end. *Gone With the Wind* brought dirty words to the purity of the silver screen.

This change in the status of taboo words is part of the dynamism of language. Robert Heinlein in his novel *The Door Into Summer* with its theme of time thwarted invents a taboo word 'kinky' with variant forms 'kink' and 'kinking' that is very much worse than any at present. The hero discovers that his audience is very much shocked when he uses the word inappropriately. Anyone who has learned a foreign language, especially one outside the Western tradition, knows that a word that seems mild can have a profound effect on teachers and anyone else with whom the word is used. The emotional charge of words is learned *en famille*, where 'cuckoo' is considered rather affectionate and 'prick' is too taboo even for the *paterfamilias*. Not that the word 'cuckoo' could be used everywhere, but if you just have to refer to your penis then that is the word you will find has the right effect on the receiver of your message.

Students of Spanish soon learn that innocent words in one country are obscene in another; even the strength of oaths varies. *Carajo* means something like 'darn' in Puerto Rico, and it is much worse than 'goddam' in Mexico. *Bicho* is a good word for insect in Argentina and a terrible word in Puerto Rico, where it means 'prick.' One would not buy papaya in Cuba, unless he wanted a prostitute, no *fruta de bomba* in Peru, where he would simply not be understood. *Chingar* is a very vulgar Mexican word that has no meaning whatever in other Spanish-speaking countries.

The problem becomes even more complicated when interlingual accidents are considered. A 'low' person would be understood as a very vulgar expression in Burma, and the name 'Lola' is a dirty pun. The word pronounced very much like the English 'low' or 'lo' means nothing but 'fuck' in Burma, and 'la,' or its Burmese equivalent, means 'come here.' The name given to a female cat who took up residence in my compound at the University of Mandalay because of a handsome tomcat was the occasion of great glee on the part of Burmese cook and Burmese driver, because the word 'Lola' exactly expressed what we thought of the cat who came to stay.

It is important to remember that the discomfort felt by one person may not be shared by another. The younger generation is in the habit of using words that would cause Victorian ladies to faint. Take the vilest word you can think of and say it often enough and it loses its meaning. As the word 'fuck' gets to be commonplace, it is no longer an act of defiance to write it in chalk anywhere. As black leaders use the word 'motherfucker,' it becomes a part of accepted speech. In the motion picture, *Where's Poppa?*, it is spelled strangely and employed as the name of a character—it becomes no longer the worst word among the variety of taboo expressions but an indication of the status, if not the race, of the speaker. To many individuals such epithets as 'kike' and 'nigger' are far more taboo than any of the words discussed above. Censorship proceedings, however, have been based on the use of taboo words, among them sacred words or ideas, for the taboo includes the sacred as well as the profane.

To some individuals, the word 'virgin' is taboo. The late Cardinal Spellman condemned the motion picture *The Moon is Blue* because the word was uttered as a part of the dialogue in surroundings which suggested sexuality rather than prayer. A euphemism is generally proposed when the word is employed to mean 'untried' or 'initial.' However, the word is too deeply engrained into the life of the community to be extricated or replaced by a euphemism. The state of Virginia was, after all, named for Elizabeth I of England, the Virgin Queen. A significant part of the Roman Catholic liturgy would have to be revised if the word became as taboo as the word 'mother' in Huxley's novel *Brave New World*.

In the ancient Jewish religion, the name of God was a deep secret known only to a few men of great importance in the tribe. It was a fearful sin to utter this secret name aloud, "in vain." The commandment loses its force if the name of God is known to everyone, as in the words "Jesus Christ." In general, in English, the name of the founder of the Christian religion is sacred and not to be used for such frivolous purposes as the uttering of oaths. In Spanish-speaking countries the name of Jesus is quite acceptable as a man's name, and some women in religion take the name *Circoncision* meaning quite literally "Circumcision."

From time to time, an author in the field of clinical psychology will prescribe oaths as a good means of relieving bottled feelings that can cause gastric ulcers, hypertension, headaches, and other psychosomatic ailments. This recognizes the emotional charge that such words carry. A good, and quite innocent method, is to utter a euphemism for the worst word you can think of, that which carries the strongest taboo. A member of the Catholic group, The Holy Name Society, when provoked beyond this limit of tolerance would exclaim "Holy Name" to serve him as well as the completely taboo "Jesus Christ." The violation of a taboo causes a distinct emotional response, intense to the degree of the taboo defied. A mild societal infraction may cause only slight titillation, but a major taboo purposefully, possibly angrily, set at naught will cause emotional shock waves that ebb and flow as guilt and defiance alternate. This occurs among individuals who have no fear of supernatural consequences. Primitive people may violate a taboo inadvertently, but even so they will experience terror in anticipating the consequences.

For instance, the Burmese believe in *nat*, the invisible spirits that inhabit lakes, trees, mountainsides, rocks, and roads. Each *nat* has to be placated in the particular way he prefers. The *nat* of the road from Mandalay to Maymyo hates the number nine. (English-speaking foreigners would understand if he hated the number eight, pronounced just like 'shit' in English with a slight difference in the quality of the final 't.') If there are eight passengers on a bus the driver will pick up a big rock, call it Mr. Stone, and give it a ride up the mountain in order to deceive the *nat*. Those not educated in Burmese animism would consider the *nat* of the Maymyo road a superstition, not the source of a taboo. Doubters are told story after story of wrecks that occurred when nine people were aboard a moving vehicle. The spot where a bus failed to negotiate one of the hairpin turns is shown as the final proof. There were eight passengers and the driver, who was careless. He simply failed to count how many he was carrying until it was too late; and the *nat* shoved the bus off the road, down the steep hillside to death and destruction. The road is dangerous enough without having an angry *nat* threatening all aboard. It winds and twists for over half of its forty-two miles.

This kind of proof is a logical fallacy given the Latin name *post hoc ergo propter hoc* meaning that once a thing occurs it is held to be the cause of a subsequent event. There is no necessary causal relationship between the eight passengers aboard the bus and the accident that occurred, although there is a good chance that the driver's fear of consequences so altered his co-ordination and speed of reflex that he failed to drive around the hairpin curve in a way that would have avoided the accident. It is poor scholarship to assign causes to human activity without extensive and difficult research.

The Paranoid Prophecy

One step beyond the simple foolishness of *post hoc ergo propter hoc* is the paranoid prophecy that because X is associated with an event Y, then Y is caused by X. This is demonstrated by the belief that widespread immorality caused the fall of Rome and the insistence that widespread immorality will cause the fall of the present civilization. In order to preserve our society, the argument goes, we must avoid immorality in every form. Granting that each of us has his dirty words, does it follow that when they are touched history is changed? The difficulty with the fall-of-Rome argument is that first of all, the barbarians who invaded were, in their minds, liberating the city, or at least punishing their oppressors of many centuries. While the glory that was Rome got trounced and its treasures stolen or ruined as the Vandals, Goths, and Visigoths had their innings, the immorality of ancient Rome had gone beyond the pietism of early Christianity into the perplexities of Christianity as a state religion. Constantine's edict making Christianity the religion of Rome long preceded the invasion by the barbarians, and according to some historians was more the cause of the fall than any immorality.

We would have to define immorality much more closely, in any case. Public morality is not simply a matter of the Judeo-Christian tradition any more. Linguistic taboos depend on the language involved, so that in a language like Korean or Japanese with verb forms indicating the relative social position of the speaker and the person he is speaking to, it is easy to fall into error and fail to observe the niceties that conventions demand. A westerner using either language has to be especially careful not to offend his oriental friends by assigning them too high or too low a station in life. The verb form carries its emotional charge reinforced by the tone of voice and the speed of utterance. In all languages of this type it is possible to utter a taboo word simply by getting the verb form incorrect.

Public morality is mostly a chimera and deserves the same kind of anatomization that is the substance of this book. But an anatomy assumes the existence of an organized body, and public morality is not so organized as may appear to the sophist seeking to find a usable idea to support his predilections. In the development of heterogeneous societies there is a diversity not only of religious but also of moral concepts. As the communication process becomes technologically more advanced, the community of this planet enlarges until we must consider a world community as the most heterogenous of all societies to date. The extent to which this community will enjoy the kind of governance of present societies is much in doubt, but one of the truisms of the communication process is that given a receiver for a message the behavior of the sender as well as the receiver tends to alter, especially if feedback occurs.

Feedback is the jargon word for a very important characteristic of the human as well as many other kinds of brains. Computers, once quite incorrectly called giant brains, include feedback loops so that subsequent activity is based on the results of activity performed. Human beings are engaged in closed-loop feedback systems almost all the time, designating the method as trial and error, the practice that makes perfect, and experimentation, as the activity may suggest. At an earlier period in time, it was not possible to examine censorship as an organized body of beliefs because there was no feedback that could delineate its structure.

But the world finds itself in one of those great upheavals of thought and behavior when experimentation is promoted and the *status quo* is under heavy attack. Censorship had its peak when Lord Cockburn (pronounced as if spelled Coburn) decreed a rule of law in the trial of violations of obscenity laws. This occurred on May 27, 1867, in the case of *Regina vs. Hicklin* as included in *Censorship Landmarks* compiled by De Grazia. The United States was in the midst of the Johnson administration with its fight-to-the-death partisan conflict over the Secretary of War and executive privilege. Not a year later, Johnson was to be tried by the Senate and miss impeachment by only one vote. Seward purchased Alaska from Russia that year. Dickens's latest novel, *Our Mutual Friend* was considered not nearly so exciting as his previous triumph, *Tale of Two Cities*. He was working on his next novel though, *Edwin Drood*, which he failed to complete before his death in 1870. Trollope's *Last Chronicle of Barset* was published that year and Wagner's *Die Meistersinger von Nurnberg* was completed. The Atlantic cable was in operation after the first successful voyage laying it had ended the year before. Only telegraph messages could be sent back and forth between England and the New World, but the communication revolution on a worldwide scale had begun, unnoticed, as Lord Cockburn said in his judgement, ". . . I think the test of obscenity is this, whether the tendency of the matter charged as obscenity is to deprave and corrupt those whose minds are open to such immoral influences, and into whose hands a publication of this sort may fall."

This is not entirely an historical anatomy, hence the twistings and turnings of law from Lord Cockburn's day to the *End of Obscenity*, as Charles Rembar calls it, are not of great moment here except as the high points illuminate a segment we might otherwise miss. The decision of the Danish Council to revoke Section 235 of the Penal

Code marked the end of obscenity in the world community. Although the law was finally passed in June, 1969, the vital decisions were taken several years earlier, and in any case a year's notice had to be given the United Nations because Denmark chose to withdraw from its treaties regarding obscenity.

This does not mean that censorship ended in Denmark. The Danes are very leery of violence, to the extent that wild animal acts with pistol, whip and chair are not permitted in the circus. Section 234 of the Penal Code was not revoked in its entirety, so that restrictions on material sold to children remain. However, all those sections dealing with pornography in printed form, in motion pictures, and in live displays and shows were revoked, as soon as Denmark withdrew from the 1923 Convention on Pornography.

In the world community, if pornography is available anywhere, it is available everywhere, above the counter or sold secretly. Attempts at import from the United States may fail because of custom and postal regulations, but there is no need for an American to buy his pornography abroad. According to Palle Birkelund, Director of the National Library of Denmark, most of the lurid Danish picture books are made from films that originate in the United States and are printed in color in West Germany. Denmark is really the marketing, rather than the production, center of pornography, and in fact, the quantity and quality of pornography is the same in Denmark as it is in the United States, depending on the cities used for comparison. Danish cities that are rarely visited by tourists have very little pornography for sale, because it is not bought by the citizens. Copenhagen's pornography business is scarcely thriving and it virtually closes down when the tourist season ends.

The United States arrived at the position where pornography is available in most cities by accident rather than by design. The law was attacked first when Random House imported James Joyce's novel *Ulysses*. On December 6, 1933, Judge John M. Woolsey offered his literate and important opinion, changing Lord Cockburn's rule of law by making the "person with average sex instincts" the test of whether the book would "stir the sex impulses . . . lead to sexually impure and lustful thoughts." "But my considered opinion, after long reflection, is that, whilst in places the effect of 'Ulysses' on the reader undoubtedly is somewhat emetic, nowhere does it tend to be an aphrodisiac," Judge Woolsey concluded. His decision was upheld in the U.S. Circuit Court of Appeals, with one dissent.

The second change began with the Roth decision of the U.S. Supreme Court handed down on June 24, 1957. A definition of obscenity was offered in the case of *Roth vs. U.S.* that has been widely applied since. In a legal sense, obscenity is material judged as a whole that is patently offensive to current community standards by exceeding the bounds of candor and shame without any redeeming social importance whatever. A spate of cases hit the courts five years later testing this definition thoroughly, and the end result of each of these cases was to diminish the power of the government to banish pornography or extirpate it. These legal battles ended with the publication of *Lady Chatterley's Lover* by D. H. Lawrence. *Memoirs of a Woman of Pleasure* by John Cleland, and Henry Miller's *Tropic of Cancer*. If community limits of candor were set by these books, then there was little in the way of verbal information in printed form that could be censored.

The paranoid prophecy had to be debated and tested when all along it was true, at least in the assumption that "obscene, lewd, lascivious, lustful" works could be said to lead to widespread sex acts, but not of a criminal sort. In fact, the authors of such legislation probably never supposed that so drastic a result would come from the censored books; more likely they would "excite the sex impulses" and if they did not do that, they would "lead to sexually impure and lustful thoughts." The early definitions of obscenity did not presume that sex murders resulted from the perusal of censored books because the rapists and murderers of the time could not read at the level the books attained. What usually follows the perusal of obscene, lewd, sex books is masturbation, but the act may follow looking at catalogues or mirrors as well, in fact may begin when the eyes are shut and only fantasies prevail.

There is a principle of scientific method that could have resolved much of the difficulty fought out in many court battles. If two independent research projects using different methodology arrive at the same conclusion, the hypothesis must be accepted until more refined research methods are available. In fact, there is not a good way of disproving such a hypothesis, and that is precisely what has occurred in the world community. The U.S. National Commission on Obscenity and Pornography and the Danish Council undertook tests of the hypothesis that pornography caused sex crimes and discovered that it did not. The sex criminal is a very complicated person who is not likely to have collected pornography and who is no more influenced by it to commit a crime of sex molestation of children, sex with violence, or sexual assault through threats of violence, than he is by the telephone book or other printed matter that he obtains regularly, with the possible exception of the daily newspaper. There is evidence that descriptions of violence do incite violent acts, especially in those who have no defenses against their murderous thoughts.

Evidence from Denmark seems to show that pornography has a cathartic effect, and if it is assumed that masturbation in private is not a sex crime, then no sex crime results. In the nineteenth century, masturbation was a dreadful sin, a threat to good health, and a social problem of some magnitude, at least in the minds of physicians and religious leaders who inveighed against it. Medical opinion had done an about-face, in this regard, and the man with sex problems who uses pornography as a stimulant is much more likely to take the edge off his sexual appetite by masturbating than he is to go out and find a means of satisfying himself by violating the rights of others and the strictures of the law.

The paranoid prophecy rests upon the moral superiority of censors who find themselves uniquely able to protect the public from the sexually impure thoughts arising from material that brings dirty words, usually those of the censors, to light. Librarians who assert a professional right to keep the stream of communication open must leave the grandstand of passive disapproval and enter the arena of conflict. Public trials are long, extremely hard on the nerves, dangerous, and frustrating. What happened in Pittsburgh in 1968 could happen anywhere. Change the names, or pretend that you know all about Allegheny County, Pennsylvania, and when a new film challenges the community standards of candor and shame, the section below will be repeated.* The emotional coloration has not been edited away, because a participant remembers that better than the details.

The Strange Affair of Therese and Isabelle

As is often the case with a *cause celebre*, the Guild Theatre case began slowly and simply with a mordant review of the film *Therese and Isabelle* by Win Fanning, published in the Pittsburgh *Post Gazette*. Taken from Violette Leduc's novel, which in itself was derived from *La Bâtarde*, her autobiography, the motion picture included music by Georges Auric and much of the dialogue included in the novel. The film dealt with lesbianism in a girl's school, this time in France. Fanning's use of the word 'filthy' excited the late Justice Michael A. Musmanno of the Supreme Court of the Commonwealth of Pennsylvania to insist that District Attorney Robert A. Duggan do something about the floods of pornography which were endangering Allegheny County. Justice Musmanno was nothing if not verbal, and he loved to see his statements in the mass media, even though his habit of mixing metaphors had gained him the Homeric standing epithet, 'the homogenizer of picturesque speech.'

District Attorney Robert A. Duggan is a Republican in a camp of Democrats. He had then been re-elected for a second term and confidently thought that the endangered citizens of the County were

*For instance, *Deep Throat*.

on his side. Very likely a majority were, as later events seemed to demonstrate. In any case, the local chapter of Citizens for Decent Literature found him receptive to their pleas that the obscenity laws of the Commonwealth be enforced. Thus moved, it seemed, by the powers of the law and a ground swell of local pressure groups, Mr. Duggan sent a group of twelve persons, a kind of *ad hoc* jury, to see the film. During the showing, which began at eight in the evening, of July 19th, the first jury—make up of members of the Knights of Columbus and Citizens for Decent Literature—came to the conclusion that the film was obscene, and one of their group telephoned Mr. Duggan to come rescue the county. He and his assistants arrived in squad cars which had travelled at top speed with sirens ululating, and while one member of the staff stopped the film, Mr. Duggan announced to the stunned audience that he was conducting a raid and those who did not leave at once would be taken away in a paddy wagon. His remarks were very effective in clearing the theatre of some two hundred potential passengers.

A week of legal struggle began, conducted out of sight of the public, ending with a hearing in the Common Pleas Court of Judge David Weiss. Judge Robert Van der Voort had refused to hear the case, and Judge John G. Brosky, it came to light, had issued an injunction against the film before the *ad hoc* jury's report was in, apparently because he agreed with Mr. Duggan's staff that the finding of the members would be such as to justify a swift injunction.

The First Hearing

On a warm July 26th, after the University of Pittsburgh's *Pitt News* had reported the dissatisfaction of such students and faculty of the Graduate School of Library and Information Sciences as wished to make known their grievance, Mr. Teitelbaum, appearing for the defense, and Mr. Paris, appearing for the District Attorney's office, argued the dubious legality of the injunction before Judge Weiss, along with Mr. Thomas Kerr, of the American Civil Liberties Union, whose *amicus curiae* brief gave the general position of the civil libertarians. In attendance were members of the Citizens for Decent Literature, of an organization called the Catholic Daughters of America, and four librarians who had organized to let their opinions be known, because some members of the Library School were aggrieved that censorship had reappeared in Allegheny County. These four persons who attended, including the author of this work, were silent throughout the lengthy argument. They were delighted that the Catholic Daughters and some Citizens for Decent Literature were rebuked by Judge Weiss when they began to take sides, vocally, as the argument unrolled.

Mr. Kerr and Mr. Teitelbaum did most of the talking. Their statements, in sum, amounted to the complaint that the statutes were vague, had not mentioned motion pictures specifically, and that the United States Supreme Court (groans from some of the audience here) had insisted that an adversary hearing was necessary before an injunction could be obtained. The hearing in Judge Brosky's chambers had not included anyone to represent the theatre or the motion picture, possibly under the assumption that there were no adversaries to morality as defined in the statutes, which, while not the best in the world, at least would serve. Despite the arguments offered at length by the attorneys for the Guild Theatre and for American Civil Liberties Union, Judge Weiss ruled that the District Attorney could enjoin a nuisance and the film could be considered that, if nothing else. The injunction stood, and that evening, the Green brothers, the owners of the theatre, had to present *I, A Woman*, once more.

Mr. Ralph Green and his brother, Mr. Millard Green, had been taken to Sharpsburg on the night the raid took place to appear before Squire Louis R. Pantone, a method used in the Commonwealth to sort out wrongdoers whose cases ought to be heard by the Grand Jury of the County. A week later they were summoned back to Mr. Pantone's little court to conduct their defense. They did so while Mr. Pantone kept watch over a manila envelop containing his decision as Squire, providently typed out in advance of the hearing. The Green brothers could not conduct a defense that would have altered Mr. Pantone's decision. It was unlikely that the squire would issue a ruling that the film was not obscene, thereby effectively destroying the case that was building. Such a ruling had been made, of course, by the U.S. Treasury Department when the film was admitted by customs, and utilizing the accepted principle of administrative finality and precedence of Federal over local law, Mr. Pantone could have ruled in favor of the Green brothers. But as matters later came to light, this was highly unlikely. The County detective force was then rumored to be involved in arrangements with the local crime syndicate, and in such a situation the general rule is not to rock the boat.

Two appeals were under way. The first to the U.S. District Court was concluded with one of those decisions that ended in two keys at once, like a confusing piece of modern music. The Green brothers got no relief from Federal sources, but the Supreme Court of the Commonwealth took the District Attorney to task for his methods. The hearing in Judge Brosky's chambers, in advance of any viewing of the film was clearly a 'star chamber proceeding' in an area where the First Amendment to the U.S. Constitution is operant. The subsequent injunction only compounded the error because it made the District Attorney a censor who never had to defend his decisions. Simply calling a film a nuisance is not reason enough to deny the public the chance to act as its own jury. No one was ever forced to see the picture, and paying admission fees is about the best evidence of a desire to see a film that has yet been devised. A patron could always walk out when he chose to see no more.

Therese and Isabelle was shown to the public while the District Attorney cast about for another method to protect it. People were flocking to the film in such great numbers that the bus-drivers announced "Guild Theatre" rather than "Murray Avenue," as had been the custom before the case began. The Circuit Court of Appeals in

New York had rendered a decision in an important and far-reaching contest. When the film *I am Curious—Yellow* was purchased for showing in the U.S., customs decisions prevented its importation. A jury trial had been held to decide the matter. At issue in the appeal was whether the jury's decision was to be regarded as final, a ruling fromwwhich no appeal could be made. The decision clarified this point when the judgement of the lower court was reversed. In the view of the Court of Appeals, a jury decided questions of fact, but obscenity is a legal question, and the jury decision is advisory to the judge, not binding. In an obscenity hearing, a jury may counsel the judge but it may not rule.

The Second Hearing

As Mr. Teitelbaum pointed out, the case represented quite a departure in American law, for the District Attorney was suing in a court of equity to enjoin the showing of the film. Heretofore, the plaintiff in such suits had been the theatre owner who sought relief from an injunction, but the action of the Supreme Court of the Commonwealth gave Mr. Duggan no other method of procedure if he wished to pursue the matter further. It is obviously easier to devote the police energy of the County toward the protection of the public from foreign films about lesbianism than it is to attack the highly profitable gambling business of the crime syndicate, then earning something over a million dollars a month.

People were interested in the question of obscenity and continued to flock to the movie to make up their minds. Opinion was about equally divided among those who thought the film neither obscene nor interesting and those who thought it either obscene or notable for other reasons. The author of this piece was especially impressed with the music, later described by Professor Lawrence Lee as "surging and panting."

Mr. Gerald Paris again represented the District Attorney. He is a black-haired young man, with an appealing manner, who was aided by another assistant District Attorney. The trial was a bewildering legal wrangle from the outset, exasperating judge, jury, and public alike. The latter did not understand the reason for secret conferences of the defense's and plaintiff's attorneys with the judge, Ralph Smith, Jr. The court reporter, a young man using a stenotype machine, shouldered his way into these conferences and put his machine on the judge's bench in order to get every word of the argument between the contending lawyers.

The plaintiff's case was heard first. Mr. Fanning reiterated his review, and after him, Miss Marie Torre, who is a television personality in Pittsburgh, gave her views. The film was filthy, they agreed. They could not be drawn into logic-chopping on the theme of community standards, regardless of the Art Cinema, which had always shown films of dubious merit and considerable sexual suggestiveness. Filth is filth, Miss Torre and Mr. Fanning seemed to say, and that was the size of *Therese and Isabelle*. This testimony was only after a delay from Friday, when the jury was chosen, until the following Wednesday when the defense was ready with its case.

Thursday morning concluded the case for the District Attorney. Professor Lee attempted to put the Aristotelian values of credibility, universality, and permanence into the law of obscenity by asserting that because *Therese and Isabelle* was obviously lacking in these classical values it was obscene. He had to read from a card provided by Mr. Paris asserting that the work was "lewd, lascivious, dangerous to public morals," before he was allowed to proceed to his own opinion. In the course of cross examination, Mr. Teitelbaum produced a copy of *Playboy* magazine for Professor Lee to inspect. This greatly distressed Mr. Paris who complained that the "disreputable journal," in his words, was being waved about in front of the jury. They seemed uninterested in it anyhow. This issue contained pictures of *The Fox*, which had played without incident in Pittsburgh despite the complaints of Mr. Fanning, echoed by Justice Musmanno and others.

The next witness for the plaintiff was the roving lawyer for the Citizens for Decent Literature, Mr. James J. Clancy, whose interest in the case was obvious because that doughty and usually self-motivated group of crusaders was determined to fight cases of the sort everywhere. That they had lost almost all of them was of no concern. Mr. Clancy could scarcely get a remark in edgewise for the objections and rulings and counter-objections and other rulings. Even his attempt at a history of obscenity law from the misbehavior of Charles Sedley in the seventeenth century was not properly shaped for insertion into the record. He did not get well started on the eighteenth century before his whole testimony was stopped abruptly. His cross examination brought on wrangles just as fierce as his direct testimony. One of these centered around Mr. Clancy's reluctance to use the word 'masturbation.' He wanted the euphemism 'self-love' to serve, and Mr. Teitelbaum demanded that he use a word that everyone understood. The case for the plaintiff ended on a note of utter confusion, as if the preliminaries had occurred last rather than first.

Mr. Teitelbaum began his address to the jury right after lunch, interrupted at times by Mr. Paris, who acted as if he had already won his case. The first witness for the defense was to have been Mr. Dana, the chairman of the Pennsylvania Board of Censors during the whole of its brief life. He had gone home. The defense opened with the author of this book, a man who suddenly discovered that the defense of liberty is an emotion-wracked, dangerous activity. Having learned in the process of his doctoral orals that anger is the worst of all mistakes, the author was careful to wiggle the toes of his right foot as an expression of annoyance while his voice conveyed sweet reason and firm control of all his feelings. The angry toes were concealed in shoes that were themselves hidden in the witness box. The stress can be gauged as two-pair-of-socks intensity, one for each day.

Mr. Teitelbaum led the witness gently through his qualifications that always rather embarrassed him despite their prestige value. The witness then went on to develop his ideas of the social value of *Therese and Isabelle*. He disagreed with the contention that the theme of the film was lesbianism and observed that Violette Leduc was an important French writer. He tried to develop social value as a characteristic of works that are unique sources of information both to people of our time and to the researchers of the future. Reviewing his testimony later, he thought of several hundred different things he could, and possibly ought, to have said.

Damage to the author's socks began as the angry toes registered silent objections both to Mr. Paris' questions and to his manner. He first minimized the qualifications far below what the university that had rewarded the author's dissertation with a doctorate would ever have condoned, then he went on in a taunting fashion, as if anything the author of this work said were suspect, the result of brains muddled by too much theory and no respect for the finer parts of the community into which he had wormed his way. The day ended with a confrontation over the word prurience, which the defense insisted the author could define, and the plaintiff still more insistently said he could not. The witness could have given the whole conjugation of the Latin verb, *prurio, prurire*, from which the English is derived virtually without a change of meaning. Further, the Assistant District Attorney was in the habit of interrupting the witness, partly because the witness tended to pause between coordinating clauses of a compound sentence, and probably also because the testimony was turning in a way that did not suit the case that had already been won, so far as Mr. Paris was concerned. After an hour, everyone including the witness was too weary to continue.

The next morning saw argument continuing between Mr. Teitelbaum and Mr. Paris over the interruptions. The judge ruled that the witness could ask permission to continue if he felt he was interrupted when he was just gathering his thoughts together. The crisis came when it was apparent that a description of a stag film was needed, but whether from prudishness or legal acumen, Mr. Paris wanted no such comparison in the record. He made hesitant approaches to the concepts of pornography and erotic realism and mentioned the Kronhausens' book, *Pornography and the Law*, but so long as the discussion remained on an abstract plane, there was no measure of what an immoral movie might be. The witness had seen stag movies while in Bangkok and in Tokyo. When interrupted, he turned in great innocence to the judge to ask permission to continue. The curiosity of the judge had been aroused, or else his legal mind, and the witness was asked to tell what a stag film is. He dictated into the record of the trial the differences between a stag film and a motion picture such as *Therese and Isabelle.*

A stag film, regardless of when it was made, focuses upon genital activity. There is very little attempt to establish character or setting, and if any attempt is made, it is patently unimportant. A work of art, however, tends to make the genital activity, usually implied rather than shown, a necessary part of the story line where it helps to develop the characterization. A stag film has no purpose other than the exhibition of genital activity, and a serious motion picture is primarily centered in the characters, the setting of the story, and the development of the plot. Following the habit of writers in the Judeo-Christian tradition, authors usually include no graphic description even of sexual events that are vital in the story. If they were included, and as will be seen below in certain literary forms they must be, the emphasis on character and on setting separates the purposefully erotic from the simply pornographic whether in a film or in a novel.

After this learned elucidation of the obvious, the witness turned back to the court, the tension of the trial fully upon him, the complexities of the subject only poorly explained, and Mr. Paris asked him if he had ever read a banned book. Quickly, rather than wisely, he admitted that he had read *Leaves of Grass* by Walt Whitman.

Everyone in the court room roared with laughter, and Mr. Paris changed his tactics. If he had pursued his air of moral superiority, he might possibly have lost the case, but he altered his approach to an elaborate politeness that served him well.

The defense had built a strong case of many important witnesses: Mrs. Mary L. Dimmick from the Hillman Library of the University of Pittsburgh, Dr. Martin M. Tweedale from the Department of Philosophy, and his wife, who had been Librarian of the Graduate School of Library and Information Sciences Library, Mr. George Sinkankas, a doctoral candidate who was youthful in appearance and had also seen a stag movie, Mr. Dana, the former censor for the state, Mrs. Rosemary Plesset who is the wife of a psychiatrist and a social worker in her own right. Each of these witnesses, representing hundreds of hours of schooling, were treated as if they were educated beyond the reach of common sense. It seemed to the author as he listened to the proceedings, that Mr. Paris put himself and the jury into the same category of pure-minded though humble folk who could tell what was dirty and what was not, and almost everything about *Therese and Isabelle* could be made offensive if it was not too openly exposed to view.

The one witness who defeated the lawyers and managed to upset Mr. Paris as he tried to maintain a genial air of sobriety and earnestness was Mr. Henry Koerner, the renowned artist. Mr. Koerner saw *Therese and Isabelle*. Others had watched, viewed, heard, observed, or noticed the film, but he saw it with the full force of an artist whose eye-to-hand coordination is far beyond what any ordinary person would have any hope of achieving. He saw the symbolism, saw the meaning of the symbolism, and he had read no books, save one, since he was twelve. The book, his airplane-trip reading material, is *Moby Dick*; and it became apparent in his flood of testimony that he saw the book as if it were a film played in a mind that understood color as the substance of thought. For instance, he said as his gestures dramatized the scene, he saw the time when Captain Ahab dipped one hand into the semen of the whale and held it aloft while with his other hand he grasped the huge penis of the whale. It was a moment of overwhelming beauty to Mr. Koerner. The people in the court room were completely overcome with laughter, even the elderly gentleman who served as bailiff. The jury was impassive, even as Mr. Koerner explained the intense visual symbolism of the motion picture.

Throughout the trial the question of what community standards meant and just which communities had the right to see the film was never resolved. Judge Smith overruled such testimony as might establish a larger community than the limits of Mr. Duggan's authority. Attempts to establish that the U.S. Treasury Department had already ruled on the question of obscenity failed, and even testimony that cities elsewhere had exhibited the film without apparent effect on anyone was ruled improper. Only the community of Pittsburgh was to be considered, and the suggestion that the good people there should be as much trusted with their moral future as with their political future seemed to pass unnoticed.

The attorneys summed up their cases and the trial went to the jury on the Wednesday a week after it began. Mr. Teitelbaum asked the jury to strike a blow for freedom especially as the highly educated witnesses for the defense thought it was a good idea. Mr. Paris asked the jury to consider the state of morality in our time and the harmful effect such films have upon us, causing, according to him, riots among students, social decay, and the general dangers which moved Mr. Duggan in the first place. After deliberating all afternoon, the jury returned with the answers to the interrogatories that Judge Smith put to them.

Their judgement on *Therese and Isabelle* was that it had no social value of any redeeming sort at all, that it was significantly beyond the limits of candor and shame established by the community, and that it appealed predominantly to a prurient interest in sexual matters. Quite clearly as Judge Smith enjoined the showing of the film, the day in the fight against censorship had been lost. Just as clearly, the adult public of Allegheny County could not be trusted with its moral future. For that one night, Allegheny County was protected by the fighting District Attorney from a French import which, if it endangered communities despite the adumbrations of the U.S. customs, was shown everywhere else without so prolonged, insistent, and ineffective a legal battle.

Mr. Duggan's wrath and legal inventiveness was at last his undoing; he should have been content with the Commonwealth's Supreme Court in the first decision. There is a law in Pennsylvania, justly famous for its lawyers, that a writ of supersedeas must be granted when an appeal is made from the decision of a court of equity to enjoin an action in the public interest. This means that no injunction is possible while an appeal is pending. Judge Smith would never grant a writ cancelling one action with another, but Mr. Justice O'Brien was in Pittsburgh, and with the aid of an electronic marvel, the conference telephone, he called his fellow justices in different parts of the state to obtain a ruling that granted a writ. The whole point of the legal battle was to obtain an injunction, but the writ permitted *Therese and Isabelle* to be screened every evening so that others in the community could make up their minds as well as the jury. Those twelve good citizens had seen the film without visible harmful effects, and only adults had ever been permitted into the theatre, so that whatever moral deterioration was taking place seemed to be out of sight, and granting the community of Pittsburgh the privilege of being made up of human beings, out of mind as well. It is a remarkable person who will assess his own moral deterioration on a continuing basis as if he were reading the gauge on a steam boiler.

Mr. Duggan was visibly angry as he announced to television audiences that evening what the action of the Supreme Court of the Commonwealth meant. The floodgates of filth were opened and they could not be closed because a court of equity was not the answer to Mr. Duggan's demands for a method that would make him an effective guardian of the public morals. This prediction proved to be accurate. The subsequent action of the Supreme Court of the Commonwealth in ruling that *Therese and Isabelle* was not obscene, that its theme was loneliness rather than lesbianism, came as anti-climax. The film ran during the whole time the case was making its way to the attention of the Supreme Court, and it finally lost its audience because anyone who wanted to had seen it. When the explicit sexuality of a Danish import offended Mr. Duggan as much as it had the Citizens for Decent Literature, it was withdrawn even though it had been shown for two weeks at another theatre. The explicit sexuality of American films was attacked, but quite as unsuccessfully; and now there is no difference in the offerings of the peep-show arcades, the 'adult theatres,' and the fare available in Copenhagen, New York, or Los Angeles.

Mr. Duggan was elected a third time by the grateful citizens of Allegheny County, even though he failed to carry the center of sinfulness, the City of Pittsburgh. His shining virtue has been rather dirtied by the revelations of Grand Jury investigations of the county detective force and the recent indictment of the numbers racket ring which flourished during the time that Mr. Duggan was doing his best to purify the County in other ways. There is a concerted attack on the dangerous floods of filth in Allegheny County, marshalled not by Mr. Duggan but by others. These floods fill the air and the water and can be measured very accurately, because they are real not symbolic. In fact, the promised moral deterioration has simply failed to occur. Bank robberies are numerous, murders threaten even the police force and burglaries are so numerous that very few of the criminals who commit them are caught, if they are ever pursued, all activated to some extent by the drug traffic.

The strange affair of *Therese and Isabelle* was one of the least significant of censorship battles, and the long description is offered for several reasons other than importance. The first reason is that censorship still prevails, and to assert that it should end absolutely is foolish. Each man is a censor for himself and for those whom he has a legal privilege to influence. The question is where this privilege is to have undisputed sway. In the author's view, the right of parents to decide what their children shall read and what movies they will see is unquestioned. Beyond that, the dirty words of one man are not to be forced off onto another. The public exhibition of material that offends must never have a captive audience. Where an act of volition is evidence of a desire to see what is offered, then the law as determined in *Stanley vs. Georgia* should prevail. Stanley was a man whom the Atlanta police wanted to arrest for something, almost anything. The only thing they could find was a collection of pornography that violated a state law. The U.S. Supreme Court ruled that the state could not maintain and enforce such a law without violating the Bill of Rights.

The second reason is that the actions of the District Attorney are exemplary of censorship battles everywhere. If censorship can be secret and has the assent of the community by its silence, then it can succeed. Otherwise, human curiosity being what it is, censorship will fail.

The third reason is that the attack on *Therese and Isabelle* finally became an attack on knowledge, a resistance to the idea that some one might learn something of which the legal establishment disapproved. Censorship prevails sufficiently in the law of libel for this author to fear making accusations he cannot prove about anyone, but the facts are clear in the course of later events. We attack in others whatever of ourselves we wish to hide from them. A swift offensive is better than any defense. Rather than protest innocence, it is much better to work out problems of guilt by finding our faults in others. The leer of the sensualist is an expression that all of us can assume when we want to. For most of us, though, sexuality is only transitorily a spectator sport, and yet the denial of the right to investigate human sexuality forbids access to one of the sources of our behavior. A Pittsburgh wag suggested making a sticker that is probably libellous despite the fact that it is completely ridiculous. "_____ is a lesbian." Fill in the name of any man who becomes upset and wants to forbid you to see a work of art dealing with lesbianism.

Finally, the law of the United States has become a silly mess, impossible for the courts to deal with except at great expense when there are more pressing problems that deserve immediate attention. Some lawyers must take the step that will move the United States the distance needed to equal the sanity of Danish law. Public morality cannot be legislated into existence, nor private immorality punished except at the expense of liberties too valuable to surrender. We have to let our neighbor go to hell in a handbasket so long as he harms no one else along the way.

King Kong is a Faggot

This book is written to explain the commonalty of the world community in its treatment of the communication process. From many different investigations we arrive at a principle of human communication. The studies of prejudice confirm what is explored here; human beings are not greatly influenced by what they read or see once their curiosity is satisfied. We cannot be made to lose our prejudices until we explore what they are and how they operate. We love to call names and deplore the state of the world. We need to find some scapegoat to take our faults. We must have easy explanations or we lose interest. Whenever possible we like to have some one else do our thinking for us. But as soon as any of these things occur, we become restive and condemn ourselves for being less than human.

The purpose of library and information science is to interrupt the flow of communication and preserve all that will provide a record of our society and a guide to its content and meaning. Librarians fight censorship because it strikes at roots of our profession, and close behind us come the information scientists with special problems of privacy and personal dignity to consider. There have always been two sides to the question. On the one side is the authoritarian view that society will decay and collapse if a tight unyielding control is not exercised over what is communicated through modern technological advances. Its opposite is the liberal view that denies anyone the special privilege of exercising this control for everyone else. Society, in this estimation, will grow and change as our human development determines.

An investigation of the argument for government control of the media of communication usually rests on the welfare of citizens, especially children. The most available medium, at present television, is subject to the most intense censorship. Gradually, the threat of books has diminished to the point where the contents of serious works sold to anyone able to read them is not vastly different, except in literary value, from books marked for adults only. A youngster who yearns to see taboo words in print can do so without too much trouble, especially if he is an adolescent. Motion pictures have been rated, in a rather complicated fashion, so that parents can expect that the local cinema hall will not let their immature young into the dark where the only lighted portion is a scene of sexual intercourse magnified to billboard size. Some parents insist that their children can see pictures rated X without harm. Research coming out of Sweden and Denmark seems to indicate that this is the case.

We assign a value to our symbolism according to the instruction of those that have first chance to influence us. Children who grow up in homes where Mozart and the pre-classical composers are the common fare always prefer this music. If country and western music is played, then the influence will be intensified as the child begins to prefer this music to all others. The Texaco Company and Milton Cross have done much to educate a generation of opera lovers, the author included. So long as the production is mechanical, does not include flesh and blood, the violation of a taboo may be intensely shocking, but it will not alter behavior, although it may be used as an excuse for behavior already tending to change.

Unfortunately great works of art do not emanate a mysterious essence that attracts the untutored eye of most of us. If this were so we could end our teaching of literature, art, and music appreciation. It is very difficult for some community leaders to understand that a work of symbolism depends upon the interpretation of symbols that must always take place within the individual. A characteristic of paranoid psychosis is the misinterpretation of symbols and the investing of harmless and insignificant signs with meanings that no one else can find. When President Nixon used the argument that immoral works must corrupt because otherwise we could not say that great works of art ennoble, he was voicing one of the weakest arguments for censorship. In rejecting the report of the National Commission on Obscenity and Pornography, he was reacting to scientific investigation of which he did not approve. In doing so, he was attempting to return to Lord Cockburn's rule of law. We must censor those works that tend to deprave and corrupt lest they fall into the hands of those who are susceptible to such influences. In the mind of the censor this is everyone less virtuous than he is. When President Nixon promised to do something about the floods of pornography, in accepting the nomination of the Republican Party, he was voicing the discomfort felt by all who believe that the commonalty are just waiting for a good excuse to engage in sexual misbehavior. One of the favorite topics of public figures is the decay of morals. Petronius in *The Satyricon* complains about the Romans who were forever asking where the sturdy virtues of the Republic had gone to in the sybaritic times of the Empire.

As a movement loses power its adherents remember the days when their strength was greatest. These are the good old days, but when moral censorship is considered, the good old days were not really unlike the present so far as human actions are concerned. Huxley's baby factories as depicted in *Brave New World* do not exist. Artificial insemination has brought its own problems to a legal tangle that has one foot on common law and another on statute law. Whatever

Kinsey reported in his *Sexual Behavior in the Human Male* was derived from the practices of men who are at the least in their late
forties. Further surveys confirm what Kinsey supposed. Human sexuality has changed very little, but our attitudes toward it are always
undergoing a change. The term 'sexual revolution' is rather foolish;
in the first place it suggests that human beings have learned a new
way of procreating, and in the second place the revolution that has
occurred is the result of the communications revolution, the broadening of the frame of reference to the point where it is congruent
with the world community. World history can no longer pretend that
the Orient came into being only when Europeans became involved in
its problems. Sociological theories have become intermingled with
anthropological methods, and the cross-cultural approach is the only
valid method when one presumes to speak of human beings. Columbus did not discover America. He announced that human beings were
living in a section of the planet of which Europeans knew nothing.
If the World Federalists have their way, the ultimate result of the
communications revolution will be a world in which the power to
make war is in the hands of an authority representing all humankind
because all humankind suffers when any war is waged, regardless of
the contestants and the causes of their belligerence.

The purpose of this book is to show that a world society will be
viable to the extent that it is based on personal liberty such as the
Bill of Rights in the United States Constitution authorizes and the
United Nations Universal Declaration of Human Rights sets forth
in even greater detail. The Constitution of Japan has probably the
strongest statement of human rights, and the most applicable to the
rest of the world, and India has the best method of protecting human
rights in its Supreme Court. An authority with the obligation of
protecting personal rights and limited in its operation so that its own
rules do not obviate what its responsibilities demand will be the
ultimate federation of human beings on this planet, each of whom
may worship his own concept of God, live in the society that suits
him best, and be at peace with all the other people of the world.

The way to this conclusion is quite tortuous and it begins in a strange place, because the model of further sections is to be found in the review of the literature of male homosexuality, with some attention to female homosexuality as well. A change that is measurable and identifiable has occurred from the period of the second World War to the present. The world is faced with such phenomena as Gay Liberation, homosexual episodes in autobiographies, and an outpouring of literary works. A topic that was utterly taboo in the Hays Code for motion pictures now appears not only in motion pictures devoted to the topic but also in sly innuendoes on the most guarded of media, television for the mass market, and in outright discussions of the topic, generally regarded as a major problem of society, something that the Gay Liberators deplore. Yet even among professionals in the production of hard-core pornography suppression operates, so that films depicting heterosexuality in the most explicit detail do not include episodes of male homosexuality although female homosexuality is commonplace.

This investigation leads to the second consideration, the other sex and heterosexuality as it has appeared in the literary outpourings of the communication revolution. To match the phenomena of Gay Liberation is the equally interesting movement usually called Women's Lib. To understand the regrouping of sexual identification, we must progress through the concepts of nudity and virginity to the idea of privacy in its expanded form as the right to determine the use of one's own body is debated in considering changes in laws concerning abortion.

Such a concept immediately puts us into the arena of the image makers and image breakers, the iconolaters and iconoclasts. This is more than showing the 'hero's backside.' For with the molding of public thought we come to the essential characteristics of censorship and suppression: the maintenance of propaganda, the preservation of stereotypes, and the limitation of knowledge as a dangerous thing.

This leads us to make a world tour from the strait-laced little island republic of Singapore to the traditional good sense of the Kingdom of the Netherlands with side trips to other places where we find some variation of the two points of view. Our comparison of these two places is based on the fact that both attempt the same result by different means. Both governments achieve the goal of their actions with the support of the people governed. Both governments take advantage of a fact that is often denied by the censors operating against the current thought of a community: pornography is boring and expensive. Erotica may be expensive, but it can never bore some people. The shadowy limbo that is the boundary between the two illustrates a dynamism of communications.

The purpose of this chapter has been to prepare the reader for what is to follow. The author sincerely hopes that anyone who is shocked by an investigation of linguistic taboos will have put down the book and will not go to further horrors beyond. Equally, those who search this book for the sort of sexual excitation to be found in some pornography and erotica should put the book down now, or use the extensive bibliography at the end as a guide to material that will prove closer to his expectations.

When the *Ulysses* case was sub judice, Mayor James Walker of New York remarked that he had never known of a girl who was ruined by reading a book. Like the misquoted statement of Charles Rembar that obscenity is in the groin of the beholder, the commonalty tend to bring a balanced view to the medium and its message, believing little of what they hear and not much more of what they see. The twelve good people were trying to do what was expected of them in judging the film *Therese and Isabelle*. They were mistaken in giving it the importance that the District Attorney tried to establish. One who attended the special showing for defense witnesses found the film deadly dull because it reminded her of her school days. All she could see were girls in uniforms marching here and there.

Censorship has always tended to advertise. That was never better demonstrated than during the strange affair of *Therese and Isabelle.* As the District Attorney sought to have his will implemented in an injunction, now on and now off as the courts played with his determination, the public flocked to see a film that did not gross nearly so much nor play so long a time in other cities. Lacking the effective advertisement given by the District Attorney, the film would have had a two week engagement, probably, and some of its audience would have enjoyed it and others deplored it. Intellectual freedom assumes that its resources are readily available and not under the interdiction of a guardian of the public morals. The history of civilization in the western world is filled with incidents based on a leader or on a government that cannot believe anyone would disagree unless they were morally inferior if not actively dangerous. If asked to define public morality, the average man of an authoritarian turn of mind would define it readily as what he believed in. That an entire tradition should establish that nudity is tiresome and commonplace while gorgeous clothing makes something worth seeing is quite beyond the understanding of the average guardian of the public American morals. It requires an investigation into the reason, found easily enough, because the people bathe together, one sex with the other, quite without any excitation whatever unless for other reasons. Nudity is so commonplace that to exhibit it on the stage is to lose the attention of the spectators. We have to learn to find sexual excitation in nudity, and in some societies it is never taught.

Human beings have to learn how to hate each other for reasons that are not an instant concern. They must especially learn that all _____ are _____ . This is the principle of stereotyping, and the extension into censorship can be seen very readily. At one point the expression French novel meant lubricous fiction. To the Catholic Daughters attending the trial of *Therese and Isabelle* before Judge Weiss, Supreme Court meant fountainhead of unwise decisions. In some circles a Hollywood party is equivalent to an orgy, especially of a bisexual nature. Even so impressive a religious leader as Saint Paul asserts in his letter to Romans, usually called the first letter, that "men committing shameless acts with men . . . are gossips, slanderers, haters of God, insolent, haughty, disobedient to parents, foolish, faithless, heartless, ruthless."

Stereotyping has especially clouded those hopes of good relations between the commonalty of different races, religions, and national traditions. When the formula that all Jews are miserly, or whatever adjective is pejorative enough to suit the speaker, is accepted, then an epithet can be applied, carrying with it the full meaning of the adjectives so that 'kike' implies everything bad about a Jew; 'nigger,' 'wop,' 'spic,' 'dago,' 'red neck,' 'fag,' 'lez,' 'square,' each having a point of reference that is the same. "All Burmans are lazy," according to information available to the author when he arrived in that beautiful country.

But the communications revolution is as much a matter of travel as it is a matter of books, periodicals, non-print materials, and instant replay television of an event seen throughout the world as it happened. When a librarian can make five trips around the world in the pursuit of his profession, then a massive change has taken place, and it is time that we realize it. This change can be compared with the changes that occurred in the society in the sixteenth century shortly after news of another continental land mass came to Europe, when the Renaissance rediscovered an ancient culture and planted a new one.

The communication revolution should speed up the process of change. After all, the world was watching television on July 20, 1969, when Neil A. Armstrong stepped onto the surface of the moon and it heard the statement that everyone had been awaiting. "That is one small step for a man, one giant leap for mankind." He carried with him thirty-eight years of life, and most importantly he brought it back with him. His statement is both biologically accurate as well as centered in the world community as its representative. If any of

Neil Armstrong's ancestry had failed in the continuation of the genes that were his at birth, he would not have been the man to make that statement. To argue that it would probably be made by now by someone else is to engage in one of the benefits of sophistry. All the science and industry of mankind were necessary to give Armstrong the chance of making that statement. He made it, and everyone heard it, and the history of the world turned a big corner, as every-one realized. We are faced, now as before, with the knowledge that mankind can destroy his planet or preserve it as home base while he visits others. What we have to fear is not knowledge but the belief that ignorance is preferable.

II.

THE HORSES OF INSTRUCTION

Male Identity

In an episode replayed as one of the highlights of the *Tonight Show* over the years, Ed Ames walked with Johnny Carson to the center of the stage where an outline of a man awaited his demonstration of skill at throwing a hatchet, a necessary part of the series on frontier life in which he was appearing. After showing how to hold the hatchet and what could be expected of it in flight, Ed Ames took careful aim, threw it, and the hatchet lodged in the diagram of the man, quite unexpectedly, exactly in the groin just where one would look to see a man's penis. With the quick-wittedness that has characterized his long stand on the *Tonight Show*, Johnny Carson said "I didn't know you were Jewish." The audience went into shrieks of laughter, practically drowning out anything else that Johnny Carson could say. What had happened released emotion, as laughter, because deep-seated feelings of both men and women were tweaked inadvertently. The wife of a famous golfer who admitted to being superstitous and as an example, explained, "Before a big game, I always kiss his balls," brought on as loud a response for a similar reason.

The evolution of human beings as a species depends upon the male genitals and the sex drive in his most important sex organ, his brain. Even in a world made up of unwilling females, the greater immediate strength of the male human being would make rape replace the complicated structures of love, marriage, and procreation. In fact, females are more than willing. They incite a man to lust be being available, as noted by the early church fathers, and encouraging sexual intercourse as much for their own pleasure as for the pleasure it gives the male. Lacking a member of the other sex for prolonged periods of time, the male, or the female, will turn to the members of the same sex for such consolation as may be derived from mutual genital manipulation.

Some great traditions derive from respect for the male organs. Circumcision may be the unkindest cut of all, as some writers have noted, but its purpose is to prevent the remote possibility that the effusions from glands at the base of the corona will cause some infection that may damage the organ. Among Jews, Islam, and American obstetricians, the ritual is greatly significant and is performed except in the cases where agnostic parents protest, threaten suit, obtain a lawyer who can send a registered letter, or otherwise make their wishes effectively known. They are sometimes overruled in their desires by hospital practices or by the actual necessity of clipping away the foreskin to correct a condition called phimosis when the retraction of the skin from the head of the penis is impossible. According to some historians, soon after becoming Adolf Hitler's mistress Eva Braun secretly reported that he suffered from this condition. It is not known whether he was circumcised at some point in his later life.

All male mammals take especial care of their sex organs, and most male mammals masturbate, according to the reports of zoologists. Male parakeets that live in lonely splendor with only a mirror for a companion embarrass their owners by masturbating against a perch. There is considerable evidence that masturbation among adolescent males is as much for reasons of testing the equipment as for purposes of obtaining pleasure and release from sexual tension. Human beings are particularly sensitive about the size and shape of their penes, and at various periods of history have been almost as anxious to suggest their existence as to hide them. In point of fact, every man has one right at the center of his body, and often enough at the center of his mind. A variety of scientific experiments have shown that a male's sexual appetite takes the third rank of priority after his appetite for food and for sleep, both bodily necessities. Some similar necessity for ejaculation can be inferred by involuntary emissions of semen if no other sexual release is available.

Kinsey published his study of the human male as a sexual being in 1948, using his knowledge of zoology as a guide to his research, rather than the theretofore popular employment of religion, psychology, sociology, anthropology, and plain supposition. It is the first systematic approach to male sexuality in human beings not polluted by man's propensity for creating mythical structures. Men invented the idea of fig leaves as a means of maintaining their privacy wishing to be judged not by their sex organs and sex habits alone. The Judeo-Christian tradition has its first man, Adam, utilizing a fig leaf as soon as he developed a sense of shame. Among most of the peoples of the world, men hide their sex organs and preserve them from harm by binding them up in some kind of protective and opaque material. Even the naked Nagas of Burma wear a kind of metal loin-plate for ceremonial occasions. Australian aborigines may be naked all their lives, but the importance of the penis is made a central part of the initiation rites that mark the end of boyhood, including circumcision or even more drastic surgery. Along with a kind of need for concealing the penis is a concomitant need for showing that it is where it should be. The sex determined adornment of males in practically every society is an extension of the external, though covered, genitalia.

At any given point in man's social history, especially in Europe, the distinction between male and female has been carefully drawn. When men wear long hair, they also wear mustaches and beards. Tattooing is usually sex-related in the societies where it is practiced, and in those few societies where clothing for men and women is virtually the same, as in certain parts of Indonesia and Africa, women walk about with naked chests. The breast becomes a sexual stimulant about equal to a pretty face in other societies. At one point, anthropologists explained this phenomenon as sexual differentiation for purposes of preventing inappropriate sexual advances. Later opinion relates sexual identification to the aggressiveness and assertiveness that characterizes the relations between heterosexual males. Among birds, the magnificent males are easily recognized by other males and driven away from territorial boundaries while females are welcomed in to stay and mate.

An inter-societal and interdisciplinary study of males in their relationships with other males inevitably centers at some point on the question of homosexuality. If, as in the view of many who seek to explain the dilemma of living and reproducing, sex and the welfare of a social group are at odds, the sexual instinct of men and women can be somewhat controlled by keeping them separated. When homosexuality enters the picture, a different balance becomes impossible. Human beings seem to be at the mercy of different kinds of double bind, that situation where each is damned if he does and damned if he doesn't. The casual homosexual activity of sailors on long sea journeys, men in prison, and soldiers isolated in a place without women is governed by stringent rules, so that sailors can be court-martialed or imprisoned, men in prison may find their sentences lengthened if they are not tried for a separate crime, and soldiers may find themselves open to charges and counter charges, all depending on the caprice of those in authority.

The reason given for moral censorship in the People's Republic of China and in various other communist countries is that the workers are distracted by graphic descriptions of sexual activity. In all these countries, homosexuality is a private vice that may be fiercely punished if brought to the attention of an unsympathetic authority, exactly like the unlucky fellow in prison, in an isolated camp, or on the high seas with an authoritarian man supervising his every action. Such activity as may take place is of a very casual nature and is defended by its participants as being of a temporary nature only, although it may be very satisfying. In the armed forces, homosexual solicitation is considered incitement to riot.

Men have been dominant in the communication process, usually refusing to give women a chance to enter into any meaningful exchange by channeling whatever is offered as meant for only another woman. Editors of children's books judge books about girls rather harshly, because boys won't read them, although girls will read books about boys. The sale is much reduced if the central figure is a girl engaged in purely feminine activity. Among almost all the societies of the world, past and present, the most important communication, that between the populace and their god, was conveyed by means of a priest. Women as senders of religious messages on behalf of both men and women seemed quite anomalous, as if one were asking a pet animal to memorize and repeat a message couched in elegant and old-fashioned phrases. Usually some kind of sexual prohibition circumscribes the activities of a priest, ranging from celibacy among Roman Catholics and Buddhists to monogamy among Protestants and Shinto priests. In some countries, priests may marry, but not if they propose to belong to a religious community of monks or nuns.

The revolution of attitudes toward women and toward male homosexuality results from a number of intense scientific studies, in effect a whole explosion of information, examining sexuality in terms of the scientific method. The process really began with a reinterpretation of medical evidence about masturbation, which was usually limited to discussions of the results of it among boys almost all of whom engaged in the forbidden practice at one time or another. Up until the end of the nineteenth century when the medical profession was re-organizing itself to take advantage of scientific discoveries, masturbation was held to be the cause of everything from acne to blindness, insanity, and yawning. Nothing was too insignificant or too terrible to escape explanation as the result of masturbation. Since every man fears, or suffers from, one or another of these physical and mental problems, there seemed to be some small amount of validation, but it was a clear case of *post hoc ergo propter hoc.* Havelock Ellis in his *Studies in the Psychology of Sex* in 1900 gave the historical background of medical opinion and showed that no harm came to those he interviewed, but in fact, almost every man carries around a burden of guilt for having masturbated at some time in his life, and no man likes to admit it, save for a few brave physicians who refuse to engage in the professional hypocrisy of the times. The physicians who condemn masturbation as harmful to health are rare, but society barely condones it. W. F. Robie, writing just after the first World War, discerned that masturbation could be proved as the cause of few if any diseases and venereal diseases were the cause of great misery and death. In a choice between masturbation and copulation with prostitutes who spread venereal disease, Robie advised masturbation. This was so much in opposition to the current thinking of the time that his books though written for the public were designated for the medical profession only. *Studies in the Psychology of Sex* was first published in the United States available only to the medical profession. It was considered obscene and prohibited in Great Britain, even though it is plainly a scientific study. It was severely restricted in its distribution until recently, although it remains an important landmark book in the history of sex research. Ellis had no experience with masturbation because some physiological peculiarity made him have frequent emissions of semen involuntarily during apparently dreamless sleep. Unfortunately this was regarded as a disease, *spermatorrhea*, by a savant of the time, Charles Drysdale, and Ellis enjoyed the terrors of guilt as much as any Victorian masturbator. Many parents worry that masturbation may harm the penis, a popular misconception of the Victorians. The solitary vice was finally scotched as the cause of anything only when Wardell Pomeroy's *Boys and Sex* advocated masturbation, especially prolonged efforts, as a good means of training toward prolonging coitus in order to satisfy the women in the boy's later adult life. When twelve years old, the author of this book was advised by a physician to whom he reported for a physical examination in order to join the YMCA that masturbation would cause weakness, inability to concentrate, moral laxity, and susceptibility to bad influences. This was in 1935, a full generation before Pomeroy's book was published in 1968.

Only the vast renewal of scientific investigation prevented the moralists from assuming the guise of scientists when promulgating utter nonsense as undeniable fact while protected by public opinion from the obloquy they deserved. Most sex manuals of the most liberal kind warned against "excessive masturbation" while admitting that the act was harmless. Excessive would be adequately defined as a little more than any given authority could accomplish in a day. A sexual athlete might draw the line at six or seven times, and the author of a sex manual who had a low tolerance for sexual activity might think that once or twice a month ought to suffice.

Masturbation was regarded as a major sin among all the religious groups of the Judeo-Christian tradition until very recently, and it is still regarded as a sin by some, though often in the charitable way that makes it one of the most forgivable because it is the one sexual misdemeanor that is most available. The tide of medical opinion has swung definitely to the viewpoint that guilt over masturbation is very harmful although the act itself is probably beneficial for several reasons. It is the male's best tranquilizer during a period of enforced sexual abstinence, especially if this is combined with insufficient physical activity. Adolescent masturbation with its attendant fantasies prepares the male for his role in the heterosexual relationship by giving him a means of control over his sexual response. Among adults, it aids concentration, as any number of writers will assert when they can be perfectly frank, by removing interest in sex for a period of time. Finally, masturbation is probably the reason that pornography is more a safety valve of society than the cause of any moral deterioration. As will be seen, pornographic writings greatly tend toward the verbalization of fantasies that are at least adolescent in their naivete and the degree of wish fulfillment supplied.

Masturbation among males in groups verges right into the exceedingly taboo and emotionally charged subject of male homosexuality. Then all the harmlessness of the act vanishes, and a sex authority is strong in his advice against such wanton behavior. Masturbation of little boys by oriental men and women in order to stop their crying is the cause of intense cultural shock among foreigners of the Judeo-Christian tradition. Even the word masturbation was permitted on television only after Johnny Carson had appealed from the ruling of the censor, whom he characterizes as Miss Priscilla Goodbody. While masturbation in private is not a crime, as tested in the Supreme Court of the Commonwealth of Pennsylvania, the act in public is one of those 'indecent' displays that offends both the law and the unwilling spectator. At a performance of *Elektra* at the Metropolitan Opera House many years ago, the author observed a man stand and masturbate in full view of the audience, in the darkened house, although only those in the balcony with him were aware of his actions. He was daring disaster by combining exhibitionism with sexual manipulation.

Very few writers have investigated masturbation as it represents the developing sense of identity in the male. Little boys handle their sex organs when they discover the stimulation it affords and in order to find a sense of security not readily available elsewhere. The habit continues, so that it is commonplace for men to touch themselves covertly when they feel momentarily threatened or know that they must exert special effort. Baseball players on television will often almost ritualistically touch their groins, possibly to assure themselves that the protective metal cup is in place, possibly also as a reaction in the wide context of the struggle before them. The masturbation that may precede a game is allied to this need for assurance.

The phallic gesture is preserved in language in such words as 'testimony' and 'testify' derived from the Latin for 'testes' still employed by some medical writers in place of the more common 'testicles.' When a man laid a hand over the testes, it signified that the truth was forthcoming lest all the 'seed' be imperiled. One of the first things Leeuwenhoek saw in his newly invented microscope was human sperm. Until more powerful magnification was available to disprove the conjecture, it was believed that the sperm cell contained a 'homunculus' or little human being much as a seed contains the sprout.

This seed could grow in the uterus, and the view of women was in part gained from the idea that at best she only served the male as a field serves a farmer. The loss of thousands of 'homunculi' is somewhat more drastic an idea than the spurt of seminal fluid containing something that closely resembles other microscopic organisms. It takes considerable faith in science to understand how conception occurs and what the male role is. Loss of semen is still supposed to weaken a man, although it is virtually insignificant so far as energy reserves are concerned. Loss of semen is about as harmful as loss of saliva.

The protectiveness men feel for their genitals is extended to the genitals of every other man. Fair fighting means that neither man assaults the loins. The ultimate sensation of rage and contempt is expressed by injuring the testicles. It is an attack on a man's future as a man. Chinese eunuchs during the period of the Ch'ing Dynasty were required to keep their amputated genitals with them at all times, their treasure. There was a brisk business in stolen jars of pickled sex organs, as often as not beginning with the surgeon who performed the operation that qualified a man to be a eunuch in the imperial court. It was the custom in China to have all the external genitals removed, leaving only a healed wound with the urethra exposed and functioning. In Arab countries the same kind of radical surgery was used for the creation of eunuchs. The history of both countries was very much affected by these emasculated men who often assumed an importance not available to the potent untouched male. The *castrati* of Italy were deprived of testicles in order to preserve the vocal range of a child with a man's increased capacity to breathe. The operation had to be performed before puberty, or the voice could change and then it was too late.

Very likely the eunuch adopted a behavior pattern already established for eunuchs that had little or nothing to do with his sex organs. As a means of birth control, vasectomy is the safest, surest, and least troublesome to both man and woman, but it will always have a fairly limited appeal because it must compete with learned, if not innate, fear of castration. This figures at length in psychoanalytic literature as an explanation for much neurotic behavior. Vasectomy affects the sexuality of a man very little; there are no sperm in his ejaculation, but otherwise he remains physiologically the same.

During the period when science had to fight religion for the privilege of investigating the sexuality of human beings, very little could be studied and less exposed to the public view. Censorship in the Victorian and Post-Victorian period, from about 1820 to 1920, prevented any intelligent investigation of what constituted male identity in the mind of the individual, even though great masses of literature prescribed what manliness should be. Coming at a time when universal literacy became the goal of English-speaking countries, the result was a curious reshaping of the ideals of mankind into a weird and confusing tangle. While Samuel Smiles and his fellows before and after gave men a certain role in life with a behavior pattern that suited whoever was writing the work, men were working out their own preferred patterns in conformity with social station and the direct or implied instruction of other men. The result is a kind of fantasy become dogma that had its peak during the first World War.

Masculinity is attractive to both men and women, and the terms used are meliorative so that 'handsome brute' is a compliment not only because of the word 'handsome' but also because of the word 'brute,' which conveys an idea of a rugged male. As Lionel Tiger describes it in his book, *Men in Groups*, conformity to a pattern of masculinity is required for membership in any male group. Men who are excessively attentive to women may lose all chance for membership in certain groups, and at one point in the Judeo-Christian tradition, it was considered effeminate for a man to spend much time taking care of his children. The hypocrisy of the Victorians, who are still among us, lies in the polarity of the behavior required for the male group and that accepted in mixed groups. A man cannot enter a female group without its becoming a mixed group. Only recently have women begun to dictate what are the canons of masculinity, although the attempt began long ago. Its success had to await the advent of intellectual freedom in sex research. It still has a long way to go.

Naked Manhood

The willingness of men to expose their genitals has varied considerably. In the April, 1972, issue of *Cosmopolitan*, in a kind of publication coup, Burt Reynolds appears in a color photograph printed to a fold-out size, just as *Playboy* shows a naked female in each of its monthly issues. The pose is very interesting. Mr. Reynolds is completely nude but his arm, not his hand, conveniently covers his genitals. He has a little cigar between his teeth as he rests on one elbow and looks at the camera with an expression that seems to give the lie to the expression *omne animale post coitum triste est* (every animal is sad after coitus) as if he had just worked his will with a most cooperative woman. Women in general approve, if the opinions expressed on various late-night talk shows is a guide, and men are vaguely disapproving. What began as a satiric thrust at *Playboy* has become valuable in itself. Copies of the magazine sold out almost everywhere, in response to the effective advertisement of the novelty. Until recently, women's periodicals were put together by men, printed by men, financed by men, and their editorial policy has generally been determined by men. The variations of the concept of sexual superiority have now reached the stage of a mass movement. If men like to look at unclothed women, should not women like to look at unclothed men? Some women enjoy it, some do not. It depends on the woman. Some men enjoy it, some do not, and none of these is homosexual.

Male beauty is not a modern idea. The masculine figure was considered entirely beautiful in ancient Greece and in Rome. Because the female lacked external genitals, which were considered an object of beauty, the female form was either clothed or a kind of modesty was expressed. The righteous friars who clapped fig leaves on the statues in the Vatican Museum had to conceal male genitals, despite the fact that in the eyes of many visitors the statuary is disfigured and only the unusual visitor is moved to sexual excitement by the sight of male genitals represented in marble or bronze. A nude Venus usually covers, or pretends to cover, her breasts and pubic region with fluttering hands, if she is not clothed from the waist down. Apollo stands upright and naked except for a small cloak thrown over his shoulders.

Michelangelo's David has so far escaped the disfigurement of pious churchmen. It stands in the Accademia in Florence high on a pedestal, completely nude. David's penis is even approximately the right size. Only in the pornographic art of the classical period was the size of male genitals exaggerated or depicted in anatomical proportion to the rest of the figure. Artists before and since have tended to decrease the size of the penis, and in all serious art but frank eroticism, the penis is always flaccid. Michelangelo created his art from reality, and his picture of the Last Judgement on the wall of the Sistine Chapel was originally painted without the convenient draperies that modern visitors see. The nude figure of Christ left no doubt that He was an adult male. Thousands of Virgin-and-Child paintings show that the Infant Jesus was male, and these have escaped the retouchers.

Pictures of naked little boys adorn many old family albums, just as male cherubs are used as adornment in St. Peter's Basilica. Until the Hays Code forbade the photography of infantile genitals, nothing immoral was seen in the genitals of children. Even in Burma with its strict code of modesty that prevents nudity from the age of eight or so onward, naked children are not considered obscene. A Burman will bathe with his or her clothing on, washing self and *longyi* at the same time, and donning the clean dry *longyi* over the wet one before it is removed. Children romp about completely naked, the objects of unlimited affection offered by all adults. The anatomy of human beings has meant that male genitals are the more often seen unless some cover is added. The female genitals can only be seen when the individual is purposefully trying to expose them. Except for the *mons veneris* and a tiny suggestion of the vulva, the genitals of little girls are neatly concealed by the thighs.

By adolescence the male has gained the stature of a man, his sexual abilities, and his need for protection of the genitals. When the Old Testament advises a man to 'gird up his loins,' it means that he ought to wear a jockstrap, the implication being that the genitals must not become a hindrance. As the sale of suspensories and jock-straps indicate, the genitals can get seriously in the way of certain male endeavors. Nothing is more painful than accidents involving the testicles. The male ballet dancer must position his genitals over his pubic hair because the thighs are in constant motion and are some-times beaten together, as in an *entrechat*. Nijinsky had to leave the Marinsky Theatre Ballet because he danced Albrecht in a perform-ance of *Giselle* without the jockstrap that would have bunched his genitals into a mound at his crotch. A princess attending the per-formance was outraged that she could see the outline of his genitals quite clearly from her seat in a royal box and demanded that he be replaced. The end result was the formation of the Ballet Russe with its profound effect on modern art and music.

Individuals learn shame from their parents, just as we are told that Adam and Eve taught shame to all of us. What causes shame varies in every society and practically in every family in a heterogenous society. Nudity is a sexual stimulant only to the degree that society decrees it is. In nudist camps, the young man who has an erection in public is considered highly discourteous, and until he becomes used to feminine pulchritude fully exposed, he may have to hide behind bushes much of the time. Shame is a part of the communication process. It results from a personal interpretation of the attitudes of others as they are expressed in the great variety of ways that human beings have of communicating with one another. In sign language, one finger seeming to clean the finger of another hand indicates shame in the English-speaking portion of the world community. The sign may vary, but its purpose does not. Some indication that an individual has earned opprobrium by his actions is essential if the behavioral patterns of the social group are to be taught and reinforced. Shame internalized becomes guilt, and guilt projected becomes a defense mechanism.

Male genitals in a flaccid state are sexually exciting only to the extent that we decide they shall be. In an erect state, the penis is the loudest exclamation of body language. In Pompeii a stylized erect penis with testicles was used as an indication of a brothel nearby. It makes a very good pointer conveying the idea of sexuality and showing the direction all at once. Consequently, while variation in the depiction of flaccid penes is an indicator of social concepts of shame, an erect penis is always consigned to pornographic works, or at least erotica of a very frank nature.

The exposed female genitals are treated in the same way. A picture of the complicated structure of the labia, clitoris, urethral and vaginal openings is as assertively sexual as the erect penis. In many men, such a picture causes an erection immediately, and such representation is always considered pornographic. In fact, it may be quite scientific, although popular manuals of sexuality were careful not to show photographs of the genitals and not even diagrams of them that would indicate their readiness for coitus. The characteristic anatomical drawing of the penis always shows it in a flaccid state, and a picture of the female organs was devoted either to childbirth or virginity.

At about the time that pornography was released from governmental control, boy dolls and girl dolls with anatomically accurate parts were put on sale in the United States. They were sold in Europe before this time, and in the opinion of many psychologists were necessary because of the child's curiosity about his own body and the bodies of others. This has been a part of the discussion of the nature of sex education, where it should begin, and who should conduct it. A curiosity about the argument over the obviously boy dolls was that the opponents were not satisfied simply to refuse to buy them, they did not want them to be sold to anyone. The matter became a question of censorship at this point. Arguments were offered for restricting or preventing the sale, ranging from the familiar prevention of moral decay to the fact that the display of such dolls in department stores was an invasion of privacy. A casual glance was so threatening, apparently, that the sale of the dolls was to be prevented at all costs. In fact, the voluntary censor is rarely satisfied with a casual glance. Intense study would better describe his reaction.

Despite the fact that Desmond Morris assures us the buttocks are the most human, and hence probably most important, means of identification in body language, no such outrage has attended the development of dolls with quite realistic buttocks. Even in families where the genitalia must be hidden from the moment of birth onward, a male baby lying on his belly with his buttocks exposed was a favority photographic memento. An adoring mother would show the picture proudly to everyone she could. Dolls that could wet their diapers had added a realistic touch to such toys somewhat earlier, but these did not cause an uproar. Some parents deplored them as much because of the cost as for any reason of their being improper.

Male buttocks have not generally been considered a sexually exciting portion of the human body, although the female buttocks have. This is in an official sense, because the censoring of the human anatomy has at times included the cleft between the buttocks. In a film showing what ought to be censored prepared by the Citizens for Decent Literature, the photographs of naked male buttocks in magazines for homosexuals were blocked out lest the people viewing the picture be offended. A popular supposition is that only male homosexuals enjoy looking at naked male bodies, and it had to be made clear that Burt Reynolds is a heterosexual. Some individuals dislike the human body, although it always attracts attention. Apparently the human body in motion is a part of the imprinting of human beings, a subject that has barely been explored. Goslings will be imprinted by any living creature about the reasonable height for the focus and range of their eyesight, and they will regard this creature as 'mother.' That all mammals include imprinting as a part of maturation, perhaps its earliest significant event, awaits further exploration, especially so far as human beings are concerned.

The study in this area has been greatly hampered by concepts of morality that have nothing really to do with the case. If we are able to see stereotyping as an immoral act, then any conclusions based on the being of another person must be inaccurate when they are not odious. Human beings, though, react to the person of other human beings around them, and usually this reaction is governed by imprinting as it is modified by social pressures. If censorship were based on what is known to be harmful rather than on what develops reactions of shock and horror on the part of the censor, or at least causes him to use those words in describing his reaction, then it might have some value. But in fact, so far the only result of censorship has been the disfigurement of statuary, the modification or concealment of paintings, and the wholesale destruction of many works. So far as art is concerned, more has resulted from the battle against censorship than from its practice, and the efforts of suppression have never been so successful as the Victorians would like.

Anthony Comstock was particularly fierce in his punishment of painters and photographers. Practically everything that was recognizably human was 'lewd, lascivious, obscene, and tended to incite impure sexual feelings.' His funny reaction to the vapid painting entitled "September Morn" did much to advertise that kind of work. Nudity in fact is very enjoyable in a warm climate on a comfortable sunshiny day. Wearing shorts or a jockstrap only makes an effort of relaxation, and it becomes a duty like labor. Freedom from the restraint of clothing is a pleasure that many enjoy, when it conforms with the dictates of society.

An understanding of human beings is quite impossible without an awareness of the sexuality that the naked genitals represent. What makes human beings all of one kind, as a biologist will tell you, is the fact that the genitals are structurally identical and the species can interbreed without producing hybrids. The threat of race is in part based on real or fancied differences in genitalia, and one of the strangest is the belief that oriental women are equipped with totally different genitals making a kind of smile from thigh to thigh rather than the 'ditch' or 'trench' or 'gash' that characterizes caucasoid women. When a renowned Chinese actress first came to the United States she answered "It is untrue," before the question could be asked. Black men are supposed to be equipped with monstrous penes, and in some part this is true, but an overall identification of race by means of sexual organ is quite impossible. In the first place, we have no way of knowing whether a pure race exists on earth or not. If we say the Australian aborigines are a pure race, there is more supposition in the statement than fact. In Ashley Montagu's terms race is *Man's Most Dangerous Myth*.

If the size of the penis were an indication of social, or even sexual, value, then some rationality might be found in the widespread belief in the southern United States that black men have as their sole purpose in life the act of sexual intercourse with a white woman, with or without force, and that the size of the penis is proof of this supposition. During the period when slavery was the accepted practice in these states, it was believed that black men were not quite human, somewhere between the horse and the white planter. A favorite, though clandestine, argument was based on the 'largness of their parts.'

Man's favorite concern is that his penis is not quite large enough. Since it gives him pleasure, he wants a little more than he has. Furthermore, penile envy is not strictly confined to women. The Japanese "Pillow Books" often included vivid representations of the penis in a grandeur that every Japanese man would have liked for himself. Privacy probably begins with a man's unwillingness to exhibit his penis or even uncover it except in the totally safe situation of the male group in which he is a valued member or in the presence of the female bonded to him by social custom and his preferences.

Some analysts have suggested that Edward Albee's play *Who's Afraid of Virginia Woolf* has as its theme the impotence of the man who is the victim of his wife's incessant bickering. The son who is supposed to be alive according to the wife and be dead according to the husband is in fact the husband's penis which has retaliated by assuming the flaccidity that is acceptable in a work of art and quite a different matter in the bedroom. If this is indeed the theme, then Albee could have chosen no better method to explore it because male tumescence makes a poor subject for two hours traffic on the stage.

One of the grimmest events in a woman's life during the Victorian period was the first episode of sexual intercourse. 'Good women,' those who had not been trapped into prostitution by the economics of the times, were supposed to be shocked by the sight of a man's erect penis, and tender husbands would turn down the lamp or blow it out rather than let their wives see them naked. The average man today may be proud of and like to display his erection to his wife. Some men passed the entire of their married life without ever having seen their spouse in the nude, even as the large families of the Victorians were created, and it was only the worst kind of low woman who would want to see her husband's sexual equipment. The Bible assured the Victorians that it was a sin to uncover the nakedness of one's father, and the nudity of the female is still considered harmful to the average boy, let alone the prospect of seeing his mother in the nude. In fact, nude families over a period of many years demonstrate that the fact of nudity is of significance only as it is determined by social pressures and the constructs of shame.

Crime Against Nature

The sesquicentennial of the Victorians from 1820 to 1970 can be divided into two periods with the trial of Oscar Wilde serving as the turning point, exactly seventy-five years after the excessive repression began. Two years after Wilde was convicted, about the time he was released and went to France as Sebastian Melmoth, the term 'homosexuality' came into common usage in English. It was employed by German psychologists from about 1870 onward. Although Smollett referred to male homosexuality in *Roderick Random*, all further mention of the subject was forbidden, and to this day, the subject causes intense emotional reaction in some people, especially heterosexual males. During much of the period, an effort was made to find the cause of homosexuality, an investigation that is rather like trying to find the cause of headaches.

Krafft-Ebing in 1887 decided that homosexuality was caused by masturbation. His writings succeeded those of Ulrichs, himself a homosexual, and the obscure Hungarian coiner of the word 'homosexual' in a pamphlet published in 1869 signed as Kertbeny, a name used by Benkert. Ulrichs refused to accept the terms in common use: pederast, sodomite, catamite, and the slang words, 'bugger' for example. He suggested the word 'urning,' a germanicized form of Urania derived from Plato's *Symposium*. Homosexual as the word to describe sexual activity among individuals of the same sex has since come into common usage. In this work, it will refer only to sexuality among males, with the convenient term 'lesbianism' reserved for the female equivalent. While homosexuals may be punished by strict laws in most of the United States and in several European countries. lesbians are generally exempt from punishment except when caught in public displays.

As the only individual who could read Latin readily, the author here while in the Army Specialized Training Program became acquainted with Krafft-Ebing. Descriptions of sexual activity were left in Latin to protect those with less education and preserve them from the shock that such descriptions in the vernacular incur. Further study of Havelock Ellis and finally of the existing literature of homosexuality became a part of Army work during the second World War. A seminar paper prepared (with the help of another sergeant) for fellow psychiatric social workers in the Camp Carson Convalescent Hospital summarized knowledge at that time. The whole of the literature boiled down to explanations as patently ridiculous as Krafft-Ebing's, because each passed off as complete truth what was a special case explained as typical of the whole variety of human experiences covered by the word 'homosexual.'

The strongest taboo, except for that preventing incest, fouled investigation into the subject to such an extent that serious scientists were considered to be homosexuals simply because they wrote on the subject. In fact, almost all of the writers who have not been apologists and many of these as well, have been heterosexual in their orientation. Despite the reluctance of legislators in most of the United States to change the laws, the taboo has disappeared in a way that will serve as a model for the further study of censorship. Suppression is complete when the subject cannot even be mentioned. This attitude prevailed in much of the nineteenth century and was changed only by the necessity of reporting the trial of Oscar Wilde. All mention of homosexuality was forbidden in the Hays Code for motion pictures, and sodomy was punishable by sentences of a year to life depending on the state where the crime was committed and its perpetrators brought to trial. This is somewhat better than the death sentence advocated in Leviticus in the Old Testament and carried out through most of Catholic Europe until the Napoleonic Code was widely adopted.

Because the charge of homosexuality is capable of being denied without being refuted, blackmailers use the laws that make homosexuality a crime even when its practice is the private activity of consenting adults. The punishment for sodomy, *peccatum mutum*, the silent sin of confessional manuals, was beheading in the case of nobles and any of several methods of torture from which death was the release for the common folk. In the uproar attending the newspaper publicity of a vice ring in Boise, Idaho, one miscreant was sentenced to life imprisonment in 1955. When no proof other than accusation was needed, blackmailers could operate against innocent persons; when proof was required, as in the case of Oscar Wilde, a willing informer could be found. A blackmail ring operated quite successfully in the United States in the nineteen-sixties and was finally exposed when various men in high places had been involved.

Johnny Carson, among other television personalities, has done much to eradicate the sting of the taboo by making homosexuality the subject of jokes, a common feature of popular humor, possibly because his orientation as a heterosexual is beyond question. It is difficult to maintain that an activity is a crime "that cries out for vengeance" and is "against nature" if it can be bruited about on television and laughed at. The tendency is seen in the words associated with homosexuality that have lost their taboo status and been acclimated as part of the vocabulary available without the need for apology when used.

Efforts of scientists to find a cause have been generally unsuccessful, because the word covers too wide a territory. There is a vast difference between the casual homosexual adventure comprising most of the one-third who reported this to Kinsey's investigators, and the fixated compulsive homosexual who is incapable of coitus with a woman. In his valuable survey, Arno Karlen indicates that a study of homosexuality is necessary if any understanding of heterosexuality is to be sought. His book, *Sexuality and Homosexuality*, includes so complete a summary that the reader who wishes to study the subject beyond what is intended here can do no better than begin with Karlen's work and pursue his sources.

A most important finding is that homosexuality is not on the increase, but rather its secrecy has vanished to the point that a respected writer can describe homosexual activities in his own life with impunity. Merle Miller's *On Being Different* is not hidden by pseudonymy or dressed up with fiction. The general result is sympathy on the part of intelligent people most of whom have known a homosexual as friend or relative or associate. Not even homosexuals recommend it as a way of life, except in a very tangential way. The prospect of universal homosexuality is more remote than destruction by atomic warfare and constitutes a threat much less dangerous in the views of ecologists than continued overpopulation.

Three currents of change converging caused the end of obscenity in the world community. First, the communications revolution has made all the men in the lands surrounded by the oceans recognizably brothers. Second, science has turned its attention to the study of mankind in all his activity, relating the present to the past without the intervention of moral dogma, and finally, legal structures are with great effort being unpinned from the assumptions of religion so that they gain support from the much more reliable data of science. These currents can be traced with considerable success in the changing attitudes toward homosexual activity.

At a certain time, all homosexuals were criminals, suspected of having a different bodily structure from others. Aaron Rosanoff was the last to attempt a scientific proof of this theorem, using studies of male hormones in the urine of twins who were reared separately. His claims rest on the tenuous comparison of statistics resulting from analysis of the sexual behavior of each twin as it relates to the urinalysis he employed. There is no way of disproving the findings if the assumptions are accepted as evidence obtained from the physiology of the individuals, but Rosanoff's statistics can be obtained by a random assortment of men willing to confide a sexual history and donate some urine for testing.

The development of the idea that homosexuality constitutes a neurosis is just about as tenuous. Irving Bieber bases his findings on the opinions of psychiatrists regarding their patients, so that at best he is using an opinion poll of experts as if it were the analysis of the patients. Such methods assume that all psychiatrists are right and that the consensus removes such minor differences as may occur. In fact, all psychiatrists can be as self-convinced as the religious leaders were when the consensus was that God would never create anything imperfect, hence the orbit of the earth must be a circle because it is a perfect figure. Homosexual activity may be a reliable symptom of neurosis, but it cannot be called a neurosis in itself.

Evelyn Hooker found that homosexuality did not assume the configuration in the results of the Rorschach test that can be seen clearly for the identified disease entities such as psychosomatic states, functional psychosis, and some diseases of the central nervous system, organic in origin but with a characteristic pattern of responses in the "ink-blot test." This was greeted with horror by the psychologists attending the meeting where her results were announced. The term 'homosexual orientation' is used here out of respect for her findings.

In most functioning occupational groups, the sexual preferences of an individual are generally of no open concern. In the university setting, only the insistent indiscretion of a faculty member can gain him any kind of attention. Homosexual physicians and lawyers function quite as happily as their heterosexual fellows, and in some occupations homosexuals are never known or noticed nor are heterosexuals. What has changed is the idea that a homosexual constitutes a threat by his very being. Until the offer of sexual activity is made, there is no reason for the average man to be concerned with the orientation of another man. Even when such an offer is made, the reaction of many men is simply a polite 'no thanks' rather than the belligerence that was formerly adopted as a proof of masculinity.

Heterosexuality is no proof of masculinity, in the sense that certain activities are considered manly and others are not. The concept of manliness gives rise to much homoerotic but acceptable work of the imagination. As the sexual roles of men and women are sorted out the identification of certain occupations with heterosexuality or homosexuality becomes impossible. Not all hair dressers and male dancers are either heterosexual or homosexual in their preferences. What has occurred is the death of a stereotype and the acceptance of individual differences.

One of the most important corrections of scientific inaccuracy occurred when Kinsey rated homosexuality on a scale from none at all to nothing else. Before that time (1948) a homosexual was an individual who had ever had a homosexual experience, as if a single adventure were enough to make a convert of anyone. Sex play that is utterly meaningless except as it is punished may involve youngsters of the same or different sex. No conclusions can be reached about sex play as a causal factor any more than other situations. Many overt homosexuals with no interest in women come from homes where a shrewish mother dominated the household in the absence, or disinterest, of the father. This is not a cause so much as it is an explanation, and the son in such surroundings has many ways of expressing his dissatisfaction with his mother ranging from occupations of which she disapproves to marriage with a girl whom she dislikes. Overt homosexuality may placate the mother because it avoids one possible mode of independence.

The removal of societal secrecy may be most important in the renewed campaign against venereal disease. Male homosexual activity is one of the chief sources of infection in the spread of both gonorrhea and syphilis. Permitting homosexuals to seek treatment without obtaining a sermonette on the evils of genital activity among members of the same sex will do much to make the infected or exposed individual willing to consult a physician. A medical degree does not confer upon anyone the right to judge his fellow man and upbraid him when he fails to meet the moral standards the physician enjoys for himself or demands of the world around him.

According to William Blake, "The tigers of wrath are wiser than the horses of instruction." The Victorians continued a self-defeating religion. Homosexuality was greeted with wrath confirmed by the

Bible whenever it served the purpose of an individual to find a weakness where he might make his assault. The return of the tigers in a new guise can only be expected. The key to censorship lies in the paranoid dilemma that provides the wrath for the tiger. If we accept the definition that participation in a homosexual act constitutes homosexuality, then we must find the sexual activity of other males, regardless of the partner involved, a homosexual experience in which the viewer participates and identifies with the male, thereby sharing his genital activity, or even worse identifies with the female, thereby receiving the sexual attention of another male. That the definition is erroneous does not matter. If you are convinced that a shape in the dark is a man with a raised rifle ready to shoot you, then the actuality of the shape is inconsequential. The paranoid dilemma rests upon a misinterpretation of sexual experience that was standard assumption until the warfare between science and religion had reached the stage of final treaty, or at least cease-fire. A sexual experience of any kind has only the significance the individual gives it unless he manages to procreate in the process. Until the sperm reach the ovum, no important change in the nature of the world has taken place. Once conception begins and is carried to its ultimate result in the birth of a child, the sexual act is a determinant of the future of everyone in some degree. In a scientific sense, masturbation is meaningless, and most homosexual activity is equally insignificant in the larger scheme of things.

In the development of a science of man, the idea that sexuality was somehow of great and mysterious importance has only slowly been defeated, and it revives from time to time. Sexual activity is pleasurable just as the satisfaction of any other instinctual appetite is the source of bodily pleasure. As with all instinctual appetites, once the hunger for sex is satisfied, nothing remains but memory. Maturation in the individual begins as imprinting and ends as identification of the self and its propensity for prolongation of life. We glamorize our sexual activity and institutionalize it to give it importance, we make judgements of eternal damnation depend upon it, but who cares today whether Havelock Ellis ever masturbated? The sexual appetite is renewed, more or less regularly as occasion and need coincide. Marriage, or pair bonding in the ethological sense, provides the maximum of opportunity with the minimum of blame, according to Bernard Shaw.

The general result of scientific study of sexual roles has been very beneficial. Children need the love of both parents and a father caring for his child is not effeminate. As the terror of homosexuality has diminished, the male finds a role at once easier and more nearly freed of hypocritical self-denial. Men whose sexual preferences have never veered from heterosexuality can love one another without any genital manipulation. Affection is often conveyed by touching, and in the Orient good friends walk hand in hand down the streed together, sometimes discussing their respective girl-friends. Even a trial run of homosexuality will prove dissatisfying to most men, and without benefit of psychiatric treatment or harangues by a moralist, they will turn to heterosexuality as the source of sexual enjoyment. For all but a small but determined minority, homosexuality is disappointing whether the attendant guilt worsens the memory or not. No one was made into a homosexual against his will though often without his understanding of an innate freedom of choice that has always determined human actions. No one is condemned to seek harmless pleasure where it cannot be found, and much of the unhappiness of homosexuals, as their literature confirms, is the result of adopting an attitude that they wish to be freed of but cannot escape. The term 'homosexual' is about as meaningless as the words used for race and offers no prediction of what such a person may be like.

III.

THE TIGERS OF WRATH

Burning Bright

The question of who shall guard the public morals assumes that the members of the public are incapable of providing for their own moral future, although the framers of the U.S. Constitution assumed the citizens could decide on what they wanted their government to be. Why the moral future of the citizens of a democracy needs the heavy hand of authority while the political future does not requires explanations that are very like the symbolic and substitutive arguments of the paranoiac. At a time when the ecclesiastical court could try offenses against public morality that were beyond the reach of the civil courts, the guardians of the public were the religious leaders. When freedom of worship is guaranteed, there is an expectation of freedom of conscience and obedience to the civil law. The development of a conscience is the result of careful education from the earliest point at which an infant's acts are considered improper and to be denied him. This varies in society from group to group. Toilet training in the Orient is much aided by the nudity of the children in places where it counts most. Even birds teach their young not to foul the nest. If sex is dirty, then it fouls the nest, and this can be enlarged to mean fouling the social order. The word 'filthy' used with 'lewd' and 'lascivious' is the clue. In human anatomy there is good reason to mix the one set of semantic contexts with the other because of the contiguity of excretory and sexual functions. Excrement is dirty and dangerous, and even the silliest tiger knows that his tracks must be covered lest his prey smell out his presence and flee. If human beings were still 'killer apes,' the fouling of the nest might be similar to the cleanliness found in the dens of beasts of prey. Someone must assume an authoritarian role if the nest of our society is to be kept clean. One of the great accomplishments of the People's Republic of China has been to clean up a country that was publicly a

69

dung heap and privately spotless. Now the cleanliness everywhere seen is a national tradition and if not next to godliness at least Marxist, Leninist, and Maoist.

This authority can come from only one source, the populace over which it is exercised. It may be extracted by force, secured by terror, petitioned by public servants, but it must be conferred. It does not reside in the governing body. When the governed decide that they wish to change the authority, they can do so consonant with the way in which they are governed. If force is the method, then a greater force is needed. If elections are the method, a new election will effect a revolution just as profound as those in history concluded only after a wild period of indiscriminate slaughter. A characteristic of revolutions is that the enemy may appear as one's own lieutenants whose protestations of innocence only confirm their guilt. The seeds of sexual revolution were planted when the civil courts took on themselves the punishment of offenses against public morality.

If the offense is committed in private, and is limited to masturbation as a kind of salute to the shock value of a given piece of printed communication, then so little damage results as scarcely to affect public morality. What may occur, and help the moral censors become virtual tigers, is a relaxation of the sense of values that makes masturbation the most heinous of sins. It is a long way from the mild rebukes at the beginning of official censorship in the United States to the twenty-five year sentence imposed toward its end by a judge in Michigan over-reacting to a bawdy little novel that included the sexual misbehavior of jurists. Public morality is not a physical reality in itself, as we might analyze the quality of air or the purity of water, but rather a supposition derived from the evidence the public provides of the state of conditioning as determined by moral leaders. In a heterogeneous society, this conditioning may take many forms. Masturbation is now regarded as beneficial rather than harmful, and the Victorian fear that loss of semen greatly weakened a man is now known to be utterly groundless. Prostitution was to a large degree condoned by the Victorian man, for some other woman than any of those related to him, as a safety valve required by society. Masturbation caused insanity, continence was harmful, and involuntary emissions of semen constituted a disease entity, spermatorrhea, quite as deadly as masturbation. The only solution, and much of the economic theorizing of the time implies this, is an occupation for women as prostitutes that provided men with the sexual outlet they needed in a socially acceptable though unmentionable way.

In a society of killers, there is only one punishment worth note, that which inflicts pain. At a time when public whipping and public executions were accepted deterrents of crime, a man named Peter Holmes appealed a judgement of the Massachusetts Circuit Court of Common Pleas that he had committed a misdemeanor by publishing John Cleland's *Memoirs of a Woman of Pleasure* and worse than that, including illustrations. The period of James Monroe's administration had continued into, if later historians are correct, the Era of Good Feeling. The capital of Liberia was named Monrovia, the Missouri compromise managed to continue slavery into the South without upsetting the balance of power as a new state was added to the Union, and Spain had ceded Florida to the young Republic. Massachusetts, where Holmes came to grief, ruled that no statute was needed to convict him of a misdemeanor and that loss of life, limb, or banishment was not a possible sentence. The same book was republished by G. P. Putnam and ruled obscene by several courts in 1962 and 1963. This time the book was put on trial rather than the publisher. On March 21, 1966, the United States Supreme Court ruled that the scant literary merit observed in the book was sufficient to rule it not obscene. However, they did not rule out the possibility that a 'panderer' might exploit the book in such a way as to make its obscenity weigh more heavily than whatever redeeming social value had been discerned in the book. From 1821 to 1966 is a long time for a book to survive, even if its value was greatly enhanced by its illegal status. With the resolution of the case of *Fanny Hill*, as the book was commonly known, the revolution was in full swing.

Clandestine editions of *Fanny Hill* appeared regularly after it was first published in two volumes in 1747 to 1749. The indefatigable Pisanus Fraxi spent some time trying to find a first edition, *editio princeps*, which must now be a very rare book indeed. The book was then published in two volumes and was reviewed quite favorably in *The Monthly Review* for April, 1750, under the name *Memoirs of Fanny Hill*. It had apparently been published only to be seized on November 8, 1749, as a "most obscene and infamous book." The warrant argues against 1750 as the date of first publication. A further problem is an episode at Hampton Court omitted from the 1749, 1784, and Putnam edition of 1962, but included in the updated edition, probably printed about the time of the first edition. This is a scene of sodomy involving a youth of nineteen and one of seventeen, described in the style characteristic of the rest of the work and either written by John Cleland or some one who could imitate his style to perfection. It seems reasonable to suppose that it was included in the edition recorded as published in the years from 1747 to 1750 by G. Fenton. Pisanus Fraxi's copy is supposed to be taken from the original corrected edition.

The work was, of course, in the public domain when Putnam decided to republish it. Soon after *Fanny Hill* was ruled to be not obscene within the legal definition of that word very many editions in paperback were issued, some as execrably printed as the numerous Victorian republications, reprintings, and re-reprintings. The Hampton Court episode is included in some and omitted in others, but in any case it contains the repugnant idea for the many censors who have worked their will on it "that ignorance of a vice is by no means a guard against it." Suppression of *Fanny Hill* was virtually complete until Putnam decided to bring it to the light of day, under the assumption that the average man was able to read it without any special subversion of his morals. However, in other suppressed works *Fanny Hill* is mentioned as the book used to initiate sexual activity. It seems very likely that the corruptibility of adolescence remembered with secret regret motivated the guilt projected by two centuries of censors, voluntary and official. It is very difficult to expunge a book, particularly if it interests anybody, and *Fanny Hill* was translated into most of the European languages during the nineteenth century. French editions of several different translations were especially numerous. A happy coincidence can be used to put the revolution into its perspective. The year that Putnam published *Fanny Hill* saw a decision rendered in the *Manual Enterprises vs. Day* case.

If moral matters could be separated from religion, then there might be good reason to put private immorality among the acts that require public trial, but religion has been a part of censorship since it developed into a system of governmental authority. Lord Cockburn ruled in *Queen vs. Hicklin* on a case that included the imprisonment of several individuals as a result of the volume the court finally banned. In large part it is a Protestant tract, as its title implies, *The Confessional Unmasked*, with a variety of subtitles: "Depravity of the Priesthood," "Immorality of the Confessional," which served as a title in the various rewritings of the work. It was derived from the confessional manual of Dens with additions from the *Moral Theology* of Saint Alphonsus Mary de Liguori, whose feast day is August 2 in the church calendar. In these and other books, the Roman Catholic Church is attacked by means of its confessional manuals meant for use in seminaries. Some were published in France, others in Ireland, and a few in England. The Protestant Evangelical and Electoral Union is the publisher of the pamphlet known as "The Confessional Unmasked" despite its many different titles. What makes these works censorable for moral reasons is their descriptions of 'unnatural acts,' as Pisanus Fraxi delicately puts it. These tracts were issued as a political move in the attempt to make confession unlawful because of the things that might be discussed. Scott, who appealed, was

a metal worker in Wolverhampton, and the pamphlet had been ruled
obscene by two justices, one of them Hicklin, who was overruled
by the Recorder. Lord Cockburn's decision reversed that of the
Recorder, and the censoring of the censors was complete. The Protestant Union had only reprinted the confession manual in order to
show how it encouraged talk of the most obscene kind. Racing
around unseen in this decision is the problem of how to prove obscenity if no example of it may be offered in evidence. The Mayor's
Court of Philadelphia insisted that such evidence was not necessary.
Lord Cockburn noted that an obscene word or even a passage, when
obscenity was not the whole purpose of the work, was insufficient
to render a book obscene within the meaning of the law. Jeremy
Collier's pamphlet "A Short View of Immorality on the English
Stage" contains passages as examples that are meant to prove his
point.

The decision that all reference to sexuality was immoral had been
made much earlier and gained currency from the time of Collier's
pamphlet in the early eighteenth century. The sacerdotal language
had always excluded references to sexuality because of the celibacy
of priests who had to subdue their sexual drive. By the end of the
reign of George III, all society had become victim to a degree of
nice-nelliness that included the privilege of fainting if something too
strong was mentioned. Society was carefully structured among the
educated and uneducated, among the rich and poor, and among the
commonalty and the nobility. The whole facade was a sham and a
fraud. The author of *My Secret Life* prowls around among the working classes, seeking virgins and, in a couple of cases, young workmen
so badly in need of money that they submit to his homosexual experiments. Nevertheless, *Tom Jones*, by Henry Fielding, was locked
up in libraries as an obscene book and even figures in a censorship
case along with a great number of other classics: *The Decameron*
of Boccaccio, *Gargantua* by Rabelais, *The Heptameron* of Margaret
Queen of Navarre, and *The Satyricon* of Petronius.

A complete translation of Petronius was not made until after the second World War, because the novel treats of the love affair of Encolpius for Giton and his homosexual relations with a fellow student, Ascyltos. At times the novel is too graphic for the tender sensibilities of the Victorians, and it may be plainly disgusting to many who are under no obligation to read it beyond the page that upsets them. But the question of the times centers around whether the best way to avoid unnatural acts is to ignore them. If by unnatural we mean as it affects the individual, whatever the act may be, then the advice is very sound. If we try to extend this over the whole range of human experience, we are in very deep difficulty. Homosexuality was not punished in ancient Greece but rather recommended, to what degree remains a matter of conjecture. The Greeks certainly married and begot young, whatever the practices among consenting males might have been, and sodomy is certainly prevalent in every society so far studied, whatever the society may decree as permissible.

Havelock Ellis served a role like that of Kinsey at a later time, but his method was quite different. Ellis collected case histories, thereby starting a literary genre, but his purpose was not sexual titillation, only the gathering of facts. Taking his case histories, the suppressed works of the time, and such monumental endeavors as *My Secret Life*, we can come up with a portrait of the Victorian period in England populated with human beings not unlike ourselves. A heuristic model of the psychosexual development of our great grandfathers, or great-great grandfathers, would not differ much from what we would derive from current case histories.

The arrogance of the censors consists in attempting to set themselves apart from all others as they insist that others will be depraved and corrupted by what incites their urges to protect society. Frequently the motivation is not nearly so honest, for even in the moral censorship of the nineteenth century there is a desire to maintain the *status quo* of propaganda that cannot be admitted without defeating its purpose. Lists of censored books will always have more readers than lists of books recommended for their high moral purpose. For one thing, the reader thinks that he belongs to the privileged group that includes the censor. For another, we would rather be shocked than elevated.

Any attempt to combine suppression with freedom of the press ends in the fantastic waste of legal energy that the history of censorship represents to date. Moral censorship when its object was to prevent knowledge of sexual acts thought to be unnatural and physically harmful generally failed because the act was readily invented by each individual as opportunity arose. Masturbation to orgasm, the pollution against which the authors of confessional manuals inveighed, is as often discovered without the help of anyone else as it is taught. Even homosexual acts may take place in boyhood without doing more than providing the individual with a knowledge that some sexual activity is painful and without enjoyment. The most treasured idea of the nineteenth century was the innocence of children, and it prevailed until Freud began to publish his works on the unconscious mind. That Freud was criticized and censored was to be expected as his investigation ran counter to accepted beliefs.

So long as society gave its applause to the censors, who represented a morality that the individual wished to make known as his own whether true or false, the burden of proof was on the defendant hailed into court for having published or sold an obscene work. When the knowledge that human beings achieve sexual morality as the result of instruction and self-control became more common, then the theme of the censors changed. Even their method changed, for the individual was no longer the object of the censor's pursuit but the work itself. When *Fanny Hill* was once again on trial, it was the book not Putnam, the publisher, that was brought into court to face the censors' decisions. In the process, something remarkable occurred as a judge decided what the community could read and what it was not to be trusted with: Shame had turned to guilt. A guilty knowledge that one had been stimulated by a book was enough to decide that others should not have the same privilege. Sexual stimulation is not only harmless, it is quite natural, and when it leads to a release of nervous tension resulting from frustration, it is beneficial. The next step is the eradication of guilt and a degree of mental health.

The Forests of the Night

Public laws preventing private immorality have been used like the laws of an earlier time meant to save society from witches. A concerted effort is made to apprehend and punish homosexuals in the belief that removing the practitioners will end the practice. Police decoys are sent out to places where homosexuals congregate, and the solicitation of homosexual activity brings the wrath of the law down on the solicitor. In the hair-splitting of courts, this may or may not be entrapment. What is virtue on the part of the police force becomes vice on the part of a publisher.

The lengthy case that at last saw Ralph Ginzburg imprisoned was decided on material that would not cause a ruffle of excitement now. His periodical, *Eros*, was advertised as pornography, although it was within the limits of community candor because it was largely historical and had considerable redeeming social merit, it could not be attacked on this basis by the United States Supreme Court. The decision, then, was that a new test of obscenity would be whether the work was offered as pornography. The pandering test, as it has come to be known, is allied to the idea of guilty knowledge, *scienter*, that is essential to convict a bookseller of having sold obscene material, especially to minors.

The case has some, but probably the wrong, merit in showing that one cannot protect with one amendment what is violated in another. Ginzburg was convicted specifically of having violated the Comstock Law, prohibiting mailing obscene material. His mistake was in too loose and frivolous a mailing list that included Roman Catholic Bishops among others who would take immediate action against him. His appeals up to the Supreme Court brought on the statement of the pandering test, and his further appeals failed. There have been several results of this protracted case, aside from the manifestly unjust imprisonment for an offense that succeeded in clarifying the law and giving it more sanity than it formerly had. The United States Postal System finally assumed a role like that of the *Kempetai*, the Japanese thought-police who were maintained until 1945. A process called "mail cover" was instituted so that inspectors could open first class mail to see whether obscene material was contained therein. It was only a short step from this kind of moral supervision to the total supervision of an authoritarian government.

Although the private letters of individuals were at times seized, their contents read, and the sender advised that he had best plead guilty to a violation of the law lest a greater wrath fall upon him, the cases deriving from *Stanley vs. Georgia* and the new postal regulations protect the privacy of the individual without restraining those who wish to obtain material that would have been ruled obscene in an extreme degree in earlier times. The great overhauling of the laws of obscenity is still in progress, but so far the Comstock Act is a dead issue. (As Anthony Comstock would have had it, all indecency, including matter advocating atheism, would be subject to seizure and the sender punished.) Obscenity laws are being changed at a time when homosexual acts between consenting adults in private are beyond the reach of the law in Great Britain and Canada and presumably will gradually be removed from the crimes on the law books of those United States that have not already followed the lead of Illinois.

At the time the postal regulations were rushed through Congress with a lack of discussion that seems quite odd now, the social classes in the English-speaking countries were well established. Censorship in Great Britain generally was in direct proportion to the cheapness and availability of the material. There is a strong and inescapable current of elitism in all censorship activities, from the moral superiority claimed by the censor to the belief that certain people are not open to the influences that would deprave and corrupt the common folk. A high-priced book of obscenity could be published with impunity while the publisher, book-seller, and sometimes the purchaser of a cheap book would face prosecution and imprisonment. Comstock's efforts for the suppression of vice are reported in his books with much of the excitement of a breathless chase by an indefatigable detective. He learned something, evidently, from the cheap novels he was forever condemning. In deciding that the Society for the Suppression of Vice did not have the right to forbid the sale of classics of which they disapproved, even though the works included the *Confessions* of Jean Jacques Rousseau and *Art of Love* of Ovid, the Supreme Court of New York County in the case usually called "In re Worthington Company" stated the idea precisely, "rare and costly books . . . would not be bought nor appreciated by the class of people for whom unclean publications ought to be withheld."

Poverty was shameful, and in a manner similar to the Buddhist concept of Karma, it was the lot of people whom God wanted to punish. The sentimental notion that virtue was rewarded, preferably in cash and with social prestige, was very much favored in the eighteenth century. It is the basis of Richardson's *Pamela*, one of the few English novels to appear in the *Index Librorum Prohibitorum* issued by the Roman Catholic Church up to the reign of Pope Paul VI. The idea that poor folk were also immoral is contained in the change of meaning of the word 'lewd' from its Old English sense of unlearned, ignorant, poor, humble, and belonging to the lower orders to lewd, lascivious, licentious matched with the word 'vulgar.' It is derived from the Latin word for crowd, *vulgus*, and came to mean improper and indecent while the adjective often associated with it, *mobile*, abbreviated to 'mob,' came to mean a crowd in exactly the sense of '*vulgus*.' *Mobile* actually means fickle. Richardson has to make it quite clear that Pamela's parents are "poor but honest." The author of *My Secret Life* decries a society in which good-looking young virgins waste their treasures on common fellows from the streets where they are neighbors. There is a great sense of *droit de seigneur* in this attitude. A cheap book that contained matter of sexually related indecency would obviously inflame passions and set all the lower orders onto a course of wanton rape.

The court in deciding that a bookseller had violated an obscenity statute was not subject to significant challenge until the Dennett case in 1930. Individuals were convicted of having used such obscene words in the presence of females as 'rump' and of allowing a cow and a bull to copulate in the presence of women and children. Gautier's *Mademoiselle de Maupin* and Radcliffe Hall's *Well of Loneliness* were judged obscene, along with innumerable paintings, drawings, and photographs, whenever they, or the obscene books of the time, could be found and the purveyor apprehended. The Dennett case finally established that sex instruction of an especially pious kind was not obscene. An earlier view would have made Mrs. Dennett's pamphlet obscene as much because it was inexpensive as because it dealt with sex. Marie C. Stopes was the victim of an accusation about as dubious as the one that brought the Dennett case into court and onto appeal. The case began after the judgement of the Second Circuit Court of Appeals reversed the conviction of Mrs. Dennett. Putnam tried to import *Married Love* from London and fell afoul of the customs regulations, just as Mrs. Dennett ran into postal regulations. There has never been a lack of censors in the United States. Mary Ware Dennett's "The Sex Side of Life" was subtitled "An Explanation for Young People." In Judge Woolsey's opinion Marie C. Stopes did the same sort of thing for adults, and he thought the book should be welcomed into the United States. Even Dr. Stopes' book on contraception was permitted into the country, although the laws of the time forbade the sale of any article, drug, or medicine that could be used for contraceptive purpose, as well as the importation of such items.

Sex as a matter that could enter into the communicative process in other than a clandestine fashion was established by these and subsequent cases. From the Dennett case onward, the only question was how. The tide of opinion had turned as the experiment with prohibition failed. The Gotham Book Mart was allowed to sell translations of works by Andre Gide, an old friend of Oscar Wilde and a homosexual himself. When the proselytizing *Corydon* was published, it caused scarcely a ripple of concern. Gide's advocacy of homosexuality fell on deaf ears, or the equivalent, ears belonging to a man happily fixated in heterosexuality. Several differences appeared in the means by which the danger to the public morals was evaluated. Price was no longer to be an indicator of safety, because it could not be shown that the rich were immune to material that inflamed the passions nor that they had become so accustomed that such material would have no effect.

A large market in undercover books was circulating at this time, and the era of the blue movie had begun three decades before. The rich were those who could afford to see or own such works and wild parties, gangland murders, burlesque, and the stock market as the gambling center of the country were everywhere in evidence. The following decade saw a reversal of all that had made the twenties roar. Depression haunted the country, the rich voice of Franklin Roosevelt unified a great majority of the electorate, and the mass media included not only books, periodicals, and newspapers but also radio and the motion pictures. The Hays Code governed what could be shown on the screen, and strict laws prohibited the importation of motion pictures that did not meet thses standards.

The Hays Code prohibited any mention of homosexuality, and a great silence on the subject prevailed, broken at times by medical and psychiatric theorists. From the content of radio and the movies except for inadvertencies, one would suppose that the millennium of public morality had arrived. Mae West had her play *Sex* closed, possibly because of the title, and Mayor LaGuardia closed the burlesque theatres in New York City. It was a sham and a fraud. The dirty comic books, sometimes called "Tijuana Bibles" were sold everywhere, especially at the Chicago World's Fair in 1932. Works very much like the 'self-publishing books' that circulate through modern Russia despite its censorship practices were much in evidence. Only the republication of these titillating works that the older generation and their parents hid about the house kept the phenomena from obtaining obscurity as total as that that befell the pulp magazines of the time. The well-heeled could purchase books that were far too high priced for the average wage earner in his struggle with low wages and the high cost of living.

In the world community, after the disaster of the first World War, the actions of Adolf Hitler went unheeded, so that the second World War became inevitable. Nazism in Germany, Fascism in Italy, Communism in Russia exercised censorship of the strictest kind. Treason consisted in publishing works that did not have the prior approval of the government and the usual sentence was death. In the comfort of the traditional American freedom of political expression, although it was conceded that the First Amendment to the U.S. Constitution did not protect obscene works, the rush of the world toward its first atomic war was apparently the work of some force beyond the power of human beings to stop. Mention of the widespread homosexuality among the early followers of Adolf Hitler would mean at the least a one-way trip to a concentration camp, and if the charge was made openly enough, to the headsman who executed enemies of the state in the traditional German fashion, in Nazi Germany. It was simply obscene in the United States. A motion picture such as *The Damned* would have been banned throughout the United States, especially in Chicago where it later showed, where the film censors prohibited showing of the issue of *March of Time* entitled "Inside Nazi Germany." Degeneracy was prohibited by Adolf Hitler and known homosexuals were put among Jews and common thieves in concentration camps. Homosexuality was rife there, so long as the inmates were not starved to death, just as homosexuality is rife in

American prisons. Adolf Hitler fired his chief of staff, von Fritsch, on the basis of a trumped up accusation by some young man secured for the purpose. Later as the tide of war turned against Germany, guillotining or hanging could follow open declaration that the country was losing the war. Nevertheless, obscene material circulating in Germany, not aimed at the Jews but rather at other religious groups, especially fanatically Nazified leaders of various religious groups, consisted of whatever the average citizen was not allowed to think about his government. That it might be sex-related was only incidental. At the present time, the Greek junta that seized the government from the monarchy and rules in a very authoritarian fashion prohibits references to homosexuality in discussions of the Periclean age.

The rewriting of history prevented frank discussions of Henry Lord Darnley's bisexuality until recently. Christopher Marlowe was treated with a certain remoteness, especially when the supposition of homosexuality was made, and no high school or college teacher dreamed of assigning *Edward Second* to a class as an example of Marlowe's interests. The homosexuality of the French court at times was concealed as well, and any reference to Whitman's "Cadmus," a section of *Leaves of Grass*, had to emphasize that the "manly love of comrades" did not include crimes against nature. Oscar Wilde was impossible to hide as securely, but focus could remain not on the cause of Wilde's ill-advised suit against the Marquess of Queensberry but on its effects.

The communication process is used to reinforce conditioning in the accepted beliefs of a society. What opposes those beliefs must be extirpated or controlled. In the view of psychiatry at the time, homosexuality was evidence of sexual psychopathy, and the broad explanation of psychopathy was widely used, even though it was evidently untrue. A psychopath was incapable of deep emotional response; he was always in difficulty with the law because he had no way of controlling his own behavior; his wish was always translated into action; he was given to violent rages when thwarted; he was incapable of foreseeing the consequences of his instantaneous decisions. Generally psychopaths had a likable, breezy, and often charming personality, and doubtlesssome of the homosexuals within the definition were psychopaths. If a single instance of homosexual activity was the definition of a homosexual, then psychopaths who were notoriously lacking in self-control would have homosexual experiences when the opportunity arose and consequently could be called homosexuals.

The ten million men who went into the Armed Forces of the United States during the second World War made the discovery that homosexual activity is available to the soldier at almost every turn. The Articles of War prohibited it, of course, and if caught a soldier could be imprisoned for several years and get a dishonorable discharge from the service. A potential draftee could be classified 4F as unfit for service if he could prove that he had homosexual tendencies, but a strong sense of patriotism motivated homosexual men, many of whom served faithfully in a long list of responsible positions, without ever giving way to their sexual preferences. A man against whom there were no charges pending could insist that he had always had, or had developed, homosexual tendencies and obtain a discharge without honor as unfit for service, the Section Eight discharge that became a part of the common speech. The second World War was one of the great unifying forces in American life, and the war effort dominated everyone's thoughts.

That something was wrong with the concept of the medical scientists at the time seemed obvious, but a few years had to pass before any significant change was observed. The military has always lagged behind other fields of endeavor in its acceptance of scientific as opposed to technological advances. Despite the growing evidence that the concept of psychopathy was less a medical explanation than the condemnation of society put into medical mouths, the armed forces tended to regard homosexuality as a character neurosis and any who could be proved to have participated in homosexual acts as criminals or potential criminals. The attitude solidified and deepened until the postwar Armed Forces became virtually paranoid in their approach to the subject of sexual deviation.

The atomic warfare was limited to two bombs dropped on Japanese cities, and the war ended sooner than anyone hoped. The period of the occupation began with American soldiers stationed all over the world, in close touch with societies entirely unlike their own. The soldier in a foreign country usually hates it, partly because he always hates his present location and regards it as only a little better than the one he is going to. While serving in the Orient, many servicemen became aware that the Asiatic attitude toward homosexuality was not the hysterical disapproval of American society. Acculturation had begun that was to end in a sense of world community, at least so far as the communication process is concerned.

It should not be surprising that the comfortable pre-war world would have to give way before the onslaught of the great changes that the first atomic war was bound to bring. The first and greatest of these changes in perception was the realization that another atomic war would not only end civilization, it would end human, and perhaps all, life on this planet. When the United States thought that it had superiority in possessing the greatest weapon ever invented, a certain arrogance could filter into the thinking of everyone. When the series of spy trials and anti-communist witch hunts proved that the Soviet Union knew as much about atomic warfare as the military leaders of the United States, another world entirely was shaping in the minds of the free citizens outside the authoritarian countries of the world.

Fearful Symmetry

In the period from the end of the second World War until the publication of the *Report of the Commission on Obscenity and Pornography*, liberty took a nose dive in many places, truth was kicked around a lot, and the image of man took on a number of highlights that had never been possible before. From one point of view, the purpose of the obscenity laws had always been to try to separate the truly pornographic from the works of literary and social value, it being assumed that pornography had no value whatever. Whenever a work came into conflict with an established idea, it might be charged as obscene. The statutes were vague enough so that Swearington, in 1895, could be charged with violating the Comstock Act on the strength of having mailed copies of *The Burlington Courier*, for September 21, 1894. The article that was lewd, lascivious, and obscene charged a "mental and physical bastard" with every form of low life then known, being a pimp, and worse than a strumpet. The man was awarded a new trial because his article was libellous rather than obscene. Whether the object of his vituperation, who had "maligned and slandered every Populist in the state," sought redress of another kind is unknown.

The statutes were held to apply to phonorecordings and the strict control of the motion picture industry extended to the rule that the troops during World War II should not be subjected to political harassment such as could be found in the motion picture that was a biography of Woodrow Wilson. It should not be shown in Army camps, although soldiers and sailors could see it in theatres operated for the benefit of civilians. The Miracle Case, as it is sometimes called, is officially *Burstyn vs. Wilson, Commissioner of Education of New York, et. al.* The Board of Regents of the State of New York was empowered to issue licenses to motion pictures so that they could be shown publicly. Such a license was issued for an Italian film entitled *The Ways of Love*, but when one of the city officials saw it, the heat was on. The controversy that raged over the film finally reached the Board of Regents who reviewed their position and denied a license. They were permitted to do this, according to the Court of Appeals of New York, but the United States Supreme Court struck down the previous decisions and then ruled that motion pictures come under the provisions of the Bill of Rights and its first amendment to the U.S. Constitution. However, what put Cardinal Spellman at odds with the Vatican was the question of whether the film was sacrilegious or not. Piero Regnoli writing in the official Vatican newspaper, *L'Osservatore Romano*, thought not, and neither did Roberto Rosselini who made the film. Anna Magnani portrays a goat tender who is seduced by an itinerant stranger whom the peasant woman insanely thinks is Saint Joseph. After being mocked by the people of the village as she is about to deliver a child, the peasant woman regains her sanity through maternal love for the child she has given birth to. This is "The Miracle" implied by the title of the segment found objectionable by many of the Roman Catholics in New York City, especially Cardinal Spellman. The United States Supreme Court decided that censorship based on religious interpretations was far beyond what the Bill of Rights would permit.

Political censorship was attempted with the Smith Act seeking to punish those who advocated overthrow by force and violence of the U.S. Constitution and the government it empowered. Communists were under every bed, and two hundred unidentified ones infested the U.S. State Department, which according to Senator Joseph McCarthy of Wisconsin, was also providing employment to men of homosexual orientation. A description of the career of Senator McCarthy is worthy of the large literature that was built up during and after his forays in the affairs of the time. Blacklists and guilt by accusation became as commonplace as any that were used in the medieval church or Nazi Germany to find and punish their respective heretics. A fascinating irony existed in that the Soviet Union was likely to punish its own kind of heretic just as brutally, or more so, than the United States of McCarthy's time. Anyone coming close to advocating a serious study of communism was likely to be labelled a communist and pursued vigorously through the courts. Westbrook Pegler assumed that the punishment was all to the good and suggested that New Deal Democrats, whom he hated, be arrested and put into concentration camps, thereby assuring the perpetuation of American liberty. In the confused ideas of Westbrook Pegler no contradiction was involved. Freedom of speech was understood to include only those remarks of which official opinion approved, and, under this definition, is indistinguishable from the thought control of other governments at other times. Taken in its larger sense, such freedom is no different from the restraints placed upon speech that was supposedly obscene. There is no reason to believe that the word 'rump' is an obscene word, especially if the local butcher can advertise specials on 'rump roast.' In fact, history would have to be rewritten carefully so that the 'rump parliament' of Cromwell's time could be given a name that was not obscene.

The fear of homosexuals reached its height when the pattern established by Alfred Redl in Imperial Austria before the first World War seemed to be duplicated by the variety of cases involving homosexuals and espionage, in the wild games taking center stage in the United States, the various communist countries, and some of the democracies of Europe. Supposedly, the Central Intelligence Agency employed homosexuals in just the same capacity as the communist counterpart agencies used them. They were not notably successful, and if true, the whole project was carefully suppressed by the secrecy of government that became even stricter than it was during the second World War. However, no cases involving censorship of homosexual literature was attempted for the very good reason that there was nothing to censor. The *Sunshine and Health* publications that had gone through the mill of liberation by the U.S. Supreme Court included naked men as well as naked women. It was the former, more obviously sexual beings, that incited the ire of the censors. Edward T. McCaffrey, who began the action ending in the Supreme Court decision in the Miracle case, used his powers as Commissioner of Licenses of the City of New York to forbid the sale of several nudist publications. This was a pattern repeated frequently throughout the country, with a variety of police and other officials acting as the local censors. They aimed their restraint at magazines and paperback books. The cheap book syndrome had taken over with the popularization of paperbacked books. They were first published in 1939, but it was not until the end of the second World War that these books became a fixture of publishing. Pornographic paperback books were being published as well.

An event of considerable importance had occurred in France, where Maurice Girodias founded The Olympia Press in 1953. Several authors immediately became contributors, including Henry Miller, Francis Pollini, Vladimir Nabokov, Jean Genet, Lawrence Durrell, and others who hid behind pseudonyms. Publishing in English in France kept Girodias free of censorship until the regime of De Gaulle began. Many of the authors found Olympia Press the only publisher willing to risk publication in its Traveller's Companion series. They were sold everywhere, in bookstores from the Far East to the Middle East and in those European countries that did not forbid importation, especially Denmark and the Netherlands. Efforts were made by Dial Press to publish D. H. Lawrence's banned novel, *Lady Chatterley's Lover*, and Henry Miller's *Tropic of Cancer*. Just as Joyce's *Ulysses* had been smuggled into the United States or simply read while travellers were abroad, the wide variety of banned books available to the reader had the effect of removing their sting. The copies were cheap in the countries where no censorship prevailed. Pornography has always been on sale in the Orient, especially in China until the revolution that put the communist regime of Mao Tse-Tung into command. The books were sold under the counter in Hong Kong and in rather depressing little book stores in Japan. They were openly available in many places.

There is no evidence at all that sex crimes were commonplace among those who had bought and read the publications of The Olympia Press. In later studies, it was shown that pornography is not a causal factor in sex crimes, and in any case, none of the travellers were made into homosexuals by reading the literature available on the subject published by Girodias. This included the *Black Diaries* of Roger Casement; *Naked Lunch* by William Burroughs; *Journal of a Thief*, *Our Lady of the Flowers*, by Jean Genet. The effect of pornography, until the publication of the *Report of the Commission on Obscenity and Pornography*, was assumed to be 'the inflamation of passions,' with almost any illicit kind of sexual misbehavior the obvious result. If homosexual literature had a causal effect on behavior, then reading it should change a man's sexual orientation. This is obviously not so. There is evidence to the contrary that rests on ground only a little less shaky. Reading about male homosexuality may encourage a man who mistakenly thinks he is fixated to change his orientation. The literature of homosexuality is to the average man emetic rather than aphrodisiac, as Woolsey put it.

The publication of *Sexual Behavior in the Human Male* by Alfred C. Kinsey, Wardell B. Pomeroy, and Clyde E. Martin brought the subject into serious consideration. Although statisticians complained about the quality of interviewing and social workers decried Kinsey's statistics, a major re-examination of the sexual nature of human beings had begun. About a third of all men have had some kind of homosexual experience to orgasm, about a sixth have had homosexual experiences over a long period of time, about three to ten years, but only a twentieth remain homosexually oriented all their lives. Along with the shocking numbers implied by these statistics, supposing the sample is valid, is the idea that one homosexual experience does not mean that an individual has become homosexually oriented. It may mean just the opposite. Kinsey confirmed what many had suspected all along, either from personal experience, carefully concealed, or from experience with men who had homosexual experience.

As a psychiatric social worker in the second World War, the author had the occasion to make a study of the literature of homosexuality. His obvious ignorance was detected by the chief social worker at the facility where the U.S. Army employed his services. Homosexuality was a significant and important part of many of the case histories of men who were in the Camp Carson Convalescent Hospital. There were almost as many kinds of homosexuality as there were men, ranging from the battlefield romances immortalized in the World War I song, "My Buddy," to the fixated homosexual soldier who wanted out of the service, after concealing his orientation for months and possibly years. The author learned of a secret world that had been misinterpreted by psychiatrists and by moralists, when the two were not combined in the same writer. Sociologists avoided the subject, and the police power of the government was armed but ineffective against those who made an obvious practice of homosexuality. In preparing a valid, scientific study of sexuality in both the male and the female, Kinsey had brought the methodology of zoology to bear on human beings so that they could see themselves without the illusions of guilt or the delusions of pride.

With an understanding of the sheer force of numbers represented in Kinsey's statistics, the gay community began to show itself openly even to the extent of accommodating the language with some of its jargon. 'Gay' is the word preferred by homosexuals in referring to themselves. At one point, the use of the word was enough to identify a fixated homosexual. At present, the word is simply a convenient short word. When gay people decide not to conceal their proclivities, they 'camp.' Finally camp, originally derived from theatre parlance, became an acceptable term. An individual who is not gay is straight. What happened was the creation of an identity that some men could live with happily, as at previous times in human history. Homosexuality is not infectious or contagious. It is apparently a fact of human nature, deriving from man's ability to experiment and to create mythical structures. The practice of homosexuality may be the only means of sexual and emotional satisfaction to some men and it may be the poor temporizing of a man deprived. Very likely, it can be controlled only by the individual himself, not by any system of laws except as they protect the young and punish physical assault and the misuse of public places.

The courts of the United States were percolating cases that included a final settlement of the nudist publications as not obscene and mailable, in accordance with the Roth decision. This was the final blow, the end of Lord Cockburn's rule, although it is restated from time to time. The Roth decision concerned an indictment for mailing obscene publications and photographs, and after Learned Hand's decision in the Kennerly case, a restatement of the test of obscenity was needed. By this time, Justices Douglas and Black consistently voted against confirming obscenity decisions, and they were joined by many other thinking persons, including federal and district court judges. Just as many opposed them, so that the test of obscenity became a crucial matter. As the case made its way to the U.S. Supreme Court, doubts were expressed about the intention of the founding fathers to prohibit obscenity even as they wrote the First Amendment to the U.S. Constitution. Franklin was the author of two short pieces that the nineteenth century would have found "lewd, filthy, indecent." What was at stake was the concept of freedom of the press, always at issue, and always subject to contention and discussion. It must be assumed that no government official is truly in favor of this freedom, although most condone it. When the licensing law of New York came under review in the Kingsley Pictures case, the idea was dispelled that an act of legislature could prevent the exhibition of pictures that display a pattern of behavior as acceptable and desirable contrary to the moral standards of the time. All along this had been the only real matter at law, for it is manifestly foolish to try to predict what will cause lustful and impure thoughts.

Lustful and impure thoughts, just like any others, are in any case beyond the reach of law if they are not communicated. To assert that a control of obscenity will end lustful and impure thoughts on the part of a large public that enjoys them is to wander in the legal provinces of cloud cuckoo land. One of the publications that was most often used for the purposes of supporting lustful and impure thoughts, probably also a spur to masturbatory impulse, was the mail-order catalogues of the time. These were often used in lieu of other paper in the outhouses that dotted the landscape at the turn of the century, and advertisements of ladies' underwear, though so prim as to be quaint today, inflamed the youth of the time no less successfully than what the youngsters, in their defused speech, call 'fuckbooks' today.

From the fine prose and the high moral purpose of the various decisions, a stranger to the actual social history would conclude that all the Edwardians were models of asexuality. Lawyers have enjoyed obscene stories as much as anyone else; telling sex-related jokes as a part of the male privilege of men in groups. The same stories printed would have fallen into the category of obscene publications and numerous laws could have been invoked to punish the offender. This raises the question of whether the obscenity statutes and the trials that arose from them were not motivated by the need of men to form male groups that excluded women and were privileged in a way that could not be permitted the general public. Beyond the paranoid dilemma, there is a problem of ethology in the communication of sex stories that has so far not been considered at any length. The concept of obscenity may be the result of male chauvinism rather than any high moral purpose. Writers who believe that the rules and strictures of censorship should be reimposed in the world community argue for a control of ideas, a shaping of thought, a belief that given the opportunity they could make the world a better place whether this was the desire of the public or not. Not even Adolf Hitler proposed his policies of violence and injustice on the basis that Germany would be other than improved by them. The contention is between authoritarianism, however masqueraded as helpful to society, and intellectual freedom that assumes no one to be capable of the decisions the authoritarian wishes to make. Democracy is repugnant to a man who cannot be convinced that he is capable of error.

The fearful symmetry of Kinsey's graphs and charts imply that there is no widespread prevalence of the ideal man conjectured as existing everywhere who needed the protection of the law to prevent his rampaging about displaying his sexual powers. We are faced with the fact that human beings have evolved as the dominant life form because they are capable of sexual activity at any time thereby nullifying the effect of the long period between birth and sexual maturity. If oestral cycles existed among human beings, the chances are that extinction would have ended the killer ape's rule of the planet long ago. As it is, this sexuality when channeled into reproduction becomes a bigger threat than any of man's enemies. When human beings have no other outlet for their ceaseless interest in sex, they will mate, and the result is the sharp peak representing the gestation period ended after an event that encourages sexual activity. The recent example of this is the huge increase in births about 280 days after the blackout in New York City and adjoining regions. This sharp increase was to be found only in those regions where the blackout left people with nothing else to do but make love and beget young.

Homosexual activity tends to occur when mammals are crowded together as several experiments have shown. An increase in male sexual experimentation with other males is likely to occur if the societal restraints are not operant, but the development of fixated homosexuality is quite unlikely in any more than six or seven per cent of the male populace at any one time. On Kinsey's closely calculated scales with seven points ranging from no homosexual experience to orgasm to exclusively homosexual experience, about half the population have no experience at all, especially if they marry before the age of forty. About half have some experience ranging from a casual and unrepeated experiment to prolonged accommodation of sexual needs by homosexual means.

No conclusions can be drawn from these facts. Considering the subsequent studies of the Institute of Sex Research, the statistics cover a period of time that becomes the more conclusive of our human status as it lengthens. Kinsey was interviewing the fathers of the generation that protested the Vietnam War, those protected by censorship laws, shielded from impure and lustful thoughts by all the powers of church and state. Censorship obviously was a colossal failure and was probably the exercise of a compulsion at a societal level rather than the result of any rational impulse. Nothing can be assumed except that human sexuality is surprisingly independent of the communication process, being served by it rather than serving communication. There are probably good reasons for this yet to be discovered as all the instruments of research are turned on the understanding of the complete human being.

The tigers of authoritarianism still rule in many places, promising to rid the land of the flood of pornography, assisting district attorneys to gain fame by posing as the guardians of public morals whatever the private life of the man might be, and pretending that lustful and impure thoughts assail the *lumpenproletariat* in a way that demands the intervention of an all-wise, all-knowing individual immune from such influences. This is only a sham and fraud and should be mocked by anyone who has a passing acquaintance with the advancement of the social sciences recently. Given the freedom to experiment, human beings will do so, and even denied the freedom they will still experiment if opportunity arises. What preserves society is not the ineffective efforts of censorship, but the general willingness of the members of the world community to be guided by morality in accord with their own best interests.

IV.

THE ROAD OF EXCESS

Susceptible Community

The *Manual Enterprises vs. Day* case began as an administrative hearing when the Postmaster General ruled that three periodicals could not be mailed because they were obscene. Herman Lynn Womack owned two of them and was the publisher of the third. *Grecian Guild Pictorial, MANual*, and *Trim* were somewhere between catalogs of male models, and the studios where photographs were made of them, and club publications featuring pictures of club members. The Grecian Guild was a membership organization that included a subscription to the bi-monthly periodical, much like professional organizations of librarians, information scientists, and others. The periodical was on sale on newsstands, where it caused some commotion among the Citizens for Decent Literature, as well as the law-enforcement officials who tried to act as public censors. Before the case ended, the U.S. Supreme Court ruled, in 1962, on the question in a way that seemed to displease everybody.

The government based its case on the fact that the periodicals were published for the use of homosexuals who would take a prurient interest in the photographs included. This sensitive concern for the homosexual seems very strange, because no effort was made to show that the magazines would cause any man to turn to homosexuality as an outlet, just that homosexuals found the periodicals appealing to "a prurient interest in sex." The District Court hearing was only preliminary to the decision of the District of Columbia Circuit Court of Appeals. The ruling that the publications should be barred from the mails was upheld because the periodicals were obscene in themselves and provided advertisements where obscene material might be found. Using the Roth decision, the defendants argued that although the magazines would arouse the prurient interest of homosexuals, for whom they were intended, the average

97

member of the community was to be the sole measure, and he would react with disinterest or mild curiosity at the most. The Court of Appeals thought otherwise: "The proper test in this case, we think, is the reaction of the average member of the class for which the magazines were intended, homosexuals." This is wide of the mark, for no one thought to ask homosexuals themselves, so that the supposition of reaction on the part of homosexuals is important if we are not to believe that the government, its attorneys, and the courts were in fact made up of homosexuals who were giving their own reaction.

The average member of the community would find the publications curious. They have the quality of photographs from an album of all the males in a family, but a strange family for the men are posed in a variety of positions always with some kind of covering of the genitals. The dorsal view is ordinarily of the nude body, with the suggestion that male buttocks are sexually exciting. The males are aged anywhere from twelve to thirty. No old men are included, and a certain pursuit of male beauty is evident. According to the testimony of postal inspectors, the studios did have obscene photographs on hand, including what are now called 'action photos.' These are actual homosexual acts at least simulated for the photographer. The court cases have simply taken the private circulation of these pictures and made them public, but in so doing, the muscle magazines have followed the life cycle of other taboo materials—girly magazines, for instance—that are valuable to the extent that they overturn a custom and are forbidden for that reason. Open publication invites competition when there is nothing novel left to show, the point at which the market becomes glutted and the bargain prices begin.

The Circuit Court of Appeals was up a legal tree, and the United States Supreme Court joined society there under the forgivable impression that all would be made clear by their decision. Several issues were at stake, including a curious re-appearance of the Lord Cockburn rule, this time with homosexuals as those likely to be depraved and corrupted. The implication would surely be that they were neither depraved nor corrupted until the periodicals came to view. This was disposed of easily. Another question was whether the Roth decision, meant to be a summary judgement that would set a test for obscenity, should be applied part by part or only as a whole. Did the three elements of obscenity work separately or only together. This caused some difficulty, but it was decided that the three elements: whether to the average person, applying contemporary community standards, the dominant theme of the material taken as a whole appeals to prurient interest, had to work synergistically to rule out obscenity while protecting the freedom of expression. This decision rose up to haunt the Supreme Court, because it found only two tests in Roth: prurient interest and patent offensiveness. There was concealed in the statement a third test, social importance. If the theme of the material taken as a whole was meant not to appeal to prurient interest but to provide matter of social importance, then it could not be ruled obscene. In the Roth decision, the Supreme Court rejected the idea that all material that stimulated impure desires relating to sex should be barred from the mail, and in the Manual Enterprises case redeeming social importance was first viewed as under the protection of the First and Fourteenth Amendments to the U.S. Constitution.

Finally, a matter of great concern was raised by the case. The action of the Post Office authorities had established a kind of administrative censorship. From the days of the first act barring obscene material from the mail, this was considered highly dangerous. It is easy to use a loose definition of obscenity to include everything that the administration in power dislikes, and an administrative decision barring material from the mail could be extended to all kinds of material finally bringing the concept of constitutionally protected individual freedom into question. Part of the Manual Enterprises case is a review of administrative censorship and an admonition on its dangers.

Mr. Justice Clark dissented in a memorable way. He observed that "The magazines have no social, educational, or entertainment qualities but are designed solely as sex stimulants for homosexuals." The question of whether Womack knew that the advertisers in his magazines had obscene photographs for sale was considered by Mr. Clark to be adequately shown by Womack's conviction for mailing obscene materials and his second indictment. If the material appealed to the erotic interests of homosexuals, Mr. Clark's decision seems to say, then it is censorable by anyone with the power to exercise this function of government.

What is not touched upon by any of the pages of elegant, if rambling, prose and excellent history, is the curious fact that a man who wishes to look at a naked man has only to undress in front of a mirror. If he wishes to see someone other than himself, there are swimming pools, gymnasia, and many other places. The average man of fixed heterosexual orientation is very little inspired by the sight of naked males, although he may be interested in the general physical development and, if artistically inclined, by the pose as it resembles great works of art. The periodicals found mailable by the U.S. Supreme Court decision may have been "dismally unpleasant, uncouth, and tawdry" as Mr. Justice Harlan found them, but they gave a sense of membership and of worthiness to the homosexuals who purchased them. These were not very many, if the circulation figures are accurate. Only 25,000 copies of the magazine were distributed and about half of these were sent through the mails. If the object of the government was to deprive homosexuals of material that they would find erotic, then a system of massive espionage and intense censorship would be about as successful as the efforts made by the Soviet Union and the Peoples Republic of China. The homosexual is quite as able to fantasize as anyone else, and the publications only serve as the verification of fantasy, including the acceptance of homosexuality as a valid sexual outlet. There is good reason to suppose that homosexual literature tends to make the activity acceptable to the homosexual and provide him with a sense of identity and worth that he cannot find in society at large. A homosexual can build a private society in which he is accepted as an individual whose sex life is like those of his fellows, a state of perpetual courtship motivating his actions within a community that is itself ready to condemn him for as many reasons as it is ready to accept him.

The fiction of the 1940's emphasized the criminality of homosexual activity and invoked the sentimental device of cautionary endings. A man either changed his sexual orientation or suffered, sometimes by being murdered, more often by suicide, and as in Gore Vidal's original *The City and the Pillar*, sometimes by committing murder. The theme of violence in homosexual fiction was much stronger in the fiction that preceded the relaxation of censorship laws. Violence is still to be found in the homosexual fiction, varying from the sadism of *Two* by Eric Jourdan, a translation of the novel *Les Mauvais Anges*, to the extreme brutality of *Naked Lunch*, by Willaim Burroughs. The popular culture of the time made the open publication of what can be called closet literature very dangerous. While various reviewers complained about homosexual novels, no effort was made to censor them, because to the average man there is nothing erotic about them. They are tiresome until actual homosexual activity is graphically depicted. Then they become intensely shocking to the point of arousing anxiety and aggressive reactions as defenses in some susceptible men.

Homosexuality is used as the key to the anatomy of censorship not out of any preference of the author of this book, but because it provides the only example of a common phenomenon that is censored even in works of pornography. The Danish picture books of homosexuality do not include women and heterosexual intercourse; similarly, the picture books of heterosexuality, even though two men disport themselves with two or more women, exclude a slight suggestion of homosexuality beyond the possible voyeurism

of men watching sexual intercourse. Involved in the problem is the
relationship of the communication process to the establishment of
identity in the individual, with considerations of mammalian imprinting, group identification, and all the half-understood or barely
imagined influences that the communication processes have on human beings. As the Kronhausens point out in the introduction to
their *Erotic Fantasies* (the underground literature that has recently
been made available on the open market for adults) the study of
sex-oriented writings reveals the intensity of the human imagination
in dealing with a topic that has always been taboo in different measure throughout the world. We might conjecture that sexuality was
freed from the taboos of the communication process only when
science became capable of studying it rationally. There is considerable evidence that even the erotic realism of such works as Rechy's
City of Night includes a measure of fantasy.

A prolonged study of Zen Buddhism leaves the author unable to
view the communication process as a means of transferring truth
from one individual to another. Our symbols and our language are
incapable of putting truth into the form of messages, and all we say
or show each other is false to the extent that it is symbolized,
whether we utilize language or photographs. Paintings and music are
the closest we can come to the transfer of messages containing truth,
but what message is sent and what received remain largely a mystery.
What makes a man wish to sit and finger his sense of awe as he
looks at El Greco's *Burial of Count Orgaz* or Michelangelo's *Pieta* or
Rembrandt's *Night Watch* is an awareness of the incredible beauty
of the world in which we live as guests of a universe that does not
need us.

The philosophic contention over the existence of an event world
and an inner world seems to be so much waste of time. Bishop
Berkeley's "Subjective Idealism" did not go so far that he gave up
eating roast beef and no longer had to use doors. In the communication process we attempt to transfer an inner landscape to another

person like ourselves. We can measure to a degree our success by the actions of the other person, but the more successful we are the more our message attains the level of signals, not unlike those of birds and other beasts who utter warnings and make noises of pleasure. As we elevate the level of communication, we approach the blurring of the content until with some messages we are at a level where language joins music and great visual art in communicating messages with a content that exists but cannot be translated into another form. All communication is bound with the concept of feedback. We cannot know that our message has been received and the contents transferred until we get a report back. If that report is the substance of the message translated into symbols that are in accord with others originally used, then we are assured that the communication process has succeeded.

This process is narrower than communication as a field of study, because we assume a transfer of message as a necessary feature, and the whole of the event world must be excluded except in symbolized form. What is of moment is not body language as posture and gesture, but the conventions that make posture and gesture the vehicles of communication, conscious or unconscious as they may be. Censorship enters into the formation of conventions, when it does not govern them, limiting the messages that can be sent and the way in which messages can be received. Our attempt to identify the anatomy of this phenomenon must utilize whatever of the communication process serves best to outline what we are seeking. A man's concept of his body and its relationship to other human beings is an object of his entire thought at times and of some of his thought all the time that undergoes as much change as the body itself. It is with the inner communication, at the level of information gathering and evaluation, that censorship begins, and as it establishes a method of governing fantasies and evaluating them, it becomes a means of asserting selfhood, of establishing the identity in terms of communication. Homosexuality was probably a threat to the early hunting groups and forbidden lest the object of the group be forgotten in the delight of naughty games.

Whatever may be discovered about homosexuality utilizing ethology and other modern disciplines, we can show that as a taboo subject with a special community the relaxation of censorship has tended at once to remove the sting and the attraction. When it loses its shock value to the community where it is of special interest and attention, then nothing is left. It can be shown conclusively that each relaxation of censorship enabled the homosexual press to be more graphic until the current picture books are no different from those produced in Denmark and are soon to share the same fate. Sales of the previous level of explicit detail mark the end of one period and beginning of the next until finally the sales include material of the most explicit sort so that no higher (or lower) level is possible. At this point marketability becomes solely a matter of quality and price.

The picture books demonstrate this. All of the muscle books have disappeared from the market, except those that actually devoted most of their available space to exercises and body building, and usually emphasized heterosexuality as healthful and natural. What destroyed the old muscle books was the importation of nudist magazines and the end of the view that the male organs are obscene. One free publication of nude frontal views of men was enough to end the interest in the books of the *Trim*, *Fizeek*, and *Grecian Guild Pictorial* sort. It seems rather a pity that the high ideals of Grecian Guild members should be lost. The periodical quoted Shelley and helped to support a Greek boy, in line with its statement of moral purpose.

The male nude publications went on sale in 1966, shortly after the settlement of the case in favor of the muscle books. *Butch*, for instance, contained articles of the up-lift kind, urging a healthy attitude toward sexuality and such virtues as honesty and friendliness. It included art as well as scenes from motion pictures it made, each asserting that the motion picture is sharp and clear "instead of the blurred and fuzzy movies being sold elsewhere." The publisher, DSI, then in Minneapolis, went through several court battles in order to continue breaking the barriers of taboos. In the course of its struggle to continue in business, the company moved to southern California and at this writing has an address in Burbank, apparently related in some way to a new firm: Hartman Associates.

At the time these magazines were put on sale, in stores devoted to erotic material, there was great shock value in photographs of a number of young men facing the camera totally nude. The erotic quality comes from the surprise, though, not from the incessant repetition of crotch art. As the viewer becomes accustomed to the nudity, he ceases to notice the genitals and finds the face the most interesting part. Significantly, this motivates the editors as well. Earlier underground picture books of this type included any photograph of any male that was nude. His face was of no importance whatever. As the acceptance of male nudes became general, and when it reached the point of being in the mass communication stream, the constraint of quality was already operative.

Questions of obscenity were generally settled in lower courts in favor of the accused. An attempt to prohibit pictures of nude males when they sported an erection evidently failed, because it is not easy to say at what point an erection occurs in a particular man unless there are pictures that show his penis in a flaccid state. The implication of homosexual activity is remote, even in photographs of two men together. A great emphasis on sport and the outdoors characterizes the work of several professional photographers. The names of the models are not revealed, and the photographic studios are not advertised. A major change of direction came with the free publication of nude male photographs.

The individual entrepreneur began selling his work to publishers of the large number of periodicals offered to the public. Evidently many of the photographs had been made much earlier and were being made available to the general public rather than reserved for the special customers of an earlier period. Even at the time draped photographs were the rule in American publications, the Swedish nudist publications had undraped and unretouched photographs. The ever present air-brush removed offending parts of pubic hair from some publications and others gave the strong implication of homosexual activity either about to begin or just concluded.

These publications are now offered at very much reduced prices because an intervening type of publication included the strong suggestion of homosexual activity without quite being an 'action photo' that represents the ultimate development. As will be seen, the photographic works lagged behind the literary, or purely verbal, works of the period, but a kind of repetitiveness characterizes the whole genre. This is carried to extremes in the publications with a scientific bent, or acknowledgement, such as the Photographers' Guild publication, *The Phallus, A Picture Study of the Male Penis*. There are, as advertised, 208 pages with over 300 photographs of the male organs, some erect, some flaccid, some a frontal view, others a side view, and the male organ of generation is depicted in every possible position and explained with text and diagrams. The book was copyrighted in 1969, and it follows other works in which the sexual organs are depicted erect as well as flaccid. An erect penis once served as the definition of pornography, but with the publication of frontal nudes, the question becomes academic, and after the publication of *The Phallus* it would seem that very little is left to explore in the depiction of male genitalia.

There were several different publications aimed at showing the male genitalia although they were ostensibly about such matters as enlarging the penis through a series of near tortures with a device called a hyperemiator, a kind of mechanized cupping apparatus that caused blood to flow into the penis in increasing amounts. This publication is copyrighted 1970 and includes textual material as well as diagrams and photographs. Entitled *Penis Enlargement Techniques*, although no certain method of enlarging the penis is offered, the publication serves its primary purpose of putting a man back into some kind of relationship with his own person. What is evident in all the publications is a sense of justification, as if men had been given the privilege of not having to apologize for being equipped with sexual organs.

Such a purpose would be in accord with modern conceptions of homosexuality as a symptom of neurosis. What may operate is a defeated sense of identity that needs constant reassurance to survive at all. This liability has effects that so far have never been calculated, but if all pornography is ready-made fantasy, then these publications are not pornography, and to the average adult male, the fifty percent of the populace that has no experience of homosexual activity, not even erotic. Every heterosexual man would find them deadly dull after a short time. A certain curiosity, once satisfied, is hard to revive, and no research is so likely to be soporific as that involving an investigation of emotions which are incomprehensible to the researcher.

The final development can be seen with the gradual publication of material that is explicitly homosexual finally reaching the point where detailed pictures of homosexual activity are accompanied by a text that is more or less suited to the illustrations. (An old European joke defines pornography as illustrations that do not suit the text.) There was a notable hesitation to publish this material because it was so obviously censorable. After the unjustified raids and illegal seizures of material during the seventh decade of the twentieth century, the fight against censorship entered the new phase of being a fight for sexual liberty as well. Because legislatures refused to take any action regarding the obviously outdated and unjust sex laws, with their Victorian pretense of a morality that no one practiced completely, various organizations formed to bring to light the unjust practices of the police and to give the stamp of group approval to sexual activities despised by the rest of society. *One*, a homosexually oriented publication with attention to lesbians as well, was ruled not obscene and allowed to be sent through the mail. These rulings in effect said that the homosexual individual was not obscene whatever the ruling judge might think of the sexual practices.

Some reason for the timorous attitudes might be found in the more flagrant police acts against homosexuals. Arrests for the purpose of obtaining bribes was commonplace at one point in New York City. Entrapment that reminds one of the practice of using *agents provocateurs* was common in many places and explained in a television program about homosexuality. As the veil was lifted on the subject, the various publishers began to compete by bringing out ever more daring pictorial material. Spartan House published *Teen-Age Masturbation* by Nicholas M. Dort. This is a rather brief pamphlet put into a magazine form on heavily coated paper about the size of typewriter paper, 8½ x 11 inches. The text is about 3500 words in length with a page of statistics, summarizing the results of interviews with 213 boys between the ages of 13 and 19. At the end of the pamphlet is an extensive letter criticizing Dort's conclusions, signed J. C. Hackney, whose final complaint is in accord with most open-minded research on the subject: ". . . you should have gone further and stated some of the many obvious advantages of masturbation, as well as the rather severe dangers involved in not masturbating . . .."

The attitude cited was only to a small degree quoted by Dort among pictures of boys with penis in hand, apparently enjoying themselves. In fact, the tendency of all men to conceal or at least minimize the extent of their masturbation accounts in part for the ferocity of law officers in pursuit of homosexuals, who are hunted down with much more vigor than are common burglars. About half of the boys described episodes of mutual masturbation. Those with strict religious training acknowledged that masturbation is sinful, although Dort found them no less active, and possibly more so, than others without such training. The indication that masturbation is used as a tranquilizer is evident throughout the text. One boy is quoted as utilizing the practice in order to stay awake while driving his car, indicating a tranquilizing effect that is not somniferous.

Hackney complains that Dort is mistaken when he states that the male anatomy does not permit much variation in the techniques of masturbation. The most extravagant variation is auto-fellatio, of which relatively few men are capable.

In 1969, Media Arts published a book much like Dort's contribution on masturbation, entitled *Auto-Fellatio and Masturbation, An Autobiographical Scientific, and Photographic Study*. A six column introduction spread over four pages with photographs that are quite appropriate to the text quotes several different authorities, including Kinsey. The case histories that follow are more of the 'confession type' story than of actual recordings or edited versions of case histories. There is the touch of the professional writer in them, but they are not fantasies in the true sense of the word. These are highly possible, if not probable, accounts dressed out with the literary devices that make them readable.

However, the book was published not for the purpose of adding to the growing literature of 'case histories,' but for the photographs that illustrate auto-fellatio and the techniques used by those capable of achieving it, something less than three or four men in a thousand, according to Kinsey. It is evident that these photographs derive from an earlier period, in some cases. The hair styles that developed in the mid-sixties are evident in about half the photographs, while in the others an airbrush has been used to make the detail clearer, and there is further evidence that the photographs were saved from previous levels of censorship. The book is rather important because it was published at a time when the average picture book, such as DSI's *Oral Genital Activity, a Photo Study of Sexual Activity Between Males* did not show the act of fellatio. There are open mouths near erect penes, but the act itself, commonplace in other publications at a later time, is not shown. The book was published in 1970, and it was apparently a failure, because the relaxation of censorship restrictions, the change of postal regulations, and the final case, *Stanley vs. Georgia* had made such near-miss erotica old-fashioned.

No method of combatting pornography is so successful as giving it a free rein. To restrict it is simply to create a special clientele for publications valued far beyond their worth. The bargain sales hit the picture book market only a year after the last restrictions for adults were lifted. The ultimate horror, to many men, was openly displayed, as available as the nearby porno shop or the postman. Unfortunately, it was also quite expensive and the post office department still went on strange crusades, punishing not the fraudulent dealer, such as House of David, but the honest purveyor. The investment of the author in matter advertised by the House of David was never honored, although the postal money order was promptly ,cashed. DSI is among the reliable dealers.

In the advertising of homosexual material, the common inducement is no longer the material and its daring but the reduced price as well. The technique of homosexual seduction as repeated endlessly in the many examples of picture book stories (a kind of photographic fiction) finally becomes too repetitive, and in any case, aside from a carefully selected example, has no value whatever, except as it is a source of entertainment to an adult. What is represented is not the decay of civilization but its-involvement at every level with mass communication and the invasion of the mass media into an area of human existence theretofore closed off to the public. Such homosexual seductions doubtless take place all the time where young men can meet each other, even if it is only a street corner, as in *L'Affaire*, Issue Two, published by All Star Enterprises in 1969. These publications are copyrighted, and the going price is quite high, even in the sales, until the market vanishes. The susceptible community becomes highly selective, but very likely it is the only identifiable group for which a market will always exist.

The Gay Dilemma

The women of women's lib complain that men treat women as sex objects. At a certain time in life, this may be true; later as the man grows older and his passions cool, it becomes quite untrue. In those societies in which sexual activity is not equated with masculinity, the cooling may be very noticeable and a relief not only for the man but for the women with whom he is closely associated. The gay community provides males who are accessible and a state of continual courtship arises with attractiveness the prize of youth and sexual solicitation its reward. In the wry humor of the homosexual community, "Nobody loves you when you are old and gay." No other indemnification would be so welcome as that of Dorian Gray, whose picture grew old instead of the pleasure-giving flesh. Though youth is prized, and as shown in *The Asbestos Diary* by Casimir Dukahz, sexual preferences may be so restrictive that any male fully matured has outgrown his attractions, its inexperience is not so much admired. A constant theme of homosexual literature is the initial seduction. Generally in the picture books, the illustrations are inappropriate for the text, but as soon as the censorship restrictions were lifted, the necessity of improving the quality required better planning and more appropriate illustrations. In some of the early picture books on homosexuality, the usual tired male and female models posed showing heterosexual manipulation in highly specific detail.

These picture books do not cause impure and lustful thoughts of a perverse nature, they confirm their existence. Any psychiatrist or social worker will assure you that individuals guard their fantasies much more closely than they do the details of their sex lives that do not arouse emotion. Perhaps more than any other 'special interest group' that has been identified so far, homosexuals feel the need to put their fantasies in written form. It rather saves the trouble of continually building new ones from the foundation up. Most of the picture book material contains stories only a cut or two above the blatant sex fantasies of case histories. The stories contained in *True Confessions, Love Machines, Manly Devotion, Muscle Up, Up Close*, and *Genitalia* are about at the same level of literary quality as the case histories found in several publications without illustrations. These are slightly more furnished with the devices of fiction than those found in Havelock Ellis or other authorities. They are at least above the level of the 'closet literature' of an earlier time.

In homosexual cant, a 'closet queen' is an undeclared homosexual, an individual who hides his proclivities, even from himself. The literature that circulated in typewritten or mimeographed copies, despite the strictures of the law, was published by various companies, notably in the Black Knight Classics, a series of over-priced small books selected by the publisher of the Grecian Guild, Guild Press of Washington, D.C. At least two of these are mentioned in various accounts of homosexual literature, and probably all of them were collected at one time or another by those associated with the Guild Press. The Kronhausens describe "Seven in a Barn" and mention others. The author saw a mimeographed copy of "Ardmore Station" years ago. "Seven in a Barn" was published in an elaborated edition with illustrations of a curious sort so that the thin story was stretched to 109 pages. The story involves a poker game the loser of which becomes the 'sex slave' of the other boys. A lengthy and detailed description of homosexual activity follows. In the elaborate illustrated edition, the characters are clearly defined with portraits preceding the text. Because of the nature of laws and their enforcement at the time, homosexual acts are simulated rather than exposed to the camera. Despite the sexual ardor of the text, the men photographed are not in a state of sexual excitement, with the exception of one model whose mid-section is the substance of one illustration.

"Ardmore Station" concerns sexual activity in the men's room of a suburban railway station. Possibly an illustrated edition exists of which the author knows nothing, but in any case a new publication "Glory Hole" shows the extent of homosexual activity in such places in photographs. Men's rooms are obviously ideal places for homosexual solicitation, as indicated by the large amount of graffiti found in some. A glory hole is a hole cut in the partition between stalls permitting voyeurism and fellatio. The anonymity of such sexual activity is highly preferred by some men, and the problem of such a facility often becomes the subject of discreet worry in the public library, as well as bus stations, railway stations, and certain washrooms in men's dormitories in colleges and universities. Once identified as a gay cruising ground, the washroom retains its character despite all the efforts of the police or the supervising authorities to change it. Only one method is successful. An attendant on duty all the time the washroom is open will either grow rich with bribes or discourage any further homosexual activity.

Raids of bars, baths, and hotels are never truly successful. The activity ceases for a time, but it is soon resumed. Angry tenants of an apartment in Queens destroyed a park in the hope that they would destroy a homosexual meeting and cruising ground. The solution to the problem seems to be a willingness to let a few places continue their catering to homosexuals and to prevent such activity elsewhere. Sexual freedom is meaningless unless it is combined with discretion and the public demeanor that will not cause anxiety in heterosexual men. Even in so straitlaced a society as the Republic of Singapore, one famous street becomes alive with transvestites and male prostitutes at a certain hour. It is a great place to see tourists, because Bogey Street is a stop on the night tours. In a liberated society like Denmark, the police will arrest men who are engaged in homosexual activity in a public latrine.

The sexual differentiation of homosexual and heterosexual men is complete in the pornography industry. Motion pictures are either straight or gay, no admixture is permitted, except for an introductory scene. In some cities, the peep shows include both kinds of films, but in others there is a strict differentiation. Theatres in New York and Los Angeles never mix the kinds of motion pictures shown. Two films of heterosexual activity may be shown, but even in a long sequence of different films, no homosexual activity between males will be shown. A kind of parlor with peep shows available quickly becomes a cruising ground and a place where 'hustlers,' homosexual prostitutes, ply their trade. Even if the films shown are completely homosexual, the customers are indistinguishable from the hustlers, except that the latter are all fairly young men.

There is a general belief that only homosexual men are interested in homosexual relations, although any man might want to satisfy his curiosity if he knows nothing about homosexual activity. The motion pictures are of much lower quality, generally, than those of heterosexual activity, and the ever-present defrauders seem to concentrate on the homosexual trade, or what they estimate is the homosexual trade. Nevertheless a kind of star system is building in the 'gay movie' business. As the competition grows keener, the producers and exhibitors must claim greater quality in the photography, in the choice of actors, and in the sexual endowment of those taking part. An individual known as Ray Fuller is the subject of several picture books and motion pictures. He has a youthful, rather innocent face and an unusually large penis. Interestingly enough, Jim Stryker, who was one of the famous models in the muscle magazines, is now a dealer in homosexual pornography, especially films.

The repetitiveness of heterosexual pornography is all the more intense in homosexual pornography. There is not even the variation in sex to relieve the monotony. Once the shock value is reduced, only the mechanics of the sex act remain, and this quickly becomes tiresome to an extreme degree. The motion pictures are likely to follow an obvious plot line, similar to that of picture books. Two young men identify each other as homosexuals and proceed to engage in homosexual activity.

It is appalling to think that the whole structure of government was at one time virtuously set on a course of eradicating such material from the stream of communication, even in the secret under-the-counter trade that at one time thrived despite all efforts to suppress it. Rarity gave the material its only value and sole reason for excessive cost. To the man of heterosexual orientation, the literature is monotonous, the films uninteresting, and the whole subject disgusting. If his initial reaction is anger, then the reduction of physical indications of the emotion generally means that such slight fascination as the material once had is completely gone.

Very likely the homosexual seeks justification for his sexual preferences in the literature, and he seeks inspiration for masturbatory fantasies as well. It is highly unlikely that he gains instruction even from the sex guides for homosexuals. These appear to be meant quite seriously, offering the homosexual instruction in the manipulation that comprises the sex acts of individuals of the same sex. A favorite theme of homosexual fiction, as well as the sex guides, is the question of the homosexual marriage. The publishers who were so fearful of advocating lifelong homosexuality should have known that this would be protected by the Bill of Rights while graphic descriptions of what sexual activity took place in such an arrangement would be prohibited. With the relaxation of censorship, books of instruction and questions relating to the marriage of individuals of the same sex are allowed freedom of circulation.

There is constant interplay between the movie producers and the publishers of periodicals. Even the *Gay Sex Guide* is likely to contain scenes from movies, as sharp and clear as any advertised earlier. The text is inappropriate because the usual action photographs show nothing that is not displayed in dozens of other magazines. The text is remarkably wooden, imitative of the dry style of the authors of health literature. This is not true of a publication entitled *Homosexual Boys* with the quite inappropriate subtitle, "A study of todays sexual mores among teenage boys with homosexual tendencies." According to the cover the book was "Researched by Dr. Albin Womac, Ph.D." Since it was published by Guild Press, although it is labelled "Homo-scientific Publications," the question is whether this Albin Womac is any relation to Herman Lynn Womack. The style of typography and layout leave little doubt about the publisher, and the distributors that put the book on sale confirm this. The book is rather less formal and shows more skill in the prose, for example: "There are no restrictions as to what can be done, nor how it should be done, so long as each participant is satisfied and rewarded in the experience." This lacks the woolliness of "In conclusion, it must be stressed that any procedure indulged in must not violate the taste or feelings of either partner." *Gay Sex Guide* (Volume 2 was the only issue examined) is not copyrighted and no publisher is identified, an indication that the manufacturers fear prosecution. From a page of advertising in the text, the publisher apparently is XXX, Inc. located in Chatsworth, California, in the Los Angeles area.

The publishers of these heavily illustrated homosexual sex instructions are much more in danger because of the photographs than because of the detailed information. There is something to be said for the cautionary tone of both publications. Although homosexual activity is accepted as desirable and natural for the homosexual, warnings are issued against 'procedures' that might be painful or dangerous: ". . . the insertion of any sharp or pointed object into the rectum is vehemently frowned upon." That the photographs are the object of the censor's wrath is indicated by the declaration in several places that the illustrated version of the Report of the National Commission on Obscenity and Pornography is itself obscene. Despite the Roth decision, several cases have gone back to the proposition that the work as a whole is 'polluted' by a portion judged obscene.

So far as we now know, such publications would only be beneficial to those men who have decided on homosexuality as their sexual orientation. If the sex guides 'dehumanize' and 'mechanize' sexual activities, as is claimed by some of the voluntary censorship groups, they operate in an area where a sentimental approach is not valid. This revealing complaint seems to advocate romanticizing and mysticizing the sexual activity of humankind for all who wish to read about it, and surely the adult is able to discern which approach he prefers without the necessity for widespread legal action that would ultimately end as wasted effort.

Any man with a Polaroid camera can produce all the sex pictures he wants of himself and any other co-operating men. The censors are reacting to their own guilt rather than protecting the public, because many heterosexual men have fantasies about homosexual experiences, and some are quite dismayed to find that a sex dream involves homosexuality. This is read by some as an indication of incipient change of sexual orientation, when it only indicates a vivid imagination and some knowledge of human kind.

To understand the motivation of homosexuals in their pursuit of pornography, the art that has centered around homosexual experience must be viewed as an attempt at justification, a revelation that the individual is not the world's greatest sinner. This technique, generalization, tends to reduce anxiety and leave the self-accusator with the feeling that he is not the only one. The homosexual press has done its best to stress that the homosexual cannot be identified except by his sexual preferences. Havelock Ellis tried to find out if homosexuals really preferred the color green and could not whistle. Homosexuals rely upon the publications of various groups to prove to them that they are not monsters, as the peculiarly hypocritical attitudes of the Victorians would insist, nor are they especially gifted because of their sexual preferences. The folklore of the previous generation was much nearer accuracy than some of the contemporary psychiatric literature when the jokes and stories described the homosexual as a man with a poor sex education.

Purely homosexual art is best when it stresses the common humanity of mankind rather than the homosexual activity that is the homosexuals' sole claim to being different. Tom of Finland, Quaintance, Colt and other artists of the muscle book era range from a near comic-book style to the work of highly skilled draftsmen. The only one whose artistic productions have continued is Colt, with an apparently thriving business. Using a soft pencil technique, he is able to produce drawings of remarkable quality, as detailed and exact as photographs but with the quality of fine art, a kind of recognizable unreality like a particularly vivid dream in black and white.

Weight lifters have been wrongly stereotyped as homosexual just as ballet dancers and hairdressers have been. Muscular development was especially important in the muscle books, but the development of a separate class of publication especially for homosexuals fills the "action-type" picture books with almost any sort of man, including some who are rather long in the tooth. What is sought in the pornographic books is length of penis. Advertisements will stress that an individual is well developed or even use the slang expression, well hung, as well as advertise the good looks of the model. Muscularity and masculinity are stressed. There is a separate class of publications for transvestites.

A favorite scene of comedy is the man who dresses up as a woman. There are many variations on the theme of *Charlie's Aunt*, one of the most successful plays ever written. British television which is generally less strictly censored showing the pranks of medical school students in a series derived from Richard Gordon's novels (*Doctor in the House, Doctor at Sea*) includes scenes of medical students dressed as nurses. An important element of the comedy is another character who is completely fooled by the masquerade, although the audience knows that the 'woman' is actually a man. This is accepted in a totally different way from operatic devices that have a woman singing the role of a male whose voice has not changed, as in *Der Rosenkavalier*, or whose disguise has a serious purpose, as in *Fidelio*. The pornography books are innocent of comic intent. Unlike the jolly smiles on the faces of those photographed while masturbating, there is a dead seriousness about the photographs of men involved in homosexual activity, explained in part by the acts depicted. Fellatio involves the mouth, in any case, and sodomy is painful, as all the homosexual literature stresses. None of the picture books examined show the transvestite homosexual, although motion pictures and paperback books sometimes use the theme.

Nudity is the general rule although a scene of undressing is usually included. This conforms with the homosexual's fascination with male strip tease. A man is vulnerable when he exposes his genitals, and the erect male organ is the central focus of the camera in all the action picture books. Those issues examined that attempt to establish character use one or two models throughout the publication. *My First Time, Rick's Tale of His Discovery and Breakthrough into Sex*, includes text as well as photographs. Distributed, if not published by DSI and not copyrighted, the volume is a kind of photographic essay including scenes of homosexual activity. The photographic sequence is difficult to follow and the few words of text do not help. The other man depicted is older and has a much larger penis than has 'Rick.' This is a boy somewhere in late adolescence, from fifteen to eighteen, more or less, although the model may be older.

If the introduction can be believed, the purpose of the publishers is not to depict fellatio but to remove the shock from sexuality as a means of reducing aggression and violence.

We offer this portfolio featuring male nudity in all its sexual variations between two consenting adults. The photography has been selected to realistically reflect life—the beautiful has not been overused and the ordinary has not been avoided. It is our conviction that the body of man is clean and wholesome and should be viewed with esteem and serenity when seen in its totality.

But to most heterosexual men, the result of looking at this book is anything but serenity if they see homosexual activity photographed for the first time. There is considerable shock in looking at a scene of fellatio involving two young men, arising from the fantasy life of many men, at least half of whom, in Kinsey's statistics, have had at least one homosexual experience to orgasm. The other half may well have fancied what it was like and rejected the notion. The whole of society arms itself against male homosexuality, which seems to be a deadly threat to the very structure of human life. Much of this is irrational, because no free man has to do something repeatedly if he is opposed to it. DSI has continuing legal problems in Los Angeles. What causes the censorious attitude is the fear that one's own erotic fantasies will be discovered. Such publications would be a definite invasion of privacy if they were forced onto unwilling customers. But they are not given away. *My First Time* was originally published in book form, lavishly printed and bound, and sold for twenty-five dollars.

DSI also published albums of photographs showing every possible homosexual act without a noticeable story line which were copyrighted in 1970. Of the eight published, all were examined, and apparently some of the photographs not used were sold to other publishers. The models keep reappearing in different magazines although the setting is the same as the album. For instance, DSI's album 1501 contains photographs very like those later published in a magazine called *Manly Devotion*, number one. Although this contains an editorial signed Robert Skully, M. D., the magazine is not copyrighted. Photographers generally take many shots of the same scene so that it is virtually impossible to say that the photographs are the same in both publications. Advertisements indicate that other photographs from the album series are used in the numerous magazines now being published.

Along with public trial, DSI claims to have suffered at the hands of postal authorities when it attempted to permit C. O. D. orders. The Collect-on-Delivery films were never delivered, and some 1500 went astray. DSI also claims that motion picture studios are raided by the police, film is destroyed, and models are arrested. This lends a strong suspicion to police corruption, because a customary method of extortion is a process of selective raids and discriminatory prosecution that encourages those who escape to offer payment against their falling victim to police intervention. As many have observed, a very good way to fight a crime syndicate is to remove the source of its income, and the Victorian sex laws offer no better prevention of moral decadence than the sane laws of Denmark and Sweden.

Probably less, because extortion is a very serious crime and the crime syndicate has little room to operate among the highly moral Danes and Swedes.

The only excuse for government is that it can offer justice and no other social organization can. When a government becomes unjust, it ceases to have stability. The fight against censorship is waged not really so that libraries, and individuals can collect such publications and films as are described here, but so that access to the publication is available to every adult, whatever his own sexual preferences might be. It is manifestly foolish to suppose that men become homosexual because they see the publications described here as the road to excess. In fact, the publications are self-limiting because of the monotony. If this were not so, increasing numbers of periodicals would be sold at increasing prices, keeping pace with the inflationary movement of the general economy. However, the opposite is true. The homosexual press is in a state of depression because of the success of battles against censorship. The best way to foreclose on such material is to give it free rein. The marketplace immediately imposes its own restrictions, and the truly valueless will disappear after sales and marked-down prices have failed to attract customers. The collection of advertisements for ten years validates this completely. "The road of excess," in Blake's eipgram, "leads to the palace of wisdom."

Oblivion Ahead

Like the homosexual act itself, motion pictures and picture books offer sterile monotony that promises barren repetition. What gave the literature its value was the repression that made putting homosexual acts into the communication process a kind of victory of identity. The Gay People of Columbia University hold a dance once a week, with the blessing of the university authorities who prefer to have no more student riots. What the confessional manuals called *peccatum mutum*, the silent sin, is now shown *in flagrante delicto*. So long as some kind of mystery surrounded the acts, they were attractive. If an adolescent gave in to his curiosity, he might convince himself that he was homosexual because of a single experiment, or experimentation over a period of time with a single person.

When the sales begin, it is an indication that the market has disappeared. The producer can then take one of two directions. He can develop plot and setting, concentrate on character rather than on the acts themselves, and very soon what results is not readily distinguished from photoplays in other genres. Or he can seek ever more startling aberrations to depict as vividly as possible. Along with the sales and the decreased prices is a decrease in quality. The fine grained coated paper of Greyhuff's albums is now ordinary coated stock, and the DSI magazines are printed on newspaper stock with an attendant loss of clarity and definition.

The process can be seen in the development of stars as well. The muscle books advertised certain men as having unusually fine physiques, and the hard-core picture books advertise the gigantic penes of their stars. Such a model as Ray Fuller can be seen in several picture books and motion pictures, in his short haircut, looking innocent and intelligent, but the long hair gives him a decadent appearance that seems to prove correct the warnings against homosexuality. In the motion picture, in which he is entirely passive, submitting to fellatio and anal intercourse, it is difficult to see the boyish charm of his muscle-man poses as he writhes on a bed.

A picture book like *The Erotic Experience*, also cheaply printed on newspaper stock, depicts other aberrations—orgies, auto-fellatio, sado-masochistic activities, and concludes with the curious sequence of pictures that show a young man attempting to stuff his own penis into his anus. The pictures of sado-masochism have the heavily staged appearance of a badly produced photoplay, and in any case, the same pictures of fellatio and sodomy abound.

A question for the librarian is whether the picture books have any research value, it being supposed that other values must be left to the individual to determine. Certainly for a library dealing with human behavior, whether medical or psychiatric, psychological or sociological, such picture books have some value, but the motion pictures are more important. The air of romanticism is preserved, and often the actors pretend to a wild delight that is apparently unreal. Everything is remarkably clean and neat, and everything is totally pleasant for the actors and, evidently, the viewer.

Only exemplary copies are needed, because the heavy repetition is seen almost at once. Even two randomly chosen picture books may contain the same pictures, or at least the same models in the same setting. The producers practice a kind of thrift, so that the *Ray Fuller Album* contains scenes from motion pictures and unused photographs from the book *My First Time.* (It has one of the few sequences that includes an older man, actually a graybeard, whose chief contribution seems to be an indication of parental approval because he joins the models, lying nude with them on the bed.)

Manual Enterprises vs. Day settled that homosexuals may be a susceptible community, but it did something more. Revolutions always occur in an era of rising expectations. The fact that a community might be worth special notice tended to give it an identity, and freeing the material from the restrictions of the 1873 Comstock Law had the effect of limiting its life. The openness with which homosexuality is discussed removes from the subject the attraction of secrecy, and the mental health of an even more susceptible community is preserved. Adolescents need to know that homosexuality is not attractive as a way of life, and that homosexual activity is not the rare preference of a few individuals but a sexual substitute available to any who have not the will to find heterosexual acceptance. Once the fear, shock, and guilt is removed from the activity, little attraction, negative or positive, remains. The change in appearance that fashions for young men have wrought argues a willingness to accept differences, an encouragement toward understanding people rather than creating stereotypes and punishing any who do not come close to fitting. Congruence of preconceived behavior patterns with models of human beings, whether assembled from physical detail or pure imagination, has always proved erroneous and dangerous. The homosexual community that creates a market for the picture books and the hard-action homosexual motion picture includes even fewer men than the number who are fixated in their orientation. Aside from the researcher, the group is made up of only homosexual voyeurs and occasional curious individuals.

What then results is a revolution in attitudes, or better yet, a development of authority within the individual, so that homosexual practices are rejected positively. This leads to an understanding that a display of affection between individuals of the same sex is not evidence of homosexuality but of common humanity. Until the stage of genital manipulation is reached, no homosexuality occurs. The important segment of the word is sexual. By depicting the ultimate stage of homosexuality, the picture books and motion pictures effectively reduce guilt or satisfy curiosity vicariously. Further, it can be supposed quite safely, that the voluntary censor is motivated by guilt. There is truly nothing to be guilty about, and the depiction of an individual's deepest secret openly tends to generalize it and reduce its pressure.

V.

THE PALACE OF WISDOM

The Cool Medium

Motion pictures, in the McLuhan view, are a hot medium, and books are a cool medium. The difference is in the need for interpretation of the latter, while the former reach conscious understanding directly. The communication process always deals with symbols, and these symbols are most direct when the actual shape of the world around us is used. The shape is most impressive when in motion, because the human being is one of the most active of animals, so constructed that he sees movement better than still objects. The shock of homosexual acts performed in a movie is far greater than the same scenes passed through the tangle of language. What we read about, we may sometimes visualize if we are not distracted by the need to interpret language. The process of reading is both slower and more provocative than watching a motion picture. Sound movies with speech included tend to enrich the communication without slowing it, so that very brief dialogue that would be meaningless in print is quite understandable and appropriate when included in a photoplay. The process is slower and more deliberate in books, but equally more lasting and impressive, because the book is freed from time as an inevitable ingredient. Cool as a medium, books are nevertheless more memorable, especially for the individual with a vivid imagination, because the action contained in a book can be delayed without losing any important element so that the reader may make comments to himself. What the individual remembers is what he says to himself with the cues derived from what he has read. The present activity of censorship groups seems not to confirm this, but the apposite reason is to be found not in the material but in the extent of its circulation. The censor is not bothered by what a few people may find interesting but rather by what, in his mind, constitutes a dangerous way of thinking on the part of the populace at large.

The conventions of censorship operate most strongly in television because it is a hot medium that goes into every home. It is quite possible that some men might use television commercials as a sexual stimulant, but there is little that can be done about it.

Similarly, little can be done about collections of pornography made by individuals and among those are what have been called "closet literature." By far the greatest amount has not been published, nor even read, for it is common when the papers of writers are examined to discover among them portions of stories, if not entire stories, that have been circulated only among friends, if at all. Such a novel as *Maurice* by E. M. Forster is a rather poor example. Although written in 1913, the next to the last novel of an accomplished author, the book was unpublished until after his death. It is not true closet literature but rather a novel that would have wrecked the author's reputation, because the title character does not suffer for his homosexuality. Closet literature that has been published is a crude genre at best, but it deserves close attention because in discovering the anatomy of censorship we perceive, as well, the history of intellectual freedom.

There are many ways to explore the human condition, and fiction is one of the best, both for the author and for the reader. Closet literature is amateur fiction that achieves a certain goal for the author, possibly a relief from nagging doubts and guilt over homosexuality. Until Paul Goodman exposed his own homosexual feelings, no writer in his right mind would permit any such worry to reach the public view. In fact, every man speculates about homosexuality as it becomes apparent that such activity abounds. The closet literature published by Guild Press has the qualities of erotic fantasy, the evidence of the amateur author, and the first tentative efforts toward developing an understanding of homosexuality. Unlike the gay novels, the homophile literature, there are abrupt changes of opinion expressed by the characters, and some are very nearly didactic. All through homosexual material a theme of sadism occurs, a necessary concomitant of description of anal intercourse.

Guild Press published a series entitled Black Knight Classics, with an explanatory subtitle, Classics of the Homosexual Underground. Like the picture books, these overpriced little volumes found a saturated market and have been combined into the standard size paperback, usually three stories to a volume, called The Lancelot Series. The same introduction is used in both series, citing *Stanley vs. Georgia* and the Danish experiment. The Black Knight series is copyrighted 1969 and the Lancelot Series, 1972. Ten of these have been examined, including "7 in a Barn" and "Ardmore Station." There is considerable evidence of fairly crude editing in the Lancelot Series, so that a curious mixture of nineteenth century cant with twentieth century jargon results.

A slave–master psychology is represented in closet literature. In "7 in a Barn" the master is chosen by a poker game. The one of the seven who has the most chips after three hundred have been distributed to each of the players is declared the master. The game ends when one player has no more chips. He is the slave. In "Porthole Buddies" the master is the Chief Petty Officer, in a naval setting aboard the U.S.S. Tarbucket. In "Boxing Camp" the master is the father, a common theme in all homosexual fiction. In "Angelo" two police officers, Gil and Bill, become involved with a juvenile delinquent and at the end of the story, Gil becomes Bill's slave. In "The Adventures of Edward" the slave–master theme dominates. The reason for this kind of erotic fantasy is readily seen in the protests of teen-agers as quoted in newspaper stories of homosexual scandals that have erupted from time to time. A young participant claims he was forced into homosexual activity, thereby excusing himself from any voluntary participation. No matter the amount of force used, the individual is depicted as wildly enjoying the sexual activity.

There have been many studies relating homosexuality to aggression and struggles for dominance. The theme of masculine dominance and of status is common to all homosexual literature, even if the slave–master episodes are not included. Especially in closet

literature, much is made of an individual's station in life. The poor
are desperately poor and the rich are intensely rich. Hustlers do not
abound in closet literature although "The Adventures of Buddy"
include his obtaining a fee for homosexual services. In the literature
of hustling, the male prostitute assumes a superiority because he
considers himself not to be homosexual. Buddy, the fifteen-year-old
hustler hero of a closet piece is completely homosexual. The purpose
of closet literature is to describe one sexual act after another with
as little setting and characterization as the picture books. Aside from
identifying the individuals more completely than the motion picture
episodes in 8 mm film or a sequence of slides or photographs, the
closet fiction sweeps from one sexual episode to another, blithely
disregarding the repetitive nature of the prose.

All the difficulties of life vanish during these sexual episodes. The
sensations are described in terms suitable for a volcanic eruption. No
one is mildly amused or displeased. Even a character who a few pages
before had discovered with some discomfort that he was interested in
men as sexual objects becomes wildly blissful in episodes of anal
intercourse, fellatio, and mutual masturbation. The realization of a
homosexual component in a character's sexual desires causes scarcely
a ripple of doubt let alone a wave of fear or guilt. "Billy Joe . . .
enjoyed it as a substitute." In all closet literature there is no fear of
the act itself, just of being caught. "Bill considered himself like a
child seeking something new just for the hell of it." In "One Man's
Meat," Kevin states, "I've always wanted to . . ., but I've been too
bashful."

Despite the insistence of all the anonymous authors that this
activity is thoroughly satisfying, one orgasm leads immediately to
another. There is no flagging of interest, no unpleasant afterthought,
no self-incrimination. However, homosexuality if it is adopted as a
way of life, represents the solution to a problem. "The Adventures of
Buddy" conclude with the father showing affection for his son. This
is what Buddy "desperately wanted." The most revealing sentence in

all of closet literature occurs near the end of "The Adventures of Buddy." "He knew that he had turned to this kind of sex because he needed affection and he thought this life would give him that affection." Buddy resolves to keep his pleasant memories and "be like other boys, now, and not be used by other people . . .."

Some effort is made in closet literature to achieve what represents true pornography, with shock leading to shock so that the reader is constantly stimulated. The most successful of this sort is the 'orgy' book, like "7 in a Barn." "One Man's Meat" begins with an episode in the showers, proceeds to an episode with a physique photographer, is enlarged with several other individuals, includes a story of homosexuality on a beach, including homosexual acts performed in front of girls, and finally arrives at the seduction of "straight boys." These are remarkably compliant, having accepted a fifty dollar fee for their services. A further technique of pornography is employed with taboo words used throughout, especially in the quoted dialogue, but nearly as often in the narrative sections. When the ultimate shock is reached, the book has nowhere to go.

"The Adventures of Edward" is strangely truncated and as a work of fiction is very poor. A lengthy opening section in the present tense describes the first master, at times seeming to be the account of some previous time in history, and at times quite modern. The master was an Indian, and his servant, a Negro named Jim, captures Edward after his escape. The story progresses to another character, a sailor named Peter, and it is easy to see why another character is added. The sado-masochism of the story finally palls, and a third character provides an excuse for more detailed and repetitious description of homosexual activity. Typical of most closet literature, the story ends abruptly, with no explanation for the first section of story, no further description of the master, and no explanation of why the sailor appears on the scene. "The Adventures of Edward" is clearly very close to an erotic fantasy, lacking all detail of setting and characterization. Its excuse for being is the recital of details about the master—slave relationship in homosexual affairs.

"A Crack in the Wall," however, is quite different. From the opening of the story, character is firmly established. Malone is a young heir to a modest sum of money left by his Uncle Charlie who kept him working on a farm. He rents a room in Springfield, Illinois, and discovers a crack in the wall, which at first means little to him. "I was very lonely. A horrible feeling of being left out of the design of God's world." Technically, the work can be called pornography because it proceeds from one shock to another beginning with Malone's masturbation, continuing with little boys, then adolescents, and a tall young man named Fred. After shaving, Fred masturbates in the bathroom, and when Tom enters there is a scene of mutual masturbation. About midway through the story, girls enter into the narrative (and the bathroom). This is a little more than fellatio described in rather basic language without taboo words. A brief episode of cunnilingus is followed by a session of irrumation with Fred and another young man, leading to troilism when a third boy enters the bathroom.

"I was desperately jealous of them. I am a lonely, frustrated voyeur," the narrator, Malone, complains. When next he discovers a youth in the bathroom, he goes to join him. He philosophizes as well as describing his first experience in mutual fellatio, the classic 'sixty-nine' of homosexual cant. "After all, I am human even if I am a homo; and I need Somebody . . . even if it's a superficial sexual contact." He ventures to assert himself with Fred, and then he watches 'normal sex.' He watches a scene of group sex with Fred, Billy, Tom, and Dick, and three sailors through a keyhole, but he decides that ". . . the bad thing is if you let this peeping, this voyeurism, become your whole sex life." The last four words are italicized in the original. "Fantasies have their place in the human mind, I decided, but I had lived too much, too dependently, on my vicarious sex thrills through others." The last lines of the story produce the author's purpose in writing it: ". . . if my story has helped any potential voyeur to stop living in a solitary sex life and to enter the world of friendships . . . then my tale has not been told in vain."

There is evidence that this is an edited version of a story written at an earlier time. Despite a reference to *I am Curious (Yellow)*, the book includes such expressions as 'golly durnit,' 'swell,' and 'gee whiz.' There is no explanation of the number of sailors who are in Springfield, Illinois, nor is there anything that would make that city a necessary setting for the story. It might be San Francisco or Brooklyn quite as easily. According to the blurb "voyeurism and homosexuality are natural and go together."

Closet literature is important because it can be paralleled with what is called 'self-publishing literature' in Communist countries where total control of the press makes censorship and suppression automatic. These homosexual stories have a remarkable perdurance, and in the present technology would be completely impossible to suppress. Although some evidence of fear of suppression can be read in the essay that serves as the foreword of each story, the free publication of the little books led to the inevitable result. When the market vanished, they were combined three to a volume, as in the Lancelot Series, generally representing a decrease in price from one-third to two-thirds. At some point, there will be no market left, and a considerable time will have to elapse before any further publication is possible. The closet literature is distinct from contemporary homosexual novels because of the use of graphic descriptions of homosexual acts, the incessant taboo words and homosexual cant and the affirmation that homosexuality is natural or normal for certain men. Although violence is included, in a mild way, it is never punishment for homosexuality but a concomitant of it. What might called 'substitutive violence' does not occur in homosexual literature. Moral attitudes were included in all of the novels examined, ranging from willingness to accept individual differences to acknowledgement of the need for love.

Obviously, as in all erotic fantasy, the closet literature scarcely records a true state of affairs, laid out in systematic order. One has to apply all the techniques of analysis used for verbal fantasies to see the real individual underneath the surface of the narrative. Suppression of these works at an earlier time did not prevent their circulating widely, although not so widely that the average man would know of them. Illustrated versions exist for several, and there is equivalent visual art now being openly published. An attempt to suppress the literature anew would simply drive it underground again where the proportional spacing typewriter, the office-size offset press, and a highly mobile publisher could indefinitely outwit the postal authorities. The result would not be the shabby mimeograph productions of early times but quite a handsome book.

The experience of Denmark and the experience in the United States is rather conclusive that the reliable key to success in the dirty book business is dependent upon governmental regulations that will procure a value that the works do not otherwise have by at once forbidding publication or importation and punishing only the most flagrant offenders. These rules are an open invitation to public corruption and such public sins as bribery, graft, and selective prosecution. The greatest threat so far to the pornographic markets of all kinds has been the freedom to publish anything that can find a market. Some Danish publishers were in open opposition to the relaxation and ultimate repeal of obscenity laws. The voluntary censorship groups have to adjust the facts to suit their protestations of public morality so that the corruption of public officials is not included. The closet literature, oddly enough, is not marked 'for sale to adults only,' a rubric common on all homosexual literature. Adolescent boys curious about homosexual experience might find some of the works seductive, but the mature individual would not. What is conveyed often is an acceptance of homosexuality as a natural occurrence that can be pursued as a way of life, with the evils of social ostracism and a barren life the inevitable result. Even so, there is something much less sinister about the homosexuality depicted in these stories than in the tales of righteous violence that abound and are openly published.

Fantasy, like masturbation, is a palliative and serves a positive function in making the emotional landscape endurable. In the quiet of the mind, wishes are fulfilled and the individual adjusts his desires to his opportunities. Fantasies in the Black Knight Classics and in the Lancelot Series have very little value as literature and not much more as evidence of amateur authorship. All have one great feature in common, they are anonymous. No author is identified with any of them, although very likely the manuscripts have been collected over a period of years. An author's name, if included, is probably a pseudonym. Equally, such works seem to have had no influence to speak of in the development of the genre of the homosexual literature. A budding author in the genre would do well to avoid the more flagrant flaws found. The reader of one or two such stories will discover that he has, in effect, read all of them, except for the odd bits of character and setting that appear from time to time.

Paperback Genre

A common experience of men in the second World War was the awakening of a homosexual component that had always existed, perhaps found expression in juvenile games of sexuality, but had never been identified. The psychiatry of the time was rather like the medieval church, full of decisions based on outdated theology and more ready to condemn than to treat. The armed forces fiercely punished homosexual acts committed so that the miscreants were caught. Sodomy was punishable by lengthy sentences and dishonorable discharge. Declared homosexuals were discharged without honor thereby depriving them of the benefits of the G.I. Bill of Rights. All this may have served to decrease incidents of homosexuality, but it did not prevent them, and the more probable result was a greater effort to hide the incidents.

A common condition was what those of us engaged in providing psychotherapeutic services came to call 'battlefield romances.' Later research has shown that men under intense stress tend to turn to each other for affection when no member of the opposite sex is available, and they will express this affection in a roundabout fashion even when the member of the opposite sex is ever-present. Soldiers fighting together fell in love with each other and expressed the love in a variety of ways. With some soldiers it was sexual activity, and with others it was not. The condition became clinically important only when one of the soldiers was killed. A profound depression set in that a little affection and understanding could have turned back. With what is now known of identity crises, a much more efficient job of psychotherapy could have been offered near the front lines, and if the work we did had no other result, at least it persuaded the Army to move its social workers up closer to the front lines so that a dramatic reduction of psychiatric casualties in the Korean War proved the point we often tried to make.

A variety of studies show that men have a strong idea of body space and resent other men invading it. In cultures where masculine affection without genital activity is expressed by holding hands and kissing on the cheek, this body space is measurably less, although it still exists except for a few companions. Male infants detach themselves from the mother sooner than female infants, and in other ways the distinct anatomical differences are matched with behavioral differences. Even so, there is a distinct need for the male infant to associate with other males, and this need is increased through the early years of life, so that a boy has generally copied the physical stance and walk of his father by the time he is four or five years old. The male body is so different from the female that a boy must learn how to use his body by observing other males if he does not want to misuse it. The center of gravity is higher, for instance, enabling males to jump higher and to run faster.

Men are much more likely to engage in sexual activity with each other than are women when deprived of the opposite sex, and adolescent males are very likely to experiment with each other before they venture into heterosexual relations. The bachelor houses of some tribes, even the boys clubs and camps of the western tradition, enable this experimentation to take place, more or less without the intervention of elders, unless it is purposefully and directly forbidden. Simply pretending that such things should not and therefore cannot occur is an ideal way of guaranteeing that some easy sexual experimentation will take place. The result cannot be predicted. Most boys give up all homosexual activity and engage in further heterosexual experimentation, and only a small percentage become fixated in a homosexual orientation.

There are vast reaches of research that were postponed or regarded as impossible during the period when literary criticism in the form of censorship had the force of law. Even the development of a significant literature awaited the explosion of heterosexual frankness that celebrated the Fanny Hill case and the unbanning of *Lady Chatterley's Lover*. Various encounter groups have exposed the need men have to touch and be touched by others, and the subdued, virtually non-existent homosexuality implicit in these groups seems to act as a release for men as much as for women. What seems very likely is that the Victorians have been feeding western civilization a thin pap of lies. The world of the homosexual as he appears in the literature that is quickly becoming a genre, identifiable and enjoyable, is no different from the world that the rest of us enjoy or deplore as circumstances dictate. Until the *Manual Enterprises vs. Day* case, no homosexual work had been censored. The dealers in homosexual pornography, when caught, chose to accept their punishment without appeal. The end of censorship brought much to light, and the only question that remains is whether such knowledge advances human progress more than ignorance did.

In 1893 a book was published in a limited edition that since has been offered as a part of the closet literature written by Oscar Wilde. This is a novel entitled *Teleny*, supposedly written at a time when Wilde was at the height of his literary powers, having just completed *The Picture of Dorian Gray* and *Lady Windermere's Fan.* If this was the work of Oscar Wilde, then he wrote it idly and without the elegance of his other works. The work is somewhat beyond closet literature, probably the work of one of Wilde's eager young disciples. The novel has considerable plot and several scenes that show the existence of parks where homosexuals met in the Paris of the nineties. The novel was suppressed until republished by Olympia Press in Paris and then republished in the United States by Brandon House. If published openly, it is possible that the novel might have had some influence on writers of the genre, but its theme and descriptions were so much in opposition to the accepted canons of literature that it was hidden from any serious attention until its period of possible influence had ended.

A much more influential novel was Gore Vidal's *The City and the Pillar*. He had written a war novel, *Williwaw*, and in 1946 decided to write a book of realism using homosexuality as his theme. Published in 1948, the book drew a storm of criticism mostly because his main character was straight out of middle class America and his mental illness, as homosexuality was fancied to be, did not affect his development as a tennis star. In the original version, Jim Willard who believes he is in love with Bob Ford after one rather mild adventure of 'kid stuff' is finally rejected and in his rage kills his friend. The cautionary ending was not decreed by the publisher but by Vidal's own sense as a novelist, and it gives artistic consistence to the story of Jim's fantasy of a love that could never be and that had to end in murder. By raping Bob in the revised version, Jim Willard achieves a knowledge of himself that the earlier book lacked. Vidal rewrote the entire book, as a line by line comparison quickly reveals, adding description and strengthening the character of Jim throughout. The book was a great success, despite the carping of critics, and its point of view was confirmed by Kinsey's book on the 'human male.'

A wave of imitators followed, and each of these serious books such as those written by James Barr, for instance, sought to show the homosexual not as a monster or mentally ill but a man in search of something that all boils down to a need for identity or its middle-aged equivalent, 'integrity.' Pageant Press, a vanity publisher, first made a book out of Jay Little's novel *Maybe—Tomorrow* in 1952. Because the author must pay not only the printing costs but the overhead of the publisher in vanity publishing, the book demonstrates a strong desire on the part of the author to see his work in print. An article of faith of modern publishing is that a good book will always find a publisher. This is untrue, and if the author is something less as a novelist than Gore Vidal who had already established himself in the literary field, then a novel like the homosexual yearnings and introspection of *Maybe—Tomorrow* will be rejected everywhere. The book was reprinted four times in the same hardcover format. It was published as a paperback novel some years later, and from the economics of vanity publishing, it seems clear that Jay Little recovered all that he had invested in the novel. This may have been influential among the writers of gay fiction, but if so, the author does not know how. What gives the novel its importance, aside from its having been more successful than many commercially published novels, is the development of character and the acceptance of homosexuality, including a happy ending. This was still the period of the cautionary tale that required death and destruction as the reward of aberrant sexuality. As in Forster's novel, *Maurice*, Gaylord LeClaire finds happiness with his lover. From a stylistic point of view, the author is not able to write without three periods interrupting his sequence of words, and he is capable of jarring metaphors ("the stars sprang shrieking into flight"). Sexual episodes are transformed into a kind of prose poetry: "It was scorching hot now and their cool kisses had suddenly turned to steam. His carpet, his beautiful magic carpet had suddenly burst in flames . . .."

A further novel, *Somewhere Between the Two*, is the story of a female impersonator, Terry Wallace, and his search for enduring love. The story is obviously based on personal experience and is a convincing portrait of the kind of life such a performer leads. A point made gently and often is that not all female impersonators are homosexual or even bisexual. The normality of life of these books is far more convincing than in many of the novels of the time. Since the substance of fiction is found in the life about us, the only way to explain why these books had to find a vanity publisher is the constraint of canons adopted by commercial publishers. The regular trade awaited the Loon series before it was seen that the public interested in such books really did not prefer that everyone die as punishment for their deviant sexuality.

The publication of *Naked Lunch* by William Burroughs brought graphic descriptions of homosexual activity to public attention. The book naturally fell afoul of the censors, and Grove Press, which published the book in the United States (it was originally published by Olympia Press in Paris) had the debilitating experience of fighting several censorship battles at once. In dissenting from the majority opinion of the Massachusetts Supreme Court decision reversing the decision of the Suffolk County judge to ban the book as obscene, Justice Reardon called it "literary sewage." The literary criticism of Supreme Court justices seems rather suspect on the face of it, somewhat like the medical opinions of postmen or the legal opinions of grocery clerks or the literary criticism of professors of law but in this case the epithet seems accurate. It was precisely what William Burroughs intended, and his depiction of sodomy is included as an outcry against capital punishment. No more gloomy and terrifying book on drug addiction has ever been written, and the use of 'literary sewage' to describe what is suicide on the installment plan seems quite fitting. This was 1966, when the Fanny Hill case had reversed the course of American publishing and the Olympia Press had run up against the French censorship restrictions. The Gaullist government acceded to the demands for closer supervision of the press on the suggestions of Madame de Gaulle. It was an old tradition in France that had once banned *Les Fleurs du Mal* by Charles Baudelaire and *Madame Bovary* by Gustave Flaubert.

The novel *Les Mauvais Anges* created a sensation in the 1950's when it was first published in France. The author, Eric Jourdan, won instant fame, because the cautionary ending that has Gerard murdering Pierre is depicted not as punishment for their sexual activity but as its reward. There is a shimmering quality of beauty throughout the novel that the translation retains to some extent, despite the title *Two* used by the publisher, Pyramid Publications. The translator, Richard Howard, preserves the French syntax to a considerable degree to provide a competent translation, not an adaptation. *Les Mauvais Anges* could be translated as "The Demons" and be much closer to the meaning in French. The word *demon* is sometimes used to describe a malicious child. Both boys pursue wickedness as a desirable means of achieving revenge, and the ideas of Gerard are much closer to those of a wicked child than they are to the usual wise participant in homosexual relations.

John Rechy's *City of Night*, however, had much more influence on the general American public, because it was a very frank description of the life of a male prostitute, the hustler who has become a stock figure in homosexual fiction. The book has a quality of realism that invites imitation, and in many respects, it is a major achievement of an author. The main character is incapable of love, a standard ingredient of homosexual literature, and his idea that he has not become a homosexual because he allows his body to be used by homosexuals apparently is the belief of many young men who find that they can gain extra income by permitting other men to engage them in acts of fellatio. The hustler is always the fellated, the customer is always the fellator. There is a strong flavor of masochism in this arrangement, especially if one considers that the customer is paying for the privilege of earning the epithet 'cocksucker.' This used to be one of the worst things that one man could call another, and it occasioned fierce battles between men when uttered in earnest. The inability of the hustler first to admit that he is engaging in homosexual relations when that is obviously a verifiable fact using any definition within reason, and second to permit himself any feeling for the customer or even his fellow hustlers, is combined with conscious grooming in order to attract 'scores,' men who will pay. Intellectual hustlers are not in demand, and the hustler points out that he would never admit that he read a book or was willing to engage in conversation above the level of arid phrases. This subjugation of self is characteristic of the homosexual at all levels, except among those men who admit that they are in search of sexual satisfaction with another of their sex.

   This admission is quite devastating and is a theme of much of the homosexual fiction that followed the ending of censorship in the latter half of the 1960's. It is paralleled by the admission of everyone that he has a sexual nature and this gives pleasure and demands satisfaction. While the average heterosexual can imagine nothing more aberrant than paying for the privilege of fellating a young hoodlum, he concedes that paying for the privilege of embracing a woman and providing her with sexual satisfaction is masculine and at least forgivable if not laudatory. Apparently, men desirous of masochistic satisfactions are much pleased by kneeling in front of young men and 'worshipping' as the variety of homosexual novels often puts it, their sex organs. The censors, in fact, were reacting not to the homosexuality in *Naked Lunch* but to the taboo words employed throughout. No effort at direct censorship was attempted with *City of Night*, and the ban on representing homosexual situations in movies and on the stage was lifted. A great number of books were being published with homosexual episodes, and the paperback market included a distinct segment of novels that were described as 'homophile' or 'gay' literature.

The change was quite aptly and significantly signalled by the remarks of Justice William O. Douglas dissenting in the case of *Sam Ginsberg vs. New York*. They have often been quoted, and they deserve further quotation here.

> Today this Court sits as the Nation's board of censors. With all respect, I do not know of any group in the country less qualified first, to know what obscenity is when they see it, and second, to have any considered judgement as to what the deleterious or beneficial impact of a particular publication may have on minds either young or old.
>
> I would await a constitutional amendment that authorized the modern Anthony Comstocks to censor literature before publishers, authors, or distributors can be fined or jailed for what they print or sell.

That was before the world community was immersed in the agony of change: riots, ceaseless protestation, and a public losing confidence in its government. The Soviet Union marched its troops into Czechoslovakia to prevent liberalization of its laws regarding publications and intellectual freedom. The blacks of the United States began a process of group identification that was repeated by students and by homosexuals. The gay community among other stereotyped groups came to life and fought back against the injustice of laws that punished the individual for his nature rather than his acts.

It has long been known that censorship is the necessary concomitant of propaganda, and that a relaxation of censorship is likely to lead to great changes in the social structure of a given society. The further the relaxation, the greater the change. While the general level of literary censorship was minimal in Denmark so that its ending of obscenity laws for adults had virtually no effect, such a similar change in one of the communistically governed countries would mark the end of the government itself. An authoritarian view of western civilization would perceive that vast changes were under way, that the rising generation of the young was not to be marched into global conflicts, that a way of life was greatly endangered and steps were required to alter the course of these changes. The authoritarian is likely to blame some abstraction for the changes, such as permissiveness, the method of his adversary, the liberal. To a liberal thinker, the changes could only end in an improvement of society. Such prophets as Nostradamus and Jeane Dixon predicted that the world would reach a watershed of history in the last quarter of the twentieth century, and everything seems to verify their prophesies.

A study of homosexual literature is enlightening not so much for what it has to say about sexuality among men but for what it says about the human condition and the males who have seized responsibility for creating the society around them. Censorship did not change anything about the homosexual, it only hid what always existed. The question in all communications is the extent to which the message represents what occurs in the 'event world' that all of us share. What now appears in our dissections of the anatomy of censorship is the unmistakable evidence that the censor is trying to deal with the homosexual component in himself by condemning what would reveal the extent of his erotic fantasies. The repugnance of the heterosexual for homosexual relations is not unmixed with a certain attraction. We are all to some extent perverse, simply because we are human beings who send one or more of our members off to explore far away places. Man's greatest attribute is always his greatest threat. Our curiosity will lead us to knowledge of ourselves that we may find quite hard to accept.

Western civilization has always tried to repose complete authority in some massive mythical structure, and there have always been men who are willing to assume the burden of deciding how to control and direct human curiosity into channels that will protect the mythical structure. For many centuries this was the local church, then it became the organization of the church, so that the Pope was the embodiment of ultimate authority, recognized after that authority had been removed. With massive conflict, the mythical structure became governments, and the struggles over ideologies of government continue to this day, but in fact, the government cannot assume a moral role any more than the church can assume a governmental role. Intellectual freedom is the opposite of censorship, because whatever may be argued as the basis for the imposition of rules on the transmission of messages, the purpose is to govern the thought of others, to control curiosity. If pornography is to be driven underground on the basis that it makes sexuality seem mechanical and depersonalized, we must forbid the curious to ask why this is the case.

The easiest way to understand a message is to suppose that you have sent it and to interpret its symbols on this basis. The argument that sex becomes mechanical and depersonalized in pornography arises from a fear of the mechanical and depersonalized aspects of sex in one's own life. The event world can never be as well-ordered and readily managed as the world of our symbology. In our erotic fantasies there are no sheet burns, weary muscles, inopportune telephone calls, or mess to clean up. The extent to which the erotic fantasy accepts the details of the event world as they impinge on the delights of sexuality is a measure of the realism, and this realism becomes instructive as the receiver of the message matches its contents with his own experience of the event world. The object of censorship has been to hide the nature of human sexuality from human beings, expecially from other men. The obscenity laws were in their deepest trouble when the irrationality of the trial of Mary Ware Dennett became apparent. Homosexual literature explores the nature of men's desires as much in terms of erotic fantasies as in the use of realism.

The Raunchy Romances

Although Guild Press published several stories, especially those by J. J. Profferes and Alexander Goodman, since collected in a two-volume work, that employed the artistic devices of later gay fiction, the genre became identifiable only with the establishment of Olympia Press in the United States, in 1967, and the development of regular series by Greenleaf Classics. Of all the publishers of gay fiction, Greenleaf has been the most successful. The publishers seem to have found precisely the kind of fiction that is most successful among the readers of this genre.

Olympia Press began a series, called The Other Traveller, to match its Traveller's Companion series. Writer's publications include the description furnished by the publisher of material that was needed. The series promised to publish the most important authors of this genre. Apparently some authors were wooed from Greenleaf, but no important new authors have thus far been introduced. Olympia Press is willing to offer a writer criticism and help him develop his abilities, up to the point where a nonmeshing of wavelength with the editorial plans intervenes. This may coincide with overstocks. The paperback distributors will refuse to accept returns when they are overstocked, and the bookstore can obtain repayment by sending the cover to the distributor. The bookstore can usually recover its expenses by selling the coverless books at a sizable reduction in price although this violates a contractual agreement. Overstocks seem to have affected Olympia Press and its new series, possibly because there is not the promise of the early days to be seen in the works published. When Olympia was the only outlet for fiction in advance of publishers' standards, or courage, some of the most important writers of the period were Olympia authors. Experimental writing is often unsuccessful and hard to differentiate from the effusions of the semi-literate. The Other Traveller seemed to be a good venture because the market is remarkably consistent. Overstocks have been heterosexual novels, and usually the overstocks are for novels that represent a previous level of candor. Olympia's distribution is not so widespread as Greenleaf's and the authors represented have no way to advance the genre except into literature that matches what the hard-cover publishers offer.

The history of the genre from 1967 to date (1973) seems to indicate that what makes a gay novel enjoyable is what makes any fiction entertaining. Strength of characterization and setting with a brisk style that moves a plot onward to a conclusion that is at once valid and unpredictable will keep the reader involved with the book. Greenleaf prefers to work with established writers, and its own stable of authors includes some of considerable talent, although success in this field of endeavor until recently was rather a pyrrhic victory. Even John Rechy was denied recognition by writers' groups because he chose to investigate the world of the hustler. The genre also has lethal elements of self-destruction that will ultimately assure it the fate of all formula fiction.

The man are always young if they are the heroes, and their bodies are always trim and masculine with muscular development that must be very difficult to describe if originality is one of the characteristics of a good author. Similarly the homosexual actions that are de rigueur require originality that is exceedingly hard to demonstrate when the same repetitive actions are to be described in the same detail, and even the pronouns become a major difficulty. A writer must inspect his rhetoric carefully so that the reader knows, as the old limerick has it, who is doing what with which and to whom. Generally, now, the novels have a happy ending. The wicked may be punished, but one of the requirements of the homophile press is that homosexuality be recognized not as a wickedness but a kind of sexual orientation that only deserves punishment if force is used or the very immature are involved. Even the raunchy romances of gay fiction seem to validate Kant's belief in a universal morality. Incest however is not a punishable offense in the world created by the authors of gay literature unless it is combined with rape. The excesses of "Boxing Camp" would bring the retribution of the plot down on the participants.

One of the most moving novels is *Like Father, Like Son* by Dennis Drew. The story concerns a policeman, Doug, whose wife dies. He believes that his son, Ralph, needs a mother and marries a widow with a son, Bobby, the same age as his own boy. In a delicate fashion, even avoiding the word 'masturbation,' the author describes how Bobby and Ralph begin to enjoy homosexual relations in their attic bedroom. Ralph resented the marriage because it separated him from his father, and when it seems that the marriage is breaking up, Ralph is happy. The two boys are discovered by Doug but the event is related only two months after it occurred when Doug and Bobby are alone in the house.

The parental permissiveness is fully explained both in the text and in the conversation Doug has with his stepson. The reader is left to fill in details only of the sexual activity. This is not very hard to do. "You got the time card. Punch in and go to work," Doug says after rolling over onto his stomach. Even though no taboo words are used anywhere in the novel, the genital activity is unmistakable, unlike the use of homosexuality in other novels of the time. Doug's adventures with Bobby continue secretly, because Doug's marriage has reached the point where Sarah is no longer interested in sex. When Sarah asks for a divorce, Doug agrees, and very rapidly he and Ralph are alone again. Ralph uses a comic book, of the sort that was sold under the counter in many places, to attract a filling station owner who is his own attendant. The same delicacy of writing is used for a restroom episode. The novel then describes Doug's encounter with a leading man in the crime syndicate, and Doug arranges to quit his job so that he and Ralph can join Vic Ponzotello on a yacht. What began as blackmail ends as a strange kind of prostitution, for Ralph is very much pleased with his lover and Doug enjoys the attention of one of the henchmen. At the end of the novel Doug and Ralph are paid off for their services and go to live in Nevada. About the middle of the novel, at the end of Chapter Six, after Doug tells Ralph, very carefully, about the arrangement he has made for them, in the words of the author of the novel, "They both surrendered to their incestuous desires. The last barrier had been torn down and each saw the other as if for the first time; as a warm, feeling human being. It was a Sunday to remember."

The book is essentially a story about a man and his son told as a homosexual romance. If a reader discounts the homosexuality, the story vanishes and its message is lost. The love of father for son is taken for granted in those happy families where both can express their love openly without the threat of incestuous relations, but in those having some kind of homosexual terror always in the way, the love may go through transformations of anxiety until it is indistinguishable from hatred. The novel ends happily with Vic off on a trip to Turkey, and the father and son ready for a new life together. Throughout the novel suspense is maintained so that it seems that it must end unhappily, and although the editing is not very good (the wrong name is sometimes used for a conversation) the story is well told.

This novel although dealing with a crime syndicate character has almost no violence in it, unlike *Brothers* by Jerry Evans and *Like Father, Like Son*. Both novels center on violence with unending scenes of homosexual activity told in taboo words. *Up Daddy* by Karl Flinders is a much more literate novel dealing with the father of twins who leads them into homosexual activity that, according to the author, is greatly beneficial to all concerned, even the father whose need for prostatic massage is enthusiastically met by the adolescent twins. At the end of this novel, both boys are happily married and revere the memory of their deceased parent. The mother is dead when the story begins and is scarcely mentioned throughout.

A Father in Shadows by Douglas Dean tells of a post-adolescent boy who finishes high school and is rewarded with a trip to La Jolla in Southern California to visit his father. The father divorced the boy's mother because he fell in love with another man and has established himself in business with his lover as his partner. Homosexual marriage is not painted in glowing terms, nor is it made to seem other than natural for the two men, with attendant problems, arising out of the father's fear that his son will come to learn that his father's friend is his homosexual lover. This occurs, as expected, just as the son positively rejects the homosexual advances of one of his father's friends. Once the dark secret is out into the open, the father helps his son to understand what has occurred. They attend church together, one of those for homosexuals in California, evidently related to the one started by Troy Perry. A member of the church, "a plain but pleasant-looking woman of approximately forty years," doffs her Salvation Army uniform and decides that her lesbian yearnings will be gratified openly thenceforward. After the church service, Dick, another friend of the father, explains to the son, "I heard there was soon to be a mission in Australia. You see, Pete, the word is really spreading! Gay guys are building a world community—but it's nothing for straight people to be afraid of. It's a community built on love and understanding." Evidence suggests that the world community will include gay guys as equal members.

Brotherly love without incest is the theme of *Brothers in Love* by Don Holliday and *Gay Brother* by James Harper. The morality that is found in all these raunchy romances is particularly evident in the latter novel. An innocent man is sent to prison to further the career of Jim, the older and dishonest brother of Roy. When Raol, the man sent to prison, is released he returns and rapes Jim on the floor of his office after holding an ether-soaked cloth to his nose. His injury is principally to his dignity. The significance of the novel is that Jim is 'straight' in the sense of not being homosexual. Morally he is as crooked as they come. As one of his nefarious associates says, "Just what you deserve, you son of a bitch!"

Don Holliday is the author of a series of detective, or suspense, stories with a homosexual cast of characters, especially the hero Jackie Holmes. Greenleaf published the stories, influenced by the popularity of the television series, "The Man from U. N. C. L. E." Jackie Holmes is the man from C. A. M. P., a word that has since become acclimated into the language from its jargon and cant usage. The central organization is called 'high camp.' Although the books have appeared as publishers' (or distributors') overstock, they were evidently quite successful. They are well written and homosexual episodes do not really occupy center stage. In most of the series, *The Man from C. A. M. P., The Watercress File, The Son Goes Down,* and *Rally Round the Fag,* there is considerable humor, especially as a 'straight' detective associated with Jackie Holmes decides to have at least one homosexual experience. " 'What'll it be boys,' [Jackie] asked softly, 'heads or tails.' " A kind of ideal society is depicted that finds a welcome for homosexuals necessary.

If the publisher's blurbs are worthy of belief, Richard Amory's *Song of the Loon* was a bestseller, and the most eagerly awaited books of the generation were the *Song of Aaron* and *Listen, The Loon Sings.* Amory explains that his "pastoral employs certain European characters taken from 'the novels of Jorge de Montemayor and Gaspar Gil Polo, painted . . . a gay aesthetic red.' " The novels are the work of a talented writer. A spate of would-be series followed, and several of the novels in this genre promised further stories that have not, to the knowledge of a bibliographer, been written or at any rate published. All three novels are longer than the average work in the paperback series, and the development of character is especially strong. The Indian characters are as well and distinctly drawn as the Europeans, whatever the provenance of the latter might be. All the action takes place in some former time in North America, possibly the last century, in the Northwest wilderness, although there is something of James Fenimore Cooper in the stories, including the anachronisms and factual improbabilities mentioned in Amory's introduction. Mark Twain would have been as critical of Amory's supermen as he was of Cooper's.

The *Song of the Loon* describes a society of homosexuals whose insignia is the loon, a waterfowl with a wild eerie cry. The society is founded by Indians and preserves some of their mystical traditions, and it is anthropologically not far from accuracy. The plot of the first novel concerns Ephraim MacIver who enters this society and succeeds in finding the meaning of love or as the publisher's blurb puts it, "new meanings to the word *love* . . . for a new self, that he must learn to love before the love of others could be fully his." The novels describe a morality based on self-acceptance, an absence of jealousy, hatred, puritanism, and racism. There are no female characters at all, and descriptions of homosexual activity are the most graphic in the first of the series. As the pages of fiction follow Amory becomes weary of describing the same activity over and over and tends rather to hint at it than to depict it, although there is never a hint that such behavior is anything but natural and normal for the characters involved.

This point of view marks the greatest area of influence, because the genre took shape with Amory's well-written fantasy. The pastoral and the sentimental novel have always been rather similar, and there is considerable sentimentality in all the raunchy romances. Amory's style moves rapidly in a stream of conscious prose in the last novel of the series, also the longest, *Listen the Loon Sings*. An attempt is made to produce speech that is like the patois of trappers and cattle-men before the end of the last century, and Amory includes verse from time to time. It has the flavor of rather awkward folksongs.

These novels could be dangerous to the man who wishes to change his homosexual orientation, because they utilize one of the fondest notions of the past two centuries. The primitive is thought to be innocent. Just as ignorance is sometimes equated with innocence, the untutored children of the wild were thought to be naturally virtuous. Rousseau was the architect of the marvelous structure that conceived of a noble savage. Unlike the hustler novels, with their bitterness and regret, in the Loon Series the man are happy with each other and find their sexual relations a means of showing and obtaining the evidence of love. If a man with sufficient desire to change his fixated homosexuality for fixated heterosexuality were to read only this kind of novel, the chances are he would weaken this desire to the point of its being a pipe dream. Amory is a convincing novelist, and some of the militancy of Gay Liberation derives from his moral attitudes.

Homosexuality expressed in the fiction available is as surrounded with moral injunction as heterosexuality, perhaps more so. The morality includes what heterosexuals should think of homosexuals. In a later novel, published by Olympia Press in its Other Traveller Series, *Frost*, a passage occurs that explains exactly what Amory means. *Frost* is a kind of suspense novel in which the title character, a Spanish and Portuguese instructor, tries to solve a murder and uncover a political egomaniac who uses reactionary politics as his means of obtaining power. This unsavory character is Frost's father, a man named McGraw. There is a kind of antithetical character, Dr. Morgan, who is the chairman of Frost's department in the college where he teaches. Frost is threatened with blackmail of the I'll-tell-on-you sort, and his friend Rip is trying to convince him to go to his department chairman and explain the situation.

Dr. Morgan doesn't strike me as the kind of man who is afraid of queers. He's established, tenured, published, and highly regarded; he's got a wife and two kids, and he's been around. He's liberal, educated, and independently wealthy. He really digs women. And *my* idea is that a man who knows damned well that he himself isn't queer isn't going to worry about the next guy. He knows it isn't going to rub off; nobody can call his masculinity into question; he doesn't have to prove himself, so he can afford to be understanding.

This is exactly the case, and Dr. Morgan provides the key to the mystery by identifying a quotation from Luis de Gongora's *Polifemo y Galatea*. The novel is a bit beyond the skill exhibited in the Loon series. Whatever the reader's sexual orientation, he would find the novel enjoyable, although a reader with no experience of the graphics of homosexuality might find the candor revolting.

Douglas Dean, mentioned earlier, is as good a novelist, along with Peter Tuesday Hughes, Dirk Vanden, Lance Lester, James Colton, and Larry Townsend. Each of these writers has a particular style and tells a good story with strongly developed characters and settings of interest. Douglas Dean is as versatile as Richard Amory, and his two volume autobiographical novel *Windows and Mirrors* is impressive as fiction, whatever the genre. Dirk Vanden excuses his not having one long succession of homosexual events in *All Is Well* in an author's note that deserves quotation in full.

In all of my previous books, sex has necessarily been the predominant theme, because whether or not their assumptions were correct, my publishers insisted on 'hot sex' and lots of it, the kinkier the better, with a little plot and characterization tossed in here and there for good measure. Olympia has allowed me far more freedom in writing *All Is Well*; the sex is still there (as it must be in gay novels as well as gay lives) but only as one of the many aspects of the story. Some readers may find the sex scenes less masturbatory as a result. I've had to make a decision—to write "just another sex book" or to test my convictions that gay people want to understand themselves and one another more than they want to jack off. After all, there are thousands of books which supply masturbatory fantasies for those who want them; there are very few books which advance the idea that being gay isn't as wretched and sinful as we've all been taught to believe it is.

There is a tremendously exciting reformation going on, all over the world, and I feel that gay people are going to wake up and find themselves in the vanguard of that reformation. But in order to "wake up" we must first understand ourselves—and that, more than anything else, is what *All Is Well* is all about.

The raunchy romances are not so raunchy after all. The books of an earlier period prepared the way for the present novels that may be of almost any kind, whether written in stream-of-conscious prose like *Clint Wins His Letter*, *Clint Scores Big*, and *Jet* by Lance Lester, concerned with science fiction like *Remake* by Peter Tuesday Hughes and *The Scorpius Equation* by Larry Townsend, involved with the theatre like *One for the Money* by Douglas Dean or the movies like *Mirror Chronicles* by Peter Tuesday Hughes and *Todd* by James Colton, suspense novels like *The Judas Match* by Frederick Raborg, and historical fiction like *Frontier Boys* by George Delacourt and *Climax at Bull Run* by Billy Peale.

The novels do not advocate violence nor the use of drugs. In *I Am Dying, Egypt*, Peter Tuesday Hughes gives one of the most impressive arguments against drugs by putting them into the hands of the villains of the piece and describing what drugs do to the hero. In *Judas Goat*, Lance Lester seems to treat the crime syndicate with the awe and respect found in Mario Puzo's renowned novel *The Godfather*, but violence is not so much condoned as explained. There is usually very little humor, except in a novel like *The Gay Haunt* by Victor Jay and *Say, Mister* by Greg Foster. There is about as much escapism as realism. *Lovers' Island* by Frederick Raborg invents an ideal society in a South Sea paradise, and *Tearoom Castles* by Dick Garfield describes the homosexual activities that take place in the men's room of a park in a small town in California. *He's Gay and Married* is apparently a fairly accurate picture of the sexual promiscuity of a homosexual travelling salesman. The realism tends to be clear reportage rather than the fictional style adopted by an author like Lester or the autobiographical style used by Greg Foster.

Whores, Queers and Others by Philip Barrows was a two volume cry of agony with psychoanalytic overtones. *Say, Mister* by Greg Foster is not a shout of joy but rather a continuing chuckle. The main character never feels sorry for himself, and the result is a novel of considerable charm. *Climax at Bull Run* is also very humorous, and even the homosexual hustler in *My Brother, The Hustler* has a kind of wit and charm about him that seems to excuse everything else. The argument that because society deplores homosexuality, we must all learn to hate people of that sexual orientation is worthless on the face of it. The exciting reformation going on around the world, that Dirk Vanden mentions, is a change in moral attitudes, a realization that there are distinct lines of authority for government and for religion, and that the individual must not expect the actions of the one to supplant the need for the other. Even the atheist has a religion, in the original sense of that word, for we are all bound by the common chains of humanity.

Homophile fiction, gay novels, homosexual trash, call the genre what you will, as a matter of accurate description, we must acknowledge that the communication process has been affected by what has been published, and whether this is good or bad depends on how one regards the changes. In a period of 'exciting reformation' not everyone will be delighted. Certainly the attitudes of Roman Catholics have been subjected to as much upheaval and change as those of other elements of society. The censorship groups that made a narrow-minded view of sinful man waiting to engage in mass rapine a fixture of dogma have so far lost power that there is little remaining of the old missionary authoritarianism dictating that an Italian motion picture was sacrilegious and therefore to be banned. Only in some countries like Ireland and Spain can the old moral censorship be found. In other countries, there has been increase in sexual sin when the right of adults to read what they wish is no longer questioned. It is not surprising that the changes in the church have come to bear upon their fellows. The extent of the change can be seen in the organization called Dignity for 'gay catholics' offering an active spiritual, educational, and social program.

This lengthy review of homosexual literature may add to the study of the homosexual in the communication process. The anatomy of censorship can be seen through this lens, for the censors are generally men, usually those in authority, with less regard for public morals than for their own pose of supernatural virtue. The chief value of the homosexual genre in fiction is that it describes masculinity in a context of welcome and appreciation rather than as the prelude to violence. When the muscular beauty of characters is established, what next follows in the homosexual novel is sexual activity with either an avowal of love or deep respect for the individual. In many of the novles, the homosexuality is almost incidental, for instance *Son of Adam*, by Llewellyn Hollingsworthy, even though the plot assumes that the hero and the villain are both homosexual as a necessary condition for the story. If there was no homosexuality, a different story would result of a plot that has been attractive since Thackeray wrote *Henry Esmond*.

The novels have gone a long way from closet fiction and case histories to the point of becoming an exacting genre where writers can develop their talents to a remarkable degree. *The Other Party* by Peter Tuesday Hughes is not nearly so good as a novel as *Something in the Blood*. A great tolerance is shown by most of the publishers so that the author can learn to write by writing. *Yours to Keep* by James Insley, for example is quite an amateur production, while *The Flesh Mast* by Rod Sawyers achieves a deep understanding of men in groups and of a common need that all human beings have for belonging in some accepting and rewarding association. The great enemy of the homosexual is not the caprice of the law, but the loneliness he feels. Homosexuals have organized so that they are no longer the embodiment of the dirty words men use to excuse their actions but a harmless segment of the human scene.

Gay literature serves a very definite and useful research purpose in producing a corpus of documentation that has put homosexuality into a new light. Dr. Morgan's attitude in *Frost* is that of most intelligent people who have no sexual fears. At some point the raunchy romances will become completely acceptable as a literary genre, and the amount and kind of graphic description will decrease as the development of character occupies the central place in the novel. There seems to be little reason to attempt anything beyond what occurs at the end of *The Gay Force* by Trock Bender, some two thousand words describing sodomy as completely as the inexperienced would ever want to find.

Publishers have become more selective and more honest. Greenleaf Classics published a series of well bound paperback books with a strange method of printing so that the removal of a paper cover would, in some cases, remove part of the story, perhaps in an attempt to reduce the number of returns. One of these novels, *Buddy*, is written with remarkable verisimilitude so that it seems to be the confessions of a homosexual, as it may well be. The *Tijuana Bible Readers* include a large selection of closet literature with an intelligent introduction, and Dirk Vanden has at least one novel in the series. Homosexuality in *Staircase* by Charles Dyer differs only in a minimal way from this kind of story, and the ultimate goal of the genre is seen in novels of the intensity and beauty of Mishima's *Forbidden Colors* and *Confessions of a Mask*. The tradition of homosexuality accepted among the samurai of Japan is explored in *Temple of Pederasty* translated by Hideki Okada from the work of Ihara Saikaku with very frank illustrations by Philip Core. Yukio Mishima committed suicide in the manner of the samurai by driving a dagger into his abdomen before a disciple could strike off his head with a sword, and commit suicide in the same fashion so that the man who beheaded him could help him to atone for the murder. These bloody ceremonies are directly from the old stories of the samurai, and the connection between homosexuality and aggressiveness seems to be a fruitful area of a cross-cultural research. A great tradition exists going back to the Greeks and the Spartans that can be compared with the ancient warrior cult of Japan and the modern Pathans of Pakistan.

A novel like *A Sand Fortress* by John Coriolan, or *Gov't Inspected Meat* by Dotson Rader, represents the other limit to the development of the genre. The search for material ever more shocking in detail must end finally with the need to integrate the sexual episodes with the substance of the story. That such novels have appeal to the general public has been recognized with the success of the motion picture made from Dyer's novel, *Staircase*, and Mart Crowley's *The Boys in the Band*. As a play and as a motion picture, the nature of the homosexual community has never been so openly displayed. Rather more is made of its frustrations than of its joys, but there is enough to show the interested public what is taking place with some millions of fellow citizens.

Bernard Geis Associates, before the firm became bankrupt, published Gordon Merrick's highly successful book, *The Lord Won't Mind*. In every way, except for length, this novel represents what the raunchy romances wish to achieve. The characters are strongly drawn, very appealing, and the plot is not only suspenseful but acceptable as realism. A psychological study of Charlie, who cannot accept his homosexuality, and of Peter whose sexual nature is awakened by Charlie, the plot traces Charlie's downfall as Peter becomes a high-priced hustler. Ultimately both men have to admit that the only thing that gives meaning to their lives is their love for each other. The characters of Charlie's erstwhile wife and especially of his very rich and domineering grandmother contrast with a kind of beautiful simplicity in Peter. Few novelists have achieved so penetrating an analysis of character as Merrick, and very few have written stories so entertaining. Scenes of sexual activity are graphic but make little use of taboo words, except those that are suitable for the action described.

The sequel to this novel, *One for the Gods*, continues the analysis of character, and the possibility that Charlie has been romanticized at the end of the first novel vanishes. This is the Charlie that each of us has known at some time, a man who is unaware of his own nature and must discover it. Peter has a much stronger sense of identity, and in the end of the novel he establishes his masculinity unmistakably. Both novels represent the latest development of the homophile genre and are much more accurate than the accumulations of case histories interlarded with psychiatric pontifications. What is most important is that graphic descriptions of homosexual activity do not detract from the story but add to it, and this did not prevent the books from becoming bestsellers. They will not be influential, except in establishing a level of quality, because they come at the end of a period of development rather than at the beginning.

The theme of homosexuality seen in all the works is the theme of humanity itself, an individual in search of his identity, discovering in the laboratory of life what the formulae of the past mean. Merrick's characters are not at the mercy of anything but their love for each other, depicted as stronger than Charlie's neuroticism and Peter's passivity. The love reshapes each man and makes him more able to create and live in a real world without shame or self-castigation. It is simply an anomaly of our times that the brief Greenleaf classics and the expansive fiction of Gordon Merrick should be separated in bookshops, the former being found only in the porno-stores and the latter among the works sold in reputable bookstores to a discriminating clientele. So far as graphic descriptions of sexual activity are concerned, whether homosexual or heterosexual, only trifling differences of phrasing and vocabulary distinguish the two kinds of books.

The purpose of sexual fantasy is to provide pleasing body sensations through purely mental activity. When the fantasy begins to explain the event world and make it endurable, it becomes art. An attempt to censor this literature would only represent the abreactive announcement that the censor has problems with his own sexual fantasies. The publishers and the market will interact so that an improvement of the message occurs to the extent that the homosexual genre becomes accepted as a literary form no different from western novels or detective stories, so far as the typifying elements of each can be identified. As the novels improve in quality, they will begin to explain the heterosexual to himself, for there is not much difference between the two kinds of men, except for their choice of sexual partner. As the sexual component of each is established more clearly without the intervention of symbolic and substitutive acts of aggression, the average man of goodwill can adopt an attitude that permits the homosexual to pursue sexual satisfactions that do not confront an unwilling spectator or invade the areas of parental privilege. Significant strides have been made in this direction already.

A Matter of Education

When a corpus of literature becomes large enough, some university will offer courses so that it is understandable and so that research can develop all the potentialities of the collection. As the National Commission on Obscenity and Pornography observed, research in behavioral science is not a matter of identifying an independent variable and conducting an experiment designed so that the results are valid and may be repeated. Truth is approached through successive studies, and to close off any area of investigation is to make truth that much more difficult to reach. The courses in sexuality and society, variously labelled, have occasioned no great difficulty until the matter is clearly identified with homosexuality. Then the voluntary censors find their most secret fantasies come to life and begin to fight, if not bravely and well at least insistently. A man who is threatened by his own erotic fantasies cannot bear to have these made public, especially the ones that the individual rejects with fear and anxiety. It is no easy thing to be called a homosexual because of the tenuous evidence of literary or research interests. A course

offered at the University of Nebraska would not have been the center
of great argument if its identification as Homophile Studies had not
been used. But the men involved were quite right in bringing the
subject into the open, even though academic freedom became a sacrificial victim of the sexual fears of the Board of Regents, who ought
to know better. These men believed a medical doctor of the area who
published what was apparently a plagiarization of Edmund Bergler's
1957 disquisition on homosexuality as his own writing in order to
oppose the course.

Evelyn Hooker of the National Institute of Mental Health recommended such courses, because she thought fixated homosexuality
was a matter of ignorance as much as anything else. No man has
to engage in homosexual activity if he does not wish to do so. Some
men invent a compulsion to explain their shyness with women or
their fears of inadequacy. Assured, perhaps by pornographic works,
that a man is a fountain of semen that never stops they find that
they have to be stimulated by a woman before a complete erection
is achieved, and this seems evidence that they are less than masculine.
The average man has to be stimulated so that he acts exactly like
some who see psychiatrists for what they fancy are sex problems.
The purposes of courses on homosexuality is to remove the threat
and fear from what can only be called a natural part of human sexual
activity. Homosexuality has been identified in every human society
at every period of human existence for which we have records. It
exists because of the inventive nature of human beings. As described
in the book *Prison Sex* by Ed Carpenter as told to Ted Baxter, when
a man is deprived of other sexual outlet, he will fantasize a woman
as he has sexual relations with another man. As the knowledge of
human sexuality grows, steps can be taken not to turn the different
ones among us into the simulacra of others but to bring about a true
reformation of unnecessary attitudes of anti-social orientation. The
homosexual cannot be included among the anti-social on the basis
of his sexual preferences alone. In the abundant evidence of the

homosexual in society, the truly anti-social may not be homosexual and the homosexual may be among the best members of society, as productive and hard-working as any of his better accepted heterosexual brothers.

The Other Traveller series includes a book by John Francis Hunter called *The Gay Insider* that offers a guide to the homosexual side of New York, from baths and cruising places to bars, orgy rooms, good places to eat, and churches. Like the *Guild Guide* published every year, this book is compiled for the visitor to New York, just as the *Guild Guide* treats briefly each of the places in all the cities identified by the men who submit information to the Guild Press. While the *Guild Guide* is simply a list of addresses with a code describing somewhat the kind of place the address represents, *The Gay Insider* also includes comment, anecdotes, and even a list of books, periodicals, and phonorecordings. The book list is especially good as it covers much not mentioned here for the simple reason that no research value for this study was discerned in many of the extant works. One of the most popular, but not investigated, is Angelo Arcangelo's *The Homosexual's Handbook*. A pirated edition exists with the apparent knowledge and disinterest of a publisher who is fierce in defending his rights, the Olympia Press. As the author of this book could not pursue the reason with any profit, the book is simply mentioned here. Equally, a close reading of *American Grotesque* by James Kirkwood showed its value for this study, as recommended by Hunter, and it forms a portion of a later section.

Such books as *Male Homosexual Marriages*, *The Homosexual Then and Now*, and *The Ways Homosexuals Make Love* are useful in giving clear descriptions of sexual activity and providing some more of the photographs that seem to be passed from publisher to publisher or periodical to periodical without regard for copyright. As the National Commission on Obscenity and Pornography states homosexual, like heterosexual, pornography is stale, vulgar, desperately tasteless and rapidly satiating. An exposure to it will convince the average man of goodwill that there is nothing very inviting about such sexual relations. Certainly there is little challenge to the basic humanity within each of us which, in this author's estimation, finds truest expression in the relationship between the sexes.

The newspapers and periodicals of the Gay Liberation, as well as such books as Donn Teale's *Gay Militants*, demonstrate the conclusion that Dirk Vanden reached as a novelist of considerable talent and experience, and this author discovered as the result of ten years of research. The world community if it is to replace war with the search for knowledge can exclude nothing that is human, whether this represents strange religions, aberrant sexual experiences, a society of men who prefer to have sexual relations only with other men, or whatever human beings have found necessary to try in a search for ways of becoming more human.

The attentive researcher formulates tentative hypotheses as he begins his investigation and at a later point he reformulates these when the method of testing them has been found. So far in describing the irrational in the communication process, we have blundered into many fields where an interdisciplinary study would be useful, and we have found some areas that can be tested by an inspection of other areas of censorship. The homosexual is the object of censorship, and of censure, because he represents what each heterosexual fears in himself, the need to surrender an image that he has been at great pains to build: a tacky structure, often enough, made of half-truths, old superstitions, outworn religious philosophy, and sheer ignorance. The realization that each of us, provided the circumstances that would make it inevitable, is capable of what we loathe most because we are a modern equivalent of the hunting parties made up of killer apes, is enough to make us protest that whoever forces this knowledge upon us must be aiming at a total destruction of society by criminal means. It is jarring in the extreme to find the substance of a sex dream that causes anxiety and depression depicted in glaring photographs or skillfully managed prose.

The censor has no interest in anyone but himself. His conception of society, if it is not an extension of his own image, does not exist. His authority is semi-divine, in his estimation, because he has such faith in it. He is incapable of error when dealing with his need for the protection of his own erotic fantasies, especially those that he puts away from his mind, as a man might turn off a television program that displeases him. Whatever disrupts the manipulated falsity of the messages he favors must be aimed directly at him as an authority and at the society he projects as worthy of his existence. Each of us is a little Hitler and never more insistent than when our view of the propaganda we always favor is threatened. The censor operates with the idea that anything that dilutes the propaganda line must of necessity be dangerous to everyone because it is displeasing to himself.

What must be settled somehow in the next quarter century is how the world community can live together in an era of peace without incurring the vast deadly silence of the peace that will follow the greatly feared *Bellum Omnium Contra Omnes*, the war of all against all. A separation of religion from government is essential if the inconclusive wars of religion are not to be repeated. Most importantly the resources of intellectual development cannot be stifled because of the fears of those in authority, whether these terrors are the net result of distaste or neurosis. Intellectual resources are too valuable for any self-styled moralist to damage whatever his excuses for his vandalism might be. Such an individual finally must realize that he has no superior virtue but is simply surrendering to impulses present in each of us. Arguing that he acts out of concern for society is so much rationalization, and it is manifestly untrue. He acts out of an intimate knowledge of his own intellectual landscape so that he can determine what he wishes to see and hear, but he cannot impose his preferences on another.

If these ideas are valid, they will be repeated as the literature of other suppressed areas is investigated, and as we do this, we shall see what means are taken to escape suppression. The homosexual press illuminates a secret area of human experience that would not even be mentioned a century ago, except among those elitiste groups given permission to discuss such things.

The effort of President Nixon to reimpose nineteenth century censorship on the twentieth century American was a vague but apparently pleasing promise so far as the voluntary censorship groups were concerned. His rejection of the report of the National Commission on Obscenity and Pornography re-enacts President Hoover's rejection of a report that pointed out what a greatly overrated and dangerous thing prohibition was, how much it had damaged the concept of lawfulness in the United States, and how little effect it had. Fortunately no concerted effort was made to bring a new wave of unrestrained Comstockery upon the unwilling nation. As a minority president, elected with less than a majority of the popular vote, Mr. Nixon wisely practiced the art of the possible and obtained changes in the postal law so that nuns who receive advertisements for pornography need not investigate beyond the sealed envelope warning that the contents might be revolting. Where volition operates there is no need for the government and its law enforcement agencies to intervene. In the long history of such intervention, the net result has been police corruption rather than a change of moral climate.

An unpleasant fact of a free society is that people who are not dangerous and are not to be admired must have their freedom too. The homosexual press could not be censored successfully even if that were somehow desirable. The result of the censorship of the past was to put a totally unnecessary value on literary works that had none otherwise. But if censorship is negative, its positive counterpart must have arguments that can be raised to show that intellectual resources can be increased by one kind of material over another. The enemy of valueless literature is valuable works. Disinterest is far more effective than censorship.

The homosexual is the victim of society because he represents a threat to the image of the men in it. He has little to fear from his fellows who are informed and educated but much to fear from those who pretend to be what they are not. Homosexual prostitution is the cause of the murders that are cited as a reason for governmental control of the private sex lives of otherwise unoffending and productive citizens. The raunchy romances that deplore violence, hatred, dishonesty, and hypocrisy in the same stories where episodes of sodomy and fellatio are described with fondness and enthusiasm, are far more moral than the romances that tell of violence and hatred as the ideal state of society. Urging violence and hatred is far more dangerous than acclaiming homosexual activity. The one is a sterile manipulation in a climate of love and the other is truly anti-social. Society can survive its homosexuals but not its crime syndicates.

Part Two

HARLOTRY AND HERESY

VI.

THE AWAKENED SEX

The Victim Temptress

Modern efforts at censorship of intellectual resources aims at depictions of women as harlots, sadists, lesbians, and incestuous relatives. Self-control, for a man born or raised by a Victorian, means courtesy to women and a firm conviction that the female human being is weaker and not so smart as her male counterpart. Taboo words are not to be uttered in the presence of women, and any woman who uses a taboo word is obviously lacking in feminine virtue. Men set the style for women and demanded certain behavior from them. Women who did not follow the accepted pattern were ostracized and Victorian novelists liked to show them aware of their misdeeds and repentant. In the erotic fantasies of every man there was the compliant woman whose sexuality would be both encouragement and support, an endless fount of eroticism, whose skill would provide the man with inexhaustible sexual energy. The unending sex acts were somehow never fatiguing for the woman, even when she was whaling the tar out of a masochistic man. Up until the moral revolution of the pre-depression decade, the image of women as either Rebecca of Sunnybrook Farm or the Scarlet Whore of Babylon was forced both on authors and on their readers.

The whore who reforms and becomes a virtuous woman occurred often enough in the west for the fantasy to have some basis in fact. Calamity Jane was a prostitute, and according to some authorities a somewhat frustrated lesbian because Wild Bill was really a homosexual. The western woman, the pioneer mother, was the most civilizing influence that the world has seen in recent times. She brought an agricultural society to the west which had had a hunter society up to that time. The fur-traders were hunters, the open range and the cattle industry of the time were a natural outgrowth. Women wanted fences so that each man would stop fighting over mythical boundaries with his fellows. She brought the church and the school, the two civilizing institutions of the west, and very early in the development of the cities and towns she insisted on a public library so that free education was a concomitant of economic development. Many of the women who settled the west were refugees from the South, escaping the defeat that had deprived them of home and family.

The revolution in men's attitudes toward women, and more importantly in women's attitudes toward themselves, spread throughout the world in the course of the next century. Women had the right to vote in the new democracies of Korea and Burma, and the women of Japan fought their way out of a role that was degrading in the extreme. The new woman of China did not equate small feet with social status so that the only ones hobbling about on deformed, but tiny, feet were old ladies. Women in Russia took such a great part in the revolution that their equality was assured, and the need for experienced and trained workers was so great that most medical personnel in the Soviet Union are women, so strictly a man's profession that the first woman doctor was graduated less than a hundred years ago. The only new thing about Women's Liberation is its institutional character. The pioneer women of the Wild West who helped their husbands build sod houses on the prairie were the granddaughters and great-granddaughters of pioneer women who settled the land inhabited only by Indian tribes at an earlier time. Women became activists of social betterment by the latter quarter of the century. The Anti-Saloon League and its axe-swinging amazons ultimately triumphed in the Eighteenth Amendment to the U.S. Constitution, one of the most ill-advised experiments in human history. Women have quite often been governors of states, although so far no woman has much chance of becoming president.

Until women began to enjoy as much education as men, there was no question who read the available, though carefully concealed, pornography of the time. It was only after women had as much opportunity to become habituated readers that a valid investigation of women's use of pornographic material became possible. Kinsey established that women were not as much excited by pornography as men, that women were more aroused by tactile sensations than by purely imaginary events whether in picture form or in written form. Until D. H. Lawrence offended the literati of his time by creating Lady Chatterley with her definite sexual needs, and her gamekeeper lover to satisfy them in a frank and earthy fashion, it was popularly supposed that virtuous women had no sexual desires whatever. Marriage was a means of begetting children with the approval of church and state, but no woman would admit that she enjoyed the act that was obligatory if pregnancy was to follow.

Gatherings of ladies, as noted by several novelists, in the Victorian period were organ recitals, usually sexual organs at that. A large number of old wives' tales were transmitted from old women to young, in the fashion of ladies' periodicals today. Women in private joked about the size and shape of men's penes and complained about their ills. The Victorian lady was, according to Mark Twain, "a featherless biped with a backache." She was often pregnant, if a virtuous wife and mother, and her husband in any case sought the comfort of a lady of easy virtue, the local harlot. For every Scarlett O'Hara there was a Belle Watling, and prostitution was tolerated because it served as a safety valve of society. Probably the Victorian wives did not like it very much, but there was not a lot they could do about it. In what Gordon Rattray Taylor calls a 'patristic society,' the males have responsibility and authority over everyone. A hierarchy like that of a flock of chickens is organized into a viable social structure, so that the cock can peck all the hens, and each of these can peck certain others in a descending order to the crippled little hen who gets pecked by all her sisters and the cock as well.

The orthodoxy of the time deplored the Liliths and offered advice on ways of correcting the sad abuses of society. The Eves did not have a very pleasant life. Sentenced to hide any sexual enjoyment lest they be classified among the fallen women, few women knew of the rapid advances of science, which were the subject of intense contention among men who decided the fate of women and everyone else. Painless childbirth was held to be sinful because Eve was punished by God who decreed that she would bring forth her children in suffering. Contraception and abortion were dreadful and hideous sins. The Comstock Law made sending information about either through the mail a federal offense. (In France, until very recently, a wife could not travel without her husband's permission, and in Italy until a few years ago, divorce was quite impossible.) In oriental countries, a woman was instructed in ways of pleasing her husband and other males, and marriages were commonly arranged to provide the best assortment of genes and wealth. In Africa, a bride had to be bought, and in India, in effect, a husband. An illegitimate child in the United States was identified as such on his birth certificate, and the word 'bastard' became a taboo word. Women who succumbed to the importuning of lovers faced either a life of prostitution or a hasty 'shotgun' marriage.

An accurate picture of Victorian life is conveyed in the fiction of the time. Women and their virtue made a good excuse for masculine aggression. Duels were outlawed in the United States, although they were thought to be the height of masculine courage and honor. Throughout the ante-bellum South, duels were fought as the virtue and chastity of women came into question. The phrase 'son of a bitch' used as an epithet was an invitation to fight because it was an aspersion on the mother. Women were, nevertheless, not the equal of men, legally or morally. It was supposed that women would succumb to men without much hesitation, and a family could protect its honor only by effecting the marriage of a girl to the man who seduced her. For those who could fit into the social system without difficulty, it was a happy and highly moral time. The standard of public ethics was rather low because sex and sin were virtually synonymous.

The Young Men's Christian Association, which supported the New York Society for the Suppression of Vice, Anthony Comstock's organization, did not have a free hand. Efforts to label atheism 'obscene' failed, and the infidel traps that Comstock warned against were allowed some measure of freedom. Those of the free-thinkers who dared to advocate free love, especially if they used such strong language as 'prostitution,' were a different matter. Prostitute was almost a taboo word because of its obvious sexual reference, and the word whore was so taboo that many women, including the author's mother, did not know how to spell it even though they could spell almost everything else. Walt Whitman's *Leaves of Grass* was banned in Boston, or at least prevented from being mailed there, because of his poem 'To a Common Prostitute.' There were purveyors of pornography, however, and many wealthy men built sizable collections, and at least one Englishman devoted himself to the pursuit of sexual pleasure and reporting on it in about equal measure it seems. The publication of *My Secret Life* by Grove Press and many of the other suppressed works of the time, including the complete works of the Marquis de Sade, reveals what Victorian England and the continent was like. No such work dealing with America has come to light, and it is possible that none was written.

While the portrait of Eve as a virtuous Victorian lady is taught everywhere in the fiction of the period, there are few good contemporary portraits of Lilith, the lady with the swansdown seat on her commode. Women began to write pornography for publication only when the Olympia Press in Paris was publishing such works for world wide consumption by readers of English. Lilith was a potential in every woman, the temptress who excited Saint Paul and Saint Augustine, against whom generations of priests and ministers inveigh, although another segment of society thought it wise for a young man to sow his wild oats, safely if possible, before he settled down to marriage. The profane love that nearly made a sacrificial victim of a man was a standard plot device.

Walter, as the man who wrote *My Secret Life* identifies himself, paints a different picture entirely. Anyone who reads Dickens should also read this book lest he gain an entirely wonky picture of the age. Attitudes such as the upper-class author displays on every page were formed much earlier, and the sentimental novels of the time make sense only when seen in the context of hitherto unreported details about life in England and the Continent from around 1840 to 1885 or 1890. Even an understanding of Richardson's *Pamela* and Jane Austen's works is enriched with this book. However, its greatest usefulness is in describing the secrets that Victorian hypocrisy successfully concealed. Unlike Fanny Hill, Walter uses taboo words in abundance to the point where they have no further emotional charge. Several of his taboo words have now become obsolete. Who would call his penis a 'pego' today?

Walter conceals his own identity and that of his various paramours who might be identified. If, in fact, only six copies were printed in Amsterdam between 1882, or 1884, and 1894, then Grove Press has done a signal kindness to students of social history by republishing the great tiresome book. The most interesting episodes, by far, deal not with his endless sexual adventures but with his ideas, opinions, and descriptions of events and places other than sexual. Unlike true pornography, this book fits into the class of heterosexual closet literature and makes effective use of character and setting, at times displaying considerable literary vigor, along with the lapses in grammar, rhetoric, and style that abound in such works.

Other collections of case histories, such as those found in Havelock Ellis' monumental *Studies in the Psychology of Sex*, confirm that Walter is quite accurate in his descriptions of his early life, except that Walter uses detail with the accuracy of Tolstoi. Sanitary conveniences were uncommon then, and the chamber pot a fixture, necessarily a movable one, of the bedroom. Some modern readers are much more distressed by thoughts of excrement standing about in the living quarters than they are by the incessant and repetitious sexuality. Despite all the 'delicacy' that made any mention of sex or of the organs of excretion taboo in polite society, there were no roadside conveniences in England and when men or women had to relieve themselves they used the nearest semi-private spot they could find.

Walter's psychosexual development includes the adventitious instruction gained from a couple of bawdy books and the assiduous interest of a cousin his own age. Together they sneak about in the hope that they will see the external female genitalia, and they have some success. They are not respecters of persons. One of the women they spy on is Fred's mother, Walter's aunt, and others are relatives. Walter develops a strong liking for women and even as a boy tries to get them to kiss him. As he matures, he employs 'smutty talk' in order to gain the confidence, or at least the acquiescence, of a young maid named Charlotte. Both are virgins until Walter succeeds in seducing her. His later experiences are, in a way, an attempt to recreate the experience. Up until this time, Walter had phimosis of a mild degree, but as was common in a Victorian household, no one knew of it, such matters being improper for a lady and unsuitable for a man, even a youngster's father. His first experience of sexual intercourse rather savagely solves the problem for him, and it removes Charlotte's hymen.

Two of the customs of the time are very well covered in the short unhappy romance of Walter and Charlotte. The 'hotel of accommodation,' where one could rent a room by the hour, and the anonymous letter, have a direct effect on the romance. Walter is glad to be able to take Charlotte to such a hotel, even when he has no money and she must pay for everything, and the anonymous letter makes Charlotte's father determined to see his daughter safely married. She is terribly worried that her husband will realize that she is not a virgin, but she is equally afraid that her love affair with Walter will result finally in a pregnancy that would ruin her life. Walter's affair first with Charlotte, then his attempts with every other servant that his mother hires, is reminiscent of *Pamela* about a century earlier. Richardson's heroine makes her master marry her before she will surrender her virtue. There seems to be little doubt that Walter would not have married Charlotte even if he had wanted to. Her social station was too much beneath his.

Walter's history goes on and on for 2300 pages in the Grove Press edition. The repetitiousness usually gets to all but the most dedicated researcher or the aficionado of this kind of literature. The reader begins to search out passages that serve to illustrate facts about Victorian life that were taken for granted at the time, such as women cleaning themselves with their petticoats after urinating. Walter is rather profligate and gambles away the fortune his godfather leaves him, commenting wryly that if he had spent it all on harlots it would have lasted longer. Romanticists of the period like to believe that it was a time of uncommon religiosity and virtue. If Walter's reportage can be taken as fact, the Victorians were dominated by sex and money in a way that is very modern. Ideas of station, social and political, govern even the moral attitudes. Walter is appalled that girls give their virginity away to young fellows in the streets when they could reserve themselves for his delectation.

In the course of his life, Walter commits all the cardinal sexual sins: seduction, fornication, defloration, adultery, rape, voyeurism, whore-mongering; homosexual intercourse, masturbation, sodomy, fellatio, and erotographia. These lead him to adopt a philosophy that is very modern and might as well be the statement of a man born a century later. In the aphoristic manner of the present-day young, "If you like it, do it." So long as no harm is done to another, whatever of sexuality gives delight is acceptable. Walter rather has to fight himself when this extends to homosexuality for which he never acquires any preference beyond curiosity, and that once satisfied is no longer enticing. His decision to tell all, even his experiments with homosexuality, makes him regret his memoirs and at times he is on the point of destroying them. The feeling of revulsion is consistent with Walter's attitude toward his own auto-eroticism and toward his brief encounters with other men. Walter's sex education is severely lacking. Books on sexuality included accounts of the horrible effects of masturbation, although he had difficulty understanding what the words meant.

Of much more significance than these books were the bawdy books that seem to have occupied an important part of Walter's sexual life to the point that Gershon Legman in the introduction to the Grove Press edition adduces evidence that Walter is, in fact, Henry Ashbee, the Pisanus Fraxi of the well known erotic bibliography. Fanny Hill encourages Walter to excesses of masturbation, despite all the cautionary literature and advice from his godfather. Walter apparently believes that masturbation is harmful, and at the very least he has guilt feelings whenever he masturbates or is masturbated. These feelings are even more intense in his few experiments with other men.

Virtually all of the book is taken up with Walter's attentions to women. A procession of prostitutes whom Walter admires assist him to experiment in every manner possible, as he says to try everything that a man and a woman can do together. Although he loses one fortune, he acquires another when he marries, and as was often the case in Victorian times, he roundly despises his first wife, who would not tolerate his insistent sensualism. She was glad that he found comfort with his 'gay' ladies, the Cyprians or Paphians he describes with such loving detail.

Walter is motivated almost entirely by curiosity and sexual pleasure. His evaluations of English and French pornography are rather like his evaluations of women. He gradually succumbs to his desires to watch the sexual activities of men and women and arranges to gratify his voyeurism. In the 'lupanars' of the time anything is possible. The height of his erotic delight is take seconds with a prostitute while the first customer's evident satisfaction remains.

We learn nothing of Walter's occupation and can suppose that he had none. He explains that he has tried to disguise the characters, and he succeeds admirably. He takes us on his travels through Europe where his sexual activities continue unabated, and finally at the end of the eleven volumes he reverts to an incident early in his history. The writing of the book is one of the fascinating themes of his story. Equally fascinating is the history of the book which was printed in Amsterdam at a hundred guineas a volume. In present day dollars, that would be around a thousand dollars a volume, rather inexpensive considering printing costs at present. Only a few copies are known. Legman traces six, although there is a story that the printer made more copies.

Henry Ashbee, when he died, left his collection of *Don Quijote* to the British Museum on condition that they accept and retain his collection of pornographic works. There was some discussion whether to refuse the bequest, even though the collection of editions of *Quijote* was one of the greatest ever assembled and could not be duplicated at the present time. With the change in attitudes since 1900, the pornographic collection is even more valuable, for it proves a point that Walter makes often. Human sexuality during the rigidities of the Victorian era was no different from the present. Under the polite society of the time was a secret world where man and women were quite as experimental in their behavior as today, in the era of swingers and orgy clubs. The difference was in the chasm between reality and the way it was reported.

If censorship arises out of a need to protect a propaganda line, then the censorship of England was the result of an elitist society maintaining its privileges. Walter is aware that he is exploiting women of the lower classes and the man who occupies a special place in volume eight, and yet it seems to him that this is the way the world is meant to run. When he rapes a girl, he manages to get her to accept money for her injuries rather than go to the local magistrate. Walter apparently has no trouble acquiring pornographic literature, and if he was Henry Ashbee, this meant buying about 15,000 volumes all over the continent.

Grove Press could only have published *My Secret Life* after the courts had decided that adult Americans were old enough to read such works and would gain information that could be conveyed in no other way. The Hicklin decision has usually been read as meaning that society is to be judged by the least informed members so far as sexual candor is concerned, but there is considerable evidence that the decision provided a discreet way for the wealthy to acquire their collections secretly. Publishers and booksellers such as Dugdale, Carrington, and Daragon found enough business to keep them alive. Legman identifies Carrington as one "Paul Ferdinando" whose business was in Paris. English dealers were in constant danger from the police, but there was no great effort to prevent the traveler of the time from acquiring the books he wanted abroad.

What Orwell called 'doublethink' in his book *1984* prevails in the Victorian attitudes toward human sexuality. Women were the weaker sex, the imperfect vessel, the temptresses who lured men from religious rectitude down the primrose path, although a certain enthusiasm for the trip is everywhere evident. A woman of the 'lower orders' was importuned by a 'gentleman' and if she surrendered, her virginity was his prize and her lost treasure. Virginity was prized above everything else, possibly because a virgin could not convey a venereal disease. Schubert died of syphilis as did de Maupassant and many others. The virtue of a girl of the lower class made her equal to the upper class girl whose virginity was guarded very carefully. While virtuous women were supposed to have no sexual appetite at all, the slightest temptation was likely to cause a girl's downfall. If the young woman yielded to a nobleman, the chances are that a life of prostitution was the only one open for her. Fallen women became prostitutes because no one would marry them, and a parent might be paid a fairly handsome sum by the gentleman who had worked his will with the maiden.

Very strict sexual roles were reserved for each sex, and it was this inflexible separatism that prevented young women from finding employment except as navvies in the sweatshops or as servants. The professions were closed to women, who were supposed not to be intelligent enough to learn what the profession taught. Parallel attitudes can be seen elsewhere in the world today, especially in the Orient. The end of censorship has brought facts into the open that were carefully guarded secrets of society during most of the previous century.

Digression in Korea

Closed societies cannot prevent the intrusion of the world community today. The communication process makes primitive man the most endangered species on our planet. It is highly doubtful that any will survive this century. The ancient traditions of the Orient were especially affected by the massive changes that occurred as the result of the war in the Pacific during the second World War. Korea is a very old country, for centuries a kingdom occupying a peninsula between China and Japan, the two powers that so often brought war to Korea that all the words of greeting contain the word for peace, 'anyang.'

The American occupation of Korea after the second World War demonstrates why the United States may win wars but always loses the peace. No one on the staff of General Hodge of the Twentieth Corps knew a word of Korean, and to General Hodge, the Koreans were just like the Japanese, the same 'breed of cats,' as he unwisely put it. The quarter of a century from the end of the second World War has seen the Korean peninsula split, apparently permanently, between the area of American and of Chinese influence. Three visits to Korea in the period of its greatest change have demonstrated for the author what occurs when the future moves in and the changes that seem desirable lead to other changes not so easily accepted. It is a case of continuing *future shock*, the apt title of a book by Alvin Toffler.

The Korean woman was among the most subjugated in the world during the period of Japanese domination. A man would not bother to count his daughters. If asked the number of children he had, he would reply with the precise number of sons and dismiss the daughters with some vague reference to 'ever so many.' A woman's life was planned for her from the moment of her birth. As a girl, she could pursue studies up to the point of being able to read, write, sing and play a musical instrument, possibly, and make sketches. Her instruction was largely in home economics in preparation for her marriage. This was arranged by the parents, and one of the worst disasters a family could face was the romances that on occasion developed between young men and women. In a proper family, the young man had the opportunity to meet his bride-to-be, under the close supervision of both families, once or possibly twice before the ceremony was performed, but the girl had no power to refuse the boy. She could be refused, however, and this would make it more difficult to arrange another marriage.

The young bride went to live with her husband's family. A strict and very complicated set of conventions, deeply imbedded in the Korean language, governed her actions from the moment of her marriage onward. She could not use the common word for 'I' without invoking severe criticism from all her female in-laws. It was quite improper for her to call herself "Bom mo's wife" because that term was not suitable until she had given birth to a male heir, and she would be considered very presumptuous if she dared to call herself "daughter of Bom mo's parents." It was even worse for her to use her given name. Most brides kept quiet and kept out of their mother-in-law's way, if possible. As soon as she could, the young bride became pregnant, and if she was fortunate, her first child was a boy. A young man who sired a girl was rather abashed, and as soon as possible he made his wife pregnant again in the hope that the next infant would be a boy. If the husband should die or be killed, the widow whose only children were girls could not attend his funeral.

A man who had sired three daughters without having a boy was given a red egg, a sign of his inadequacy as a male, and he endured as much disgrace as his wife.

However, with the birth of the first boy, the bride assumed a meaning and role in the family, to the point that she would enjoy a grammatical structure in the language addressed to her indicating that she was above the level of animals and female servants, the lowest order of living creatures. With the second or third boy, the woman would find that her husband, if he was rich enough, would marry a second wife. Some women looked forward to this event because it would give them somebody to fetch and carry for them. A woman who yearned to exercise the tyranny she had observed in her own mother-in-law could do so only with second wives and daughters-in-law. Wealthy families set the style for all others, and the hope of social mobility was in the concubinage offered as the only respectable future for a girl whose family was lower in station than that of an interested young man.

The families of farmers were not so strictly controlled, and even among the upper classes, all was not misery and unhappiness. In many families, the mother-in-law was anything but a tyrant and the daughter-in-law might be fonder of her than of her own mother. However, this was rather an exception, because some girls committed suicide rather than surrender themselves to the meaningless abuse of the families whom their fathers thought suitable. There was no divorce, only disgrace, and a life of unbearable indignity. One girl said that marriage only represented a deep black hole from which she knew she could never escape.

The Japanese altered this to a considerable degree by bringing universal education to the Koreans, partly so that they would learn the only approved language, Japanese. It was strictly forbidden to speak Korean in public and somewhat dangerous to use the language in the home. The Koreans did not intermarry with the Japanese to any great extent. Those that did wanted to go to live in Japan, but the Koreans regarded this as a form of treason. They appeared in the traditional costume whenever they could, and all the efforts at integration were diluted by the Japanese attitudes of superiority. The Korean was not as badly treated as the Ainu in the north of the Japanese islands, but very nearly as badly as the blacks in the United States during the period preceding the second World War. As the war began to go badly for the Japanese, they relied more and more on the Koreans to serve as guards in prison camps and as service personnel. The moment the Japanese announced their willingness to surrender, the Koreans tried to take full possession of their country.

In the first years of the American occupation, a Korean girl who showed an interest in the foreign soldiers was instantly ostracized. She was in danger of this even though she did no more than speak to an American in public. There were only three kinds of women, the virtuous wives, or daughters, who would kill a man rather than show any sexual interest, the Ki-sang, paid entertainers like the Geisha of Japan, and the prostitutes. The soldiers did not help their case by saying "saek-si iddewa" which cannot be accurately translated. It means something like, 'come here, young bitch.' Very few marriages occurred in Korea and then only between the most liberated girls of the most independent families. Virtuous young women would not consider marriage to a foreigner.

With the invasion of North Korea in June, 1950, the former social structure began to crumble. Another great influx of American soldiers in a period of utmost trial led to many mixed marriages, to the extent that the American forces in trying to discourage such activity did not welcome the possibility of a large number of Korean brides and made marriage a complicated pursuit of permissions and affidavits. The occupation by American army forces has continued since the ceasefire, and many Americans now live in the Korean community. Korean women who married Americans are no longer ostracized. Women now work, if not on an equal basis with men, at least without most of the hampering restrictions.

There is a cleavage between the 'old ways' before the Korean War and what now prevails. The Japanese and the Koreans have always taken an open-minded attitude toward sex. In Japan, nudity is considered uninteresting, and like the nineteenth century European, Japanese and Korean men relieve themselves without shame along the side of the road. The language of both countries has a double set of words, one of which is for polite use and the other is coarse and reserved for men alone. The chief difference between the social station of women previously and now can be seen in the number of women who attended university courses before the Korean War and after. There are many more women in the professions, because of medical schools that opened for women only, such as that of Ewha University. Most of the men's universities are now co-educational, and at least one woman educator, Luise Yim, created a university entirely through her own effort after the Korean War. Helen Kim, the President of Ewha University, was almost as famous as Syngman Rhee, during the period of his ascendancy, and she is still remembered with great affection by the Korean people.

As the waves of changes roll on, very likely the Korean woman will gain a status like that of the Burmese woman, who was never subjugated at all, and who had the vote from the time the British first allowed the Burmans to form a parliament. From the beginning of Burmese independence women served in the government as members of parliament and as cabinet ministers. In the Burmese civil service, women have an exactly equal status with men, and in such industrial activity as exists, women are managers and executives as often as men. The Burman cannot conceive of a social structure that would put the women in other than an equal position with the men, and in the villages, the women are generally the managers of money. The bazaar shops are managed by women, who treat their husbands with respect and encourage idleness on their part, supposedly because the men are not as shrewd or efficient in the bargaining.

Burmese women do not change their names when they marry. In any case, Burma has no system of surnames, and there would be little point in a woman changing her given name. Rules prohibiting ownership of property, found in western countries, have never existed in Burma. There were never any rules against interracial marriage, and a large community of Anglo-Burmans and Anglo-Indians enjoyed equal status with the Sino-Burman and Burmo-Indian groups. During the period of the Burmese democracy, no laws could be passed that would affect any of these groups because of their number and importance. When General Ne Win seized the government and instituted a military dictatorship, he gained the approval of the Burmans by forcing the Indians and the Chinese out of the country. His latest moves have been aimed at the Anglo-Burmese groups, some of whom were highly placed officials in the Burmese government. Even though the Burmese had considerable prejudice amounting almost to xenophobia, this was never intermixed with sexual discrimination. Both men and women become extremely modest before adolescence, and nudity is considered horrible and characteristic only of animals.

Anthropological studies of an amazing variety have undertaken to explain marriage customs and generalize from them to some sort of statement about man as a creature whose social activities are built upon his physical nature. Only the ethologists have come close to a systematized statement that seems to stand the test of cross-cultural and cross-species examination. Human beings are generally monogamous when possible, an activity called pair-bonding. Their mating is never as brutal as that of weasels, for instance, but even the early investigators such as Mantegazza commented on the experimentation of human beings that is rarely seen in the rest of the phyla of animals. In fact, much of the knowledge of animals has been gathered from special cases such as those in zoos, so that statements about animal behavior are quite inaccurate when they are not also anthropomorphic. The sentimental view of animals, often used to substantiate suppositions about human beings, depicted them as virtuout as little reverends in a Trollopian romance. Every variation possible can be found in the history of mankind, from polygamy and polyandry to the multiple suicides of literature resulting from frustrated passion.

The change of lifestyle that can be seen in the Orient is duplicated in western countries. Communal marriages, ready divorce, group sexual activities, and trial marriages are so commonplace that an Anthony Comstock would run himself ragged trying to keep up with, let alone censor, all the literature dealing with these possibilities. The swingers' clubs have institutionalized the promiscuity that Walter enjoys in his autobiography. Single men are a problem among the swingers' groups, as noted in issues of *Swingers' Life*, but throughout the pages is an acceptance of sexuality as so much fun and games to be enjoyed by like minded people who can use the advertising section of the periodical to make their desires known. Membership enables a person to put an advertisement in the publication and await answers.

The issue at hand includes an article by a reporter signed Donna Swanson about a couple who have adopted swinging as a way of life. They are very contented with their life, and they enjoy meeting a great number of people. Sexual activity has become a kind of social cement, among the swinging groups, and it is not a detriment to their communication with other, non-swinging, couples who are friendly with them. Melody and Mike believe that their marriage is improved by their having a free-wheeling life among those who share their views of entertainment. They do not advise their life-style for any but those couples in agreement and able to communicate with each other. They do not force their ideas off on others, but rather believe that they have a right to pursue pleasures that are at least harmless to the individuals involved, whatever such delights might do to concepts of public morality.

Since these couples use the postal services extensively, and the United States mails to this day seem to be governed by prudes, an effort is made from time to time to invade the private swinger's life and haul him into court for having violated the Comstock laws by sending obscenity in the form of private letters through the mail. This is truly discriminatory prosecution, because for every couple advised to plead guilty and accept a sentence and fine, there are thousands, if not tens of thousands, who use the first class mail for the purposes of communication about a subject that seems no more obscene to them than eating or drinking. Sexual freedom, it seems, is as much a human right as any other.

Not all readers agree, and the position of opponents can be adequately demonstrated by the following letter, quoted in its entirety as published in *Swingers' Life*.

Dear Ed.—I saw your magazine on a newsstand and I was horrified. To think that people would actually advertise for sex. It's these kinds of people that are Communists and you probably print all the stuff they use in schools for sex education. My husband and I have been married for 16 years and at first he was like all men but he found out that sex wasn't all that important. He has a traveling job that keeps him away from home during the week but on weekends we do other things besides act like animals and he's happy. I hope you Communists end up in front of a firing squad of good men like my husband. (signed) Anonymous!!!

The editor asks if anyone knows any traveling salesman jokes. The woman who wrote the letter is probably unaware that Communists enjoy no more sexual freedom than she would find permissible. Censorship in Communist countries is strict enough to gladden the hearts of all the volunteer censors and the pornography that some people enjoy is strictly forbidden and, if it is anywhere to be found, is probably like the closet literature of the homosexual press. Like all special interest publications, the periodical focuses on what interests the membership and quotes opinions that confirm the beliefs advanced in its pages. A medical opinion that finds sexual abstinence rather dangerous and not so healthful as sexual activity is given space in the magazine denied to opinions like those of the author of the letter quoted.

At one time or another, in one country or another, a special or privileged class has favored social activities like those of the swingers. The Neapolitan monarchy, for instance, or Japanese business men, or the Chinese nobility, or the inhabitants of South Sea islands, or the tribes of Africans as reported in various studies. The swingers have not discovered anything new. They are simply claiming an old and honorable tradition as their own. It is not the Judeo-Christian tradition, but freedom of worship implies a freedom from the moral constraints of any particular religion.

The changes observed in social structures may seem to be minimal to the casual foreigner whose ideas are governed by much more advanced societies, but they are as vast and important as what are really minimal changes in his own social climate. The change is toward diversity, toward allowing for special cases without social ostracism, toward equality before the law without a loss of individuality. Such changes always operate against a privileged class whether of oligarchs or the arbiters of taste. Instantaneous world-wide communication has meant that closed, even xenophobic, societies are of brief duration.

The revolution that took place in Burma on March 2, 1962, has continued with many problems to this day, although an armed force along the border is making a strong bid to re-open the country to the west. There are rumors that an international crime syndicate is financing the attempted revolution. If so, the reason is obviously the ideal climate for the opium poppy found in the northeast sector of the country. A nation that would be immune to the international agreements that would prevent large-scale and open cultivation of opium poppies, and would export the refined drug into international criminal channels, would represent a reliable source of heroin for the illicit drug trade around the world.

The status of women in remote areas like Burma is of vital importance elsewhere, so that what occurs in one place in the world will have repercussions elsewhere, and the only question is how great they will be and how soon they will begin. The rebuilt city of Seoul looks nothing like its predecessor, but the monuments of past eras tie it securely to the civilizations that have come and gone. One of the most beautiful is Nam Dai Mun, the Great South Gate, beyond which in previous times those condemned to death were beheaded. Now the amazing structure is surrounded by tall buildings constructed according to architecture developed in Europe and the United States. If any spot in the world truly summarizes the vast change that has occurred since World War II, it is the beautiful old Korean architecture of the Great South Gate standing in a traffic circle, as serenely beautiful now as it was centuries ago. Yet, concealed amid the thick traffic and surging crowds, is primitive mankind still ruling essential elements of life.

In almost all the languages of the world, the word for mother is virtually the same, whether Burmese *ameh* or Korean *omah*, and the word for father is very similar. Babies throughout the world learn to say 'ma-ma' and 'ba-ba' to their adoring parents and at some later date listen to their own children uttering their first words. At the time a child is experimenting with vocal sound he learns to produce all the possible phonemes in all the languages of the world, even the variety of click vocables in African tongues. He learns more than a language from his parents, he learns a cultural tradition that is about as fluid as the language. Along with changes in the attitudes and expectations that men share with women are changes in the native language. Twenty-five years ago, when the American experiment in military government was at its height, an effort was made to change the practice of teaching thousands of Chinese characters to the elementary school child, because the Korean language has an alphabet developed by a Yi king, in 1449, about the time that Charles the Seventh was expelling the English from France, having been crowned

King of France with the help of Joan of Arc. The Korean alphabet was absolutely forbidden by the Japanese in the course of their censorship of the entire language. It is, however, a remarkable linguistic achievement, possibly the only well-engineered alphabet in the world. An appeal to national pride was successful, and despite the feelings of the older educators that a great tradition was being lost, the youngsters in the renewed and Koreanized schools were given books that taught them the Korean alphabet first. They learned rapidly, as is the wont of children, and the Korean alphabet enjoyed a revivification it richly deserved. Chinese characters were taught later, and very successfully, because they represent a kind of brief form of a word that may be rather long and ambiguous in the Korean language.

Today the Korean alphabet is everywhere, on signs, in the newspapers, in books, and on the checks the waiter writes in a restaurant. Literacy was vastly increased by using a far simpler way of teaching the language. The American educators who promised that this would occur were motivated by much scientific study of reading and the way children learn. Their opponents were motivated by the traditions of an elitist society, so that the great argument, increased literacy, would have fallen on deaf ears if the government were in the hands of an elitist oligarchy. At every point in acculturation and culture-exchange, the challenge is between an elitist group and the egalitarian ideals that have dominated American thought from its earliest days. An especially unappetizing prospect was that boys and girls would have the same education and the same opportunity to learn. The older educators were quite aware that this meant a great change in the position of women in society, and the argument was rejected, though it often represented a fruitless digression that took hours to resolve.

But it happened just as the Americans said it would. The Koreans should have known that an official inquiry would annul the sentence of death for witchcraft and heresy imposed on Joan of Arc, and that, even though she had been burnt at the stake, as much for political as for religious reason, her spirit would everywhere inspire men and women. Korea had its own Joan of Arc in Queen Min who was murdered by the Japanese because she rejected the idea of Japanese hegemony over Korea. Whenever the argument about women got hot and heavy, the wiser among the Americans would resurrect Queen Min and this served to stifle the remaining objections of the older educators.

What the moral revolution is teaching us is that women can do much, given the chance, that men cannot do. In an episode of *All in the Family*, the difference in center of gravity between men and women was demonstrated by a simple experiment. Three paces back from a wall, against which the subject places the top of his head, a man cannot straighten up with a chair lifted off the floor in his hands, but a woman can. The process of developing a world community, without the imposition of irrational restrictions, will demonstrate that in many other ways, aside from being mothers, women have talents that men do not have.

Mother is a Lady

All the great religious leaders of the world, including Jesus Christ, had mothers. Jesus was the Son of God, according to Christian dogma, and had no mortal father, but in order to be a man, he had to have a mother. The Lord Buddha, Gautama Siddhartha, was born under quite miraculous circumstances, the son of a king and queen. He was married and sired children of his own, at least a son, before he set out to find how men could escape the wheel of birth and rebirth. The founder of Islam, the Prophet Mohammed, was a man in all respects, the son of virtuous parents, and the father of several children so that some families can trace their lineage back to the Prophet. The mothers of saints are particularly honored by Roman Catholics, and many have been canonized as saints. In the beautiful art of the world, the most enduring representation is a mother with a child.

In the view of most sexologists a man learns his appreciation of women from his mother. She is the most beautiful and necessary creature in his life up until he is an adolescent when he transfers this affection to a young woman. Men tend to seek in other women what they recall of their mother, not solely in physical appearance, although that may play a part, but also in personality. Mothers represent the final idealization of virtuous womanhood, and every social structure provides for special privileges to women who have borne children. A very deep system of perceptions arises from the initial experience of a child with his mother, how deep and how perduring is still a matter of serious investigation by some of the most talented scientists in the world, involving several different disciplines ranging from anthropology to zoology.

More importantly, human beings learn to communicate with each other because they must communicate as helpless infants with their mothers. Comparative studies of primate behavior reveal that the human infant learns a system of signals very early in life and perfects and extends these for purely biological reasons. There is an international dictionary of sign language that makes one method of communication at an elemental level possible for everyone. This signaling probably begins during the fetal stage of existence when the bliss of the womb is characterized by the snugness of the amniotic fluid, which cannot be compressed, and the unceasing heartbeat of the mother. In the trauma of birth the uterus begins tremendous contractions, as the strongest and largest muscle to be found in humankind, that makes the uncompressible fluid a strait-jacket and a threat until it flows out and the child is expelled from its safe haven.

The effort to find the peace, tranquility, and safety of the womb is unconscious and unremitting throughout life. According to Desmond Morris, especially in his book *Intimate Behavior*, the signaling of crying and smiling systematically becomes a method of communication without bodily contact through childhood and early adolescence until the need for mating establishes itself and then bodily contact becomes important once more to the individual. Studies of infants by psychologists have established that the need for bodily contact differentiates between the sexes very early in life and explains the generally superior feminine use of language at an earlier age than found among boys. The male infant is willing to go further from his mother than the female, and the female keeps establishing contact by using the surrogate of language or other signals. Little girls who have company all day learn to talk quite young and use language for purposes of establishing contact that serves in place of the bodily contact that all of us need throughout our lives.

Many of the signals that mother teaches us have a social origin that changes as slowly as the language itself. Touching the crotch is a sexual symbolization of inner feelings, and the little boy is taught that he must not handle himself in this way. The mother is probably unconsciously aware of the incestuous nature of such signals, and her rejection of them establishes the virtues of her motherhood all over again. The need for love is so strong among human beings that a sense of belonging to no one is equivalent to the utter despair that precedes suicide. Mother love has a biological as well as an emotional explanation, and the patting, crooning, rocking movements that a mother uses to calm a fretful child reassure both the infant and the mother.

In an experiment with children confined to a nursery where the nurses were always too busy to pick up and comfort the babies, the nurses were as distressed as the infants, many of whom died from lack of attention. A film was made of the nursery, and it is so moving that men and women alike weep as they watch it. An appeal to save infants regardless of their race or parents is successful to both men and women and represents one of the standard methods of gaining sympathy. The infant signals by smiling and inviting attention and by crying and demanding it. Adults respond to such behavior almost instantly, and significantly the race of the individual is of no matter.

The system of signals offering sexual and non-sexual messages is as much a part of life as eating and sleeping. The social context and the cultural modification of essentially biologically motivated signals affects each of us, designating this signal as acceptable and that as not acceptable, so that we permit the male to caress other typically male parts of his body, his mustache or his jaw, but the need for love shown by rubbing the penis is taboo. It is too strong a signal for public use, and it may have caused fights between males in the past. The seductive mother is often described in psychoanalytic literature, but the seductive child is not. Seductive children are not sexual in their advances but are demanding of love, a biological as well as a social necessity.

So dependent is all our civilization and society on motherhood that in past ages, it has been almost a crime for a woman not to bear children. In the primitive societies of the South Seas, where knowledge of sexual reproduction was lacking, a woman who menstruated was considered to be wasting possible baby-making substance and made to do penance in a special hut. In ancient religions most of the sexual restrictions were meant to insure that maximum reproduction occurred in a society where male aggression was directed toward other societies and the environment rather than toward fellow males. The role of woman was so much that of mother that any other virtuous role was impossible. Women were not encouraged to develop and enjoy their sexual capacities because it distracted them from the role society needed for them. Mothers spent most of their lives pregnant, and as strictly censored as frank details of sexual intercourse were methods of contraception. Abortion was a felony because it decreased the numbers of the tribe, and many physicians were sent to prison for the crime even when the evidence was shaky.

Women have declared their liberation from the role of breeders, the fertile field in which the male plants his seed, by insisting that each woman should have the final say whether she will produce or not. This has caused further conflict with Roman Catholic dogma, and the anxiety and emotion generated establishes that a complex of unconscious and even censored ideation is operant. On the grounds that the unborn child has rights as well as the mother, as opposed to the idea that a woman can secure an abortion when she discovers that she is sentenced to an unwanted pregnancy, Roman Catholic theoreticians and laymen besieged the legislatures proposing change in the abortion laws, and in the case of New York succeeded in getting the law repealed, although the act was vetoed by Governor Rockefeller in a way that commands respect as much for his political courage as for his honesty. Other legislators hate to lose the Catholic vote. The debate was resolved in the courts.

In the author's view, speaking as a Roman Catholic, the Church is absolutely wrong and actually illegal in its efforts to impose its dogma on the general public. There is a dedicated segment of the laity that are more Catholic than the priests or even than Rome, and it is this segment that insists on the moral philosophy which states that fetuses are alive and fully endowed with rights at the moment of conception. To take human life is murder, hence abortion is murder. The argument is acceptable if we agree that human life begins when the sperm cell invades the ovum, and further that at this point all the rights of the individual are in effect. This means that a woman has no rights whatever when pregnancy begins and must continue it, whether she likes it or not, until it terminates in childbirth. A fully acceptable argument is that the woman has the inviolable right to determine whether or not she wishes to carry a pregnancy to term, and if she chooses not to, then she may procure an abortion without endangering her health. If a physician wants to, he may abort a patient without attempting to discover whether or not she is pregnant by using a treatment for another set of symptoms. The net result is the same.

Where two equally good arguments contend, then freedom of worship requires that both be acceptable. No Catholic woman should be required to have an abortion, even if the pregnancy endangers her health, and no other woman should be denied one, whatever her Catholic sister may think of the matter. And when a church uses its funds to lobby against legislation, it should lose its tax-free status, just as certainly as this loss of status should attend lobbying for government support of Catholic schools. In Pennsylvania, at least, the Roman Catholic hierarchy saw fit to devote some eighty thousand dollars to lobbying activity, a plain violation of the law. No organization should be permitted to violate a law from which it draws benefit.

Contraception with the advancement of science has gone beyond what some Catholics call Vatican roulette. Church dogma requires belief in a curious set of philosophic principles called 'natural law.' Again, as a Catholic, the author is heretical to the extent that he regards the whole complicated philosophical system as so much balderdash, Betty Martin, and my eye. The natural law is God's plan for the universe worked out in nature itself. Unfortunately, it is unknowable. If it exists and science enables us to know what we know of science, then science should discover the natural law even more effectively now than in the past. If not science, then there should have been some revelation of the natural law by God himself. Unless the Church is willing to accord God-like status to Saint Paul and Saint Thomas Aquinas, then so far there has been no revelation of natural law.

Using the philosophy of natural law, it is the opinion of the church fathers that contraception is a deadly sin because it is in conflict with the will of God. A moral argument would insist that God's will is done in any case, and that human beings can put themselves in conflict with it only in a symbolic, substitutive sense. Preventing childbirth by artificial means is possible only because God has willed that it be possible, otherwise we must amend our ideas of the omnipotence of God. If we could not prevent childbirth by artificial means, we ought not to be taking pills or other medications for headaches, stomach upsets, and constipation. In any case, all but the most single-minded Catholics seem to honor the dogma as they pay it no attention or at best offer lip-service. Demographic studies show that Catholics have about as many children as the social attitudes dictate. Some devout church-goers are genuinely unhappy about the necessity of denying church dogma in order to survive. They forget that church dogma is a great deal like the philosophic idea of an arrow. At any one point in its flight it is standing still. Church dogma has changed radically in every century of its existence.

The great attention paid to over-population in our world has put the idea of natural law rather at a disadvantage so that it seems to recall the conflict between the fundamentalist views of nature in the nineteenth century. This reached its height in the Scopes trial when a teacher was the center of a confrontation over the right to teach evolution. Over-population is only a part of the problem, because a much more powerful argument is in the behavior of the women who carry a pregnancy to term despite their desire not to have other children. The child so born generally enjoys the lavish affection of the mother to the extent that it is finally accepted. The most common crime of women is infanticide and this kind of murder goes undetected more often than any other. If the infant's signals for unceasing attention cannot overwhelm the mother's countersignals of disapproval and disaffection, then it may die or survive only in a warped form. It is far better to allow women to terminate unwanted pregnancies in a medically safe environment than to sentence a fully-developed infant to the slow death of maternal hatred. Only a sentimentalist would insist that the infant has a means of communicating so powerful that it can overcome any interruptive mechanism of the mother.

Social and other pressures operate against childbirth, including the health of the mother. In the Catholic view, this has no possible bearing on the matter, but it makes a religion of love rather like the juggernaut religions of India to insist that a woman have one child after another because it suits some medieval concept of the church that she destroy her health rather than be spared another dangerous pregnancy. As a Catholic, I regard this as murder much more foul and despicable than abortion.

This intrusion of the author in the nominative case of the pronoun would be unforgivable if the point at issue were the Catholic Church, not its opinions of its rights and the opinions of non-Catholics regarding the Church. It has seemed to be a monolithic structure in which the laymen march in blind obedience to the priesthood, but this has never been the case, and in fact, the priests do not march in an obedience that is very blind or willingly given. When dictating the basic behavior patterns of its willing adherents, the Church has a right to describe what is acceptable and what is not. When involved in a pluralistic society, the Church and its members have no right to impose their dogma and beliefs on others who have not chosen to become converts.

Cancelling out the hundred odd years when Protestant groups maintained an affiliation with the governments of the United States and western European countries that was operative to the extent of decreeing what dogma would be taught in supposedly non-secular schools obscures the fact that most Protestant churches until recently believed that contraception was immoral and the Comstock laws of the past century simply made legality of a moral decision, until the tide of public opinion worked a complete change. Human volition is completely operative in the matter of producing children. Everything of our physical structure and social organization is aimed toward the perpetuation of the species, but the need of the individual to participate completely is always a question that he and his mate must settle together.

The bodily signals that affirm sexual readiness are either accepted or rejected by those who observe them. These bodily signals are only in part biologically determined, in part conscious, and in part socially conditioned. When a child invites an adult to hold him, in his desire for body contact, he is partaking of a general need felt throughout life. The man who embraces his wife is re-enacting the parent-child love in a new context. The recognition of this need and satisfaction of it accounts for the belief that one homosexual can automatically spot another. What he recognizes is the assertion of readiness to engage in sexual activity and a set of bodily signals that are determined generally to be directed toward a member of the same sex when they would ordinarily be directed toward a member of the opposite sex. Sex appeal is in part physical structure and the subtle emphasis of certain parts of the body. The red lips of the modern woman, according to Desmond Morris, meant to attract attention to the mouth, have a further importance in reminding males of the vulva and the almost similar labia majora and minora. Further the breasts of a woman are emphasized in some cultures and constricted in others. Korean women were required to bind their breasts so that the short upper jacket would fit, otherwise the breasts would protrude, producing a sexual signal stronger than social customs allowed.

The extent and subtlety of the communication process has only recently been investigated, and the towering structures of communication are always subject to control to some extent. The only question is by whom and for what purpose as represented in the nature of the control. We learn to refuse some messages and accept others as early as infancy, and we continue this choice of cognition throughout our lives. Ignoring a signal is different from preventing it, and the mother who ignores her wailing child is not censoring his crying, while the mother who beats her child is. Children demanding attention generally signal this with unmistakable clarity, and even so the attentive and loving mother can hear her child crying long before anyone else notices it. When the mother begins to instruct her youngster not to touch himself and not to use certain words, she has begun the process of self-censorship that amounts to the most effective control of the communication process yet discovered. The mythical structures of mankind only extend the parental control and provide it with gigantic emphasis, but the world is not made up of governments, it is populated with individuals.

The moral revolution has primarily touched motherhood and made new demands on the most complicated task a human being can face, that of instructing another human being in how to behave as a human being in a society that has not yet determined precisely what behavior is most desirable. A pluralistic society requires that the possible diversity of behavior be recognized and accepted so long as it is not destructive to human life and its artifacts. The aim of modern censorship is to put the responsibility on the parents for the way their child is reared and for his understanding and use of the communication process in order to secure love and survival for himself, maintain an identity, and fix his social status where it is most rewarding to him.

If we assert the right of every individual to intellectual resources, we must assert an equal right to privacy and the inherent privilege of rearing our young to understand where in the pluralistic society each of us fits. At some point, the youngster begins to manage his own life, and at this time begins to exercise his own control over the communication process, both as sender and as receiver of messages. This process has begun with the parents, especially the mother, who confers a sense of rhythm on her infant with her own heartbeat which the fetus hears by the sixth month. All of music and poetry spring from this early process of learning the steady seventy-two beat a minute rhythm that governs all of human life.

As opposed to the old days of imperialism rather than exchange, the industrialized nations of the world are learning from other customs and societies whatever is lacking in our tangled and complicated world. American parents are now much more affectionate with their children, and some have begun to use carriers strapped to the parent like those used in primitive societies so that the child rides with his head against the parental back listening to the comforting heartbeat. An oriental baby is never put down, except to sleep, until he demands it. This was also the custom in western society until recently.

The development of encounter groups is an outgrowth of an expanding vision of human beings, going back to pre-natal days. Intensive study is beginning to reveal how much we rely on the sense of touch, and how damaging a no-touch world can be. The touch of one person by another in a non-aggressive manner has been an assertion of friendship for all of mankind's development. According to Desmond Morris, this becomes sexual invitation only by stages, through five of the twelve he discerns, as much asexual as motivated by sexual expectations. What the mother teaches the child is the value of each of the twelve stages except the last, actual copulation. As the child grows older he is not allowed the intimate touches, such as fondling the breast, and he is never allowed to fondle his parents' genitals, although the parents have that privilege, at least, in washing the youngster. Finally, the adolescent boy or girl is at the stage of trying out his ability to communicate sexual desire with a member of the opposite sex.

We inhibit those displays that would signal sexual desire when we do not intend it. Two men who inadvertently look each other over thoroughly do so in some way that will not make their interest evident to each other. To openly inspect another man is a sexual invitation in certain circumstances, 'cruising' in the homosexual cant, a word that has come to be used for women who invite sexual approaches by staring at a man. The smile, once thought to be the result of gas on baby's tumtum, is now understood to be purposeful behavior like throwing the arms about, and is one of baby's methods of communication before he has full use of his vocal chords and long before he has mastered the complexities of language. From smiling follows verbal exchanges and the first tentative touches. A situation of sexual parley completely in gestures can accompany meaningless exchanges of small talk, as it usually does in societies where there is strict inhibition of sexual words and phrases. Walter confesses in *My Secret Life* that he likes the bawdy talk that accompanies a sexual act, and in describing in detail his numerous seductions, the use of taboo language is an important element in reducing the resistance of the woman he wishes to make love to. He does not recognize the non-verbal signals, but he wishes to overcome the verbal resistance that always is a prelude to seduction, except among 'gay' ladies. Virtuous Victorian girls, and those of the present-day as well, fend off suitors who attempt to use bawdy talk in order to gain sexual acquiescence.

The mother reproving her son for using 'bad words' is in part motivated by patterns of inhibition she has been using for years. Bawdy talk, in her mind, belongs in the bedroom, if there. Some mothers are appalled at the idea of the sexuality of their sons, defending themselves against incestuous ideation before it reaches consciousness. Incest involving mother and son is the most taboo topic and most taboo experience of human existence. It is strictly prohibited everywhere, and the possibility is permissible only in those pornographic works that must use this as one of the final shocks for the reader. In the motion picture *The Damned* a scene of incest was included, accounting for the X rating the picture received. As might be expected, the violated mother became quite mad as a result of her mistreatment by her son. This is used to explain the complete moral degradation of the early Nazi movement that included scenes of the homosexuality among Ernest Roehm's brown-shirt troops.

Sigmund Freud and the early psychoanalysts explained the psychosexual development of children as an Oedipus complex or its feminine equivalent, an Electra complex. Further studies have shown that love of son for mother and mother for son does indeed account for emotional processes throughout life, but that father-son relationships are equally as important, and present investigation seems to indicate a much deeper biological explanation for characteristics of behavior that have gone unnoticed until quite recently.

The liberated woman of modern times in the world community has the right to choose her mate and decide whether she wants to live with him all her life or not. Biology requires that she endure the miseries of pregnancy and childbirth, but if she desires, she can desert the infant and let her husband, or mate, rear the baby. Usually mothers need the first few months after childbirth to recover from its effects. Childbearing in the modern view requires very careful planning and a clear separation is made between sexual intercourse as enjoyment and as the necessary preliminary for childbirth. The result has been an acceptance and demand for contraceptive devices and medicines that are effective but have no harmful side-effects. Women who desire children but do not want to have a man in the house all the time, not so unusual in such liberated societies as those of Sweden and Denmark and some areas of the United States, may choose a lover, become impregnated, and then give the man his walking papers.

What has decayed in such societies is not morals but uniformity. There is a potential for diversity in human society that only freedom of intellect can realize. With diversity comes a decay of stereotypes as well so that the son of an unwed mother is not a bastard. He might be a very pleasant and thoughtful gentleman, and the son of firmly wed parents may be a bastard, a thoughtless ill-tempered stingy man. As our stereotypes change, our epithets change meaning. A son of a bitch is no longer the son of a whore, and a son of a gun is not the bastard son of a soldier. The parenthood implied in the epithets has been lost. Whoreson is no longer a pejorative with any force because it is obsolete, and even the stereotypes of motherhood have changed. As seen on television, the mothers in commercials are younger and better looking, and the 'mom' of Philip Wylie's excoriations is a heavy set middle-aged woman.

The awakened sex is not only women but also men who are smart enough to see what is happening. Women's liberation is male libera-tion as well. A tired professor on a bus does not feel any urging to give up his seat to a young woman although he would do so instantly for a pregnant woman or one with an infant in her arms. Women have always been the compliant sex, more readily taking what was offered as the ideal role for themselves with less question. They are closer to the social norms than men and generally more conformist. Asserting a liberated viewpoint urges men to become more diversified in attitudes as well as life-style.

This is not meant to be an argument for the benefits to be derived from a relaxation of censorship restrictions, because the relaxation is a result rather than a cause. What has occurred is the rapid formation of the people of the world as a world community because the advances in communication technology bring cultures in close proximity. In the time that it once took to go from London to Paris, a traveller can go from New York to San Francisco, or from Hawaii to Tokyo, or from Tokyo to Hong Kong with time to spare, or from Ireland to New York. Using commercial airlines, an adventurous man sped around the world in less time than it takes a train to go from New York to Denver. The marvel of television using satellites as relay stations makes the entire world an audience of spectators who watch a United States President in Peking, and who also observe the cleanliness of the streets, the uniformity of the people, and all but taste the food prepared for banquets.

We are drawing closer to a full understanding of what censorship is when we realize that in today's world complete control of the communication process is impossible. The wife of an Italian journalist can shout 'freedom for Vietnam' at the Bolshoi Theatre where President Nixon had gone to enjoy a performance of *Swan Lake* as the guest of the Soviet Union. Not even the smallest child listening to the world news would miss the story if he could understand anything of what was being said. We are in the process of re-enacting the experience of mankind at earlier stages of his development. As the threats to civilization are understood, some are mythical and others are known perhaps too late.

During the Middle Ages, the Church regarded curiosity as a sin. Thomas a Kempis in his manual of devotion gives prayers that a person may use to prevent his falling into this sin. We now regard curiosity as at least an academic virtue, if not laudatory everywhere. We limit the extent to which one's curiosity may extend by strict rules of privacy that originate in the first experience of life that each of us has. Our body space is defended, what messages we wish to receive is determined in advance of receiving any at all, and what messages we send is governed by canons of acceptability. There is no point in arguing that all messages should be received and all sent. Communication does not exist where there is no one to receive or reject the message, but it takes place even if the message is rejected. That is how the canons of acceptability are formed.

Censors have always fallen into the mistaken belief not only that are they motivated by a sincere concern for the well-being of society and all its individuals, recognizable everywhere, but also that no one defies them. A censor is only an arbiter who uses the legal structure to make his decisions effective. Literary criticism is censorship without the force of law. Deciding upon his own preferences, everyone is an absolute authority. Censorship succeeds to the extent that it is limited. If the individual limits his censorship to himself, he can never go wrong. There was no need for the bishops who received Ginzburg's advertisements for *Eros* to read them thoroughly. They fondled their shocked sensibilities and then had to proclaim that they had been shocked. But bishops by tradition and religious authority are responsible for their flocks, and each has the right to proclaim that some part of the communication process is dangerous to faith and morals.

VII.

SENSUOUS EDUCATION

Sex as a Home Study Course

Cross-cultural and cross-species investigation of human sexuality has fairly well determined its nature, although many mysteries remain to be solved. Sex is determined by the sperm cell which either has a male chromosome or a female chromosome. Because the ovum has one chromosome, always female, the difference in sperm cells means that the male cell will develop as a male and the female chromosome will cause a female to develop. So far as our heritage of hormones is concerned everyone is bisexual. The external genitalia begin to develop early in fetal life, and the testicles of the male descend into the scrotal sack before birth. Sexual maturation begins with the growth of pigmented hair in the genital area and concludes with menstruation in females and in seminal ejaculation in males. Procreation is possible at this point but not desirable. Sexual activity reaches a peak in men about their twenty-first year, according to Kinsey, after which a slow lingering decay of sexual powers occurs, which are always quite limited. However, one ejaculation may contain over a hundred million sperm cells. During her lifetime, a woman will produce about 480 ova. In phase with the lunar month, the female loses the lining of the uterus, the cause of menstruation, and regains a new lining in which a fertilized ovum may be implanted. Fertilization takes place in the Fallopian tubes where a newly matured ovum has about three days to be fertilized or lost. If fertilized, it moves into the uterus where it is implanted in the lining of the uterus and chemical changes begin so that all the physical processes of the women supply the fetus. The birth cycle ordinarily begins after forty weeks of pregnancy, and the woman, like all other mammals, is ready to sustain the newly-born with food from her own body. Breast-feeding has ordinarily been a necessity through much of human history, and it may be of great importance in the psychosexual development of the infant.

207

This brief summary represents several decades of intense scientific study, and in many places this is the substance of courses in biology or physiology. Sex education, when introduced into the elementary school curriculum has caused great excitement. Groups within the community, who have every right to decide what their children can learn and cannot learn, deplore instruction that runs counter to the story about the stork or the cabbage patch. If the instruction goes no further than what is given above, it is hard to see what harm is done the child by learning fact rather than fantasy; there are many who can adduce evidence that fantasy is harmful and that fact is not. The trouble begins when a bright child wonders how the sperm cell gets to the Fallopian tubes in the first place. The reason that any mention of childbirth, pregnancy, or even virginity, was taboo is that all these imply copulation, and this would cause shame and a guilt reaction that was intolerable to the parents or other adults concerned with educating the young. During the Victorian period, women were confined during the last stages of their pregnancy because such immutable evidence of copulation was considered immoral.

When the trial of Mary Ware Dennett established that sex instruction might arouse the sex impulses, which the law sought to prevent, but that the overall intention was valid education, the moral revolution was well under way. The opponents of sex education have been fighting a losing battle ever since. They are trying to defend official hypocrisy that made sex education a matter of the blind leading the blind for many years. A fortunate boy would get a straight answer to a question, without the intervention of birds and bees or dilution with homilies on the sacredness of marriage. He would often be the instructor for a whole neighborhood of boys. The danger of venereal disease was not used as advocacy of male virginity, rather as a good reason to exercise caution in one's activities. Somehow he would acquire a respect for human dignity as represented in women, and he would learn that masturbation is not harmful, it just never should be public. In the minds of the parents, the boy was being prepared for what seems to be a necessary part of human life, pair-bonding.

This is the ethological term for a generally monogamous attitude of human beings. Whether, in sum, men are less monogamous than women has yet to be determined, but the evidence, even in sex-oriented fiction, is that given the right set of circumstances and body chemistry, a couple will become bonded—attached by emotional ties deeper than their own understanding. This bonding is sought by homosexuals and lesbians, as well as heterosexuals, and when it occurs is remarkably durable. Marriages of sixty years are not unusual, and the author knows of two women who have lived together for twenty-eight years, as firmly bonded as any couple of differing sexes. They live next door to another couple, a pair of men, who have lived together for twenty years. They are friendly in an off-hand way, like neighbors, and enjoy the company of another couple, a man and a woman who have been married for thirty-five years. From any practical social point of view, each of the three couples has made a significant contribution to society. Only one is purely a housewife, and her childlessness has never bothered her or her husband. In view of present difficulties with the young, she is just as happy, she says, never to have had a child. One of the six is an engineer with forty years of experience, another is an accountant, another is a librarian, another is an interior decorator, and the only other one to be accounted for is a very highly paid commercial artist. The reader is challenged to match the profession with the sex and with the mate. It is quite impossible without more clues than the author will give.

That bonding extends deeper than sexuality although dependent on it is a very recent discovery likely to remove the cynic from his assured position of 'biological urge with sentimental smear.' The bonding goes beyond sexuality so that transsexuals may remain married after they have changed their sex, not only in dress, but in actual anatomical structure. Mrs. Paula Grossman is a good example.

The massive literature of sex is tending toward the training that is found in learning other games and pastimes. It has now surpassed the literature of bridge and almost equals that of music appreciation. The purpose of pornography has always been to incite sexual impulses and the goal of erotica is to explain them. Both are useful in the marriage that represents a true bonding of a couple. Pair-bonding survives everything but separation, protracted mental illness, and death.

Pair-bonding tends to be reinforced by sexual experience, and because the nature of the bonding repeats the pleasurable experience of the infant and the mother in a sexually mature relationship, sexuality remains a method not only of strengthening the bond but making it more delightful. Pair-bonding is a source of joy that, finally, is understood to provide for sensual experimentation in a protected environment, and whatever of polygamy may incite the male, the average woman with some understanding of herself, a lack of shame, and love for her husband provides an infinite variety that can please the most active man. A free society permits much more experimentation than a closed or strictly authoritarian society, and freedom of the press, especially when voluntary censors must operate without the cooperation of the law-enforcement agencies, leads many to write on marriage providing something more than instruction, encouragement, at least, and some times entertainment. The tendency has been for these marriage manuals to match the moral climates of the time. *Light on Dark Corners* is as much a guide to sexual ethics as it is informative of the genital side of human experience. The ultimate goal of all instruction is human enjoyment in this lifetime or another. When the world could offer nothing but sickness, old age, and death, then another better world was the reward for certain behavior patterns. In order to give an air of authority to the instruction, a higher authority is cited, often a deity. In the witty remark of Ingersoll, "The noblest creature of man is an honest god."

When the deity to be propitiated is not of our own creation, we see it as funny. Roadside shrines, are, to a Southern European, reminders of his faith; to a Northern European they are indicators of another culture. In Burma the villagers build little shrines to propitiate the *nats*, the invisible spirits that guard trees, mountainsides, lakes, and other natural features. In Rangoon, at the edges of a city that was becoming thoroughly modernized, there were *nat* shrines, most of them including the little gifts of flowers, fruit, and coconuts, but in one of them, during the hot season, some thoughtful Burman put a can of baby powder useful in soothing prickly heat.

The early marriage manuals tended to reinforce the social concepts of the time, propitiating the arbiters of morality, and there are counter marriage manuals for any that advocate a kind of change. At about the time that D. H. Lawrence asserted a sexual need on the part of women, theorists of sexuality who used their own prejudices rather than scientific method began issuing instructions, especially to men. A man was a kind of pleasure-giving creature whose highest duty was to satisfy his wife. A man who read such works could become performance-shy, always threatened by an ejaculation that preceded his wife's orgasm and ended his pleasure too soon. In place of the priest in the confessional making decisions about the morality of one act or another, there were psychiatrists whose pronouncements had the force of canon law.

There has always been an authority blessing the marital state with words. The Church reluctantly accepted marriage, while insisting that chaste celibacy was preferable, and virginity the most desirable of all. Marriage became a sacrament, the outward sign of an inward grace, only in the twelfth century, but it has always been a public announcement of special privilege, with whatever gods are in vogue duly propitiated. During the Middle Ages, marriage was a civil affair, a way of arranging property and determining the amount and kind of dowry. Divorce was about as easy as marriage, and the custom of attending mass immediately after the civil ceremony eventually became a nuptial mass with the ceremony presided over by the priest. What began as a kind of sale in Northern Europe ended as an indissoluble sacrament, as binding if performed in a church in the presence of a priest, as birth or death so far as the Church was concerned.

Pair-bonding is seen in many different animals and in birds. Swans are monogamous and so are chinchilla. Horses that work together for many years develop an attachment so intense that one will die of despair soon after the death of the other. If circumstances of society only make a virtue of a natural state, then marriage ought to be the social aspect of pair-bonding, but this has been the case in only about half the marriages performed in the United States. Marriage has become an institution protected to some extent by the state, and at least surrounded with as many property transactions as it was during the days when it was a civil contract. Government has taken over not only the commercial but the moral aspects of heterosexual pair-bonding.

At the time the Church gained complete ascendancy with the regularization of canon law, all sexual activities came under its purview as well as control of heresy, so that such sins as sodomy and heresy were intermingled, and equally adultery and masturbation were controlled by canon law, not as causes of divorce so much as crimes against the authority of the Church. Impediments to marriage so that it could be annulled as invalid were rather fewer than popularly supposed, and to this day, such impediments are difficult to find and hard to argue through the chancery of a diocese. If the Church was reluctant to accept marriage, it has never accepted divorce. A faithful member of the Church is required not to marry again if he is separated from his wife. A civil divorce may be permissible, but remarriage is not, and if it should be attempted, then it cannot be in a Catholic Church and is null and void, so far as the Church is concerned. The solution for many Catholics is simply to quit the Church.

By the end of the Protestant reformation, the power of the church had been vastly diluted and passed largely to the civil authority which gradually gained a power equal to that of the Church. The old marriage manuals for the use of confessors, designating this as sinful and that as not sinful, became enacted into laws by a council of men anxious to proclaim their sexual morality. The laws in the United States that prohibit oral-genital activity make no exceptions for the sexes of the individuals, and married couples can be arrested and tried for violating these laws. In maintaining laws regarding obscenity, the civil authority was taking over the duties of the Church, and civil heresy is a criminal offense in countries where democracy prevails, even though freedom of the press is guaranteed. Most of the new countries that gained independence after the second World War failed to understand the concept of freedom of the press, so that their recent constitutions will usually read "the freedom of the press shall not be restricted except in accordance with law." Individual freedom assumes that the civil authority is not the ultimate authority.

The reassertion of the civil character of marriage began in England under the Puritans who denied that it was a sacrament, but Puritan England did not accept the ideas of one of its greatest philosophers, John Milton, whose work on marriage is contained in *Doctrine and Discipline of Divorce*. Until quite recently, England had divorce laws as strict and difficult as Italy's. As women have gained equal status under the law with men, divorce has been more easily obtained. The pioneer women of the American west shucked husbands who failed to meet their standards, and of all the states, Nevada is one of the easiest in which to obtain a divorce.

Marriage is a matter of mutual consent, and when the consent is no longer given, then the marriage should end. There is little need for the court setting in which most divorces occur, because the ritual of the law is of importance only when the property aspects are settled. At the present time in the United States, a man is foolish to marry unless he is willing to work hard to make a success of his marriage and has found a wife who is willing to work just as hard, because property settlements invariably favor the wife. New York maintains a debtor's prison for men who fail to meet alimony payments as required by the divorce courts.

Men who are married to women who enjoy sex and love them in the bargain have every right to become uxorious. The sex books that described human sexuality in normative terms and decreed that a woman must have an orgasm every time she makes love with her husband were no closer to reality than the old marriage sections of confessors' manuals. An even more foolish rule was that which demanded orgasms at the same time for man and wife, thereby removing from the sexual act one of its great joys, the awareness that one's own activity has caused the height of enjoyment to another. *The Sensuous Woman* is a much more profound treatise on love than any of the sex books written by psychiatrists and physicians of other specializations. A woman who takes the author "J" to heart will find that she has a very happy husband, and throughout the book she will learn that her sexual rights and her husband's are the same.

Pair-bonding tends to strengthen and give each of the individuals involved greater happiness. One of the greatest discoveries of the liberated people of the United States is that certain couples are not separated by engaging in orgies but are more firmly bonded because of them. The tendency of each partner to want a new and different experience from time to time is worked out in a climate of social acceptability, at least for the individuals who participate. Swinging, as it is called, is apparently an approved lifestyle for some couples. A modified form of this can be found in the advice of "J" on how to find a lover, the assumption being that a housewife need be no more faithful than her husband. If he likes an occasional night with another woman, then his wife has rights too.

The Sensuous Woman and *The Sensuous Man*, by "M," are highly successful, especially with young adults, because they leave out most of the pretense and nonsense of earlier sex books, some of which were written for the medical profession. The 'sensuous' books are practical manuals of sexual intercourse as a way of 'having fun.' The idea is foreign to the Puritan, who did not object to human sexuality just to the idea that it could be enjoyable. No move has been made to censor these books, although they both recommend masturbation and do not blink at adultery and group sex. Robert Chartham tops off the series with a book entitled *The Sensuous Couple*. The purpose of all these books is to undo what a long succession of censors has done.

Until recently the best books on sex have been imported. Even *Married Love* was imported from England, and Marie Stopes was writing primarily for the phlegmatic Britisher, who is just as sensual as any other human being. This book gave way to Van de Velde's *Ideal Marriage*, a book that in Edward M. Brecher's history of sexual research, *The Sex Researcher*, is described in a chapter entitled "He Taught a Generation How to Copulate." Several hundreds of thousands of informed couples acquired the book and moved rapidly away from the misconceptions of the Victorians to an understanding of human sexuality that was both delightful to themselves and encouraged a healthy attitude on the part of their children. Not surprisingly, happily married couples tend to rear children who achieve happy marriages themselves. Children of hypochondriacs tend to become hypochondriacal themselves. Schizophrenia is not inherited, but it can be taught.

Van de Velde's book was important in providing authority that fellatio and cunnilingus are not immoral or perversions but represent a part of our mammalian heritage. Not even the Catholic concepts of conjugal propriety rule against such behavior, the only requirement is that the sperm be deposited in the vaginal channel of the woman, in order to meet the misconceptions of natural law that have become frozen as dogma. Fellatio to orgasm, then, would be sinful, but fellatio that is discontinued at some point and the ejaculation properly located becomes blessed. From the author's point of view, no man in his right mind ought to discuss his marital life with anyone, least of all with a professional celibate who has only a foggy notion of what he is talking about. A man should discuss his sexual problems with his wife, and if she is unwilling or incapable of understanding, then he must conclude that the depth of pair-bonding he desires may be quite impossible. The worst effect of censorship is felt when it reaches into conjugal love and stifles communication. Implicit in all the instructional manuals, but recognized fully by David Reuben, is the realization that the most important sexual organ among human beings is his brain.

It is the brain that is capable of synthesizing former experience and recreating it, and it is the brain that enables a man to gain an erection and enlarge upon his physical responses so that he can learn to control ejaculation and using all his skill create an intensely rewarding experience for a woman and thereby for himself. Men derive intense pleasure and a strong sense of identity and ability from finding themselves skilled as lovers in the eyes of their women. It is possible for a man to achieve an erection completely involuntarily, indeed to have an orgasm as the result of a dream. The brain and its processes are as much a physical fact as the digestive tract. When we discuss the communication processes we are discussing only a part of the whole human being, not a separate part from the rest of his entity but a vital and essential element in his life. Men are quite frail in their sexual abilities, and a woman can easily cause a penis to wilt by rejecting the man who offers her his body as her plaything. What governs sexual performance is more than a biological drive, it is a climate of willingness and acceptance and a matching both of tastes and talents. Where no discussion is possible, the ideal of the Puritans is the only kind of sexual activity that may occur: a woman lies prone and a man gets himself situated above her, supported on his knees and elbows, inserts his penis into her vagina and manipulates his buttocks until he ejaculates. This is animalistic, not the fanciful and prolonged sessions recommended in each of the "sensuous" books. Man is chiefly distinguished by his ability to make much of the equipment he has, to extend his muscles and his senses, so that he can fly to the moon and let his fellows on earth see him there.

Censorship becomes ingrained, so that a virtuous woman becomes less than human, shocked by taboo words, unable to touch her husband's penis, and genuinely horrified if, in his tenderness for her, he would rather use his tongue than his fingers to stimulate her clitoris and vulva. Fingers have fingernails that can accidentally be quite painful. Unable to say what bothers her, unwilling to use words that say exactly what she means, the couple manage to continue the pair-bonding at a level of civility and politeness, especially if the man finds some outlet for his sexuality that his wife knows nothing of. He is, in fact, very lonely, offering a gift that she cannot accept. If he continues to be a loving husband in the face of her disinterest and neuroticism, he ought to be canonized for heroic virtue.

The great censors, however, have all been men, and in the past, having control of society, they have decreed what behavior must be punished and what is permissible. Men are as unwilling to communicate their needs as women, and the average animal-level lover wants a woman to respond to his nudge, cooperate a bit, and provide him with an orgasm. What happens to her is not his affair, and he becomes irascible and possibly brutal when his wife tells him that she has wriggled her last wriggle if he does not recognize that she has rights too. A woman who tolerates a man that claims his satisfaction and gives her nothing is practicing a heroic virtue that is really quite silly. She should explain to her husband that he is a lousy lover, makes her feel like an animal and that he needs a thorough course in sex so that he can become at least halfway human. She should provide him with the course if necessary.

Some couples become so open and frank with each other that they find almost unbelievable bliss in their sexual relations, and this is the end that the various sex educators advise their readers to achieve.

However, not everybody has the same need for and talent for sexual ecstasy. For many people, sex is enjoyable, not a matter of constant effort, and they are just as happy as the sexual athletes that seem to be the ideal to the sex instructors who write books like *The Sensuous Couple*. Robert Chartham, to give him credit, believes that each couple should find both time and place that are likely to provide them with greatest enjoyment. Chartham, especially, dwells on the difficulty of communicating with one another and the reluctance to change the level of candor even though a man and a woman are about to be joined as one flesh.

Training the most important sexual organ has been at the core of all censorship of 'obscene' materials. Public morality in the simplistic view consists of individuals who do not use taboo words following a set of inhibitions that tradition has decreed preferable. Inhibitions are indeed desirable but each has its time and its place. To reach into the marriage and decree that one act is sinful and another is not, when anything that promotes love ought to be encouraged, is to give marriage with its evident difficulties a further and unnecessary obstacle course to run. It seems that the anti-sexual attitudes of the Church become formalized into a pattern of anti-marriage, demanding incessant childbirth, regardless of the health of the mother or the economic status of the father, and forbidding them to derive any pleasure from the act of procreation. Married couples were breeding machines of the laity, some of whom became priests.

In the forty years since Mary Ware Dennett was exonerated from committing a federal crime by mailing her pamphlet to Mrs. C. A. Miles in Grottoes, Virginia, the opinions of the public have changed greatly. *Ladies Home Journal, Cosmopolitan*, and other periodicals for women usually include a great deal of information about sex, and the general attitude of the public has tended to acclimatize taboo words so that a public broadcast station can retain 'bare-assed' and 'pregnant' in its production of Arthur Laurents' "Invitation to a March." The play deals with a woman who falls in love with a married man and bears his son, who is the liberated spirit to contrast with a son sired within wedlock. Both sons want Norma, the ingenue, as a mate, but one offers a life so regulated that Norma falls to sleep when she tries to talk about it. Television represents the level of candor that the public will accept. Probably some viewers objected to the taboo words, including the word 'virgin,' but the level of candor established for the public is about where the average viewer wants it. Reading material is candid to the extent that it is sold in public places not just for adults, and the pornography and eroticism that were once heavily tabooed are now openly available. This relaxation of inhibitions must have its effect, especially on married couples.

The open publication of research works by Masters and Johnson followed in a tradition begun by Kinsey. Havelock Ellis was one of the most important researchers, but his works were generally for the medical profession only. Popularizers like Albert Ellis, to be distinguished from Havelock Ellis, have taken the medical information gathered from many sources and explained it in their own works. Albert Ellis believes in sexual intercourse as a healthful exercise, and his moralizing is generally along lines that represent community feeling at present. Research work is much harder for the individual to judge unless he has made a study of the field. At one time, physicians believed that the public could not understand their literature. But the popularizers have generally proved that such is not the case. The literate public is not easily fooled, and each will derive what he wishes from the work. What Masters and Johnson show is that orgasm is a vital physical function of the body. Their research into the causes of sexual difficulties is no less imposing as research although it has not gained the attention of their earlier book.

Inge and Sten Hegeler in *An ABZ of Love*, translated from the Danish, provide information on almost every subject that has some relationship to sex. The book is arranged alphabetically by topics, and throughout the authors maintain an air of good sense and compassion that even obtained enthusiastic reviews for the book in

the homosexual press. The book was issued in two different print-
ings, the earlier one lacked certain illustrations, including one of
cunnilingus and several of erect penes. The book had considerable
circulation, although it never appeared on bestseller lists. In several
respects it is better than David Reuben's *Everything You Always
Wanted to Know About Sex but Were Afraid to Ask* which sold a
million copies in hardcover and over six million in paperback. This
is especially noticeable in the sections dealing with homosexuality.
The Hegelers adopt a mild attitude, rather assuredly compassionate
without attempting to moralize, and David Reuben cannot conceal
his distaste for the subject and for the individuals involved, whom
he evidently regards as both sick and sinful.

Neither book is offered as science or art, although Reuben makes
many more scientific claims than the Hegelers. If the common failing of popularizers of sexual research is a moralizing attitude, then
Reuben's Judeo-Christian attitudes operate against him. He moralizes
in a covert fashion all the way through the book, most openly, when
he discusses homosexuality, so that his book represents an improvement on, rather than a change from, *Light in Dark Corners.* In places,
Reuben seems to be advertising psychotherapy, as in his section on
male impotence. A man who ejaculates too quickly is offered only
the expensive solution of prolonged psychotherapy without more
discussion than is necessary to designate one solution after another
as impractical. Chartham is a great deal more practical in this respect,
noting that the clenching of the buttock muscles usually precedes
ejaculation, a man can simply swing his buttocks without the thrust-
ing that accompanies the orgasm in the male. The sensuous books
provide the answer. Some men should have two or more orgasms.

Both books, however, are most useful in destroying the effects of
censorship over many decades. So long as society maintains an air of
secrecy, guilt, and shame, there can only be great need for books that
reduce the net effects of these attitudes. They are not easily lost,
although books like *The Sensuous Man* and *The Sensuous Woman*
help.

At each stage of his development, man has put his sexuality into the service of an organized mythical structure, so that a denial of sexual activity has served religion, warfare, and political systems. Tracing the history of human sexuality is equally tracing a history of religion and of social structures. At a time when the communication revolution is making a massive amount of information available on all kinds of societies, there is a lack of mythical structures that can claim the universal approval of the world community. The voluntary censors in the United States wish to preserve the Judeo-Christian tradition and hold that it accounts for the American way of life and our system of freedom. However, the perpetuation of a mythical structure has never been possible on the basis of terror or police action. A willingness to cooperate is essential if the system is to survive, and the cooperation achieved only by authoritarian rule is likely to last no longer than the force that can be brought to bear on the members of the society.

Censorship is most effective when it is secret, and it cannot be truly effective if more people than those of an elitist group are given permission to peruse censored materials. If these materials are left to the public, the marketplace takes over and those works that have the most value at the time are the ones that gain widest distribution.

Burning Sappho

The education of women has never put such strong restraints on homosexuality as the training of men. Although males in homosexual activities are taboo in pornographic films, unless the film contains nothing else, lesbian encounters are standard fare. The Danish picture books ordinarily include two men and two women, or one man and two or more women, and a common element in most of them is cunnilingus between the women. Books on lesbian activity are purchased and used primarily by men, just as scenes of lesbian activity in standard erotic films are enjoyed by men. Many men cannot endure the sight of another man engaging in sexual intercourse. That men are sexually aroused by the nude bodies of women has been one of the standard assumptions of humankind. This is not always the case, and the experience of nudist camps and nude encounter groups indicates that something more is required. The women must be in a sexually ready condition.

All mammals and birds have sexual displays indicating a readiness to copulate, ranging from the 'presentation' postures of chimpanzees to the squatting of fowls. Much of human activity is of this display nature, and the censorship of 'lewd and indecent' dances was occasioned by assuming that the dance is sexually oriented. All dancing has a sexual motivation, the stately minuet as well as the fast-moving fandango. The waltz was considered lewd because men held women in their arms, and the tango was thought to be at least daring because of the proximity of sexual organs and the sensuous rhythm required in the performance. Belly-dancing utilizes the symbolism of the naval, according to Desmond Morris, but even more it duplicates what a man can see when he is making love to a woman in the frontal positions. He feels her hips meeting and accentuating his movement but he sees her midriff in motion.

All sexual display is ambiguous to the extent that it is not meant as a specific invitation. The bumps and grinds of the burlesque dancer, if performed nearby, become very like the dances that became popular in the sixties. Some of the older generation thought the romance had gone out of dancing when men no longer held women in their arms, but it has a much easier anatomical explanation. In all dances, the more the hips gyrate the greater the distance between the partners. South American dances require a movement of the hips, and the partners are at about an arm's length from each other. If they were closer, they would be grinding their hips together in open and unmistakable prelude to sexual intercourse.

Western society has tolerated women dancing together because no threat is seen in such activity, and men are quite willing for a woman to be excited by another woman so long as she meets his demands for sexual intercourse. Studies of lesbians conducted by the Gay Liberation Front, as well as sociologists and psychiatrists, show that the level of bisexuality is much greater in women than in men, so that a comparison of fixated homosexuality in each of the sexes is less revealing of differences than might be assumed. Lesbians are willing to marry and beget children, and some of them become frustrated but faithful wives, leading lives of quiet desperation with at least the protection against prolonged sensual contact with men that an average marriage affords. The man who takes no time to excite his wife is doing her a favor by getting his sexual needs satisfied as quickly as possible.

Censorship of lesbian writings began with *Fanny Hill*, with its early encounters, and continued through *The Well of Loneliness* by Radcliffe Hall because descriptions of lesbian lovemaking are very exciting to some men. A significant number of men become almost painfully aroused by the sight of two women engaged in tribadism or cunnilingus. The tribade has been a classic element in pornography because two women lying one on top the other, face to face, rubbing their sexual parts together, seems to scream for a confident man to take the place of one of them. Scenes of female masturbation have about the same effect. One of the first indications that censorship was fighting a losing battle was the inclusion of masturbation in motion pictures, such as *The Fox*, and then the clear indication of lesbian masturbation in *The Killing of Sister George*. This would never be permitted if the plot concerned two men rather than two women. A scene of mutual masturbation between men is still homosexual pornography and very repugnant to about half the males who might see the picture. Something like half the women would find the scene very exciting sexually and would react in a variety of ways.

Women have much more opportunity to express affection publicly than men. One of the most significant changes in social custom has been the male embrace now permitted on television and in the movies. Women have kissed each other, in accord with Christian tradition, for centuries with no implication of lesbianism. A lesbian encounter does not begin with an expression of sisterly affection but with manipulation of the clitoris and stimulation of the breast. If brotherly kisses became commonplace, a homosexual encounter would begin with manipulation of the penis and stimulation of the male nipple.

Pair-bonding among lesbians has been more often the rule than among homosexual men. Reuben reports that lesbian prostitutes use their earnings to support a mate, and lesbian prostitutes generally prefer to receive male customers because they are less likely to have an orgasm with men. Pair-bonding between women may have no sexual overtones at all, a matter so little investigated that a comparison of the same possibility with men is very difficult to make, although the pair-bonding of heterosexual men is not at all uncommon, in fact is quite an accepted fact of human life. The sexual need of an individual could be registered on the same scale as Kinsey's six degree statistical measure from virtually nil to incessant. Pair-bonding may include two individuals who fall at any point on the scale, but very likely a good hypothesis is that the pair will both have approximately the same sexual drive.

The assumption that two women living together are lesbians is made less often than that two men are homosexuals. The author knows of two men who have lived together for years who actually have little or no sexual activity, and after one rather tiresome attempt at homosexual relations gave up that aspect of sexuality as both boring and unnecessary. One of the men masturbates occasionally, and the other visits a prostitute once in a great while. The lack of a strong sex drive is considered a blessing by both men. Sexual pair-bonding between women is possibly much more commonplace than is supposed.

Lesbianism has not developed a literature similar to that of male homosexuality for the reason that it has never been as taboo a subject nor as readily identified as a threat to society. Ballerinas are not assumed to be lesbians, nor are nurses, because men need the comfort of a pseudo-mother when sick and the excitation of the female body in movement is considered a heterosexual, not homosexual, invitation. The Victorian laws that punished homosexuality applied only to men because Queen Victoria could not bring herself to believe that women would engage in lewd behavior with each other unless they were prostitutes, and that group of women provided society with a valuable release for otherwise dangerous repression.

Schoolgirl crushes were accepted as a feature of a life that led to marriage and childbearing, even in Victorian times. It was rarely necessary to explain that a girl ought not handle the genital area of another girl, because none of the writers on sex could imagine this happening in any case. Girls were understood to have a natural 'god-given' modesty that prevented their being sexually active with each other. The literature of lesbianism written for women, of which *The Well of Loneliness* is still a good example, except for its cautionary ending, stressed the social rather than the sexual aspects. A sympathetic attitude toward lesbianism is much more common among the educationally sophisticated segment of the community than at lower levels of intellectual attainment. The books about lesbian love meant as pornography are for the most part written solely to stimulate men. Lesbian literature is much more filled with statements of hatred of men than homosexual literature gives space to a hatred of women. A further difference is in the nature of the dislike. Homosexual men take exception to women as social beings rather than as sexual beings; that is, disgust with pregnancy is rather rare among homosexual men while disgust with the social aspects of motherhood is common and disgust with wives is nearly universal among lesbians. The statement that 'only a woman knows how to make love to another woman,' is duplicated by a similar conclusion, though not so frequently advanced, that only a man knows how to provide sexual pleasure to another man. Almost all writers on female homosexuality feel constrained to mention that a penis is not available in a lesbian relationship and to describe dildoes and other substitutes. Hetero-sexual women cannot understand how lesbians obtain sexual and emotional satisfaction otherwise. The penis is so much the organ of pleasure that its lack seems to deprive a relationship of one of its most pleasurable aspects, although lesbians do not use dildoes solely for a sexual reason.

It is just this lack which makes lesbian pornography and literature desirable to men. The usual pornographic work expounds on the vast size and inexhaustibility of the penis, and this is a profound threat to some men who see the writing as a standard rather than as a fantasy. If the male in a pornographic novel drives his willing (or demanding) female companion to incredible heights of ecstasy, then is able to repeat the activity again and again, always with fountains of semen spurting as climax after climax is reached, then the reader believes that his once or twice having reached a halfway measure of such sexual virtuosity is an indication of his unworthiness and lack of true virility. Lesbian literature offers something better than implied threats; the details of women providing sexual thrills for each other invites the reader to compose his own fantasies of how he would change the mind of each women with his own superior personality and sexual performance if he had the chance. A significant amount of the lesbian literature is accompanied with sado-masochistic writing as well.

The man who watches a lesbian act is engaging in pure voyeurism. He cannot participate in lesbian activity because it would automat-ically become heterosexuality at that point. Some mammals will show that the estral cycle is beginning by what has been called 'homosexual' activity, seen in cattle ranches, for instance, when one heifer tries to mount another. Young animals, in fact, engage in sexual play with any object that is somewhat like their natural mate, and female animals are often very attentive of each other, cleaning the genitals and engaging in caresses that are characteristic of the prelude to sexual intercourse in the less belligerent of animals. The love-play of elephants goes on for hours.

Lesbian literature provides men with a good understanding of what 'turns women on.' The rough embrace and bruising kiss may be tolerated but the attitude that a woman exists for the sole pleasure of being available to alleviate a man's sexual need is what turns women off men. The outstanding characteristic of both homosexual and lesbian literature is that the couples are devoted to giving pleasure to each other. The homosexual provides sexual gratification, even to a man who considers himself to be exclusively heterosexual when women are available. This attitude is sometimes found in lesbian literature but is especially common in heterosexual pornography. Lesbian literature centers upon the unfeeling emotional attitude of sexually excited men who are not aware that their sexual partners are women with pronounced emotional and physical needs.

Narcissism in women is much more readily tolerated, if not acclaimed, because of the physical excitement it provides men. Very beautiful women are depicted as cold and unresponsive until they meet the hero with whom the reader can identify. The distance from lesbian literature to the accepted fiction of heterosexually oriented individuals is much shorter than from male homosexual fiction. Beautiful women are a standard part of fiction, they invite lengthy descriptions that handsome men never get. The excessively beautiful woman is somehow dangerous, a threat to everyone concerned, and from Helen of Troy to the modern cinema stars a significant literature is devoted to their faults and flaws.

What is involved is fantasy that satisfies the male ego, even though the bulk of fiction is read by women. Heterosexual women soon learn that the male ego and sexual performance are very closely related. An erect penis is subject to wilting with a word of criticism. Lesbian literature dwells upon the adoration of one woman by another, situations that bring sexual ecstasy and joy to the participants. The very handsome youth of homosexual literature is a kind of sex object that the dominant male enjoys. The difference is as distinct as directions outward or inward, and the possibility of important research into the attitudes expressed in each of these literatures arises from a comparison of the relationships involved.

The "sensuous" books are remarkably like the graphic descriptions of sexual activity in homosexual as well as heterosexual fiction. Such sex researchers as Sha Kokken, Frank Caprio, Albert Ellis, and Alfred Kinsey omit, or note only briefly, that the male nipples are highly erogenous, although they dwell at length on female breasts as a sexual exciting area. Only the lesbian literature fully explains that love for a woman consists not only of sexual stimulation of the sort the woman finds pleasurable but also of learning what that sort is and discovering each peculiarity with a sense of joy and announced delight. A woman and a man need to be highly valued in the eyes of the sexual partner, and love is something more than a series of bed exercises.

So akin to lesbian literature that there seems to be no point in separating it is the fiction that describes masochism. The butch female, bull-dyke, character in lesbian literature is so much like her sadistic sister in masochistic literature that the two seem to be cut from the same cloth. Masochism derives its name for Sachar Masoch, a novelist who wrote in German during the period of the Austro-Hungarian Empire. The name was adapted to describe a man who delights in maltreatment at the hands of a sadistic woman. *Venus in Furs* is usually the novel cited, even though this is a historical fantasy with Catherine the Great of Russia as the main character. There is little evidence that Catherine was particularly cruel to men. She was certainly no lesbian, as the records of those retained to provide her with sexual pleasure give a man about six months at this job before he is promoted to some higher position.

Masochistic novels written for the porno-book trade are as repetitious as other novels, featuring a woman with high-heeled boots and a whip who keeps her slaves or paramours in a collar used ordinarily for large dogs. The slaves are constantly punished, much to their exquisite and joyous sorrow. A great problem exists for the authors of this genre of literature for the point of view must be that of the victim, who at the same time both enjoys and suffers the maltreatment. A strong current of virtue runs through the novels. Discipline is seen as an abstract good that would please the most repressive of authoritarians. The only real difference between this kind of novel and the sado-masochistic homosexual novel is the sex of victims and of their tormentors. There are essentially lesbian novels, such as the *Story of O*, based on masochistic episodes, and there are heterosexual novels, such as the numerous nineteenth century English novels of flagellation. Corporal punishment becomes a sexual thrill both for the victim and the administrator, and the English public schools with their beatings trained several generations of men to enjoy a caning.

By investigation of such literature, especially its greatest author, we come at last to the central issue of censorship on both an individual moral plane and in the world community, at least so far as censorship of the works of harlotry is concerned. As will be seen, the censorship of heresy derives from the same impulse, and the works of a single author undertake an explanation of this side of humankind, present in all of us, the most self-defeating of human activities. Yet in the pursuit of knowledge, all the intellectual resources of humankind are necessary.

The Prince of Hell

In the depths of the Bibliotheque Nationale is a caged area admission to which is strictly limited. A person trying to borrow a book, for use in the library only, is usually refused if the work he wishes is sequestered there. It is still possible to peruse the work provided the reader is willing to fight French bureaucracy far enough and long enough, but this is something like swimming through an English channel filled with *blanc mange*. The caged area is called *enfer*, literally 'hell,' and it matches similar areas in other libraries. Great research libraries always have a 'hell' where restricted works are kept, and the greater the library the more strictly is hell guarded.

The collection of Henry Ashbee in the British Museum is kept in a restricted area, and only a scholar of the most prestigious qualifications is ever allowed to investigate the works. Part of the reason is that the books are very rare, and, as every librarian knows, a rare book is meant to be seen and admired as an artifact; it is not meant to be read. Every regime in France since the Revolution of 1789-95 has suppressed the works of Donatien-Alphonse-Francois, the Marquis de Sade; although his name is often employed in the word 'sadism.' The Bibliotheque Nationale and de Sade's writings developed at the same time. It seems fitting that the wildest, freest spirit of all time, who has left a record not only of his life but also of his fantasies, should be in 'hell.' De Sade was the prince of pornographers, the philosopher of anti-societal monstrosities, the dramatist who held a mirror up to nature and observed not the gentle creation of a wise and benevolent deity but series of catastrophic events that care not a whit for the life of any man nor indeed for whole civilizations. Nature as depicted in his writings is sadistic, taking a wicked delight in earthquakes, volcanic eruptions, floods, tornadoes, and in creating cruel societies out of the evil nature of man. De Sade is the ethologist who sees the predator in man more clearly than anyone else. Desmond Morris' *Naked Ape* is indeed a killer, but one who has learned the arts of keeping peace with his own kind, or at least enough so that utter destruction is somehow avoided. Ardrey's investigation into archeology confirms the predatory nature of early man, and recorded history from Herodotus onward re-affirms this predatory nature at every turn.

Taking sexual pleasure in the suffering of another is so commonplace it is admired, but only if the pleasure is couched in terms that seem to avoid all sexuality. When a District Attorney advocates public executions, almost wistfully, he is simply asserting that the populace deserve the kind of sexual thrills that the social order provided up until the middle of the nineteenth century in Europe and at the present time in many countries. The civil war that established the People's Republic of China was attended with executions of landlords following mock trials asserting both the ultimate power of the state and the mythical power of the people. There is nothing mythical about death, however it is inflicted, nor about torture.

These are what the Marquis de Sade celebrated and attempted in his own life. Just how sadistic the Marquis was remains a mystery. There is no evidence that he ever killed anyone, but he was very cruel in his dealings with prostitutes, and he managed to agonize his high-born wife so that his absences were a great relief to her. The King and Queen had given permission for the marriage, a mistake so far as the young captain of the Burgundy horse was concerned. Louis XV was one of the worst monarchs France had, and even his grandfather, Louis XIV, was not a marvel of intelligence and foresight. Both men prepared for the holocaust of the Revolution by pursuing policies that placed absolute power in the hands of the nobility and of the Church. Despite de Sade's position, he was soon in difficulty, because his father and mother-in-law, the de Montreuils, could obtain his arrest and imprisonment without trial. He married because his father insisted that an alliance between the two families was essential to the economic well-being of his son; de Sade was in love with another though less wealthy woman. His wife seems to have been quite long-suffering and virtuous, trying to protect the Marquis from the various people who lodged charges of poisoning and other cruelties against him. At one point, he was condemned to decapitation for sodomy, along with his valet, a man named Latour, who was to have been hanged and strangled for the crime. The sentence was revoked only after seven years, and then de Sade was held under a *lettre de cachet*, a legal procedure available to the King for holding a subject in prison without charges or a trial.

Of some writers it can be said that their characters are more real than themselves, but none of de Sade's characters ever lived so daring and heavily punished a life. De Sade spent thirty of his seventy-four years either in prison or in an institution for the insane. He was in the Charenton Asylum when the citizens of Paris stormed the Bastille, and he suffered from the Revolution in that all his personal effects left behind in his cell in the Bastille were pillaged and burned by the outraged populace of Paris. At last, released from Charenton, he begins his career as a writer, having lost all his other resources.

This is the period of the Reign of Terror, when the blade of the guillotine rose and fell regularly in a crowded public square separating the head from the body of some forty to fifty persons a day. On September 3, 1792, some ten thousand prisoners were slaughtered. Nothing in de Sade's writing could equal the wholesale bloodshed and horror of the two years in which the people of Paris gained revenge upon the nobility, and each other, for the misfortunes they had so long suffered. The age of reason had become the age of irrationality, and even de Sade, who had been for a time a magistrate, was imprisoned on apparently false charges. The freedom of the press that saw the open publication of his novels and plays did not exist in fact, because a letter he had written much earlier was suddenly brought forth in accusations against him. He seemed to have belonged nowhere, because his play *Le Suborneur* was hissed off the stage by Jacobins on the grounds that its author had been an aristocrat. He was held in prison for two months short of a year and escaped the guillotine by only a day. He was due to be tried on the twenty-seventh of July but for some reason was overlooked, and of his twenty-eight fellow prisoners who were tried, only he and six others escaped being guillotined that day. The next day Robespierre, the author of the Reign of Terror, was himself decapitated by the blade that had been operating since April 25, 1792. In a year of public executions, several thousand persons had died by an instrument that provided even the common folk with the death reserved for noblemen.

De Sade was a revolutionary, but the Republic he helped to found, whose clutches he barely escaped when almost everyone was liable to sudden trial and immediate execution on the basis of accusation alone, had never been able to decide whether he was an *emigré*, one of the noblemen who had fled from France. His sons actually were, but they did not have to account for the desertion and emigration. De Sade's property was sequestered, and he lived in endless poverty from the time he was released from prison and the shadow of the guillotine until he died. He was imprisoned in Charenton because of his writings in 1801 at the age of 61. Napoleon was then First Consul and later as Emperor he decided to keep de Sade at Charenton Asylum. While incarcerated, de Sade organized theatrical performances in which the inmates performed his own plays. These attempts at theatre were recognized as therapeutic by a far-sighted physician of the time. De Sade never left Charenton, despite various efforts to have him transferred to a prison. His chief crime was having written *Justine* and *Juliette*.

The first American edition of the most important writings of the Marquis de Sade was published by Grove Press in three volumes, including essays by Simone de Beauvoir, Pierre Klossowski, Jean Paulhan, and Maurice Blanchot. No effort was made to censor the books anew, although they had often been censored in the past and any bookseller from 1801 to 1962 who was found to have them in stock was liable to arrest and imprisonment. De Sade could not have imagined a more fitting way to honor his literary efforts. Virtue ought to be punished, he preaches in *Justine*, and vice rewarded, he explains, in *Juliette*. At times when the government of France is caught between one repressive regime and another, the canon of de Sade's work has appeared, and there have been at least two excellent biographies, of which the definitive one is by Gilbert Lely. De Sade has been one of the most influential literary figures in the history of French letters and in the world community. His position as the prince of hell has earned him an influence based on the myth of his writings among those who have never read anything of his works. The possibility remains that further works of his will come to light, as did *The 120 Days of Sodom*, the manuscript which Sade supposed had been lost when his cell in the Bastille was robbed and its contents stolen or burned. It had been found by a man named Arnoux de Saint-Maximin and come into the library of the Villeneuve-Trans family who sold it to a collector in Germany at the beginning of this century. Iwan Bloch, the German psychiatrist, acquired the manuscript and published an edition so filled with errors as to be unreadable. Maurice Heine obtained the manuscript in 1929 and after two years of patient effort, published what can be considered the original of the work.

Olympia Press published the English translation, read by world travellers during the fifties and sixties, although other editions were available. The translation by Austryn Wainhouse and Richard Seaver of this and other works by the Marquis de Sade ranks with the great literary efforts of all time, including Samuel Putnam's translation of *Don Quijote* and C. K. Scott Moncrieff's translation of *A La Recherche de Temps Perdu*. *Justine* and *Juliette* have inspired hatred, admiration, and understanding among those who have read the works, but the cornerstone of de Sade's literary method and his philosophy is found in the 1785 work with the strange history. Some of his manuscripts were burned after his death, by his son, and possibly some of his writings have been expunged from all the libraries of the world even though they made their way into print, but the odd circumstance that saved the first complete statement of de Sade from the fires of misunderstanding, and passionate devotion to contemporary myths that beset the nineteenth century, entices an attitude of superstition that de Sade would have hated.

Simone de Beauvoir admits that de Sade is undeniably the worst reading one can find. No self-respecting pornographer would have dreamed of such a melange as de Sade serves up in *Philosophy in the Bedroom* with its equal measures of atheistic anti-humanitarianism and instruction in sexual perversions. As literature to invoke masturbation, the work is suitable only for adolescents who can skip about and make a fantasy out of such pieces as can be read for their sexual content alone. Nor would any philosopher of the time dream of including sodomy, fellatio, tribadism, along with arguments for murder as the privilege of those in authority, especially infanticide, and an incisive view of legal murder as so little different from the premeditated crimes for which it is invoked as to be unworthy for purposes of punishment. All this mixture is found like conglomerate in a consistent view of nature as uncaring, unapproachable by argument and rationalization, and no more to be propitiated by our prayers and petitions than are the *nats* of Burma. De Sade would have been almost as delighted by the earthquake that destroyed a pagoda in Pegu as he was by the desecration of the altars of Catholic churches in Paris.

The main characters in the work are the adumbrations of the anti-heroes found in later fiction, much later. The post second World War produced heroes who were "born treacherous, harsh, imperious, barbaric, selfish, as lavish in the pursuit of pleasure as miserly when it were a question of useful spending, a liar, a gourmand, a drunk, a dastard, a sodomite, fond of incest, given to murdering, to arson, to theft, no not a single virtue compensated that host of vices." Because they are wealthy and titled, no one dares to suspect the characters of all the crimes they commit because they feel a thrill. The Duc de Blangis is described in terms that are used in pornography, with the expected huge penis and capacity for endless ejaculations, as much as fifty times a day. His brother, however, is a bishop who is devoted to active and passive sodomy. This man is described as having "a foul mouth and ugly teeth, a hairless pallid body, a small but well-shaped ass, and a prick five inches around and six in length." The Marquis de Sade helped to acclimatize taboo words in French, although at the time he wrote such language would never have been tolerated. The bishop is not standard for any pornographic work. He continues the anti-hero concept, and is matched by the President de Curval, who is described as procuring a girl by involving her father in a crime so that he is executed in the public square at the moment the daughter loses her virginity in order to save him. Both mother and daughter have been poisoned, in any case, and the President's delight is increased by his treachery. Here too there is no similarity to the characters in standard pornography. The President is described as "a satyr, flat-backed, with slack, drooping buttocks that resembled a pair of dirty rags flapping upon his upper thighs." Finally there is Durcet, but his portrait is lacking because it was to have come from other man-uscripts that have not been preserved. Only a short paragraph of the small chubby man is available. Again unlike the pornographic ideal, "his prick is extraordinarily small, 'tis scarcely two inches around, no more than four inches long." The huge member is one of the characteristics of the standard pornographic work.

Although de Sade describes the pleasures of "the four villains at length," and he elaborates on their delight in sodomy, he proceeds to describe women with great enthusiasm. The men are married to each other's daughters, except the bishop who provides a daughter, so that all of them may engage in incest and adultery with perfect ease. The bishop does not care at all for women and has only one experience of heterosexual intercourse, in which he engaged for the sole purpose of begetting an offspring so that he might enjoy incest at a later date. All are beautiful, but Julie, the President's wife and Durcet's eldest daughter has a bad habit of never taking a bath. ". . . she had the worst-decked mouth, the foulest teeth, and was by habit so dirty in every other part of her body and principally at the two temples of lubricity . . ."

The novel concerns the plan for the eight principals to secure four women who were experienced in "the most furious debaucheries," who would describe the simple passions, one hundred fifty of them, followed by an equal number of unusual passions, then "the most criminal whimsies" and finally the tortures that delight libertines. These precisely numbered tales were to be woven into the story of the life of each of the ill-famed raconteurs. The four women are described rather briefly, but not so briefly as eight candidates for defloration, chosen from among some dozens who had been kidnapped. Each had to be high-born and flawless. One girl was rejected because the gum over one tooth was higher than elsewhere. All were between twelve and fifteen years of age. There are eight boys as well who are not described physically but the lineage of each is carefully traced, along with the circumstances of their abduction which cost the four villains considerable treasure but were not discovered. The names of male servants indicate their attributes: Hercule, Antinous, Bum-Cleaver, and Invictus. These fellows are what you would expect to find in standard pornography, and de Sade calls them "fuckers." They range in age from twenty to thirty. Then some of the women servants are described, and by this time the eager reader is ready for more plot and less description.

What he gets is a long description of the locale in which the adventures are to take place, and then a section entitled "Statutes." These regulations provide for the sexual satisfactions of the four villains, except that the eight girls and eight boys are not to be violated until the month of December, so that "by the augmentation of a desire incessantly inflamed and never satisfied" the "lascivious fury" of the four villains may be provoked. An ominous regulation provides that no one will relieve himself except in the chapel, outfitted for that purpose, and then only after he has secured permission. The Duc de Blangis makes a speech from the dais where the storytellers will sit. It is a kind of recruitment or enlistment speech, different in verbiage, but amounting to what the new recruit or inductee hears from his superior officers. "In short: shudder, tremble, anticipate, obey—and with all that, if you are not very fortunate, perhaps you will not be completely miserable." Desertion is impossible, and not only are the individuals whether wives, hired storytellers, abducted youngsters, or "the fuckers" completely in the power of the four villains, but they are advised to anticipate orders before given, to leap to the chance of obeying a whim. Religion will be fiercely punished, and any who do not abhor worship and "abjure this infamous God," will be scrupulously examined. The word is used in the sense employed by the Holy Inquisition and the other law enforcement agencies of the time. The descriptions of the principal personages is reviewed, and in the form of a journal the work begins in earnest.

The manuscript was not finished, so that we see the writer at his efforts throughout the work, and notes at the end of the first part show how de Sade would have amplified the work if it had not been lost. Even so, the method he has chosen allows him to direct words to himself through the mouth of the President, for instance, reproving Duclos, the first storyteller for not including sufficient detail. Duclos continues her story regarding the lubricity of priests who delight in having her urinate in their mouths, and one of the principal elements in the story develops around urination and defecation.

The story is interrupted by the description of the activities of the libertines, their rages and cruelties, and by a summary of plans they have for further excesses. Duclos continues her story of prostitution from the age of twelve, and the chapel interludes become more important to the story. The modern reader cannot follow the story too long without feeling that he is being subjected to the vilest literature ever written. Unless an individual takes delight in prolonged descriptions of the eating of excrement, he will find the novel beyond his comprehension and certainly beyond enjoyment.

This is just what de Sade intended. He was writing for an audience, supposing that he was ever released from the Bastille and that his writings could be published, however clandestinely. At the end of the first part, he includes a list of his mistakes, but if he wrote the work as quickly as he later said, then it is amazing that he could keep all the details of character and setting so well in mind. The remainder of the book is a draft, or more properly an outline, elaborating day by day as wide a variety of tortures and sexuality as has ever been set down in writing. The whole manuscript took thirty-seven days to complete from the twenty-second of October onward. Possibly the notes and papers that were lost completed the work for the Marquis de Sade, but so much as remains enables us to understand what has made his writings so influential in the history of modern literature.

De Sade is the pathologist of the human spirit, recording in detail everything evil that man can do, and by attempting to put a sexual evaluation on it all, he can find only torture and death worthy of his attention, for the simple love of Fiton and Sophie is violently punished, and the exercises in sexuality become so monotonous that even the Marquis tires of them. Sexuality itself seems harmless and even enjoyable as it exists normally in human beings. The reader is not convinced that the Duc, the Bishop, the financier Durcet, and the President, a kind of superior court judge, should be allowed to prey upon society in the fashion that they demand as their right. In order to have an orgasm, they are willing to sacrifice almost anyone or anything. But is an orgasm that important even for a man of prestige and wealth, if the description is not redundant?

De Sade wrote anti-literature in an age of sentimentalism. His are the first novels of philosophical intent that do not rely upon anything except his fantastic imagination. Very little of what he describes, he experienced. He provides the only means of understanding the French Revolution, one of whose goals was the proclamation of the rights of man. The freedom of the press was included in these rights, but it was as slow of realization as in the United States. The book was written two years before the Constitution of the United States was adopted and six years before the Bill of Rights was included. It had to await the social and moral revolution that followed the first of the world wars before it could be published in anything like an authoritative edition, and that was in a France already mortally sick and a ready prey to the advancing super-righteousness of the German Thousand-Year Reich. The motto of the Hitlerian government could have been "shudder, tremble, anticipate and obey." What the Marquis de Sade describes as happening to his forty-six characters is almost an allegory of the madness that reigned in

Germany for seven years of peace and six of war. Adolf Hitler's dream of an "Aryan" superman ruling Europe cost the lives of something close to thirty million people.

A student of history always has difficulty understanding how the populace of France could turn so violently against their governing class, how the teachings of the Church for centuries could be so quickly forgotten, its bishops and priests abused and killed, and atheism enshrined as the goal of all mankind. De Sade's works were tolerated as examples of the depravity of the nobility, and the moment that another elitist regime began, the works fell under the ban again. De Sade is not arguing against society as he depicts each horror only to attempt in the next passage to exceed it. He is showing how society operates, and he uses human sexuality because nothing was so capable of effecting the series of shocks that would open minds to the philosophy that he wishes to explain. The Marquis de Sade was a moralist, as rigid in the depiction of his moral ideals as any that preceded or followed. Just as a Satanist is a religious man, and a Communist a politician, so the Prince of Hell was a moralist; beyond the evil he preached as desirable for his characters was the evil he saw in the society around him. The French Revolution was ready to accept his divulgations as literal fact. Had not most of them suffered incredibly at the hands of the aristocrats, who were forgiven crimes that would have meant instant death if committed by a peasant? In an age of brutality and insensitivity when public execution was the established order of things, the list of capital crimes included theft, forgery, and a variety of sexual crimes from sodomy to adultery and rape. Advocating all these crimes as the right and privilege of a noble few, who scarcely deserved anything but the torture and death they inflicted on others, was a way of showing how the people of France had tolerated feudalism beyond the point of usefulness.

The 120 Days of Sodom precedes the Revolution that is shown as inevitable because of the highest ranking men of society. His writings are the ultimate heresy so far as the Church is concerned. Everything that it teaches as right he teaches as wrong, and into the bargain writes defamatory descriptions of its priests and bishops. No horror could exceed what de Sade imagined except the horrors of society at that time, repeated often. His works can be re-interpreted today and compared with any period of history when an elitist psychology reaches its ultimate fulfillment. The revelations concerning Stalin were like toned-down scenes from a Sadian romance; and the behavior of the Russian nobility before the Revolution that brought them death and imprisonment is almost a replaying of the French Revolution in another place with a different cast.

The mistake was not to have allowed the publication of the works of the Marquis de Sade during the nineteenth century when the horrors that were a game of sensuality in his stories were in fact the common events of society, at times encouraged by religious leaders. The Indian mutiny of 1854, the U.S. Civil War from 1861 to 1865, included horrors so like those that de Sade describes that we are surprised only that the sexuality commonly a part of them has been concealed. In the Marquis de Sade they are revealed. Even in our own times, police torture includes attacks of a sexual nature, and the usual fate of a good-looking young man (or woman) imprisoned with hardened criminals is to be raped in one of those sodomitical orgies that de Sade describes with such loving detail. We can add a new hypothesis to those that the investigation of censored material has provided so far.

De Sade shows us handsomely, in his view, by incessant repetition, that frustration leads to aggression, that violence and sexuality are intimately intertwined among human beings as among mammals fighting among themselves, that man the predatory ape preys upon the fellow members of his species for a sexual purpose, and that such violence asserts a means of communication when no other is permitted. De Sade's writing is the natural outgrowth of that turn of mind that has come to be labelled Puritanism but is in fact characteristic of all systems of belief whatever the country and whenever the period. If this hypothesis is valid we can find it supported by other works. In the sense that in dealing with the anatomy of censorship we also discover the anatomy of heresy, and that which makes heresy possible, we will discover that the arch-heretic is a most useful member of society. He is a kind of social purgative that enables us to understand both the ills and fevers and to take measures to remove the cause.

   To the nineteenth century mind, de Sade represents the ultimate in depravity. Sensuous education is not complete until the limits of sensuality are known. The ugly monsters who people de Sade's stories provide vicariously the experience of a Gilles de Rais or Neill Cream to the reader. He need not sodomize an infant so that he can have an orgasm during its death throes. The record of humankind is incomplete without its strangest geniuses, and the Marquis de Sade was this if nothing else. His influence will never be completely known, for the number of persons who reject the act that bears his name after having read his works is far greater than those who would use his works as a guide to sensualism, if any exist. Human beings learn less from the books on sensuality than might be supposed. They satisfy a need of their most important sexual organ, their brain, but that does not mean that they will work themselves methodically through the list of positions in a book for a sensuous couple, or man, or woman, nor will they dream of engaging in the violence of de Sade's characters.

   There is good reason for censoring a book that so illuminates a period of history, because it runs counter to those written to prove some kind of point: to show the glory of a nation and the wisdom of its leaders, to make the national goals seem reasonable and inevitable. However when the Marquis de Sade is read throughout, however hard a chore that might be, including his biography, and the works of those who have studied and reported on the French Revolution and the Napoleonic wars, along with other memorabilia of the time, memoirs and diaries, contemporary accounts and letters, a picture emerges that differs from the official histories.

The modern writing of history would insist that the literary works of a period, especially the commonplace works, be studied along with the productions of the geniuses. It is no occasion for wonder that the young graduates of college are so well-informed and so critical of official hypocrisy and injustice. Having access to such works as *The 120 Days of Sodom* broadens the mind even if such works turn the stomach.

VIII.

TO TURN A TRICK

Erotica

When all investigation of sex was discouraged and the results censored, the traditions of folklore with its bawdry and the commercialization of sexuality provided some education for men. Women were left in ignorance among themselves. In Georgia it was a crime to tell a dirty joke in front of a woman, and elsewhere it was very bad manners. Dirty jokes, bawdy humor, immoral songs, and the verse-form devoted to the obscene, the limerick, were a part of the repertoire of every man and used to entertain a group of males when they found themselves away from women, as they often did, enjoying each other's company. The parlor of a good whorehouse was a jolly place, where men could buy drinks, fondle the girls, and tell bawdy stories, before and after they spent as much time as they liked in private. The fancier places in the Wild West gave out souvenir coins, or sold them, some of which have survived despite women who would have thrown them out if they could.

Virtuous women hated prostitutes, because for no good reason they envied the ladies of easy virtue, but not for their sexual activities. Prostitutes lived idle lives, earned their living on the flat of their backs, dressed in fine clothing, and enjoyed the company of husbands more often than wives. One of the great victories of turn-of-the-century domestic warfare was the agreement that kept the husband home in the evenings. One night a week he could go out on the town, but otherwise he was expected to stay home and listen to the wife's complaints or accompany her in a round of social activities. Pair-bonding took second place to economic conditions.

Men have always lived on the food provided by women. The hunter groups could not be relied upon to furnish meat for every meal. The women gathered edible fruits, roots, leaves, and stalks, and the vegetarian dinner was more often the case than not. Women also trapped small game and birds, and there is considerable evidence that farming began as a female occupation. Planting your own seeds saved a good deal of walking and searching. It was not particularly effeminate to take over a woman's duties and help her with them. A man's hunting activity was more often motivated by warfare than food-gathering. A hunting party would kill a great cat that threatened the community, or the tribesmen who invaded the territory, and only occasionally would they go after big game. Not many big animals are edible and all of them are dangerous. Better a meal of vegetables and grain than a gourmet feast of wild buffalo especially if it could be chased and killed only at the risk of the lives of the hunters, one or two of whom might be left behind in mute evidence that one was either quick or dead when hunting big animals.

The physical needs that account for the continuance of life are in this rigid order, food, sleep, and sex. In the experiment conducted during the second World War, the conscientious objectors who participated were starved systematically. As they used up body fat and came closer to death by starvation, they lost all interest in sex, and when their diet was changed they regained their interest. Studies of sleep indicate that it is a vital necessity, a physiological process that the brain requires in order to remain in working order. While resting the muscles is healthful, without total relaxation and the dreams that discharge the overloaded circuits of the brain, death will ultimately ensue. The brain has to dump some of its files from time to time. A man who has had to keep awake for more than a day or two begins to confuse the external world with the fantasies that the brain is constantly creating, and he has no interest whatever in sex.

But granting that he has enough food and enough sleep, a man is interested in sex, and if the seminal vesicles fill, he will produce an emission of semen involuntarily. This was considered immoral in the medieval church. (The author was recently informed that some priests who act as confessors in seminaries will regard involuntary seminal emissions as evidence of immoral thought on the part of the

seminarian.) When science and government took over moral responsibility for the community, because religion had been denied the use
of force, seminal emissions were considered evidence of disease if
they occurred more than once in a few months. The common Victorian term for ejaculation was 'spend,' and a sex dream ending in
seminal emission was a 'cheating dream.' The accepted Victorian
practice was to visit a prostitute when one's sex urges began to be
troublesome. There was widespread belief that an absence of sexual
activity was harmful in several ways: it encouraged masturbation or
seminal emission, it caused seminal losses at stool, the involuntary
emission of semen during defecation, probably a psychosomatic condition because it is very rarely seen now as a separate complaint. The
wakefulness and pain that may accompany long periods of sexual
continence are harmful. There is considerable evidence that a man
can learn to control his seminal emissions to the extent that he can
use this as a sexual outlet in view of restrictions on voluntary masturbation. To the Victorian, a visit to a reliable prostitute was much
better because it restored a man's image of masculine identity and
strengthened his ego. Young men were often shocked out of their
wits by being thrust at a prostitute by a father eager to provide him
with sex education. As a laboratory method there is nothing to
recommend the practice. Prostitutes are notoriously coarse, often
rather long in the tooth, and not at all the idea that a youngster has
of femininity as provided by sexual fantasies.

Interest in sex is as much intellectually grounded in curiosity as it
is a desire to use the physical equipment. Erotica has in all ages and
languages, whether as an oral tradition or in written form, provided
the satisfaction of curiosity and the explanation of sexuality in all
its wide varieties of influence. It differs from pornography in the way
that the limerick differs from other verse. Erotica includes pornography, a highly restricted form that must follow a certain pattern if
it is to be successful. Erotica may arouse the sexual impulse, as may
anything else, but this is incidental and not the calculated reaction
on the part of the reader that the author wishes to obtain.

Strictly interpreted according to the etymology of the words, pornography is the writing of whores, and erotica has to do with Eros the god of physical love. In later mythology, Eros was the son of Ares and Aphrodite, or using his Roman names, Cupid was the son of Venus and Mars. The Roman name was also Amor, Latin for love, while Cupid is derived from a verb meaning 'to desire.' In earlier mythology, his name was Protogonos, a Greek word meaning 'first-born,' because he was the oldest of the gods and the first child of Chaos, who was not so much a god as a condition, the unfathomable space from which everything arose, including Tartarus and Gaea as well as Cupid-Eros-Protogonos. He was worshipped in the Dionysian festivals, and the Roman sculptors usually portrayed him as a child with wings or as an adolescent boy. Eros never assumed a feminine form.

Through the history of civilization in all its languages and records, the erotic runs as a constant theme. "The Song of Solomon" is erotic verse, some of the most beautiful ever written, celebrating the love of a man for a woman and the kind of love that is returned. In the Spain of *El Siglo del Oro*, when the greatest writers were producing works of imagination that remain as the classics in Spanish, nuns were not permitted to read this work, and San Juan de la Cruz was imprisoned by the inquisition because he translated "The Song of Solomon." It is as impossible to remove the erotic from the record of man's past as it is to remove the evidence of sex from his body. A male body is structurally different from a female body, from pre-frontal ridge between the eyes, to length of the humerus and tibia, from the breadth of the shoulders to the width of the pelvis. Every cell of a male body is male. Life is essentially erotic.

All biological comparisons must be made by statistical methods, for there is no absolute male or absolute female, there is a degree of maleness that may verge quite closely to female, so closely that it is sometimes a great problem to identify which sex the individual has. Corrective surgery can sort out the distinctions more effectively, but it cannot change a male into a female. In the case of Stanley Gordon Hall, who was a transsexual, that is somewhere between male and female in his physique, the decision was that a mistaken identification at birth had labelled him male when he was, in fact, female. He has born his husband two children, and we must in honesty concede her the right pronoun on this basis alone. The bisexuality of individuals is the constant state, physically, as well as emotionally, and the preponderance of male or female determines the category into which custom and physical evidence place the individual. There are now very good tests to determine the sex of those persons who are so nearly in balance as to be of indeterminate gender.

Human bisexuality was celebrated in classic times by the numerous statues that provided a female body with male genitals. The moral revolution was truly underway when women began wearing trousers, or trouser-like clothing, and it achieved its zenith when men resumed the long hair that had been one of their traditional privileges, indicating a leisure status. At the same time, most men wore beards and mustaches so that the sex difference was still unmistakable, despite similarity of clothing and hair style. Quite significantly, those countries with strict censorship for a time discouraged or forbade long hair on men and refused to permit tourists to enter the country if they sported flowing locks. They were correct in their interpretation of long hair as a revolt against the established order that their censorship also protected.

Singapore makes a good case for study of this phenomenon. The little republic maintains strict censorship and prohibits importation of obscene works of any kind, especially motion pictures for public exhibition. *Irma La Douce* was finally released to the local theatres after years of deliberation. No widespread collapse of public morals ensued. Dealers in pornography ply their trade in secret, taking precautions that they will not be caught, but without any large number of customers. The republic is following the preferences of the voters who see no reason to waste limited funds on material of

such restricted usefulness. The Chinese outnumber all the other eth-
nic groups, and publications in Chinese are about as numerous as
those in English. Malay and Tamil are the other official languages,
each with a significant amount of publication, and all submit to the
canons of taste prevailing in the society. A newspaper was closed
down, its license revoked, when it was proved that the paper derived
at least a part of its funds from the People's Republic of China. In
the sense that a license is required for publication, if not for the
individual work published, there is limited freedom of the press. The
newspaper criticized the prime minister, one of the few that did,
although the press has the privilege of criticizing any public official.
The paper was in deep financial trouble, because no newspaper com-
petes with the Chinese press easily, and the English newspapers that
have been published for decades are well known throughout the
world. *The Singapore Daily Mail* is one of the best sources of information on economic conditions in the whole Malay archipelago.

The government of Singapore rejected a bid by the U.S. authorities who wanted to make the city a rest and recreation center for
troops stationed in South Vietnam. The gin mills of Bangkok and the
experience of Penang were enough to set the government firmly
against a large influx of soldiers, seeking prostitutes and saloons, who
would bring crime and moral degradation with them. The island of
Penang has some of the most beautiful scenery in the world, miles
of beaches with cream-colored sand stretching down to the clear
blue sea of the Straits of Malacca. The city of Georgetown is a kind
of small-size Singapore, with a few great hotels and busy markets.
When the prospect of thousands of overpaid soldiers from the United
States was raised with the local authorities, they rejoiced until the
men arrived in pursuit of a huge influx of prostitutes of all national-
ities followed by a thriving crime syndicate. After a few months of
dealing with drunken, disorderly, and wounded soldiers, the Kingdom of Malaysia, the state government, and the city of Georgetown
kicked them out. They can go to Penang but only as private tourists.

In the future, historians may cite as one of the worst effects of the prolonged Vietnamese war the internationalization of the American crime syndicate. Information about this development is necessarily lacking, because nothing has been more closely guarded, and the person who knows enough to cite details probably has a short life expentancy. Wherever drugs, gambling, and prostitution abound the crime syndicate moves in to manage the business and derive the major profits. Until recently, the American crime syndicate refused to deal with drugs on any large scale, but some secret agreement was reached, as in Mario Puzo's novel *The Godfather*, and the unfailing source of raw opium in northeastern Burma was located along with trade routes through Thailand and Laos to Vietnam. But equally the raw opium can be transformed to heroin and shipped through Malaysia with the free port of Penang almost beckoning the dealers in drugs to use its excellent facilities and corrupt its public officials.

Prostitution has always been associated with the criminal element in a society, except in countries where it was legalized and the professionals subjected to regular medical inspection. In the United States, prostitutes are generally managed by the crime syndicate, and so far as the health of the professional is concerned, the prostitute is subjected to regular inspection and in a situation where venereal disease is rampant may require the customer to pass a 'short-arm inspection,' reminding the veteran of military service of his days in the armed forces. Prostitutes tend not to be carriers of venereal disease because they have regular medical examinations that the amateurs never get.

Because of inexperience, the author cannot make any statements about the modern prostitute not found in the autobiographies that at least seem to be accurate reflections of life in the United States. A constant fear of the late nineteenth and early twentieth century was the white-slaver, who drugged young women and abducted them, forcing them to serve in foreign houses of prostitution. If any such places exist in the Orient, the author is unaware of them. The countries where such houses might exist have very strict immigration rules so that the prostitutes would have to be smuggled in like spies or saboteurs. In any case, orientals do not prefer Caucasian women, who smell bad in their estimation, and are not good in bed. Oriental prostitutes, however, are very skilled in pleasing the customer, and they prefer to spend the night with him, unless he will pay for no more than a half hour or so. Apparently there are not so many perversions as are reported in such books as Madame Sherry's *Pleasure Was My Business*. This book fell afoul of the Miami authorities who banned it, possibly on the basis that it was too factual. There is nothing obscene about the book, except that it deals with prostitutes and their customers. The whorehouse may still exist in some places, but a combination of willing amateurs and the call-girl business have generally replaced it.

Prostitution is a common reason for arrest. In places where the crime syndicate and public officials play games of corruption, prostitutes may be arrested or establishments raided in order to encourage a higher pay-off by the crime syndicate to the police. Organized prostitutes and crime syndicates can hardly exist without the cooperation of the public authorities, especially the police. In places where anti-vice campaigns are waged, there is a very good chance that a cynical police force utilizes the good intentions of the morally upright in order to increase the percentage of the amount paid by the customer that finds its way into the pockets of public officials. Whether the relaxation of censorship has helped the business of the brothel is unknown. One can speculate that it increases business by making men eager for sexual activity, but there is much evidence that those who purchase or use pornographic material do so as an end in itself not as a means of exciting their heterosexuality. For obvious reasons, the crime syndicate has opposed the relaxation of censorship restrictions for the same reason that the legalization of gambling was opposed: it destroys the illicit business that forms the basis of the crime syndicate's income. Banned books sell at high prices.

Erotica is now openly sold in drugstores as well as bookshops, and pornography finds only a saturated market, so that only an exceptional work of pornography will attain the sale that is commonplace for such works of erotica as *Couples*, by John Updike, *Myra Breckinridge*, by Gore Vidal, or *The Love Machine*, by Jacqueline Susann, and these works have not had nearly the sale that Mario Puzo's *The Godfather* has enjoyed. The total of all sales of erotica is probably still less than that of the mystery, wild west story, or thriller where the object is violence rather than the depiction of sexual activity.

Pornography, as can be seen from the above is not concerned with writings about whores or even by whores, but represents a series of emotional shocks that cause the reader to respond with sexual excitement. Probably pornography is effective only in a climate of repression, and when the discussion of sexuality is open and accepted what tends to invade is not emotional shock but emotional pleasure. Sex and comedy have always been intimately associated. The bawdy limerick is funny because its last line produces the twist that causes us relief in the form of laughter. When comedy is reached in erotica, it bears no further threat, and despite the fact that the author and the publisher of the *Sex Life of a Cop* were each sentenced to twenty-five years imprisonment, the book is funny when it holds both police and the judicial system up to ridicule. The sentence was later revoked, because the book while trashy and obscene to many was not going to cause nearly so much disrespect for the law of the land as the actual cases of bribed judges. In the case of Madame Sherry, and very likely in many other cases, the censorship proceedings reflect an official attitude rather than a response to a threat to public morals. Certainly public morality begins with incorruptible officials. In Thailand where bribery is a way of life, avenues of saloons and the numerous houses of prostitution along with the incessant crime represents degradation of the public morals. Singapore's strait-laced view of immoral literature does not account for the cleanliness, swift punishment of crime, and generally moral attitude of the heterogenous society but the incorruptibility of the public officials does. A special branch of the police are in the position of having access to every secret file and document with special privileges of investigation, so that a bribed official has but a short time to enjoy his ill-gotten gains before he is subject to trial and imprisonment. The knowledge that the government is determined to end what was accepted as an old Chinese custom has made bribery rare and widely condemned. In the huge projects to provide adequate housing, there was considerable trouble at first with gangs of thieves, but the vigilance of the police gradually so reduced the profits that the terrorization of the people who rented apartments steadily decreased as the members of the gangs were sent to Changgi Prison. If any of the police force had shown a willingness to be bribed, the Singapore of today would still be like the ramshackle city of twenty years ago. Any society can rid itself of a crime syndicate by making public corruption the most opprobrious of misdeeds, the most impossible to conceal, and the most swiftly punished.

Pornography

The special kind of erotica that can be called pornography must follow a pattern of going from a simple and permissible act to one that represents the ultimate in sinfulness. This naturally varies with the readership at which the author directs his work. If masturbation is regarded as the most heinous sin, then it will come toward the latter part of the work, but if it is considered not sinful at all, the work will begin with masturbation. Certain taboos are very strong and virtually universal, among them incest, bestiality, and profanation of the sacred, in that declining order. A work of pornography that began with incest and worked its way on to masturbation would reflect a society with a curious set of values. There are two major types of pornography: heterosexual and homosexual. Homosexuality represents a taboo subject to the heterosexual man to the extent that an episode of homosexuality, as in *Adam and Eve* published under the pseudonym of Marcus van Heller by Olympia Press and widely pirated, will be so brief as to be negligible and will find the hero in the active role. In a work published by Olympia Press after it became an American publishing firm, *Bishop's Gambol*, an episode of homo-sexuality barely intrudes at all where it is used to establish the main character as a kind of anti-hero; typical graphic description that is a necessary part of homosexual pornography is omitted in the few examples available.

A pattern can rapidly be established by an investigation of the market as censorship is relaxed. First comes a period when almost anything can be sold, including the closet literature that is written to relieve the feelings of the author. As the tastes of the readers become more educated, the closet literature gives way to pornographic works that include all the taboo subjects in one story. Gradually, as these saturate the market, the fiction begins to specialize in one or another sexual preference. There are fetishist novels, incest novels, bestiality novels, sado-masochistic novels, and the aberrations become more lurid and strive for greater emphases. Specialization in one aspect or another of human sexuality is possible only when there is a signif-icant number of readers who are willing to pay the inflated prices charged for the material.

However lurid the material may be, whether fiction or nonfiction, it is derived from human experience. Even when the sexuality be-comes as bizarre as in a surrealist painting, it is derived from common experience and its appeal is to a common drive. While all valid autobiographical material can be called only erotica, much of the 'case-history' material is fictional and skillfully written pornography. Except that taboo words must be used to increase the emotional shock, the true confession material published for the past fifty years and popularized by the Macfadden Publishing Company was case-history erotica very close to what is achieved by pornography. One way of achieving the emotional shock necessary for a work of fiction meant to arouse sexual impulses is to say that what is going to be described is very shocking. Rather than recoiling, the average reader will eagerly turn the page and be properly shocked. A typical attitude is an author's begging forgiveness and repenting of his misbehavior. This establishes the work as erotic rather than pornographic, because a necessary part of pornography is the happy violation of taboos, and a work that includes repentance and regret can no longer deliver the shock the reader is waiting for. An individual who hates to read about human sexuality will find pornography obscene to the extent that he considers obscenity and pornography synonymous. Erotica, because it involves descriptions of human sexuality, will be regarded as obscene and therefore pornographic.

The three useful words finally resolve into a semantic blur even though they are especially necessary in the practice of librarianship. Every profession develops a jargon to serve as a kind of intellectual shorthand making communication easier and more effective. The volunteer censor who proclaims that Jerry Rubin's book *Do It* is pornography immediately labels himself an offended reader with a poor vocabulary. Individual taste is completely operative in obscenity. What is my obscenity may not be yours; each of us has his taboos and cannot bear to have them violated. An amazing discovery of recent times has been that sexual taboos are learned and quite tenuous because sexuality is not entirely responsive to the communication process. But aggression is, and scenes of violence may encourage aggressive behavior. While no one is physically harmed by loving genital activity, aggression can easily end with a loss of life or limb.

As used here erotica includes all works dealing with human sexuality. Pornography is a special form of erotica meant to arouse the sexual appetite of the reader. In order to accomplish this, the author moves with skill from what is acceptable to what delivers severe emotional shocks but of a sort the reader can accept without discarding the rest of the story. He writes what the reader wants, delays the emotional shock and because it tends to identify the act with an individual when the pornographer must show the universality of the act. Typically a work of pornography begins with a scene of masturbation and ends with an orgy, having progressed through scenes of heterosexual fellatio and cunnilingus after vivid descriptions of sexual intercourse in a variety of positions. Final orgies are described so that they represent the review of all the previous sexuality, and the incest theme may be brought in, as well as bestiality, if the reader is schooled to expect severe emotional shocks from such description. At one point, when the Catholic Church reigned as the moral supervisor of all Europe and much of the new world as well, profanation of the sacred was a necessity. *The Autobiography of a Flea* uses the wicked priests, bishops, abbots, acolytes, and deacons as the male characters who violate the willing and cooperative Bella.

This brought such works under the view of the Church in two respects. *Ex professo* pornography has always been taboo and reading it an occasion of sin. This gained the authors of such works recognition by the Church. To describe the mischief of priests in works of fiction is the sin of causing scandal. Such heretical views of the Church would never have been tolerated during the period of its ascendancy, before the reformation made the works popular, although such works doubtless circulated as closet literature.

Priests were described as wicked devils in the anti-Catholic literature of the time, and it was commonly assumed that priests used the nunnery as a kind of religious house of prostitution. Protestant groups continued the fight long after the victory had been won, so that examples of this kind of libel exist for the campaign against Al Smith for the Presidency in 1928. The Republican Party did not publish the worst of the material, but it was certainly approved by the less broad-minded leaders. A tunnel going from New York to Rome for private conferences with the Pope was shown in photographs. The entrance to the Holland Tunnel served as the model for this bit of fiction. The resurgence of the Ku Klux Klan in the 1920's was important in the defeat of Al Smith. Some anti-Catholic families found the "Ave Maria" terrible because the word 'womb' is mentioned in it.

In the prolonged warfare between Catholics and Protestants, still going on in Northern Ireland as this is written, each religious group accused the other of hideous crimes. However, aside from minute details of theology, the average Buddhist or Hindu found the religions exactly alike. Hinduism, in particular, approves of a wide variety and latitude of beliefs, and Buddhism has as many sects as Christianity, if there are not more. Catholics have tended to confuse unity with centralization, and obedience to the Bishop of Rome, the Pope, is considered a mark of Christian morality. In the anti-Catholic literature of the nineteenth century, Protestant exegesis often explained that the Scarlet Whore of Babylon was actually the Catholic Church, especially the Holy See in Rome.

However, none of the immoral literature of the time was used as evidence against another religious group. Just as Roman Catholicism has in common with Communism the practice of strict censorship, and the censorship of Ireland is as active as that of the Soviet Union, granting that the subject matter censored is sometimes different, the censorship advocated by Anthony Comstock and Charles Sumner, working for the Young Men's Christian Association, was Protestant in nature. Much of the pornography that gained prison terms for the seller or printer was of the 'closet literature' variety, very crude and far from the standard that would be openly sold at present. When the Olympia Press set up its business in New York City, its large list was taken over by several different publishers. A few works had been republished under copyright in the United States, such as *Lolita* by Vladimir Nabokov. The Olympia Press edition was on sale throughout the world long before the standard American edition appeared. Such novels as *The Double-Bellied Companion* by Akbar del Piombo are close to standard pornography and were widely pirated because of the peculiarities of American copyright law. The general novel of sexuality, as close to pornography as the formula will allow when adjusted to the requirements of the market, gave way to novels dealing with the oddities of sex. Each earlier stage of candor was then sold at reduced prices.

It is now too late to claim that great harm has resulted from this kind of publication. Many writers see the re-awakening of interest in the occult as a direct result of the relaxation of censorship and the defeat of old obscenity laws. Obscenity has become a legal definition of certain works that usually are tried in the lower court and released by a superior court. Studies of sex crimes have shown that availability of pornography has little if anything to do with the rate of sex-related offenses. In Denmark, where there are rather fewer punishable sex acts than in the United States, there was a sharp reduction in the number of sex crimes reported to the police. This is somewhat different from the statement that sex crimes decreased. This is unknown everywhere if the statement means that acts so labelled have decreased in number, but if a crime is committed only when the miscreant is caught, then the number has decreased everywhere without regard to the status of censorship within the community. Sex crimes are rather rare in Singapore and mostly of the commercialized sort. Prostitution is strictly forbidden and punished when the evidence is sufficient to procure a conviction in the Singapore courts. Houses of prostitution can be controlled rather easily, but the private semi-professional is beyond the reach of the police.

What has increased everywhere are crimes of violence, in part a response to the incessant instruction of television which can show little else that interests viewers as much. Danish television will not show American crime stories, horror stories, and ghost stories. Nude Danes do not cause a flutter of disapproval, although actual sex acts would never be shown, but scenes of violence, the usual gore of a Hollywood detective story, would be strictly controlled by the Danes. In this case they have more evidence that harm does result. Society is not in the least disturbed by adolescent (or adult) masturbation, but assault, murder, and mayhem disturb society to its foundations. If an especially gory motion picture, *The Godfather*, for example, is imported then restrictions on the age groups that are permitted to see it are strictly enforced. The American rating system was taken from many European examples of the same procedure. The Danish psychologists have produced considerable evidence that violence communicates violence, but that sexuality cannot be so deliberately and readily structured.

Pornography loses its appeal. The satiation rate is very high, and finally is the reason for the replacement of general novels of sexual activity by special novels. Significantly, case histories of all kinds may come close to being actual pornography, but they are generally instructive and, whether fiction or nonfiction, are written with an effort toward verisimilitude that includes the use of taboo words.

Real case histories might include taboo words that offend the professionals who must deal with them. However, the social worker or psychiatrist who shows shock when his patient produces a taboo word is likely to lose rapport with the patient. The censoring of case histories does nothing to improve them, and verbatim reports would need not only censoring but heavy editing. Taboo words, do not, in fact designate a work as pornographic although it might well be considered obscene by an individual. Fanny Hill does not use a single taboo word in her letters. Her language is as pure as Pamela's, but what she describes is purely sexual while what Pamela describes is not. Pamela, after all, includes a list of clothing and other interesting details, but Fanny Hill is forever commenting on some man's 'engine' or other euphemism for penis. Fanny even avoids medical terminology, which she may not have known.

Pornography can be written that contains no taboo words, but this would be a *tour de force* in a field that has been as thoroughly thrashed over as the form of the sentimental romance. There are still buyers for this kind of fiction, but the general public has long ago lost interest. Pornography represents a drag on the market, a type of material that fails to amuse or please and becomes repetitious in the extreme. Only a person who is interested in one or another oddity will buy material, and as the speciality literature reaches the extent of its readership, a further reduction in new titles will be seen. Even homosexual literature, probably the most enduring of the types, will improve in quality so that homosexual romances will, in due time, become a standard genre as varied and interesting as the heterosexual novel. It is highly doubtful that this kind of fiction will ever have much appeal to those heterosexual men whose component of homosexuality has been reduced to virtually nothing by experience and preference. Sophisticated readers of homosexual fiction will require that it rise above the level of the Olympia Press publications in its Other Traveller series to the quality attained by Gordon Merrick in *The Lord Won't Mind* and *One for the Gods*.

It is quite clear that pornography is a self-defeating type of material, and that vivid illustrations of sexual intercourse are instructive but soon tiresome. Censorship of sexually oriented material is unnecessary for the world community, although one community or another may decide to limit its investment in such material. Communities, like libraries, have the right to decide on their own policies of selection without fearing that they are engaging in censorship. Denmark is quite within its rights to censor material dealing with violence, and probably wise, and Singapore and the Republic of Ireland are within their rights to censor material that would represent an investment they do not wish to make. Unless nations restrict travel in the world community, they cannot prevent citizens from visiting Denmark or Hong Kong, whichever is closer, where the censored material is readily available, though less so in Hong Kong than in Copenhagen. In a large heterogenous society, New York City would greatly decrease its tourist trade by closing down the pornography stores and theatres. Many people visit the city because it is Sin City and such material is readily available. In a democracy, the majority will rule honestly only by their behavior in the marketplace so that voluntary censorship groups need some other means of displaying their sexual purity. The individual should not be subjected to unwarranted invasion of his privacy by having his sealed mail inspected. An individual who orders pornographic material, or sexually oriented material from whatever source, should have it delivered faithfully. There are a few compromises as foolish as requiring that postal authorities serve in lieu of moral censors.

Erotica is available according to the taste of the individual, and the only difficult word left to be defined is obscenity. Erotica represents one of the great achievements of human beings, as well as one of his most enduring artistic inspirations. Sexual intercourse has been depicted in cave paintings, in Egyptian tomb decorations, in Chinese drawings, in Indian sculpture, in Greek ceramics, in Pre-Columbian pottery of the New World, in Roman interior decoration, in medieval church decoration, in Renaissance paintings, in drawings by such renowned artists as Rembrandt, in furniture decoration and other wood carvings throughout the ages, and in photographs dating from the invention of photography. The nineteenth century experiment in hypocrisy was a digression from the central interest of humankind rather than an improvement of morals, and the voluntary censor is motivated not by considerations of the public good but by deep-seated feelings of guilt and superiority fighting each other for dominance. Very difficult problems of human communication must be resolved before we can get beyond the stage of a macro-anatomy of censorship. The micro-anatomy demands assistance from ethologists, sociologists, anthropologists, and psychologists. The scientific advances of the past quarter century have made this book possible, and we are now able to define obscenity.

Obscenity

Despite the lengthy efforts of the United States courts to make this word into a legal shibboleth, obscenity is a useful concept but one that is for the most part misunderstood. The legal definition need not detain us here, for such cases as now involve obscenity face review by higher courts, and unless public officials with a great need to prove sexual virtue (and to obtain publicity) can manage to revive the public's interest in such fruitless pursuits, it is nearly a dead issue. The purification of public morals by chasing pornographers can be viewed as a great masquerade for those heavily involved with the crime syndicate who must find some means of proving their ability without offending their masters.

Take the last ten years of *The New York Times* and compare the evidence of police corruption with anti-pornography crusades. A remarkable fact emerges. If there is a police scandal, expect some announcement that a crackdown on obscenity is necessary. In the recent revelations (1972), front-page stories of raids on three theatres in the Times Square area shared space with the announcement that a new squad of detectives would prevent the pay-offs to the police that had become a business expense of contractors.

Obscenity as a legal issue was put in proper perspective by the case of *Stanley vs. Georgia*. Robert Eli Stanley was suspected of illegal gambling activities. Instead of the evidence they wanted, the police found pornographic films in his home. Stanley was convicted of "possessing obscene material." The United States Supreme Court reversed the decision of the Georgia Supreme Court on the grounds that the Georgia law was unconstitutional. "If the First Amendment means anything, it means that a state has no business telling a man, sitting alone in his house, what books he may read or what films he may watch. Our whole constitutional heritage rebels at the thought of giving government the power to control men's minds."

Nor is obscenity in the groin of the beholder. It is in the brain of everyone as a part of our ability to communicate. What is obscene is the class of messages we reject without any attempt to understand or give an indication that we have received the message. This is the inherent danger in preventing the advancement of knowledge; the rejection of messages may end as the stagnation of ignorance and the obscenity of today is likely to be the wit of tomorrow. This is the typical attitude of the heterosexual man toward homosexual pornography. The attitude of the censor is quite different. He finds a fascination in the material, is on the alert to spot something that fits not his concept of obscenity but his concept of negated interest. He denies any usefulness to the material and wishes to protect the public from it, but at the same time he searches for it, making comparisons of this with that, drawing conclusions not on his own behalf but on behalf of everyone. It is quite impossible for him to believe that everyone does not agree with him. Everyone is an excellent censor for himself and his children.

If the reader will pause to think a moment, he will realize what it is that he hates to hear or see. He may have no experience and only imagine that he will react in such a way that he can say the material is obscene for him. The purpose of a message is not only intellectual but emotional. Great verse does not engage the mind alone but also the whole concatenation of feelings that make us human beings. Music is capable of communication because it excites an emotional response. The same is true of paintings and sculpture. For most of this book, we have investigated sexually oriented materials because censorship has centered on them for the past two centuries. But now the concept of the obscene is being understood with much greater scientific vigor than before.

The obscene as sexually related material is censored to the extent that it represents a signal the receiver of the message does not wish to accept. The reason that nocturnal emissions caused such distress to the medieval church was less the loss of seed and the regulations of Leviticus concerning this but the vivid dreams that accompany this sexual experience in a man. The dream, in Freud's concept and as shown by later studies, is the preserver of sleep. Hidden ideation, the imaginings of the brain that are consciously rejected, reappear as the physiology of the body seems to respond to sexual stimulation. It is all internal but nevertheless is there and is equivalent to the sexual fantasies that commonly accompany masturbation. By rejecting sexual material the individual is first of all rejecting masturbation fantasies. Very little sexual material is intellectually stimulating, and if this is the case, then it is not sexually stimulating. Our canons of taste arrange a value scale for sexual signals, as indicated by Desmond Morris. This value scale is in constant revision, but at some point the male must achieve an erection in order to continue with the object of all sexual signalling, manipulation of the genital organs. When women wore long concealing dresses, emphasizing the buttocks by means of a bustle, men tried to catch a glimpse of an ankle. The sight of the long women's drawers that covered not only the pelvic area but the thighs and lower limbs as well was very exciting to the male deprived of one of his favorite sights, a pretty girl.

This sexual signalling can be seen in male homosexuals and in lesbians, each sex having its own set and its own pacing for the sending and receiving of messages. When a man becomes aware of a sexual signal offered by a homosexual, he may react with aggression or with a reaction that substitutes for aggression. As Jim Bouton relates in his books, not all sexual signals have homosexual content even though they are employed by homosexuals. It is only the revelation of homosexual orientation that makes the signalling effective. In *Ball Four*, the baseball players, as a joke, began kissing each other. It has no more sexual content than any other joke and is accepted by the players in this fashion. The Commissioner of Baseball, however, who reacted to the publication of the book and would have suppressed it if he could, found it highly suggestive and thought that it would defame the important big business that the game represents in the United States.

In the sequel, *I'm Glad You Didn't Take It Personally*, Bouton includes further anecdotes involving homosexuals who make passes at ball players. Quite typically, Bouton is unaware of any homosexual baseball player, and those who became the victims of practical jokes, in which a homosexual is sent to a certain player's room, reacted with fear, a typical substitute for an intense aggressive reaction.

Lapsing once more into the first person singular pronoun, I was very much displeased that the key to the study of censorship lay in the field of homosexual literature. I knew immediately that many men will assume homosexuality on the part of anyone who shows the slightest interest in it (women apparently don't if they are at all sophisticated). I reacted with a coarse tremor, axillary sweating, and other signs of anxiety that in myself always indicate aggression carefully concealed and suppressed as my parents taught me to do. I had to teach myself to understand homosexual literature by writing homosexual novels and comparing my own reactions with what I felt when I watched the relaxation of censorship that could be easily measured in homosexual literature. There was nothing else that could explain the attitude of the censor as it applies to all of us and nothing else that could penetrate the prevailing mysteries that surround the concept of the obscene. A young colleague who read two of these novels put the first down half way through totally repelled by the graphic description of sodomy that I had managed to write. His wife, who read the novel at the same time was as repelled as he, but she did not conclude that I was a homosexual, while he did. It was a relief for him to say this to me, signalling acceptance and understanding, because he is no more homosexual in his preferences than I am. He wanted me to know that he and his wife would continue to respect me even though I fell into a rejected category and they had found my novel obscene. The reaction is exactly what has been found in many other studies, and the novels served the purpose of a test instrument also in gaining a first hand impression of the homosexual book market.

One publisher rejected them out of hand, without further consideration, and another prefers to deal only with established authors. A third, Olympia Press, rejected a novel but encouraged a rewriting. When this was submitted, the usual three-months delay brought the novel back because the editor was faced with a non-meshing of wavelength, as the letter of rejection put it, when the probable answer is to be found in the failure of the series to make a market for itself, as was hoped when the series began. Just what would have happened if the novel had been published must remain a topic of speculation, but I feel relieved every time I think of the rejection.

Obscenity is what the receiver of a message will not accept because it is indicative of a set of signals that he does not wish to see. Fiction, like all art, creates an event world in the form of symbols that all of us can understand. In doing so, the reader identifies with a character and goes through the experience of receiving and rejecting signals. The average reader has always liked a little sexuality from time to time because it makes the event world of the novel more similar to the event world of which he is aware. His preferences will reject an event world in which he cannot associate himself with the transformed reality of the symbols he finds. But the symbol is not the reality. As Hayakawa puts it, "a map is not a territory," the word rose is not the flower we find and smell and touch and possibly taste. Rose petals are delicious. A wild strawberry in the woods is one thing in the sentence I am writing and another in reality.

The law of obscenity must be changed to conform with the broadening of the world community to include all mankind, and its limits are simply this: no one has the right to invade the privacy of another with messages he does not want to receive. Putting brown paper over the windows of dealers in pornography protects the right of privacy of passersby. Canned music in a library violates the privacy of readers. Insisting that all the viewers must watch a program that they find boring, or obscene, violates privacy just as much. If some national television used the satellite system for an unremitting broadcast of pornographic movies, there is not much that the present world community could do about it, but so long as television sets can be turned off, there is not much harm that could be done by such a broadcast, and even if the sets were left on, the chances are only that worldwide masturbation among those who like the sexual activity would occur. The net result would be so close to nothing as not to matter.

Governments that try to assume the moral teachings of a church as statute law invariably reduce the effectiveness and respect for law that is in substance the only source of a lawful and orderly society. A government cannot punish crimes that can be committed in private between consenting adults without anyone being the wiser. To apprehend and convict a person of such a crime is as flagrant an example of discriminatory prosecution as can be found. The criminal is guilty of being caught and whatever remorse he feels is solely for not having outwitted his pursuers.

The world community can provide for a millenium without war, famine, and pestilence using the technology available and such a minimum of international structure as would scarcely change the present bureaucracy of the United Nations. But each society must be allowed its privilege of informing members and no society can be given the privilege of maintaining captive audiences. In the business of communication, the government can only insist on correct labelling. The obscenities that each of us find in the stream of communication can be shunted aside at the point where there is greatest assurance that the message is obscene, the individual himself.

This is not censorship but the exercise of freedom. The U.S. Supreme Court has observed that freedom of the press means that hateful theories and ideas have the right of publication, though no one should be forced to read the resulting material. Devout atheists who wish to raise their children as atheists object to the religiosity of American life, with its deist mottoes on coins, on the walls of the Senate, and especially religious observances in the public schools. Madeline Murray, especially, fought long battles through the courts so that her children would not have to endure prayers that seemed antithetical to the beliefs that they were taught at home. Efforts to amend the U.S. Constitution have proven unsuccessful because the House of Representatives cannot agree on the prayers that should be allowed. In fact, no one prevents, or can prevent, praying anywhere so long as it is done silently. What the court cases provided was that public prayer was not to be forced upon the children, the most exemplary captive audiehce our society provides, especially in view of the laws regarding truancy. Education is compulsory, and secular schools must teach what seems best for the world community and the local non-sectarian society.

A similar problem arises with sex education which is viewed as the work of "communists" or other bogey men. There is a great difference between religious education in the schools and sex education. The latter is limited to elementary biology that has never been prevented and is simply accomplishing one of the purposes of education, to provide an understanding of the event world in which all of us live. Some groups adhere to the belief that the world is flat, and in the face of tremendous evidence, maintain their belief. To such a group, compulsory education that includes the evidence collected from space exploration is directly in opposition to all that the society holds dear. A sincere belief that sex is a mistake on the part of an otherwise omniscient deity and that all sexual activity is dirty and disgusting represents a point of view that a parent may wish to instill in a child. Unless there is a sufficient number of persons willing to provide separate instruction inculcating this idea in the children by creating a private school for that purpose, then the public school has no choice but to provide sex education in accord with valid scientific studies of human sexuality.

The only rallying point of the world community is science, and the only epistemological ideal must be the scientific method. It is sufficiently strong to correct the errors of the past and provide for the increase of what we know that we know. But the events of the past few decades require that along with scientific method we understand the principles of suspended judgement, as explained by Bertrand Russell. Until a fact is known absolutely, we must be able to take a position of no position, asserting neither the truth or the falsity of a proposition. Science, for all its contributions to technology, cannot do more than disprove hypotheses. The predictions based on experiments remain predictions, subject to incalculable chance factors. When a beautiful theory is developed, a subsequent discovery may cast it aside. All our knowledge is speculation worked out, if at all, in the event world. We are motivated by faith, whether it is faith in the validity of revelations or the predictions of science, based on experiments designed with the greatest likelihood of providing predictions in which we can repose all our trust.

The censor is one who would limit investigation because its results might be damaging to faith and its concomitant in the mental landscape, morals. If a man's morals are the motor that runs him, his faith is the fuel that supplies the motor with energy, and we are all instructed in faith from the moment that we develop sensory receptors, some weeks before birth. Our faith comforts and supports us and gives us the opportunity to provide for our bodily and emotional needs. A government can have nothing to do with either characteristic. It can only provide justice by maintaining control of physical power. Government has always been limited by the consent of the governed, demanding total consent, as in Nazi Germany, or securing such consent as it can, as in Great Britain and the United States. A government cannot destroy its constituency, and a constituency can only alter the form of government. When the ecclesiastical courts of the middle ages were finally put out of business by the rising middle class of the post-renaissance period, governments took over the job of providing moral direction. In a democracy there is constant danger that the majority will provide for laws that exceed the rights of government. A vote on the only true religion would not make whatever the choice might be the only true religion, it would only display the religious convictions of the electorate. The United States at present must fight its way through a massive structure of laws that have lost their meaning and usefulness, and one of the great aids in the battle against crime will be a reform of the legal system.

Governments cannot discern between orthodoxy and heresy, they can only dispense justice on the basis of what exists in the event world. If a government decrees that the life of an individual cannot be taken by another citizen, then it must not take the life itself. What is justice for the citizenry is justice for the members of the government who cannot justly constitute a privileged class. Governments are forgiven all kinds of nonsense, but in a world threatened by its own power, allegated to this governmental authority and that, the world community must centralize the power and limit its use to specific instances. In a world where the furthest person is only micro-seconds away so far as communication technology is concerned, intellectual freedom is not a privilege but a necessity.

Censorship is belief that one's obscenities must be the obscenity of all. The voluntary censor who enters the library and demands the removal of a book is trying to force the obscenity of one person onto all the others. So long as volition operates, then there is no need for censorship. To the extent that volition becomes inoperative, then some control of the channel of communication is necessary, but this need not be censorship. In this view Singapore is exercising its selectivity rather than censoring material, and when the people of Singapore decide that they do not wish to employ police time in the pursuit of pornography, then the law can be changed. There will be very little effect on the public one way or the other, because pornography is the most self-limiting of all literary forms and the swiftest in reaching satiation on the part of viewers when pictorial. Erotica to the extent that it explores the human condition factually and entertainingly is enduring. Rabelais made a good story of his erotic masterpiece, and Boccaccio offered entertainment even in passages that were once left in Old Italian. Censorship cannot define the obscene in terms that everyone can accept, because it is a matter of taste. The Marquis de Sade's characters eat excrement with the joyful cries of delight or murmurs of appreciation one would expect from gourmets. They endangered their health, but so does a person who jogs along a highway taking deep breaths.

IX.

MASQUERADE FOR WOLVES

Political Orthodoxy

When Richard Nixon defeated Jerry Voorhis, and became a representative, his campaign was a masterpiece of half-truths that his opponents still recount as evidence of unfitness. The voters in 1946 elected him, whether because of his campaign or despite it remains unknown. The Alger Hiss—Whitaker Chambers case involved him during his four years in the lower house, and he won his senate seat by asserting that Helen Gehagan Douglas had voted the same as Vito Marcantonio. He could prove this by showing the record of roll-call votes in the House of Representatives. Vito Marcantonio, who was indeed a leftist, if not a card-carrying Communist, voted with the majority very often, especially in considering the private bills that account for half of the roll-call votes.

His assertion that Mrs. Douglas was the dupe of the Communists was challenged repeatedly, but ineffectively, by her campaign managers. The United States wanted to believe that the use of atomic energy in warfare was the privileged technology of English-speaking nations. The danger of spies from the Soviet Union never seemed greater. Nixon provided the impetus for the campaigns of Senator Joseph McCarthy against Communists in the government.

Nixon was elected, and his opponents like to believe that he won because of his campaign strategy, composed of red-baiting and communist scare techniques in about equal proportions. It is entirely possible that the electorate thought that Nixon was a candidate of greater promise and elected him accordingly. If so, there was very little Mrs. Douglas could do. She was the star of the motion picture made from H. Rider Haggard's novel, *She*, but she was not a communist. Subsequent events proved that Nixon was indefatigable in his pursuit of office, sometimes despite his own aspirations, and his

273

last campaign proved to be his most effective. He scarcely campaigned at all in comparison with his unceasing previous efforts.

American history is filled with episodes that are similar. Richard Nixon went up and down the length of the United States campaigning vigorously for Dwight D. Eisenhower, his running mate, promising to get the communists and corrupt dealers out of government. *The New York Post* disclosed that as a Senator Richard Nixon had benefitted from a special fund organized by a group of businessmen to take care of their Senator's office expenses, which are much greater for a Californian than for a Virginian for reasons of distance alone. Richard Nixon faced a nationwide audience to account for this rather shady private fund. Television had entered politics at the time, and in his "Checkers" speech, he disclaimed any impropriety in the fund. Dwight Eisenhower promised that his aides would be honest men, "as clean as a hound's tooth," and the electorate voted overwhelmingly in favor of their war hero and his running mate.

James G. Blaine's disclosure that Grover Cleveland had sired an illegitimate child was greeted with a counter-disclosure of massive corruption on the part of Blaine and his fellows, and the Teapot Dome scandal did not prevent the election of Calvin Coolidge who had been Warren Harding's running mate. The American electorate is remarkably insensitive to evidence of political corruption. A persistent story that Warren Harding's grandfather was black was successfully suppressed, and the results of Woodrow Wilson's collapse on the stage of the Pueblo, Colorado, municipal auditorium were kept from the public as well, although there was no reason for not disclosing them.

Richard Nixon's two defeats, for the Presidency in 1960, and for the Governorship of California in 1962, seemed to end his career, but his campaign for the Presidency in 1968 discounted all the past and presented a "new Nixon." How new is now recorded in his visit to Peking. The People's Republic of China was at one time the arch-enemy of the Republican Party, though less so fo the United States government. Senator Knowland of California campaigned as vigorously against "Red China" as he ever did against any of his Democratic opponents. What is at work is the politics of change when the natural urge of everyone is to hold fast to what is comfortable and to reject any change that would mean a re-ordering of ideas and beliefs and lives.

This conservatism is explained in Alvin Toffler's book, *Future Shock*. All evidence predicts that the last quarter of the twentieth century will introduce such vast changes as will leave many people disoriented in their own culture, having lost their moorings as time sweeps us onward into a fully developed world community. Culture shock as a characteristic of individuals who find themselves disoriented in a foreign culture was identified among the many technicians and advisors sent by the United States first, and then by other countries, to assist the underprivileged in the world community to enjoy the benefits of modernization. Anyone who has lived in a foreign country can recall when the foreignness of the place no longer excited curiosity but became a threat to well-being.

A sense of emptiness and frustration quickly becomes a feeling like the anger of a wasp in a bottle. One seems to be separated by walls of glass from the external environment, imprisoned in his rage but incapable of being heard. The aggression gives way to a profound depression in which the only clear thought is the awareness of the futility of one's efforts. One is deserted and rejected by the entire world, and the sole remaining hope is an end to the tour of duty or tranquilization through quantities of alcohol. One good reason to have technical advisors accompanied by wife and family is that bodily contact reduces the anguish, and the comfortable excitement of sexual intercourse can make the culture seem almost friendly again.

The more widely one travels, the less the shock, and the more readily one accepts and deals with the phenomenon on a rational basis, the shorter the duration of the shock. It is still likely to occur, and in the days of jet travel may be accompanied by the disturbance of the circadian rhythm that governs our physical processes, so that one seems to be suffering from a disorientation not only in space but also in time. The realization that this phenomenon is common and can be occasioned by any major disruption of the tranquil succession of days enables us to understand the anguish of an older generation as the young adults re-order the world in which they dwell. *Future Shock* has its concomitant in what might be called *moral shock*. It is this shock to the emotions and ideas that excites the censor in each of us. As we understand that we are pursuing the pleasure of sexual excitement in turning the pages of a pornographic work, we feel less moral shock, and finally none at all. In the couplet often quoted we finally embrace the vice. Sexual excitement is pleasurable, but the sexual appetite is jaded quite as readily as any other, and sexual satisfaction from an orgasm leaves us nothing to look forward to. Prostitutes hate to have orgasms because it makes their work harder. It is this characteristic that makes pornography self-limiting and inconsequential.

Moral shock also occurs when a hero is exposed as a human being. As culture broadens and science finds a better method of explaining the event world, we demand less of heroes, so that the humanity of a man may be his best feature. Religious leaders would find a medical description of the birth of Jesus displeasing in the extreme, and questions of his miraculous birth, as opposed to his miraculous conception, are raised among theologians who would like to believe that he "shot forth like a sunbeam." No stretching of the vagina, no flood of water, no blood, and especially no birth of the placenta. Folk literature is filled with stories of mythical figures in the throes of sexual intercourse, even when these figures are the modern equivalent of Mars and Venus, such as Queen Victoria telling Prince Albert as they make love that the pleasure is far too good for the common folk.

Public figures create their images with the assistance of public relations specialists, so that a politician may wish to project his wisdom, heterosexuality, and common touch. If a black man or a woman might never become President of the United States, granting no change of attitude on the part of the electorate, then a known homosexual has even less chance.

Anything that tends to destroy the image is censored. General MacArthur, when he had full power to command those who took his photograph, allowed pictures only of his better side. He exhibited it freely for those who could not readily locate it. It was the right profile view that tended to show strength of jaw, breadth of forehead, and clear-sightedness of vision. Adolf Hitler, who enjoyed the same privilege, reviewed all photographs and destroyed those that seemed like the allegorical painting with his "*fade et immonde visage*" as a French writer put it, transformed into the noble expression of a knight in armor. *The Great Dictator* was not only forbidden in Germany, any picture made by or including Charles Chaplin was also forbidden because of his having insulted the Reichs Chancellor. President Franklin Roosevelt prohibited pictures of himself in a wheel chair, although there are many of him seated in a car.

Fact magazine, one of the many ventures of Ralph Ginzburg, went out of existence when Senator Goldwater sued because of an issue that reprinted the opinions of psychiatrists stating that he was not mentally fit to be President. This was libel, according to the judgement, and the periodical had struck below the belt. The electorate voted for President Johnson in large numbers, but it is highly doubtful that voters were influenced so much by the issue of *Fact* as might be supposed. All evidence shows that such material does not form public opinion, it solidifies it. No amount of preachment can make a man change his mind, least of all if it is the utterance of a stranger in a strange place. Printed works have even less appeal. The pastor of a church is believed because he says in private what he preaches in public. He loses his congregation if his private utterances, or actions, do not confirm what his sermons announce or explain.

Image-making often requires that the individual who is projecting the image convey sincerity, sensitivity, and genius. The image gives this appearance, and a demonstration of human emotion may destroy the image entirely. Senator Edmund Muskie lost his following when his emotions got the better of his good judgement and he wept in public. The electorate does not want a crying man to be President. Governor Thomas E. Dewey was advised in his campaign of 1948 to speak in broad generalities that would not lose him voters already convinced that he should be elected. His vapid speeches bored everyone out of his wits who was not already a part of the campaign, and the willingness of President Truman to take to the small towns and byways and "give them hell" probably won the election for him. Governor Dewey was a shrewd and highly competent administrator who looked, according to Tallulah Bankhead, like the little bridegroom figure on top of a wedding cake. He sounded like it and his speeches are remarkable only for their lack of content.

"Beware of false prophets," Jesus warns, and for much of the history of the communications revolution, the governments of the world were preoccupied with political censorship. Freedom of the press and freedom of speech came to most of Western Europe only during the revolutions of 1848 and were not adopted until the post-Hitler governments in Germany and in Austria, although there were interludes of free communication from time to time in both these countries. The secret police of Russia was unable to prevent the Marxist-Socialist underground from publishing newspapers, and during the second World War, underground newspapers were printed in almost all of the countries occupied by the Germans. Freedom of the press has the advantage of bringing the critics of a regime into the open. Criticism of the government is a way of life in almost all the English-speaking countries, and the critics are effective to the extent that the electorate has decided to seek confirmation of attitudes already assumed. Suppression of the press is effective, as in Czechoslovakia in 1968 by the Russian armed forces, only for the public distribution of material, but private or 'self-publishing' literature may still exist, as seen in the closet literature of homosexuality.

An attempt at neutrality in the United States in the first years of the first World War required that publications and newsreels show no favoritism toward one side or the other. Today television news programs have the same requirement forced upon them by the government using the threat of a suspension of franchise. Some attempt at distinguishing between news and commentary is made, although it is impossible in human languages to remove all evidence of bias. In the United States, the Federal Communications Commission exercises considerable authority because it may refuse to renew the license of a radio or television station. The legal system of the United States provides for review of decisions made by federal organizations, but this may be a very expensive procedure. Political censorship in the United States has usually been combined with suppression of 'obscenity,' and this has included the performances of Lenny Bruce whose irreverent style of comedy and social commentary utilized a vocabulary that included taboo words. Political censorship has attempted ostensibly to protect religious or minority groups. Efforts to diminish anti-semitism by refusing air time to known bigots have been somewhat successful, and the arbiters of taste have made such words as 'kike' and 'nigger' virtually taboo.

The local public library is even more open to the pressure of social groups wishing to prevent circulation of material that is unfavorable to one of their leaders or to their philosophy. School libraries are especially subject to censorship of this kind, and every librarian must study the means that voluntary groups have of forcing their opinions on everyone, whether by theft of books or by campaigns against the librarian. Much more attention is centered on the efforts to suppress the circulation of anti-Catholic works, such as Paul Blanshard's books on Catholic influence in American public life, than on the failure of the librarian to provide a collection that includes both the conservative and the liberal points of view. The publications of the Devin-Adair kind of conservative may be overlooked as the librarian follows the general preferences of the public at the time. Research libraries collect much more effectively because they tend to purchase anything that can be fitted into the collection on a particular subject.

Just as the moral censor wishes to prove his virtue by forbidding others to read works of which he does not approve, the political censor wishes to remove a danger to a public official that such works seem to represent. This can be done only if all the channels of communication are strictly controlled, preferably owned by the government. In recent times governmental secrecy and the right of the taxpayer to know where his money is going have come into direct conflict. The growing disillusionment of the public over the protracted war in Viet Nam has brought about the spectacle of the Attorney General of the United States attempting to stop publication of material in two of the leading newspapers of the country. *The Pentagon Papers* did not represent the first attempt of the United States authorities to practice *censura praevia*, the characteristic activity of authoritarian regimes. The Department of Justice prevented the publication of the original Valachi papers and required the editor of them, Peter Maas, to write a volume based on the confession of Valachi omitting all those sections that disclosed the methods of the Federal Bureau of Investigation. A former CIA agent, Robert Marchetti, was prevented from publishing his memoirs on the basis that they would reveal secret facts that Marchetti had sworn not to make public. Early travellers to South Viet Nam, especially American government personnel, military and diplomatic, were required to sign an oath promising not to discuss what they had seen in Viet Nam.

Such acts protect corrupt officials as well as governmental secrets. Every organization claims the right to review what is written about it by its employees. After a man leaves the employment of a company, he may describe it in very unflattering terms. The Federal Bureau of Investigation under J. Edgar Hoover was especially sensitive to any kind of criticism. Attempts to suppress publication of unflattering stories were limited to non-public and extra-legal means, such as visitations by agents, letters to publishers, and even telephone calls made by the Director. *The FBI Story*, written by Don Whitehead, tells the officially approved story of the agency, and such books as *The FBI That Nobody Knows*, tells another. Agents were required to refer to Hoover as something a little less than deity and more than man. Public criticism of The Director was reason for instant dismissal.

Secrecy has always presented a problem both to the public and to the government. Electronic surveillance is claimed as a necessary tool of law-enforcement, and only very recently have domestic subversives been provided with the protection of a court order, secretly secured, before their living quarters, offices, and telephones may be monitored. The secret police of Imperial Russia, and of Imperial Austria, were always listening over someone's shoulder, but revolution could not be prevented. Modern methods are much more effective. The regime of General Ne Win of Burma has successfully stifled criticism by means not unlike those of the secret police of old. Anyone who criticizes the general publicly, even as a joke, is liable to be arrested and interrogated by the special police. The government has taken ownership of everything, including the newspapers and periodicals, the bookstores, the libraries, and schools, so that added to its control of radio, it has complete authority over all forms of communication except the private remarks of citizens in secret. Burma is a Marxist state, and at one time the government of the United States was in the anomalous position of fighting communist guerillas in Viet Nam and providing aid to the Marxist government of Burma. As the Viet Nam war became something more than a guerilla action, the United States government offered as the reason for its involvement the need to fight communism in Southeast Asia, which somehow was a military action in Viet Nam and a diplomatic maneuver of offering foreign aid to General Ne Win's government in Burma.

In countries accustomed to freedom of the press, the effort of the government to prevent publication is widely read as an indication that the government has something to hide. This is so often the case that it is not a bad hypothesis. Every government has much to hide, and almost all public officials wish to keep their image intact, even though apparent falsehoods are revealed everywhere, as in the claim that American troops are being withdrawn from the Viet Nam war when they are transferred from South Viet Nam and restationed in Thailand. The action taken to prevent publication of the Pentagon papers was seen as an admission that the United States government had been involved in the kind of misprision that wrecked its image as a peace-loving nation.

What has emerged from the relaxation of moral censorship is a concept of privacy that is gaining some stature in the courts as a right that is implied by the Fifth Amendment to the U.S. Constitution. Electronic surveillance could be used to enforce absolute obedience to the sex laws now found in most of the states, but the cost would be tremendous and the social value is entirely doubtful. A public official who requires the populace to love him and punishes those who give evidence that they do not, like Stalin, may utilize all the equipment that electronic technology has invented to secure evidence of affection, and disaffection, but he cannot control what takes place in the minds of the populace. Freedom of press and speech is the most effective social release that a government can have, and the tide of public opinion can be stayed for a time, but it cannot be turned except by face to face confrontation. As methods of communication have grown less expensive, means of controlling them have increased in over-all cost because the widespread communication of forbidden ideas requires little equipment and no great investment of time and money. Underground newspapers have sprung up all around the country as the regular newspapers have sought to prevent the expression of ideas that seem to be radical and reflect something other than the canons of popular opinion.

Some of these newspapers are attacked as obscene and dragged· into the courts in an effort to suppress them. Abbie Hoffman's book, entitled *Steal This Book*, was published at the expense of the author and when already in print distributed by Grove Press. All over the country, voluntary censorship groups are trying to get the public library to stop putting the book on the shelf, if it can be found there. Jerry Rubin's book, *Do It*, is also addressed to the young revolutionaries of our time, but it is an easier target because he uses the liberated speech of the younger generation with greater effect. *The Berkeley Barb*, one of the first underground newspapers, was purchased by the Richmond, California, library much to the horror of one member of the community. A lengthy, and successful, campaign was waged against the librarian, John Forsman, so that the library would not tend to support what was considered an obscene and dangerous publication. We can assume that wherever there is a group enjoying an elitist status and special privilege, there is a center of conservatism that is endangered whenever it discovers an open challenge to the authority and status of the group. A deep conviction of infallibility helps motivate most censorship attempts.

An interesting question would be how many libraries subscribe to *Screw*, the most important of the newspapers that combine a highly liberated attitude toward sex with considerable social comment. *Screw* has already had its days in court, ordered not to be the means by which people can solicit the public to commit illicit acts. Sangamon University in Springfield, Illinois, has a library so fitted to the needs of its community that it includes *Screw*, despite some gulping and shrugging on the part of the more conservative faculty members. The students think it only an indication that the library is fulfilling its function in providing them with intellectual resources. It would be a remarkable anomaly if the University, devoted to a search for fact and a dedication to the advance of knowledge, should exclude an influential part of the communication process from its library. The National Library of Denmark, serving also as University library, has a large, ignored collection of Danish pornography.

It is unethical for a librarian to attempt to make the collection express his own convictions, and it is unethical as well for him to provide any special person with the right of censorship over the collection. The librarian must serve the entire community even though a portion of it may have hysterical objections. In an academic setting, the principal group of users is the student body. If the university exists only to set forth and elaborate a particular religious or political view of the world, then the librarian must follow the prescription for the collection given him. The student who enrolls in the university knows that he is obtaining an education of a particular kind, and the librarian who accepts employment must be willing to carry out the policy of the university authorities. A secular university, however, is dedicated not to any particular philosophy or religion, and its liberality is likely to be offensive to everyone because it represents no one. Only a foolish person would invade the university library and demand that certain books be removed from the shelf. Not even the Nazi regime in Germany nor the Stalin regime in Russia attempted anything like this, because censorship strikes at the well-spring of knowledge. Scientists have a corresponding ethical obligation to allow the expression of opinion. Science cannot offer proof of anything, it can only limit alternatives.

History has suffered greatly from every destruction of records. The reason may be purposeful obliteration, as in the case of Mexican pre-Columbian writings destroyed by the priests who brought their only true religion to the Aztecs, often with the auto-da-fe as the final method of convincing the populace of the verity of the only true religion. The destruction may be accidental, as in the fire that consumed the Alexandrine library. Chinese history had to survive the destruction of the first Chin Emperor, Shih Huang-Ti, who ordered the destruction of all written records in 213 B. C. If man had an infallible means of predicting his future, than a censor could employ this to destroy whatever was worthless. But the falsity of prophets is known only from the results of their prophesy. A fig tree does not produce thistles. The record of man's past is a prologue that introduces a drama the outcome of which leaves us in doubt. The course of increased knowledge has enabled us to make better judgements about our fellows, expecting that the hero must have a backside, and every human system be somewhat in error. Political orthodoxy is an impossibility unless the growth of knowledge is stopped at its source.

Scientific Orthodoxy

The Stalin regime suppressed any work on heredity that differed from the statements by Trofim Lysenko that renewed Lamarck's contention of environmental influences transmitted to subsequent generations genetically. For twenty-five years Lysenko was the director of the Institute of Genetics, and his ideas constituted a scientific orthodoxy that Russian biologists were required to support, despite the orthodox view elsewhere. Until denounced and replaced by the Kosygin regime in 1965, Lysenko was the only source of genetic truth in Russia. This story is often told by American scientists who wish to demonstrate that scientific fact is not a matter of public support or governmental approval. However, the United States can offer a demonstration of scientific orthodoxy almost as blatant as the Russian model.

In April, 1940, while working on a book that would suggest Akhnaton and Oedipus as identical figures, the real Pharaoh having given rise to the Greek mythological king, Immanuel Velikovsky wondered if the Israelites' Exodus from Egypt could be explained as a great natural catastrophe. This intellectual puzzle remained as private entertainment until Velikovsky noticed that the miracle of the sun 'standing still' in the book of *Joshua* in the Bible is described as having been preceded by what can only have been a shower of meteorites. He began to collate evidence from many widespread sources, utilizing the libraries of the United States where he had resided since leaving Palestine just before the second World War broke out. He completed his manuscript and gave it to Harlow Shapley, the most important astronomer in the United States. Dr. Shapley was very

busy and gave it to several of his colleagues to read, including Horace
Kallen, who had already acclaimed Velikovsky's breadth of research
and independence of speculation, very valuable characteristics of a
scientist. Kallen recommended the book to Shapley who refused to
read it on the basis that its sensational claims were "pretty obviously
based on incompetent data." Velikovsky wished that certain spectro-
scopic analyses be made to test some of his hypotheses. He was
directed to ask Walter Adams of the Mt. Wilson Observatory or
Rupert Wildt of the McCormick Observatory. Eight publishers rejected the manuscript, probably because of its footnotes, and then
Macmillan accepted the manuscript with the payment of a small
advance on royalties. The manuscript was read by several different
scientists, including Gordon Atwater, then Curator of the Hayden
Planetarium. Horace Kallen, among others, found the work exciting.
"If his [Velikovsky's] theory should prove valid, not only astronomy but history and a good many of the anthropological and social
sciences would need to be reconsidered." Eric Larrabee was com-
missioned to summarize the book, and in January, 1950, *Harper's*
magazine published the first information on Velikovsky's work. It
caught the imagination of the public, although Shapley had written
Macmillan on January 18, expressing his relief that a publishing
company famous for its scientific books was *not* going to publish
Velikovsky's book. James Putnam, the Senior Editor, replied that
Macmillan was not going to publish *Worlds in Collision* as a scientific
text but as the statement of a theory that scholars should know
about. Shapley thought otherwise.

As everyone in Academe knows, there is nothing stronger than the
old-boy circuit. Friend and classmate talk to each other and compose
fixed positions that assure one man of a job and another of failure,
that bring one idea into widespread discussion and sentence another
to obscurity. The old-boy circuit has always operated, not as a privilege of astronomers, or of scientists, but as an example of the elitist
classes in American academic life. While Macmillan was going ahead

with publication, Shapley plugged into the circuit, and his friends responded immediately. *Science News Letter* published a report of Shapley on behalf of fellow astronomers that Velikovsky had written "rubbish and nonsense." If so, he wrote it remarkably well and his sources are as close to unimpeachable as can be demanded of anyone. He might have used the original source material, rather than translations, but no one could expect a man, however learned, to know Chinese, Egyptian hieroglyphics, and ancient Mexican languages. Cecilia Paine-Gaposchkin, a member of Shapley's staff, wrote a rebuttal in advance of having read the book. This was published in *The Reporter*. If academic blame must be assigned here, Mrs. Gaposchkin committed a major sin so far as librarians are concerned.

Shapley's old-boy circuit had faulty connections, one of whom was Ted Thackrey, of *The New York Post* and then editor of the New York *Compass*. He was startled by the emotionalism of Shapley's attack on Velikovsky, personally as well as for his ideas. But George Brett of Macmillan was filled with doubts even though the book became a bestseller almost as soon as published. When Shapley and Whipple, among many of their friends, began to boycott Macmillan salesmen and threaten never to purchase any of the textbooks published by the firm, James Putnam, who had worked for Macmillan for twenty-five years, was fired, as was Gordon Atwater from his position as Curator of the Hayden Planetarium. Doubleday took over the publication of the book, because the firm did not publish textbooks and was not vulnerable to the retaliation offered by the astronomical establishment. Some librarians gave the book the same treatment accorded science fiction, and not a few refused to buy it on the grounds that it was trash.

Five years later a companion volume, *Earth in Upheaval*, was published, confirming with geological and paleontological evidence what the massive research of ancient texts had unearthed. As the exploration of space became a reality rather than an aspiration, Velikovsky's hypotheses were not refuted. Almost all the others were. Every cosmological and astronomical theory regarding the origin of the earth and the solar system had to undergo major revision when it was not altogether reduced to unconfirmed imaginings and discarded, and this included Shapley's own work. A man who was considered the antithesis of the dedicated scientist was revealed as one of the most important scholars of our period, and to the glee of Yale men and us alumni of Columbia, Harvard was proved once more not to have a privileged claim on all fact and verity. Shapley's activities wreck a career that is otherwise an example of dignity and devotion, and he should not be judged by his hysteria alone. Tough as it is to swallow, Velikovsky's cataclysmic theory of the solar system and its evolution is about the best we can entertain for the present.

Significantly, the restitution of Velikovsky's reputation began with students who wished to hear his theories, even if they might be wrong. The best available report on the whole affair is to be found in a student publication, *Pensee*, offered by the Student Academic Freedom Forum in Portland, Oregon. If the students of our universities are capable of withstanding the pressures of the old-boy circuit when they attempt to produce scientific stagnation, we need not worry about the advance of knowledge.

While members of Shapley's old-boy circuit were boycotting Macmillan's salesmen, the unlikely possibility that Velikovsky was correct in his powerful speculations and hypotheses ripped through the scientific and philosophical world. Bertrand Russell published an important essay advising a state of suspended judgement regarding the great questions of science and the unproven hypotheses of our time. Unproven in the sense of untested, because a test does not yield proof, it only fails to disprove and tends to support a hypothesis. As predictions made by Velikovsky have been investigated and shown to be true, he has not been acclaimed one of the greatest scientists of his time. Borrowing from his discredited work became the favorite activity of some scientists, because new careers were available in some of the suggestions he made for investigation. A major revision of our ideas of the history of the world was overdue in any case.

"All fruitful ideas have been conceived in the minds of the non-conformists, for whom the known was still the unknown, and who often went back to begin where others passed by, sure of their way. The truth of today was the heresy of yesterday." Velikovsky is only reiterating what scientists have always said, but he followed his own advice. Among the complaints against Velikovsky is that he challenged the celestial mechanics of Newton, the evolutionary theory of Darwin, and it was concluded that Velikovsky was therefore challenging reason itself. But Newton was a man like any other, and Darwin was not provided with divine intuition. In their times, they faced criticism as fierce. The warfare between science and religion during the nineteenth century was waged over Darwin's concept of unlimited time and changes in genes resulting from the competition of the species. Cataclysms and catastrophes cast doubt on his neat ordering of the events of time. An orderly universe was one of the favorite assumptions of scientists from the time that Laplace announced this idea to the French Academy. The year was 1773, and to the placid world of the eighteenth century, nothing could happen to change the stability of government, the correct and inviolate ordering of societies and sciences.

The idea of an orderly universe is essential if science is to hope to make accurate predictions. We can calculate the eclipses of sun and moon only because we believe that the orderly sequence of events that our mathematics predicts will take place as expected. It was thought that Laplace, with his concept of celestial mechanics, had explained all that was needed of the underlying principle of the universe, and Newton's mathematics could account for all. Newton did not attempt to include anything but gravitation in his concepts, nor did Laplace suppose that meteorites fell from the heavens. A world visited by matter from outside its atmosphere is not as orderly as one would wish.

In reading nineteenth century science, the underlying assumptions must figure into an evaluation of the validity of theories offered. Theory in the nineteenth century was a composite of fact and hypothesis meant as an explanation before the last details are known. Electromagnetism was thought to be a characteristic of the earth, and the discoveries of Marconi were essential before the electromagnetic character of the solar system was understood, and beyond the solar system, the electromagnetic character of the universe. Even Cecilia Paine-Gaposchkin, whose rebuttal of *Worlds in Collision* in various articles continued, had to confess in the September, 1953 issue of *Scientific American*: "Ten years ago in our hypotheses of cosmic evolution we were thinking in terms of gravitation and light pressure . . .. Tomorrow we may contemplate a galaxy that is essentially a gravitating, turbulent electromagnet." This is just the assumption that Velikovsky made, against which a mighty attempt at censorship was launched.

Evolution was a most welcome substitute for religion, because agnostics and atheists could take comfort in the orderliness of a universe that might argue the existence of a divine being, or might not, but in any case made science the only valid source of prediction. Religion, based on revelation, was therefore discarded because its adherents asserted that the Bible as the Word of God could not be in error and when Genesis said six days, it meant six days. Only a little thought would have revealed the inherent contradiction in the statement. The word day must be used figuratively, because if a day is the rotation of the earth on its axis, from point of origin back to point of origin, then there being no earth, there could have been no day. An omnipotent god was in the embarrassing position of being bound by earthly time before he created it. If cataclysms can occur, then a person who can read the tarot cards or a crystal ball is about as good at predicting as the scientist. The news that a pair of giant star clusters had collided behind the constellation Cygnus and were emitting radio signals like cries of distress failed to warn the Harvard astronomers that such things might occur, and if in one galaxy then the possibility was universal. By 1952, the titanic collision of the galaxies had been verified.

It has always been the dream of scientists that the last fact would become known and the details could be filled in by patient doctoral students, working out tables with mathematical computations in order to earn their degrees. But such an assumption requires that we repose great faith in all our tools of communication, and the whole course of science has been a process of proving that language is very faulty as a medium of scientific communications, that mathematics is at best shaky, and that every logical system so far devised is capable of producing a contradiction that cannot be resolved with logic. As facts are known, theories must change, and the originator becomes a historical figure not a prophet for all times. It is much safer to repose faith in human ignorance than in human knowledge.

The most profound argument that can be raised against censors of all kinds is that the present state of human ignorance requires that everyone have a chance to communicate regardless of present canons of taste and methods of proof. Psychiatrists reacted almost as hysterically as the Harvard astronomers when L. Ron Hubbard's book *Dianetics* was published. The hydrogen bomb was tested in the Bikini Atoll at about the same time, and a short time later the Montgomery, Alabama, non-violent revolt against racial discrimination began. The violence erupted later, especially when Martin Luther King was assassinated in Memphis, Tennessee. No attempt was made to censor L. Ron Hubbard and the development of his science became, finally, a religion, Scientology.

The contention between the people who believe that some, if not all, unidentified flying objects are visitors from extra-terrestrial regions of which we know nothing saw a growing literature, at times disfigured by governmental restrictions on pilots who reported chasing and failing to catch what seemed to be flying saucers, and also being chased by such objects. An open investigation would have left the proponents without the argument that their opponents were seeking to prove something or were hiding scientifically valid proof. Claims that individuals had been inside the space vehicles were offered along with refutation of the argument that such things were known only in the present age, long after Orville and Wilbur Wright had proved that Simon Newcomb's mathematical calculation of the impossibility of heavier than air flight was good mathematics but poor prophesy. Pictures were uncovered of medieval towns turned out to view a flying saucer, or possibly a flying trencher.

Science was being challenged as never before, but it was making more progress than ever before. Whole divisions of science underwent major revision, and the prospect of outdated material was matched for the librarian by floods of new material. The information explosion was underway. So long as the publication goes unhampered, we reduce the extent and danger of human ignorance. One of the most threatening events in modern American life occurred at the time when Velikovsky shared the disrepute of L. Ron Hubbard. Academic freedom was at its low point because certain professors were labelled "controversial" and fired. Usually the reason announced was political unorthodoxy, such as communist affiliation or sympathy as detected by associations to which the man (or woman) belonged. If all the professors of the association were fired, there might be less reason for supposing that scientific unorthodoxy was the real reason. Owen Lattimore underwent an *Ordeal by Slander* at the hands of Senator McCarthy who could not have had less interest in Lattimore as a scholar. McCarthy needed a victim and Lattimore was handy. He had written a book, which even Job noticed was a good tool to use against an enemy, and he was called to account for his unorthodoxy before the United States Senate, never one of the centers of scholarship.

The fear of being labelled "controversial" is one of the most effective means of censorship known. Velikovsky urging the students at Princeton to dare was predicting the modern student, who seeing the state of present society is much displeased, thank God. Where controversy is not welcomed, stagnation results. The orthodoxies derived from human sources are always fallible. Whatever the reason for an entrenched position, whether vested interest or personal pride, only the open discussion provided by controversy and inspired by it can bring us closer to what the facts are. In order to understand how the universities got themselves into a mire of privilege to such an extent that student rebellion was needed to spark a reform, we need only follow the course of a developing scientific discovery. Velikovsky's efforts would serve as one starting point, but another quite as readily at hand is the debate concerning vitamin therapy. A very valuable book is Roger J. Williams' *Nutrition Against Disease*, in which the hostility of organized medicine in the United States to nutrition therapy is carefully explained. In defense of the many physicians who are dedicated only to curing the ailments of their patients, we trace this hostility to sources other than vested interest. A part is the nature of scientific publications.

Williams cites hundreds of articles in a far-reaching assortment of scientific journals, along with a few popular accounts. This massive amount of literature cited is only a portion of the literature investigated. The average scientist working in the field of nutrition must cover literally l. undreds of publications if he hopes to keep abreast of developments in his field. Usually this is impossible, and he does well to pursue investigation in the limited confines of his special interest. If he is investigating, for instance, vitamin C and its relationship to synovial tissues, a fairly broad field, he may have to keep abreast of publications in a huge assortment of journals. Most scientists cannot devote such time as they can spare away from their laboratories to perusing journals. They rely on personal exchanges with other scientists. If they are fortunate enough to be situated where there is an exceptionally good library with an exceptionally hard-working librarian in charge who will screen the publications, they will enjoy a current-awareness service that brings to their attention the crucial articles of interest to them. Even so, the development of the literature lags behind the level of investigation, so that a journal is usually at least a year out of date and a textbook about six years at the time when a new edition is issued, if it is not delayed considerably.

Medical schools are now so crowded both with students and with material to be learned that the formulation of medical curricula has become a major worry of the profession. While granting that their students do not get the courses in nutrition that they should have, professors of medicine can find no room left in the curriculum that will provide for the amount that could be learned. The better professors in medical schools offer inspiration to continue as scientists and as healers. A true evaluation of vitamin therapy must await lengthy experiments that, following the general pattern of experimentation, are ninety percent unsuccessful, even when correctly designed. Not all vitamins can be purchased without a prescription—Vitamin K is the notable exception—but many can, and Americans are always dosing themselves with something, so that the medical profession prefers to await further developments rather than rush in while the matter is subject to hot controversy. At some time in the future, when biochemists have more reliable information, the medical profession will have to put vitamin therapy into the curriculum and make human nutrition as significant a part of medical education as animal nutrition is in agricultural colleges. However, money is involved with animal nutrition and not with human nutrition so far as the medical profession is concerned.

Money is heavily involved in the drug industry, and despite the defense of the dedicated physician there is no avoiding the fact that vast sums are spent on cough drops, aspirin, and an immense amount of febrifuges, laxatives, and tranquilizers. "The body at best is a bundle of aches," as Edna St. Vincent Millay puts it, and the average person dedicates a good portion of his income to an attempt to minimize if not cure the aches. A cheap vitamin like C, for instance, which can be purchased without a prescription, is hard news to the industry that makes special compounds guaranteed to alleviate the symptoms of a cold. If, as Linus Pauling shows, vitamin C is a preventative and the need for the vitamin varies widely from individual to individual, then the drug industry has received a major setback, and one that manufacturers would be willing to fight, employing physicians who can support their claims with the authority of a medical degree if not the exact scientific detail needed.

The Federal Food and Drug Administration enters into the picture, and some venality can be supposed in the handling of various drugs, especially thalidomide. One of the most curious but effective instances of censorship arises from the Food and Drug Administration which can prevent the publication of works that advertise a device proven to be ineffective if not fraudulent. This power was employed against Wilhelm Reich, who had nothing on his side. A former communist in Germany, a psychoanalyst, and a proponent of sexual activity as a means of psychotherapy, Reich thought he had discovered a vital force, orgone energy, that flowed through the atmosphere. He developed orgone energy boxes and some of his writings support this theoretical approach to mental health by means of simply constructed devices. It was never shown that the theory was erroneous; there may well be a vital force of which we know nothing, nor was it shown that Reich made the purchase of his orgone boxes an essential element in the treatment. He scarcely even sold them. However, the evidence was sufficient for Reich to be sentenced to a federal prison on the basis that he refused to cease his scientific publication and was thereby in contempt of court. His books were seized and burned in a display of what appears to be medieval religiosity in the service of science.

Dianetics was a best-seller and though widely condemned by psychiatrists, a whole school of therapy was devised on the basis of its suppositions and rather loose-jointed hypotheses. Hubbard often uses the expression, "this will be proved later," thereby making the whole system suspect. Scientific nicety would have him test his idea and reluctantly adopt it pending better tests. Orgasm therapy, however, has since proven quite accurate and many of Reich's dangerous and supposedly fraudulent ideas for which he died in prison, are now accepted by a school of psychiatry utilizing his approach.

Professional education is always suspect and usually lags behind the most recent advances in the sciences that support it. Library schools avoid any mention of computers when there is no professor available who can understand the literature of information science, and the profession was most reluctant to speculate about the effect that computers would have on libraries and on the communication industry. Scientific heresies, whatever the field, are never welcome among those who lay claim to an orthodoxy. Pettenkorf devoted his life to a theory of the origin of cholera and could not be expected to welcome the experimentation of Robert Koch. The germ theory of disease was suspect in its entirety, and Koch was simply a young upstart who was wrecking the results of thirty years of scholarship and scientific effort. That further scientific work proved Koch right and Pettenkorf wrong is just the hard luck that visits all of us, so far as our pride is concerned, but the good fortune of knowledge itself. The harm would have been in preventing Koch from publishing his scientific studies because they were in conflict with the accepted ideas of the time.

Certain facts are now apparent about the transmission of knowledge, the communication process so far as fact is concerned, that were not suspected when the great debate between the Darwinian theorists and the religious leaders took place. First, language is a faulty tool of communication, and the reality of language is not the sort that will support life or shelter a person from a storm. Second, information is anything that a human being uses as input in the development of his thinking, and any potential source of information must be kept and made accessible. Third, we have no way of knowing the extent of our ignorance. Consider knowledge a beam of light in the darkness; outlined in the light are all the things that we know that we know, and as the beam of light sweeps from one side to another, at its edges are all the things that we know that we do not know, but beyond in the infinite blackness are all the things that we do not know that we do not know. When mankind is able to descry where his ignorance lies, he will have become as nearly omniscient as he can hope for.

Orthodox History

In the year 213 B. C., the ninth of his reign, the first Chin Emperor Shih Huang-Ti ordered the destruction of all histories and commentaries on them, all the works of Confucianism and Moism, and he forced the acquiescence of scholars by threatening condign punishment of those who did not submit. Several were put to death, and the book burning effectively ruined the history of China. Confucianism survived, because of the custom of having a student memorize the entire work, and the beautiful couplets of Taoism as well. Much of Confucianism was reconstructed and many of the books survived, despite the efforts of the imperial police. Official histories were written which recorded the glories of the Chin Dynasty, even though its beginning had marked the violent end of the Chou period. Shih was a great authoritarian, and the works of Confucius deal with the relationships of human beings: the ruler with the ruled, the father with his sons, the master with servants, relationships among brothers and between men and women. When Confucius was asked what he thought of the principle of returning good for evil, he replied, "What is good? What is evil? Better to return justice for injustice." Such a philosophy would displease a tyrant.

To lapse into autobiography again, I was the beneficiary of a remarkable history course. The period was from the Renaissance to the second World War. Each student was required to know two languages besides English. Some of us had French and Spanish, others

Italian and German, and still others French and German. Everyone who knew Spanish knew Italian as well, or practically so. We read and reported on the major events of history, but always from the wrong side. The Italian accounts of the Reformation differ so greatly from German that only the names and dates seem the same. The Spanish Armada seen in Spanish accounts seems to have been a different fleet from what the English fought off. One of the most interesting is the report of French journalists on the American Civil War. They were appalled at the carnage and could never understand why such small differences should occasion a desire for secession and a willingness to fight to the death over it.

Any reference librarian will inform a reader that differences exist in almost every fact to be found. History is a great deal like mensuration, we approximate but never reach accuracy. These details are frequently used to degrade a historical account that is objectionable to the critic more because of the opinion of the historian than because of small differences of fact. Histories usually have an object other than the reportage of fact, and it is this that creates the bias and excites the critics. A good history seeks to disprove a hypothesis, but histories have often been written to prove a hypothesis, usually that the country is glorified and its honor increased.

The assassination of President Kennedy, then of his brother Senator Kennedy, and of Martin Luther King has become so mysterious a matter because of governmental secrecy, suppression, and censorship, that the historian of the next century would be quite justified in hypothesizing Department of Justice involvement in all three assassinations as part of an official conspiracy. The gadfly (and best source for our future historian) would be Harold Weisberg among whose books on these assassinations is *Frame-Up* devoted to the James Earl Ray case. The historian of the future might outline his history this way:

"On a hot night in the city of Athens, Georgia, a group of right-wing extremists meet to discuss the deterioration of the traditional South. Among the members is an agent of the Federal Bureau of

Investigation. He advises them that there is a way to act, that the Director is not sympathetic to the pro-communist pinkoes that make up the civil rights movement. A debate on who is the most important man to remove from public life reveals that several are considered very dangerous: Martin Luther King, Malcolm X, and even the Senator from Massachusetts who is running for the Presidency. Plans are laid to kill civil rights leaders in the South, and the conspiracy discussed is temporarily shelved. With the election of President Kennedy by a very narrow margin, the conspiracy is revived. His vice president is a Southerner and could not fail to be sympathetic to the cause. Police connections throughout the South insure help with the assassinations. When President Kennedy orders an investigation of the bombing of a Birmingham church, the fully developed plot is ready.

"In order to preserve the most important part of the conspiracy, a fall guy must be found for each of the four principal assassinations: Medgar Evers, Malcolm X, and Martin Luther King, and the President of the United States. For this assassination a pro-communist has been found who will make an excellent dupe, a man who has been around New Orleans, is known to the police there, and who has the requisite lack of a strong emotional constitution, so that he would easily be hypnotized. The whole affair must seem to be a communist-Jewish plot. Attempts on the life of a noted right-wing general prove to Oswald that his friends are ready and willing to help him. He is told of arrangements for his escape after the assassination and the plan of the President's motorcade is given to him. It has been arranged to pass through Dealey Plaza where the Texas School Book Depository where Oswald works is located.

"At some point after the shooting, all telephone service will be interrupted, especially long-distance calls. Radio announcements over the police networks will get a patrolman to Oswald who will be given a plan of escape that will lead him into a police trap where he will be gunned down. But Oswald does not cooperate. He loiters at the entrance to the building and then quietly makes his escape. He plans to expose the entire conspiracy and hides in a theater where he cannot be killed. His arrest takes place as a tide of national emotion over the assassination reaches its height. A friend of the police is needed who will kill Oswald before his trial, lest he say anything that might expose the conspirators. A bar-owner who is relatively harmless and very unstable is selected. Primed with ideas of sparing the President's widow the necessity of appearing in court, Ruby shoots Oswald, as planned. Ruby is arrested and as nearly as possible kept from revealing how he developed the idea of shooting Oswald. Sentenced to death, he becomes insane and dies in prison.

"In reviewing the assassination, and planning the campaign of a true conservative, the conspirators see the many mistakes that were made, most of all in the openness with which everything was done. The police network has proven itself very effective and has not been used properly. Chance remarks considered dangerous require one killing after another, all made to look like accidents, but increasing the possibility of discovery. A propaganda campaign is mounted to assure that the commission appointed to establish guilt in the assassination of the President will leave off its investigation at the point where Oswald's actions become irrational, concluding that rationality must not be expected of a man who has committed so horrendous a civil crime.

"Malcolm X is gunned down without difficulty, and so is Medgar Evers. A fall guy is found for the next important assassination, that of Martin Luther King, reasonably considered the only man who can unite the black community. James Earl Ray is helped to escape from prison, is given money and is made totally subservient to friends who assure him that he may be called upon to perform a service, but even so he will be protected. Arranging the assassination is very difficult, but a means is found whereby Ray will be stationed in a boarding house across from a motel in Memphis, Tennessee, where the civil rights leader is expected to go in aid of striking black workers.

"While propaganda could be used in the assassination of the President it was highly dangerous in the case of Martin Luther King. The black community had erupted when King was killed, and worst of all, Robert Kennedy began to campaign for nomination of the Democratic Party. The conspirators also found that their arrangements for Ray, who could be trusted even less than Oswald, were now bringing focus on the police of three countries. The Canadian police, misunderstanding a suggestion, discovered Ray and traced him to England. An attempt to get him to safety having failed, the man was arrested and subsequently extradited to the United States. An arrangement was made to have him plead guilty, which he would find assured him of a life sentence, or less, and ultimate freedom after the furore had died down. Robert Kennedy, as planned, was assassinated by an Arab immigrant, and the conspirators settled back to the denial of evidence and censorship and suppression of works that might reveal the facts."

Historians ordinarily make up with reasonable supposition what they cannot find precisely documented, labelling their suppositions carefully. From Weisberg's book, the record of the suppression of evidence, of censorship, is very clear. This is not Weisberg's supposition but is photostatic reproduction of actual documents. Weisberg's accounts of his difficulties with the Department of Justice, which refused him the records of a public trial in defiance of the law, make one of the most interesting accounts of official efforts at censorship.

At some time in the future, when the people involved are beyond the reach of lawsuits and prosecution, some of the facts of the assassinations will become known. Then in a kind of justice what is not evident will be supposed, and there is no way to make the assassination of Martin Luther King the work of one man, working all alone. There is even considerable doubt that he committed the crime, despite his plea of guilty. Significantly, Weisberg's book is published by Outerbridge and Dienstfrey of New York, with the original plates made from typescript. Weisberg rushed his book into print, and it makes fascinating reading for those who like to see the opposition have its say. In this case, the official reports are about as trustworthy as those regarding the Viet Nam war in the early stages of that disastrous adventure. The credibility gap remains between the official statements, evidence of suppression, and the combination of evidence and supposition that make up an opposing view.

When the supposition is confirmed, in the manner of the Velikovsky affair, not only the single piece of evidence but the whole theory tends to be confirmed. As Weisberg shows, official censorship will seem to aim at trifles, and the Freedom of Information Act which became law in 1967 is not included in official concepts of law and order. The Justice Department, quite obviously, is selective about the laws it wishes upheld, reserving some that must be followed by others but may be broken with impunity by officialdom. This is no different at all from the bank robber who stops his car at a red light on his way to commit a crime, nor from the police car that pulls into a no-parking space for the convenience, rather than necessity, of its passengers. Official censorship and suppression tend not to encourage law and order but to add to the disrespect for the law that is the most important influence in a lawless and disorderly society. A point often made in official propaganda issued by the Federal Bureau of Investigation is the lawfulness of its officers, and even clerks. In fact, there is evidence of widespread lawlessness used as shortcuts in the investigative procedures of FBI agents. This lawlessness is concealed, and much official censorship is aimed not at protecting national security but at concealing private misbehavior.

Weisberg recounts rather blandly how his telephone was tapped, even though he could not have qualified under any known rule for such activity. The Department of Justice has taken a very liberal attitude toward electronic surveillance for its purposes. When Weisberg decides that he will sue to obtain the public documents held by the Department of Justice, there is an almost immediate response from officials there, even though Weisberg was talking in private with his lawyer, a man named Fensterwald, whose office one assumes was bugged. In a murder case that draws great attention from the public, the right of privacy is violated widely. There is no way of redressing such violation.

One of the strangest cases in American legal history is recounted at length by James Kirkwood in his book *American Grotesque*. This is the story of the attempt to prove that Clay Shaw, a man altogether blameless theretofore, had in fact conspired with Lee Harvey Oswald to kill President Kennedy. Allegations of homosexuality made the trial a rich spectacle, and a great many people in the United States wanted to believe that President Kennedy's assassination was the result of a conspiracy. Despite a web of evidence, rather thin on the face of it, Shaw was acquitted only to be rearrested on charges of perjury and re-acquitted. It was his nemesis, District Attorney Jim Garrison, who fell afoul of the police and was subjected to the kind of hounding that seems an American custom. The crucial elements in the trial do nothing to reveal a conspiracy and the speculation continues.

Frame-up is a history of a trial as well, but there is little doubt that much has been suppressed that ought to have been made public, and *American Grotesque*, another account of a trial, shows that much was made public that ought to have been suppressed. The difference lies in a man's right to think his own thoughts, live his own life, and within the law take his place in society without the fear of discriminatory prosecution. Shaw denied ever having seen or talked with Lee Harvey Oswald. That made the prosecution's case very shaky because it could never be proved that Shaw was lying when he made this statement. Shaw had met President Kennedy and "believed in him." He did not want the President to die. The cross examination, supposed to disclose all manner of unpleasant things about Shaw took sixty-five minutes and dealt only with rather slight innuendoes that could not have affected the trial much even if they had not all been denied. This cross examination made the whole prosecution case seem as weak as it was subsequently proved to be. Jim Garrison was attacking the Warren Commission by means of Clay Shaw, a man whose prestige in the community should have offered better protection, and in a just society who should never have been brought up before any judge, whatever his prestige.

In periods of great disturbance, records are likely to vanish, and the work of the historian made especially difficult, if he aims for validity, and rather suppositious if he fills in with deduction what ought to be documented. Protecting the right of privacy of an individual ought to be the first concern of government, as in many cases it is, but during the McCarthy episode, the government began investigating supposed communists and it seemed that National Security had become a kind of national goal demanding the sacrifice of anybody who stood in the way of its accomplishment. Orwell's totally collectivized society in his novel *1984* shows history continually having to be rewritten as the official position shifts. Something like this always occurs when through consensus a government is thought to be above the constraints of justice, one of which must surely be the reliability of evidence.

During this period there emerged the picture of the conservative as a person who favored a strong government and stronger police, taking whatever steps are necessary to maintain an orderly society, with rather less law than is possible when the citizenry are reluctant to obey the laws they are given. Stronger police forces, better prisons, fiercer punishment have proven ineffective so often in the past that it is a strange example of preservation to find the whole system recommended again. The typical conservative in the United States favors capital punishment and opposes a relaxation of the rules regarding abortions. Killing a fetus is far more reprehensible than killing another adult human being. The conservative favors strict censorship and control of the media of communication while he opposes government intervention in 'free enterprise.' This is a catch-phrase to cover a kind of laissez-faire economics. The conservative almost rebels when civil rights are furthered by Supreme Court decisions, protecting racial equality and equality of the sexes, strict rules of evidence, and the separation of church and state. However, his protests are almost as loud when strict rules are enforced preventing the pollution of air and sky and prohibiting the use of dangerous chemicals.

His opposite is in almost an anomalous a position. He favors tight governmental control of business and industry, high taxes for revenues to be spent on a variety of social projects from education to rehabilitation. He favors very broad civil rights limiting the government in its dealings with citizens with very strict rules of evidence and prohibiting the government from interfering with communication media while providing a wide variety of educational programs on public broadcasting. He would invade privacy to protect the environment. He would censor programs that preach racial inequality. To both conservative and liberal, society is sick and needs the treatment that each would provide.

A librarian must keep the works produced by each group on the shelves and protect them from the depredation of users who represent one side or the other. The librarian has to assume a middle role, exercise suspended judgement, be totally neutral inside the library. Outside, he rather misses an understanding of his community if he does not participate. One librarian found that an unflattering biography of Mary Baker Eddy was so frequently stolen by Christian Scientists that he ordered the book by the case lot and simply replaced copies as they were stolen while trying to increase his security arrangements. It was rather sad to see dignified members of the public trying to spirit away the book when they would regard other kinds of theft as a disgusting form of misbehavior.

Each society has its heresies and its heretics, and the writing of history demands that each have an opportunity to have his say. The predictions of such men as Edgar Cayce, whose fifteen thousand 'readings' represent a most valuable form of documentation, are verifiable as time passes. Significantly, heresy has become much less a threat to the Roman Catholic Church after the Second Vatican Council. *Incrementum Doctrinum* implies that there is a search for truth in which all participate so that a knowledge of heresy becomes impossible if it stays this side of denying the essential dogma, of which there is very little. No Catholic, for instance, is required to believe in the miraculous deeds of the saints.

Moral censorship on the part of Catholics is more often determined by the society than it is by the Church. Masturbation in the Dutch catechism is not regarded as sexual sin so much as it is considered evidence that an individual has not attained sexual maturity and needs to learn how to share his sexual drive with a wife. Homosexuality is not considered the vile sin and utter abomination that a poor translation of St. Paul and Genesis would imply. The whole concept of homosexuality as a poorly understood human phenomenon is conveyed in remarks that indicate an awareness of modern psychology. The homosexual Catholic is advised to consult a psychiatrist and a spiritual advisor to discover how he can live with his sex drive and be a contributing member of his society.

Italy, Spain, and Ireland have strict moral censorship, arising not so much from Catholicism as from the traditions of censorship and modesty that have prevailed for centuries in those countries. Belgian, Dutch, and Danish Catholics are no less devout, but they are not endangered by the relative freedom from censorship in those countries, ranging from the utter liberality of the Danes to the rather more conservative attitude of the Belgians. The question seems to be whether the Church can accept the fact that it is a religion for adults of many traditions. There are very many catholic churches, some allied to the Holy See in Rome, some directly under its authorities, some heretical resulting from priests whose views were not accepted by the local bishop and who chose to leave the Church rather than follow them. In its re-awakening, the Catholic Church is getting close to the tolerance, patience, and acceptance of Hinduism and Buddhism. The whole idea of heresy may be lost along with such problems as simony in the years to come, even though the heretical group centers around a priest who preached that only Roman Catholics had any hope of going to heaven.

It is now apparent that man is reordering his concept of himself, that the communications revolution has forced upon us a new image of humankind, not the least like the image developed by nineteenth century science. In those days it seemed that the last problems of physics and biology had been solved. History as decided by Bishop Usher was untrue, of course, and it was not just exactly 4,956 years from the beginning of the universe to the date of Usher's calculations. History in the Darwinian view was a long, very slow, and completely orderly succession of subtle changes, so slight as to go unnoticed as the long millenia passed. The movements of the planets had been calculated and they followed the laws of gravity as determined by Newton and explained by his successors. The survival of the fittest accounted for the coiled-spring anatomy of the felines, and the comforting prospect of a succeeding billion years stretched before the imagination of scientists.

No wonder that Velikovsky was rejected when he first offered his hypotheses of a solar system designed by a succession of unpredictable cataclysms. Edgar Cayce's readings became almost as important as the lifelong efforts of the most exacting scientific genius. The old idea of an elitist society began to crack and fall apart. As scientific discoveries have given mankind more power to control his future, they have required understanding of human abilities and knowledge. The philosophy of science is now as important a study as the history of religions, and they are strangely similar. Granting absolute power to anyone would only provide for absolute corruption. Even if B. F. Skinner can assert that the future of society demands controls that are, as he puts it in the title of his book, *Beyond Freedom and Dignity*, his position as a Harvard man makes him suspect. Is he another Harlow Shapley decreeing scientific orthodoxy? No wide

ODOX HISTORY

movement to elect Skinner as the controller-designer of the new world has begun.

One of the most moving events in mankind's enlargement of his knowledge occurred when television pictures of the earth as seen from the moon were sent back to be spread throughout the world, instantly, and later in permanent form. Visit your local library and you will see the earth as God sees it, as the passengers on Unidentified Flying Objects see it, as Cayce saw it in his trances. It is

A pendent globe, hung on the reach of space,

A tiny jewel, glowing with time . . ..

We can understand why *Fate* magazine had a circulation of many tens of thousands, and would have more if it were better known, and why hundreds of books on astrology are available. Twenty years ago, it was exceedingly difficult to acquire a set of tarot cards, and today the local store, Sign of Aquarius, offers very many, of many different designs. When mankind faces a black future, prophecies abound. Rarely have so many prophets been so much in agreement as at the present time. The planet earth will undergo vast changes again causing widespread destruction. An effort was made to silence Cayce, efforts were made to prove his work rubbish and nonsense, but the method of judging any kind of prophet is by evidence that previous predictions have proven true. Einstein, one of our greatest, predicted the atomic age with a formula that proved true, just as his predictions about the nature of the universe are proving true. It is not surprising that Einstein and Velikovsky were friends; both had suffered at the hands of the scientific establishment at one time or another. Interest in Cayce has grown constantly, and the doubts that began in 1910 when stories of his abilities reached the newspapers have constantly diminished.

For one thing, although a very religious man, Cayce never forced his ideas on anyone. He had an interpretation of Christianity, but this was never a new church. He found the ideas of reincarnation developed during his trance states quite foreign to his beliefs and had to work hard to understand them. Reincarnation is the basis of both Hinduism and Buddhism, accounting for the way the soul struggles to perfect itself, and it serves admirably in lieu of external punishment and its alternate external bliss to warn a person that every obligation must be met in full. It is not, as some Catholic writers suppose, the reason that there is a lack of reverence for life in the Orient. Life is indeed revered, but the same human motivation that enabled the Christian nations to make war on each other, to permit widespread starvation, death by disease, and public executions, prevails in the Orient. Poorly developed social responsibility is not characteristic of the East any more than it is of the West.

There is no real warfare between science and religion, because even the greatest scientist has only faith to assure him that an experiment will produce the same results, time after time. There are always exceptions. We are reaching a period of understanding where we realize that science and religion conflict in the way that one hand conflicts with another. They can cooperate as well as conflict. With this knowledge, with a conviction that all men are brothers, there is every possible reason for so constituting the world community that war is impossible and that the advance of knowledge is a most important human goal. Knowledge is used in its widest sense, meaning all of man's artifacts and the universe in which we live.

This brings us to the last bit of dissection we need in order to establish the anatomy of censorship, even though we cannot be as fine and detailed as we would like. Every human being is constantly sorting among messages, rejecting some, accepting others. He censors for himself what he does not want to receive. He has no right to censor messages for other adults. Wrong ideas, foolish ideas, rubbish and nonsense, moral threats, and personal pollution all describe some of the greatest works of mankind. We can label, but we must never destroy. A relaxation of censorship where the right of privacy has full power to operate in accordance with volition on the part of the individual will not harm society. It will hasten an understanding of the world community and its members.

X.

INTELLECTUAL FREEDOM
AND THE WORLD COMMUNITY

Beyond Good and Evil

To assure yourself that you are a member of a world community, take a trip around the world. If you are an American, you will feel that you have never really left home when you return. During the course of the trip, especially in primitive areas, you may feel disoriented and confused, but whatever aggressiveness you feel will be directed at conditions rather than people. The Archie Bunker in all of us subsides to meaningless memories in the presence of children, and the urge to sustain, feed, and comfort that rises strongly in the presence of a child in need of help. The African baby becomes your own, as does the Korean, Singaporean, Indian, Iranian, Greek, Italian and Danish child.

Beyond the humanity common among all of us, there is the importation of American artifacts, methods, sciences, and ideals. Almost all of these are American because we of the United States developed them last. There are parks and libraries, universities and museums, schools and playgrounds, motion pictures in theatres and over television, and the music we listen to in the United States can be heard almost everywhere, whether it is the great outpouring of German composers or of American folk poets who, like the minstrels of old, sing their poems. The Viet Nam war has become an obscenity to many Americans because it is so foreign to the American ideal of a peaceful nation, advocating and propagating peace and plenty around the world. An age of isolationism is possible only in a country like Burma under General Ne Win. Foreign journalists are refused visas and the terrified public refrains from anything but gouging the tourists. Any traveller who returns to the "cleaner, greener land" finds that his old friends would endanger themselves by renewing acquaintance. Only those who travel under the aegis of the United Nations are free of suspicion. The press and radio are completely controlled as Burma attempts a kind of socialism that is strange to Russian as well as Chinese theorists.

How great the interchange has become can be reckoned only by comparing modern America with its earlier stages of development. Only a little over a century ago, Japan was even more firmly closed off from the world than Burma is today. Knowledge of its culture became generally known in the latter half of the nineteenth century where it first exerted strong influence on art. The rise of the Japanese militarists and subsequent defeat in the second World War hastened the era of close cooperation. The victors helped to rebuild the country they had tried to destroy, and we gained as much, or more, than we contributed, just as the Japanese recovered more than they lost excepting human lives from the sum. In the propaganda of World War II, the Japanese was a buck-toothed bespectacled little monster whose chief delight was in torturing Americans. How little convinced the public was can be ascertained by the behavior of American soldiers who made up the Army of Occupation. They found the Japanese women very attractive, and many interracial marriages resulted. The little buck-toothed villain was gone, nudged aside by the Red Chinese villain who tortured Americans in North Korean prison camps.

The Korean war marked one of the most important developments in world society. The United States did not go to war, not officially. The United Nations united for peace, as the Russian delegate walked out, and the war, although fought with American soldiers and American equipment, was conducted by the United Nations. At the time of the war, a visitor to the military graveyard in Pusan was not allowed to take his camera into the walled area because of a few graves in one corner where Russian pilots were buried. The world community did not want to hear that American and Russian pilots were conducting dogfights over the skies of North Korea.

Nor did the world community want to learn that the Secretary General of the United Nations was an important figure in a country that had become Marxist if not communist. U Thant was not welcome in Burma after the socialist experiment began, because he would unite the dissident elements who might then overturn Ne Win's government of the military and replace it with a new democracy. On the strength of his promising not to return to Burma, a large number of important political prisoners were released, including all those held in the jail in Insein, a suburb of Rangoon. U Law Yone, the editor of what had once been *The Nation*, went to meet U Nu who had been released from prison and allowed to leave the country. U Thant continued as Secretary General and the government of U Ne Win was as safe as any tyranny can be.

Tyrants die like any other human beings and the nature of a tyrant makes it impossible for him to pass his power to another tyrant. Just as he must exercise strict censorship in the hope that it will amount to thought control, he cannot allow an heir to gain sufficient power because the heir will dispose of the tyrant when he can. Tyrants have lost ground and are allowed in very few places. The last tyrant of a large country was Stalin, and he died and was degraded. His sins were recounted by the first successor who dared to expose what life was like under the authority of the man whose smallest whim was a matter of life and death to tens of thousands of people.

Not that there are no longer those who would like to be tyrants, who feel some kind of special ability to make decisions for everyone. The world is full of people who would like to do the thinking for others, who are denied their role in life if they cannot exercise thought control over the populace. Like Robespierre some love the concept of humanity but cannot accept the malodorous reality of mankind. The blade of the guillotine is a means of maintaining authority that could not be gained any other way. But Robespierre lost his power and his head. Others, like Adolf Hitler, believe that

they are the leaders of a chosen race who will bring about a millenium of superiority for their people and install a *Pax Germanica*, or
whatever. To question the right of the tyrant to accomplish his goals
and to doubt that his methods will succeed if the value of the goal is
accepted is to face the ultimate punishment. In the early days of
Hitler this was the sword and block, traditional in Germany. Later
when skilled headsmen were lacking, the guillotine was used. To such
tyrants, censorship is a vital necessity and the use of capital punishment to prevent fouling the propaganda lines is accepted by the
public that is either in accord or too passive to take those steps that
will end the reign of the tyrant.

The public exercises censorship by its attitude alone, and no superman is needed for the public to appoint and protect a guardian
of the public morals, such as Anthony Comstock, to ferret out material of which they disapprove. In Nazi Germany, during the period
when Hitler was undefeated, a chance remark might be reported
and the luckless person who offered the statement in the presence of
a virtuous Nazi might be subjected to the severe interrogation of
the Geheime Staats Polizei, the Gestapo of countless thrillers. The
attitude may be unquestioning and unquestioned, right because it
seems right, so that the thought police of Japan, the Kempetai, are
performing a public service. Mankind has always made his greatest
advances of knowledge by challenging his own axioms. Such prophets, however, have a difficult time in the comfortable periods when
all of society is armed against them. The wife of Sir Richard Burton,
Isabel Arundel Burton, a devout Catholic, put the unfinished manuscripts of his translations and books into a bonfire in order to save
her husband's reputation. She was in error in believing that it could
only survive the constraints of his own time.

Moral censorship, like political censorship, attempts to preserve a
fixed idea of society. To most heterosexual men the literature of
homosexuality is repugnant because of their attitude toward homosexuality. It always has a certain attraction, a kind of memory of

younger days, and if each man outlives a homosexual period when he hates girls, then a return to that period seems to re-install juvenility and its blunders. The homosexual has been persecuted because he represents a stereotype composed of one's own doubts about himself. The censor is never harmed by the works he censors, although it is his opinion that the average public will be harmed. He sees society as a group of faceless individuals who will be led to commit sex crimes by the sexual material he reviews and rejects. He has an enviable opinion of himself, for if he needs advice on some material, he can ask the help of a fellow superman. It is easiest to be a censor when the canons of public taste rule neatly between what is acceptable and what is not. As the canons become confused allowing one thing and prohibiting another, the work of the censor becomes more difficult.

When the Watch and Ward Society of Boston made the expression "banned in Boston" equivalent to a good review of a sexy book, the advertising that is accomplished along with censorship gave a value to some books that they would not otherwise have had. *Ulysses* by James Joyce so fascinated Americans who visited Paris that a Helen Hokinson cartoon has one of her plump ladies at a French bookstall asking, one imagines in her best highschool French, "Avez-vous *Ulysses*?" The relaxation of censorship so far as *Ulysses* is concerned marked a milestone in the history of moral censorship in the United States, and the movie made from the book went unharmed and untouched, beyond the reach of the censors because it was evidently for the educated public alone. Rembar believes that the cases involving *Lady Chatterley's Lover*, *Tropic of Cancer*, and *Memoirs of a Woman of Pleasure* mark the end of moral censorship in the United States. John Cleland's novel *Fanny Hill* as it is popularly known, has been so widely and severely censored, and so many men have served jail sentences for selling or possessing it, that the publication of the novel by a reputable American firm must be a benchmark in the beginning of moral, social, and political change. Permissiveness is the major mistake of an authoritarian and a permissive society is one that is bound to develop without his special help, therefore awry. The hope that something could be done about the pornography flooding the land was realized.

When the case of *Stanley versus Georgia* was decided in the United States Supreme Court, the right of the individual to possess pornography was equally the right to purchase it. There was some indication that not everybody was shocked by what some called obscenity. A famous blooper on television is recounted in the film *Out of the Blue* made by Kermit Schaefer who collects such mistakes. The night man on a television station, identified only as Channel Six, thinking that he was alone decided to look at some hardcore pornography using the station's equipment. He broadcast the films for all to see. Schaefer's production shows the films while the voices of callers are heard. The switchboard operator is unaware that the programming of Channel Six is out of the ordinary and only gradually catches on. One elderly female voice insists on knowing the name of the film, a sensuous male voice attempts to turn his praise of the programming into an obscene telephone call, a bartender calls to complain that he cannot close his bar because his customers won't leave so long as Channel Six shows the movies that were then on. A woman calls to compliment the station because her husband "sure got his natures" by watching the television. Two callers were incensed. One who identified himself as Father McManus protested that scenes of perversion, "fornification," and copulation were being sent over "God's airways." Another, a politician, promised that he would call the Federal Communications Commission and see to it that Channel Six lost its license. The switchboard operator finds that she is being victimized and calls the manager of the station who tries to believe that she is having delusions or is mistaken, but whatever, cannot be correct. Her story is literally incredible until he turns on his television set and sees that she is quite accurate in what she supposed. He advises her to tell no one. The station is unidentified in the film, and the newspaper

accounts blame a bored production man for the blooper. The pornography is not very good. One can always judge the reality by
the clarity with which erection, penetration, and ejaculation are depicted. This trio of sexual physiological processes constitutes the
ineluctable material of all pornography, but men are readily aroused
by just the suggestion that a sex act is taking place.

There is very little good pornography available, still, and most
of it is overpriced. Films are unedited, the sound track and the
local theatre's patched-in music sometimes conflict, and what little
story exists is lost in the scenes of sexuality that rapidly become
boring almost to the point of being unendurable. The sexual appetite
is as readily jaded as the appetite for food and it becomes educated
as well, so that pornography accepted despite its crudity is later
rejected, and the suggestivity of sex is more impressive than the
depiction. So far this hypothesis has been supported by the events of
the marketplace for such material.

Pornography cannot be identified by other means than those that
establish the material as formula-fiction, following a pre-set pattern
leading from shock to shock on the part of the reader. Its purpose is
sexual arousal while the purpose of erotica is explanation. The trend
is always away from the crudity of pornography toward the artistry
of erotica. This can be seen in the homosexual literature with its
easily defined types, closet literature meant to relieve the sexual
feelings of the creator, crude novels reaching finally the sensitive
interpretations of a major writer. As the novel comes closer to reality
and tells the story with more interesting content, it must leave the
purely graphic depiction of homosexual acts. The number of these
almost determines the quality of the fiction. There must be many if
the author does not wish to lose his reader, apparently, but the
difficulty of making each original and beautiful is usually too much
for all but the most skilled authors.

There is no question that pornography causes sexual excitement.
Men do get "their natures" from reading or viewing pornography.

There is no evidence that this causes any physical or emotional harm. Masturbation, which commonly follows the use of pornographic material, is now considered to be healthful rather than harmful, and ethological studies show that male creatures masturbate when deprived of another of the opposite sex but same species. Even that bastion of sexual puritanism, the Roman Catholic Church, is revising its attitudes toward homosexuality, masturbation, and heterosexual acts that are sexual but not copulative. In doing so, the Catholic Church is not attempting something new but returning to previous periods in its social leadership.

The communication revolution now enables an adult to be his own pornographer, and the government would have to engage in a massive system of espionage to prevent this. Governments should not be in the business of making moral decisions in any case. A government should be strictly limited to dispensing justice and protecting privacy. The history of western civilization may be summarized as a search for a supreme authority. First the Church and then Government has been tried and found wanting, for the supreme authority can only be found in the citizen himself, participating in the developing culture of a world community.

The censor has tried to suppress material that degrades an individual, especially a hero, but this has proved both unsuccessful and unnecessary. In a desperate attempt to protect his own fantasies, the censor prohibits the fantasies of others and even if the truth is told will prohibit that on the grounds that publicity will endanger public morals and the welfare of the government. But communication rarely creates opinion, it only confirms it, and public morals would not be harmed by pornographic materials so much as they are harmed by governmental secrecy meant to hide mistakes, protect the crime syndicate, or confirm a stereotype. When the motion picture industry, television, and the newspapers never showed a black individual in the role of anything but a servant, a stereotype remained fixed. Advertising companies rejected black faces because it was thought that the public would not accept a black person as one to formulate an opinion for him. Textbooks on American history regularly downplayed the role of the black community in the development of American culture, and the end result was a protest long overdue and still continuing.

We are able now to say that censorship indicates that there is something to hide, usually facts unpalatable to an elitist group. The superman who can do the censoring is always a representative of this group and acts on its behalf. None of the cruelties found in the literature of sadism are worse than those practiced in the name of religion, the government, or a privileged class.

Censorship is not something that must be learned. We are always busy censoring material for ourselves, and the canons of taste both in the choice and use of words as taboos arise from a complicated structure of sexual signalling. Pornography and erotica cannot be separated by means of the taboo words, as can be seen by the report of an experiment below. Nor can we ever make erotica unattractive. Using the right methods, as determined by prevalent canons of taste, erotica will always fascinate us because it depicts an experience of reality in an acceptable fashion. The ultimate protection for many people is to concede the right of choice to some superman who will determine what messages one can receive and the ones that must be rejected. The censor aims at the group that wishes to belong to an elitist organization that is considered above the constraints forced onto others. Censorship and a belief in it are a way not only of establishing one's own privacy but also of participating in a privileged society. To some, who cannot endure the loneliness of the mind, this is a vital necessity.

There is a need for bodily contact established early in life, and the users of pornography are generally those who have lost the right to this contact through some circumstance of life. It is not strange that the audience in a theatre showing heterosexual pornography is not made up of the dirty old man type at all, nor is it strange that the graffiti in the men's room may consist of offers of homosexual experience. Even the superman begets his children like the rest of us, uses his penis for urination and may touch it to reassure himself of his own identity. Pornography is a surrogate for the most important form of bodily contact an adult may have. Denied one kind, an individual will find another. A novel like *Gay Vigilante* describes this need even more accurately than in the author's, Frederic Raborg's, previous novels.

A valid hypothesis is that men tend to censor what would disclose the underlying current of homosexuality in all of us, whether arising *faute de mieux*, through casual choice when heterosexuality is more pleasing but unavailable or requiring too much effort, or by habituation, or from factors of which we know virtually nothing. For oneself, censorship is an exercise of the right of privacy. When extended to others beyond the family group or its equivalent, it becomes an indication of a troubled sense of identity, a need to prove one's own virtue, an assertion of a superman status we each ought to be very reluctant to have attached to us, for what makes us all human, beyond the fact of our capacity to interbreed without producing hybrids, is our common ignorance.

At each stage in our development, we tend to believe that we can go no further. Don Quijote's cry of despair becomes a protection: *"No puedo mas."* Very often in the past, we have complimented ourselves on the extent of our wisdom, never suspecting that one discovery is likely to be the disproof of a whole comforting set of theories. We must constantly revise not only our conception of nature but our image of ourselves, conceding to each the right to be mistaken without being punished so long as no harm is done another. Satanism poses no threat until the Satanist believes that he must murder others as a means of worshipping his god. The witch who uses spells and incantations to harm a person from afar is beyond the reach of our laws because no one can prove how effective these have been even if the victim falls ill on schedule. At one time the sequence of events would have been enough to cause a court to follow the injunction of the Old Testament: "Suffer not a witch to live." In the process of the trial anyone who defended the witch was considered to be in league with the devil as well. No one would have dreamed that the laws were wrong, the methods of gathering evidence not only cruel but silly as well, and the results unjustified.

It is rather a shock to realize that our concept of the universe until space exploration began derives from a time just prior to the Salem witchcraft trials in 1692. Newton's theories were published in 1685 and remained largely unrevised until the late fifties and early sixties of this century. Samuel Sewall, the judge at the witchcraft trials, later regretted his part in them. Newton was knighted and buried in Westminster Abbey, and we have since honored him for his many mathematical achievements and his contribution to physics. Witchcraft trials were given up in the English-speaking world only in the eighteenth century. (The last was in Scotland in 1722.) Since that time a variety of crimes partake of the nature of witchcraft, conducted in private with no known harm to the individual involved except what can be supposed by a process of thought usually an example of the logical fallacy, *post hoc ergo propter hoc.* Such crimes are useful to an authority that must rule by tyranny rather than by the consent of the governed restrained by limits on the powers of government.

The Information Avalanche

Librarians and information scientists are fond of the expression "the information explosion." The analogy is poor in several respects. An explosion is soon over and done with. An avalanche begins in the distance and gathers in strength as it courses down a mountain, burying everything in its way. A library is not a collection of books; it is an organized means of obtaining information. The extent of the information avalanche is unknown, because the method of organization, bibliographic control, is unequally applied to materials. Many billions of words are carefully recorded and then lost to information seekers. Whether these documents are of the importance of Mendel's theory is unknown. The original work was published in an obscure Prussian journal and reposed unmolested on a shelf until forty years later when two independent researchers came to the same conclusions as Mendel. It rather boggles the imagination to try to suppose what the history of science would now be if Mendel's works had not suffered from the poor bibliographic control of his period.

Weisberg's criticism of the Warren Commission Report on the assassination of John F. Kennedy was published at his own expense, prepared evidently by his wife and friends, because he had very little money. The camera-ready copy was made from typescript prepared without proportional spacing. Even so, Weisberg's charges of concealment, improper investigation, censorship, and actual destruction of evidence remain unchallenged and available. In the preface to *Whitewash*, Weisberg recounts his experiences with publishers. He is praised and rejected on all sides. Apparently publishers would not touch his book with a barge-pole because of "a lack of interest on the part of the public." This was the most common of the excuses offered, and Weisberg suspects some kind of conspiracy. He is advised to rewrite his book as 'sensationalism.' He chooses quite a factual method, criticising the report on the basis of internal contradictions, omissions, the determination of the Commission to find that Oswald was indeed the guilty party despite the problem of a picture, apparently of him, dressed in the shirt in which he was arrested. Another man claimed to have been in the spot where Oswald seems to be standing, on the first floor just as Altgens snapped a picture that followed the first shot by a few milliseconds and before the last shot was fired. Lovelady, the other man, was wearing a shirt with broad stripes. A further difficulty is the surveyor's report. The first shot was fired and hit President Kennedy as the car passed the fourth stripe in the road. It came from behind, but it could not have come from the sixth floor of the Texas School Book Depository because a tree blocked the way. The Altgens picture shows a man on the fire escape of the Dal-Tex building, apparently in distress, and an object projecting from the window just below him. It may be an arm, it may be a rifle. The President is clutching his neck, as described by the wife of the Governor of Texas, Mrs. Connally.

To write his book, Weisberg had to go over the twenty-six volumes of testimony, which was only a part of all the evidence collected about the events leading up to 12:30 P. M. on November 22, 1963, at the section of Elm Street in Dallas where the President of the United States was killed. The Commission's report is lengthy, but the entire collection of evidence is less than complete, as admitted by the Federal Bureau of Investigation. The autopsy reports are to remain secret until the last of the President's family dies. The autopsy report on Officer Tippit, who was shot by somebody, but whether Oswald or not cannot be finally determined, was released after much delay. Oswald's autopsy was performed briskly about an hour after his death at the Parkland Hospital in Dallas, and the physicians even took note of his black eye and bruised lip. Weisberg supposes that Oswald was subjected to police brutality.

On the face of it, Weisberg has a better case than the Warren Commission, Oswald makes a more credible dupe than an assassin, because Weisberg accounts for more of the evidence in a satsifactory way without omissions and mistatements. The government's whole case is wrecked by evidence of doctoring of photographs, such as the Zapruder film and the aerial photographs shown in Weisberg's *Whitewash I* and *II*. In order to arrive at the truth of the fascinating story of police, of the assassin (or assassins), and of the murders of almost everyone connected with the case, when they did not die accidentally, a historian will have to read through the collection that began to be assembled within milliseconds of the assassination itself. An appalled nationwide television audience watched Jack Ruby shoot Oswald, and the documentation grew as the doubts multiplied. Oswald denied that he had killed anyone, and on the basis of

Weisberg's defense, a jury would have a difficult time finding him guilty. Weisberg states that Oswald made a good suspect because everyone wanted an explanation of why a President had been killed, who had done it, and how the crime was committed.

To add to all these problems there are the numerous warnings given by Kennedy's friends and associates, including leading mystics, like Jeane Dixon, and political advisors, like Adlai Stevenson. The author of this book is in the unhappy position of being one of the prophets. On the day of the election and later he observed that a President elected during a year divisible by twenty died in office. This is true of all the Presidents of the United States, except for Zachary Taylor, who died in 1850, the last Whig to be elected to the Presidency. Presidents Harrison, Lincoln, Garfield, McKinley, Harding, and Roosevelt all were elected in years divisible by twenty: 1840, 1860, 1880, 1900, 1920, and 1940, and all died in office. Three were assassinated, so that a presumption that Kennedy ought to be very careful was valid not so much as prophecy as possibility.

A total search of all the literature surrounding the assassination of President Kennedy is probably already beyond the ability of anyone with less than several years to spend even supposing that the files of the National Archives were to be opened to the investigator. This is a rather easy example, because almost all of the documentation is well controlled and available. In other fields, the difficulties mount so that a study of space exploration from original sources would be impossible for any individual at the present time. In the development of the equipment, tens of billions of words have been written, In the experimentation and final achievement of on-the-spot exploration of the moon, the total of original sources could not be housed in any but the largest library nor its contents known except by very sophisticated computer techniques. One of the best ways to hide information is to put it among the vast outpouring of the offset presses, private communications media, and typewritten reports. As the information avalanche gets underway, we must realize that at present we are far up the mountain not down in the valley. The avalanche is rolling onwards gathering material as it accelerates.

Technical assistance and the development of underprivileged nations has as its goal enabling the populace to join in the world community as equal and valued members. In remote places around the globe a search for knowledge has been gathering speed since the end of the first atomic war. When the nuclear bombs destroyed Hiroshima and Nagasaki, mankind realized that his only way to peace and plenty was through education. It is the nature of the human animal to go out and explore his surroundings, to use the organ that gets about one third of the nourishment of the body, the brain.

To accomplish this massive tutoring of a world's population, the primary business of numerous world organizations, librarians have worked in very distant places in order to share their American contribution to the development of new disciplines. An effort has been made to remove the barriers between nations so that whatever can be exchanged by way of information will not meet unreasonable resistance, so that the Chinese ballet may follow the Russian ballet to the United States, and a folk-dancing group from the United States may perform in the Soviet Union. At every meeting of public officials from different countries, there are assurances that the people love each other. President Nixon so assured the Chinese leaders, and the Chinese people so assured the United States over its television system.

As the world grows closer in its communication, the possibilities of war are reduced, and if we had only the composure of Darwinian evolution to look forward to, we might assert that man had nothing to fear but man himself. Velikovsky's theories come at just the right time to make human beings apprehensive again. Edgar Cayce died on January 3, 1945, and the first manuscript of Velikovsky's work was completed about a year later. The statements of each are in remarkable congruence, for Cayce's prophecies become probable taking into account Velikovsky's reconstruction of history and Cayce's track record as a prophet. Mankind has reason to fear that the kind, placid earth will go into a rebellion that will make our wars seem like the nonsensical adventures of very bad children. If Cayce is correct, a succession of natural disasters will beset humankind, each more terrible than the last.

A painful example is at hand in the first hurricane of the 1972 season, concluding its last destruction as this is written. Agnes is the worst we have known so far as damage to the United States is concerned. Pennsylvania has just suffered the worst flood in its history, and Pittsburgh the third worst in its history, despite the monumental work of flood control that followed the worst of all, the March 17, 1936, disaster. Without the dams and reservoirs that trapped a great deal of the water that would have flowed down the Allegheny and the Monogahela rivers, the flood would have been by far the worst ever known, with a crest of about 48 feet, six feet higher than the 1936 peak. A massive amount of information is available about Agnes and her wanton ways from the time the hurricane began in the Caribbean until it finally drifted out to the Atlantic in the northeastern section of the country. Even with spectacular improvements in meteorology, including satellite photographs, the people of the Pittsburgh region complain that they were given insufficient warning. The predictions of the meteorologists should have been made much sooner.

What is emerging from the information avalanche is a new concept of human beings, their approach to and acceptance of information, and from this we gain a new appreciation of humankind. Culture shock, future shock, moral shock are all the same experience, a feeling of disorientation, of having been removed from the familiar and set down in a strange place. "To force upon the fellow man truth which he cannot live, means stirring up emotions impossible for him to carry; it means endangering his existence; it means kicking off balance a well-set, even if disastrous way of life." Wilhelm Reich's almost paranoic work, *The Murder of Christ*, from which this quotation was taken, was published in 1953. It is a strange work which was included among those the Food and Drug Administration listed specifically in its evidence that such books constituted labelling "of the article of device, and which contain statements and representations pertaining to the existence of orgone energy . . ." and demanded that it be withheld from the general public. On August 23, 1956, and again, on March 17, 1960, agents of the Food and Drug Administration had a book burning which may have satisfied them but otherwise had no effect whatever. Reich's books were withheld from the general public, as the injunction required. In the final article of the injunction a clear case of *censura praevia* is displayed:

"(9) That the defendants refrain from, either directly or indirectly, in violation of said Act, disseminating information pertaining to the assembly, construction, or composition of orgone energy accumulator devices to be employed for therapeutic or prophylactic uses by man or for other animals."

Farrar, Straus and Giroux have begun republishing the works of Wilhelm Reich, daring the federal government to take action. Strictly speaking, the publishers are violating an injunction. Reich was sentenced to two years in prison for doing the same thing, and he died in the Federal Penitentiary in Lewisburg, Pennsylvania, on November 3, 1957, eight months after his incarceration of March 11, 1956. The penitentiary also housed Ralph Ginzburg. Reich fell victim to his own injunction. He apparently kept forcing his truths on his fellow man before they were ready, and he must have thought of the persecution he endured in the United States as similar to that of Giordano Bruno whose refusal to renounce his belief in the Copernican system of astronomy caused the Inquisition in Venice to have him burnt at the stake in 1600. Bruno serves as an example in Reich's work, *The Murder of Christ*.

At the present stage of scientific discovery, no one is able to say that Reich's idea of orgone energy is untrue. It may be unlikely, but that is often a defense against having to accept a "truth which [we] cannot live." Reich may have been, as his biographer, Michel Cattier, suggests in *La Vie et l'Oeuvre du Docteur Wilhelm Reich*, ". . . *Un paranoiaque tellement typique qu'on croirait avoir affaire a un cas tiré d'un manuel de psychiatrie.*" (a paranoid so typical that a person believes he has come upon a case taken from a manual of psychiatry.) Reich believed that orgone energy was an ocean of space, that ether and even God were identical with this energy, and he saw the spiral nebulae as star systems in the ecstasy of orgasm. Ether has been disproved, but the existence of electro-magnetism in space is now a scientific fact, and even if galaxies do not have orgasms, they may crash into each other.

Cattier suggests, and the idea occurred to many at that time, and later, that Reich was the victim of McCarthyism, and the mad pursuit of communists. Reich was a communist at one time, but when the Stalinist puritanism was decreed as law in the Soviet Union, he deserted communism. His subsequent flight from Adolf Hitler in 1934 from Berlin and in 1938 from Europe was also flight from his former association with the German communist party. Cattier notes that censoring *The Mass Psychology of Fascism*, *The Sexual Revolution*, and *Character Analysis* was not because these works touch, here and there, on his ideas of orgone energy but because of his revolutionary beliefs. All his books were withdrawn from circulation, and to this day, it is difficult to find a copy of *The Mass Psychology of Fascism*. *The Function of the Orgasm* is virtually a classic and has very greatly influenced the development of sex research. Editions published before the book-burning are considered rare books.

Reich now seems to be the prophet of the younger generation. His use of body movements to diagnose neurotic ailments foreshadows the development of kinesics, and his view of the origin of sexual suppression in *The Invasion of Compulsory Sex-Morality* as an economically motivated social restriction has yet to be disproved. His attacks on the family are so fresh that they seem to have been written yesterday in support of the experiments in communal marriage. His advocacy of sexual experimentation by adolescents in a sex-free environment is duplicated by Robert Rimmer in his book, *The Harrad Experiment*. There is little reason to reject Reich's ideas, if his books can no longer be censored, because they are revolutionary. Even his belief in the orgone boxes that forms the basis of the Federal case against Reich was not for the purpose of defrauding the public. He sold them as a convenience more than anything else, and they were an experimental tool not a miraculous cure-all. The box did not create orgone energy, it only trapped it as it escaped from the human body and redirected it.

If Velikovsky's rejected ideas have since proven a boon to researchers, then Reich's ideas are a fountain of ideas exposed by later writers and these works owe their existence to an interest in the Reich case dating from the period in which it was taking place. As Reich states his purposes, the whole of his investigation is meant to account for and deal with the irrational, not only in the individual human being but also in society as well. Reich became interested in the social aspects of psychiatry because he could not escape them. He was associated with Freud and had qualified as a physician at a time when psychiatry was just beginning to investigate the sexual nature of human beings with any degree of freedom. He became interested in the adolescents in post-war Austria who were in full rebellion against their families, and it seemed to Reich that something had to be done about the society in which the youngsters were attempting to reach maturity. His tract of land in Rangely, Maine, was once besieged by townspeople who thought Orgonon, as Reich called it, some kind of center of evil. His motion picture made for the communist party of Germany was shown secretly in the United States, equipped with a narration by a female voice speaking English in warm encouraging tones ("Fuck happily, comrades . . .."). It has only very recently been shown along with information about Reich, in the film *Orgone*, celebrating Reich's ideas of freedom of movement as indicative of mental health and the object of mental hygiene.

Some of Reich's work can be put into a class with some of the poetry of Ezra Pound, who was as much—or more—a fascist than Reich was ever a communist. Cattier's suggestion of a paranoid can be gained readily from the writings without reference to Reich's life, the number of disciples that took him seriously and the articles contributed by scientists and physicians to his periodicals. If Reich had offered himself as the Messiah that he and his disciples believed he was, if he had given all his writings a religious rather than a scientific meaning, if he had offered his orgone boxes as the tools of a religious cult that would improve the health of true believers, the Food and Drug Administration could not have served as the arm of punishment for the United States government. Possibly he could not have been touched, although the desire on the part of his persecutors to subject him to punishment and to ban his works was intense.

But the anatomy of censorship can be seen clearly in Reich's complicated views of society and in his description of the struggles of adolescents. Censorship begins in the family and should remain in the family. The various cults of true believers require the rejection of the family as the basic unit of society. However, an enormous amount of research now convinces some scientists that human beings are gregarious animals that need a family, or its surrogate, as a means of achieving self-regulation. Reich does not oppose the family as a unit unless it is so sick as to educate children into the family neurosis, diagnosable by what he calls 'armoring.' This is a spasmic contraction of the muscles, the opposite of relaxation, and is used to express hatred, rage, contempt, anger, and all the other concomitants of human violence. The sex act then becomes a matter of anger, and representations of the sex act cause anger. Reich saw that the use of language by his patients led away from the trouble, but that bodily movements exposed it. Feeling, he said, is identical with a sense of being alive beyond the confine of words. As nearly as it can be put into words, Reich is offering the meaning of Zen, the mystical experience, the purpose of meditation.

Censorship in the healthy family group consists of teaching the canons of sensitivity to the rights of others. What is taught is the right of privacy, and this is learned at about the time the individual begins to experience puberty. Much of this book has been devoted to an investigation of censorship of sexual material, because in the period since the American Revolution that has been the center of suppression in society. Since the end of the first atomic war, the center has shifted toward political orthodoxy, enlarged to include medical and scientific orthodoxy. Reich protested that the federal government had no right to prevent his investigation of what he calls natural law. He was conferring upon himself the right of privacy he advocated for parents in dealing with the adolescents in their care. Since Reich's time it has become apparent that human beings begin to achieve a separate identity along with a power to propagate. The active sex life begins much earlier, but it is effective only when biological maturity is reached, at about the age of eighteen. Premature ejaculation, Reich notes, is not unusual when the youngster has only a few minutes for his sex act performed standing up with all his clothing on. An openness toward sexuality will do much to allay the curiosity that drives the adolescent.

Reich had the misfortune to run up against a much more powerful clique than Shapley's old-boy circuit. The medical profession in the United States is a center of conservatism, and the psychiatric wing is barely tolerated. Reich was regarded as a perpetrator of a fraud, but he profited very little from it. He was unlike the usual fraud who carefully observes the protocol of the Food and Drug Administration. He did not carefully state that his orgone box was meant to influence the spiritual well-being of the individual. He said that it would cure cancer, rheumatism, and neurosis. He offered the wood and metal box as a means of curing diseases and the medical profession took arms against him.

The Food and Drug Administration gradually assumed a moral role in society. It was formed to deal with false labelling, misbranding, and fraudulent advertising of the nineteenth century when the government recognized that babies were addicted to soothing syrups containing large amounts of opiates, ladies were addicted to the alcoholic content of patent medicines, and the ghettoes of large cities were filled with the human residue of a massive self-medication experiment that ended in phenomenal addictions. Later the Food and Drug Administration became enmired in a moral problem. Does a person have the right to medicate himself to death? So far the answer is that he may do so only if he uses approved medication. Any individual can commit suicide by swallowing a sufficient number of aspirin. Unwanted babies can be dispatched this way by murderous parents as soon as the infant can crawl well enough to obtain an aspirin bottle, left open by mistake.

The heroin addict commits suicide more slowly and devastatingly, supporting a crime syndicate and the law enforcement officials by depradation beyond what he does to himself. Human beings are permitted to kill themselves by smoking, by drinking alcoholic beverages, and by eating food that is empty of nutrition while providing calories. About this and other means of suicide the law can do little, but it can forbid the use of certain drugs. Marijuana fell under the ban of the government only in the period of the thirties, largely as a result of the efforts of a single man. A member of the Urticaceae family, *cannabis sativa* grows to a large plant in temperate regions, and the fibers may be used for making rope or fabrics, a kind of linen, and even lace. Sisal hemp which has a stronger and longer fiber is now more widely used, although the old jokes about smoking rope once had much more meaning than may be recognized today. The wild stands of marijuana are probably the result of accidental propagation after the cultivation of *cannabis* for the purposes of making rope was discontinued. To lapse into autobiography again, I can remember the marijuana cigarettes that were used by Mexican Americans in Colorado when I was a boy. They were despised by us gringoes because they were typical of that community. (An elderly aunt of mind still thinks that 'dirty' is a required adjective before the word Mexican.) A study of Spanish convinced me that my mother was right, Mexicans are fine and honorable people, filled with love of family and earnestly trying to be good citizens. Those not fitted by this evaluation were members of another class entirely that included Irish, Jews, Italians, Negroes, and some of us Caucasoid-Mongoloids who had gone into the business of criminality.

Songs that seem to popularize the drug culture have been censored and may not be performed on television. This does not include the familiar Mexican song "La Cucaracha." Very few people know the meaning of the first stanza: "*La cucaracha, la cucaracha,/Ya no puede caminar,/porque se falta, porque no tiene,/marijuana que fumar.*" A fairly literal translation would be: "The pothead, the pothead, now he cannot walk, because he lacks, because he does not have marijuana to smoke." Part of the subculture that despised the drug supposed that constant smoking of marijuana would result in utter dependence to the point that the addict would be incapacitated by a lack of the drug. I would rather take two beatings a day with a knobbed stick than smoke a marijuana cigarette, but there is no evidence that the long term effects of smoking marijuana are harmful beyond what may be the result of smoking tobacco. Certainly a knobbed stick would do much more damage and not being a masochist, I would find it unpleasant in the extreme.

Reich believed that he deserved the Nobel prize for his discoveries in physics and in medicine. His incarceration and the censoring of his books was as much acclaim as he received in his lifetime. No one would suggest that Nietzsche's works be censored because he ultimately became schizophrenic, and there is scant evidence that Reich was as paranoid as his disciples and his writings depict him. He had great pride in his work, believing that he had discovered a mode of treatment that would cure almost anything. What he had rediscovered was that faith can act as the most effective medicine in the world. There are hundreds of individuals who are willing to swear that an apparition of Padre Pio cured them of every sort of affliction.

Faith healers have been working effectively for as long as we have written records and probably even before. Christians can find that the healings of Jesus were effected by means of the individual's faith, and it is a poor physician who believes that his ministrations alone account for the recovery of his patient. The American medical profession has, in the estimation of many, almost nothing besides its scientific achievements to be proud of. The unmasked greed of its professional organizations is enough to cast doubt on the virtuous image cast over the airways. Like the legal profession fighting no fault insurance, the medical profession has seemed to guard its financial prerogatives much more closely than its just rights as healers.

It is the first rule of scientific investigation that one cannot prove a negative proposition. It is sufficient to say that orgone energy has not been discovered in the form and manner described by Reich, but it is quite wrong to say that it does not exist. We do not know. It may be something that we have identified and named something else, and if so, then Reich's descriptions of it are inaccurate, but he cannot be imprisoned for the crime of suggesting that an unknown exists. If so, then we must also imprison all of our religious leaders and most of our scientists as well. A world-wide and historical view of censorship will show that it has always been fiercest when the orthodoxies of science, religion, and a political system are challenged. The great book burnings have never really included works of the imagination, whether they are sexually oriented or not, because even the sexual-censorship campaigns of the nineteenth century can be argued as evidence of economically motivated sexual suppression. Reich was very critical of the Comstock Act of 1873 and viewed it as a kind of sexual suppression motivated by economic considerations.

The information avalanche is inspired by many thinkers who, like Reich, have challenged our fundamental axioms. In a very prophetic way, from his earliest days as a practicing and respected physician and psychiatrist, Reich saw that individual ills are also social ills, that a freedom to experiment was an essential element of the maturation process and should be protected by society. The guilts and fears associated with sexual suppression accounted for most of his caseload and led him to open mental hygiene clinics where he could deal with sexual problems before they blossomed into full-scale neuroses. Reich's earliest writings precede the acceptance of psychosomatic medicine, and his later writings foreshadow the development of a biological explanation for the functional psychoses. He is later than Adolf Meyer in this suggestion, but he is rather more accurate, providing a means of therapy without being able to account for the sequence of biochemical events that make it effective, rather like physicians who are at a loss to explain precisely why a drug is effective but can show the results as a kind of test, what amounts to the history of medicine from its beginning. (Digitalis, for instance, was used in treating dropsy long before there was enough medical science to explain that slowing the heartbeat enabled the blood to reduce the water accumulated in the tissues and assisted the kidneys in ridding the body of excess fluid.)

Reich is prophetic as well. "Truth knows no party lines, nor national boundaries, nor the difference of the sexes or of ages or of language. It is a way of being common to all, and potentially ready to act in all. This is the great hope." An uncritical person receiving a message when the family group is enlarged to the society of which he is a devoted member believes that he must accept the message completely or reject it completely. Hoffer's description of the *True Believer* attaches the paranoid dilemma to the formation of mass movements in a way that Reich's work confirms, in part. There are always messages that the uncritical person finds not only undesirable but dangerous to others. The censor is above all a true believer in something, who must defend his virtue by opposing the exposure of others to whatever he finds threatening.

Reich actually never intended to be the sort of creator of a mass movement that he condemned. He takes pot-shots at politicians wherever possible, not unlike scientists at almost every stage in the development of science. However, he sees a role for three separate social entities: religion, government, and education. He would make the family whatever group the individual finds his most productive means of working and fulfilling himself in a loving relationship with his fellows. "Let each keep to his own domain," he advised. A close study of Reich would have convinced the managers of post-war society that no writings may so readily be dismissed, least of all those of Reich, Velikovsky, and many others.

Toward a World of Peace

The events of the quarter century following the end of the first atomic war have convinced most of the knowledgeable people of the world that another would mean the end of the world community as we now know it. For all its faults, its the only one we have. Like children born into a quarrelsome family, we find it better than any other each of us can imagine because it is the only one we have any direct experience of. The fact that Grandpa, or Papa, can take the family weapon and murder all of us is a grim conjecture, especially as we come to learn that such things happen. We become more worried if Grandpa and Papa each have weapons and keep buying more and more ammunition. The object of destroying each other that motivates them scares the hell out of us kids no matter whose side we are on. We must pressure our elders and betters to sit and reason together, stop buying ammunition when we really need food, clothing, and medical care, not to mention books, movies, and games. When our Chinese uncle gets into the act, we can really become terrified at the possibility of a holocaust, even if we sleep in an upstairs closet. It is one house, one family of man, and it is bound to occur to the bravest among us little folk that the thing to do is to seize all the ammunition and guns, by one means or another, and lock them up good and tight so that no one can get to them unless all of us can have them at once. Instead of wasting money, let's spend it on things we really need. We don't really need to kill each other, because a merciful life will do that for us, eventually, one by one, and usually, if not helped by someone, quite gently.

In defining the anatomy of censorship, we must of necessity define the anatomy of intellectual freedom, for the one is so much the obverse of the other so nearly that we can define censorship as a restriction placed on intellectual freedom and intellectual freedom as characterized by the absence of censorship. In doing so, we come to see that the world community may yet be able to fulfill the prophecies of Nostradamus, *Revelations*, by Jeane Dixon, the Great Pyramid, Edgar Cayce, Wilhelm Reich, the World Federalists, among others. We can achieve a world at peace.

There is a world community already, and it is rapidly achieving what is needed as the first step, the development of education to the point where it unites us rather than separates us. Science is a unity that depends upon credibility. Its methods are universal because they are supported with the endeavors of philosophers. The institutions of education have found worldwide acceptance, aided by such investigators as Jerome Bruner. Librarianship has a universality to the extent that it can be considered a non-national profession, in Lancour's happy phrase, and museology is a course of study available in several universities, along with archives and records management. Travel and education have always been recognized as two terms connoting one purpose. As world scholarship develops, with the purpose of enlarging our knowledge, the xenophobia of the ignorant will become virtually sinful. In order to protect education, we must provide intellectual freedom. To gain this freedom we must endure the restrictions imposed by the right of privacy.

Religious institutions are becoming as widespread as educational ones. In order to pursue studies within the religion, the two often coincide. There are missionaries of many different faiths now, not only those of Christianity. The failure of Christian churches in the United States to address major social problems popularized forms of

Hinduism and Islam that would otherwise have been unattractive. Ethical societies share with religions the right of describing moral conduct, the acts of the individual in the privacy of his home and in his thoughts. To preserve freedom of worship, the right of privacy is an essential protection, but to gain this religions must give up the right of censorship over matter that does not pertain to a particular religion. Similarly, religions may not impose beliefs on others who are not members nor may they include as rituals whatever would be destructive of life among their members or among others. Religions can survive only if there is a wall of separation between them and the state. They may tax only their own membership not the members of other religions. Any activity that is conducted in order to gain support by competing with secular institutions must be taxable if taxes are justly extracted.

The concept of a world government has fascinated the nineteenth century mind as it grew into twentieth century man. Supposedly the wars of 1914-1918 and 1939-1945 were conducted to prevent any one group from 'ruling the world.' In fact, a world government could not rule the world, it could only rule other governments. Communist countries have devised the best system of local government. In China, the leader of a relatively small number of people becomes the representative in a larger group. The old ward system of government worked best when there was one party only. A return to the old political methods which made the will of the individual felt to the topmost level where the government had the right to rule can be seen in the reformation of the oldest political party in the world, the Democratic Party of the United States. The success of the federal system in the United States depends upon restrictions in the power of government at every level and on the ability of each individual to influence decisions made in his behalf. It has fallen completely apart when attempts were made to impose moral restrictions by means of laws. All the laws that protect life and property have a foundation in concepts of justice, but moral legislation can never be made just.

The result of unenforceable laws is discriminatory prosecution and exemplary punishment, both forms of injustice.

Governments cannot enforce morality, they can only dispense justice. The authority of the law resides in its ability to use force to maintain justice, but this force must be limited at every level of government. The government cannot rule the sex lives of its citizens except as an act would deprive another person of his rights. Because certain funds to be distributed fairly require the protection of force, the government supports welfare and educational institutions not otherwise supported by religious groups. A government cannot wantonly take the life of a citizen nor can it impose its authority on governments outside its own structure. The government cannot impinge on the freedom of worship, the right of privacy, nor restrict the intellectual freedom of the populace.

Because commerce can only be successful when protected from violent or unfair exchanges, the government must protect commerce without favoring any particular institution. It cannot permit monopolies not under the direct control of the general public, so that it requires fair competition. It must establish the value of the medium of exchange, and it must be ready to make the fluctuations of commercial activity affect the well-being of the citizenry as little as possible. It distributes the goods that cannot be fairly exchanged and provides for the support of those who cannot act in the commercial exchanges because of age, infirmity, and incompetence.

Deliberating on government as a means of securing the individual's right to life, liberty, and the pursuit of happiness, one comes to the conclusion that government cannot punish individuals, it can only secure a change of behavior, hence the government should not · have prisons as a means of enforcing laws. It is highly questionable whether anyone learns from punishment, and a change of behavior is precisely what education is all about. The government should require compulsory education and re-education if the individual fails to observe the elementary rules protecting the rights of others. Prisoners might well be in a kind of college, unless their misbehavior results from actual illness, in which case they should be in a hospital. A government should have control of no more means of enforcement than are necessary to conduct its operations, consequently the power to enforce popular respect for the government in power sufficient to change it only by just methods must reside in some worldwide authority that has the *force majeur* but can operate only within a very restricted and limited area. A world police would enforce the laws of a world authority that settle conflicts between governments properly in a world court. Yet the world authority should require that the elementary principles of justice be practiced down to the authority with the least power and fewest subjects.

When Jefferson and his drafting committee set about writing a declaration of independence for the English colonies in North America, they presumed to speak for all mankind. "We hold these truths to be self-evident, that all men are created equal, that they are endowed by their creator with certain unalienable rights, that among these are life, liberty, and the pursuit of happiness, that to secure these rights governments are instituted among men, deriving their just powers from the consent of the governed." For most of its history, the United States has been content to serve as an example and has not tried to force its way of government on any other nation. This is just as well, because the development of laws in the United States has not always pursued a just or wise course. No experiment in history taught the world so much as the protection of the moral crusaders against alcohol by means of an amendment to the U.S. Constitution and the organization of law enforcement agencies to enforce laws derived from this change in the fundamental law of the country. The agencies swiftly became the most corrupt in the history of the country and breaking laws derived directly from the Eighteenth Amendment became the privilege of the citizenry, from President Harding down to the local beer manufacturer, frequently one's uncle if not father. Moral crusades that require an invasion of privacy to be effective are unjust and lead to a corruption of the agents of the government and a disrespect for its laws.

Similarly, the economic experiment in the Soviet Union has shown that communism as practiced there and everywhere else has great trouble making an ethic of work effective. This is not because the workers are aware that they will not starve if they do not work but because they secure no rewards for their work. Communism, in the perception of the New Left in the United States, is state capitalism. An effective work ethic requires immediate reward. "From each according to his ability to each according to his needs," rewards needs and taxes ability. Protection of the disabled is largely a matter of finding work for them that will prove rewarding. The ownership of the means of production by the workers employed does exist and has been highly successful where an efficient manager has been selected to make the work of the participating owner-workers productive and competitive with what is offered on the market.

This is offered not as a great change but as an assessment of the trends of rational development in the affairs of men, worldwide. It is not offered as great work of originality. Practically all of it comes from other sources of which the author is unaware or which are so generalized as to be impossible to quote fairly. Almost all the elements of world government already exist, except that the arms of war are still held by individual governments in the world community. This has led to an arms race which may be very satisfying to the leaders of the governments but is enormously costly and totally wasteful, not only of the lives and well-being of the citizenry but also of the planet itself.

Environmentalists have begun to see that their faith in the inexhaustibility of our planet is naive and dangerous. Governments and the efforts of industry to support governmental policy do more to consume the resources of the planet than any other institutions. Considering what we know of the moon, Mars, and Venus, we are wealthy beyond our wildest dreams on Terra Firma, provided with infinite variety and a self-perpetuating system of necessary goods and resources. After reading Velikovsky and the predictions of Edgar Cayce, it would be interesting to ask an ecologist to compare the writings of both men with other work in the same area. The belief that evolution is not chaotic is one of the great faiths of science today. There is valid reason to hold this faith, but there is no ineluctable proof.

Our concept of the family is changing along with our ideas of almost everything else. Homosexuality is no longer a hidden shame and arguments over the 1972 Democratic Platform included some discussion of whether the Democratic Party should go on record as favoring homosexual marriage. One Iowan complained that in place of blood, sweat, and tears, the Party would be dealing with dope, sex, and queers if it did not change the emphasis of its platform. The worry over the drug laws, the development of Sexual Freedom Leagues, and the open discussion of sexuality extending to the point of making such flagrantly sexual oriented words as 'pregnant' and 'virgin' proper on the television screens runs concurrently with efforts of the local police to 'do something about the dealers in pornography.'

It may be that changes in the law will be delayed, that the arms race will continue despite treaties that would end the madness if enforced. But the men of my generation should remember that immortality has been granted neither to us nor to our fathers and our sons are growing up in a world that has been enjoying a communications revolution.

>   "I runne to death and death meets me as fast
>   And all my pleasures are as yesterday."

John Donne observed in the first of his Holy Sonnets. If we accept Carl Rogers and his belief that human beings are good and that enlightened self-interest is beneficial to all, then we must agree that whatever may characterize the world of the future, it will not be the dominance of any moral code or legal structure as we now know them. The information avalanche makes eclecticism the easiest of viewpoints to assume on any subject, and all our orthodoxies are beyond good and evil. They are doctrines in development, true so far as is known in any one point of time but likely to be altered by later discoveries.

In periods of revolution there is least censorship. No authority can assume the office of censor when many factions contend with about equal success. Censorship is more often whimsical than arbitrary and it is the work of an arbiter who is more carefully schooled in the past than in the current acceptance of canons of good taste. The censor protects society from the dangers of his own fantasies, rejecting what he would not have known as the playthings of his mind. Given a set of premises, the censor will reject all that does not logically follow, but in so doing he can be rational only to the extent that the given premises are rational. Extensive logical development from an irrational premise does not yield a rational conclusion. If this were true, we would have to judge de Sade as one of the great rationalists of what is called The Age of Reason. In the French Revolution and in the Russian Revolution an attempt was made at a sexual revolution, but what was achieved was a moral revolution worldwide while Russia returned to its peasant puritanism and a legal revolution when Napoleon's code exempted from the law the sex acts of consenting adults in private.

We are in the midst of a legal, political, and moral revolution, according to the White House Conference on Youth. The relaxation of censorship is at least a symptom if not a result of this. Attempts to stop this revolution may have dire consequences, because it is overdue. The century of the Opium Wars and imperialism, of child-labor and public executions, of involuntary addictions and legal monopolization of resources, of boom and bust economics, of prostitution and moral censorship had to be left behind amind the world wars and massive dictatorships. An awakening was bound to come, fortunately before the great rivers and beautiful lakes are killed and become cesspools as monuments to industrial and governmental greed. A revolution is a re-ordering of priorities, and the French and Russian revolutions attempted this in all spheres of human life.

The United States has been a constant revolution, the perfect example of chaotic evolution in political structure. It now keeps pace with Denmark and the Netherlands in the freedom of expression, even for voluntary censors who would achieve their preferences at the expense of the public. A re-valuation of human life is taking place that would extend the connotation of the word man to include both sexes and all manner of sexual preferences. The younger generation, finding the morality of their parents objectionable, have been re-assembling a moral code. It is quite wrong to believe that the majority are immoral. In sexual morals, the code goes "Whatever turns you on, but don't use force or violence."

There are many dangers before us. We can destroy our planet with another world war, by carelessness and greed, and even by simple disinterest in conservation. We can blight mankind with a new set of orthodoxies that cannot be challenged and must be accepted worldwide. Some new cataclysm in space may cause the planet to explode and become a series of arid meteorites pursuing each other in orbits like those between Mars and Jupiter. We have no way of knowing whether a pandemic is now in the making, evolving in some hitherto harmless microorganism.

But there is as much reason to hope. The progress of man has been toward a greater understanding of himself and of his universe so far as he has the power to know it. One of the marvels of the revolution so far is the emphasis placed on love, one of the reasons that moral censorship has become an insoluble problem. There is no separating human love from human sexuality, although it is very easy to separate violence from both love and sexuality. We have discovered new kinds of love beyond that which enables us to live together as a human family. Love is the theme of non-violent demonstrations. It has taken us much time and suffering to realize that we have much more as human beings to bind us together in a loving relationship than we need entertain that might separate us. Acceptance of diversity and love of variation are characteristics of human beings who can die of monotony and must dream to remain alive. To force obedience is not nearly so great an achievement as to earn respect, and the rights of each of us is endangered when the rights of any of us are threatened.

Whether the film *Out of the Blue* is the record or the re-enactment of a pornographic film blooper, the Sermonette on Channel Six offered the pre-recorded voice of an Episcopalian minister with views of a nude young woman in the throes of sexual ecstasy. One is reminded of a theme of science fiction: God delivering messages to mankind over the airwaves he created. Of course, the authors of those stories wrote God's script for Him. The U.S. Supreme Court decision of June 21, 1973, is a new effort at producing morality by God-like control of corrupting thoughts. Yet the best advice any of the religious leaders offered concerning temptation is very much like the professionalism of librarians who organize recorded knowledge and turn the user loose amidst it. All who are involved in the communication process can play God with greatest authenticity if they only quote the Lord Buddha: "Go thy way and work out thy salvation with diligence."

The End

NOTES

All references and quotations are identified here, including rather oblique allusions and supporting information. Title unit entry has been used in order to simplify further references. The first reference or citation gives the title of the book, the author, the edition, the publisher, place and date. Series, if important is included, or an additional title page or volume title, as needed. The page number of a quotation follows the entry, following the number of a volume and a colon, if necessary, for instance:

72-2. *The encyclopedia of erotic literature*, by Pisanus Fraxi; reprint of original edition; Documentary Books, New York, 1962. *Centuria librorum absconditorum* . . .. 2:86-111. (Henry Ashbee *pseud.* Pisanus Fraxi.)

Further references to this work will include the item number, 72-2., which gives the page of the text where the work is first mentioned and the number of references on the page. Rather than use the hallowed devices of academic authorship, *op. cit.* and *loc. cit.*, a further reference will include only the author, reference number, additional title page if necessary, and volume and page number as above, for instance:

74-1. Pisanus Fraxi, 72-2., *Index librorum prohibitorum* 1:422.

Index entries include only the page number of the text where the work is mentioned or alluded to. This is equally the bibliographic citation within an entry or two. All the titles of works are entered as well as authors so that the index is also an author index to the notes.

Chapter I., Don't Touch My Dirty Words
The Irrational in the Communication Process

3-1. *Language in thought and action*, by Samuel J. Hayakawa; 2nd ed. Harcourt, Brace and World, New York, 1962. pp. 184-187.
3-2. *The silent language*, by Edward T. Hall; Doubleday, New York, 1959.
3-3. Canon Law 1399.3: "Books which have for their principal or one of their notable purposes to attack religion or right morals are also *ipso iure* forbidden." And 1399.9: "Books which purposely treat of, narrate, or teach lascivious or obscene matter are *ipso iure* forbidden."
3-4. *The Valachi papers*, by Peter Maas; reprint of original Putnam edition; Bantam Books, New York, 1969; Q4849.

3-5.   *The Pentagon papers*, as published by the New York Times, . . . by Neil
         Sheehan and others. Quadrangle Books, New York, 1971.

4-1.   *Three essays on the theory of sexuality*, by Sigmund Freud; ed. and
         trans. by James Strachey; Basic Books, 1963.

4-2.   *Studies in the psychology of sex*, by Havelock Ellis; Random House,
         New York, 1936; 4 v.

5-1.   *Intellectual freedom issue, A.L.A. Bulletin,* issue of Nov. 1953, 47:445-
         491, especially President Eisenhower's letter Dr. Downs, 47:484.

5-2.   "John Cotton Dana," by Julia Sabine; in *Encyclopedia of library and
         information science*; Marcel Dekker, New York, 1971. 6:421.

6-1.   *Portnoy's complaint*, by Philip Roth; Random House, New York, 1969.

6-2.   *A Latin dictionary*, by Charlton T. Lewis and Charles Short; Oxford
         Univ. Press, 1879, 1933. p. 498. Cicero condemns the word in *Orator
         ad M. Brutum* and *Epistulae ad familiares.* Horace's surprisingly mod-
         ern use of the word occurs in his *Satirae.*

7-1.   *My secret life*; introd. by G. Legman; Grove Press, New York, c1968.
         11 v. in 2.

7-2.   *The Spanish curate*, by John Fletcher; in *Beaumont and Fletcher*, ed.
         by J. St. Loe Strachey; Scribner, New York, 1923; v. 2.

8-1.   *Strange fruit*, by Lillian Smith; Reynal and Hitchcock, New York,
         1944.

8-2.   *The catcher in the rye*, by J. D. Salinger; Little, Brown, Boston, 1951.

8-3.   This and other publications such as *Color Climax, Intercourse in Colors*
         are published by NB of Copenhagen, although copyrighted by Color
         Climax Corporation.

8-4.   *Georgia Code Annotated*, 26-6303, prior to the 1963 Act amending it,
         the statute covered (1) use of opprobrious words or abusive language
         "to or of another" and tending to cause a breach of the peace, and
         (2) the use of such language in the presence of a female or of any
         person who shall communicate it to a virtuous female. The penal code
         of 1895, section 396, carried a similar provision.

9-1.   *The anatomy of dirty words*, by Edward Sagarin; Lyle Stuart, New
         York, 1962. p. 50-60. The word 'shit' has been traced in English to
         the period of Chaucer. 'Excrement' as in *Bible. O.T. Deuteronomy*
         Rev. Standard Version, 23:13, came into the language in the sixteenth
         century. The common name of the small American heron, *Ardea
         virescens*, is shitepoke, always an epithet in the author's family.

9-2.   *Gone with the wind*, produced by David O. Selznick, 1939.

9-3.   *The door into summer*, by Robert Heinlein; reprint of original
         Doubleday edition; New American Library, New York, 1959. p. 78.

10-1.   *Tabus linguisticos*, by R. F. Mansur Guerios; Organizacao Simoes
         Editora, Rio de Janeiro, 1956. A discussion of linguistic taboos

ranging from Latin America to the original Latin, this book does not
provide a clear guide to Latin American complexities of propriety.
The most taboo of Portuguese words are omitted.

11-1.   *Where's Poppa?* produced by Gerry Tokofsky and Marvin Worth, 1970.

11-2.   *The moon is blue*, produced by Otto Preminger, 1953.

11-3.   *Brave new world*, by Aldous Huxley; Doubleday, Doran, Garden City,
N.Y., 1932.

12-1.   "Burma," in *Encyclopedia of religion and ethics*, ed. by James Hastings;
Scribner, New York, 1911. 3:21.

The Paranoid Prophecy

13-1.   There are several theories to account for the fall of Rome, for instance,
The outline of history, by H. G. Wells; 4th ed. Macmillan, New York,
1940; pp. 399, 412; where slavery and its effects on moral principles is
held to be responsible. Citizens for Decent Literature, Cincinnati,
Ohio, in recent brochures does not mention the fall of Rome, although
early writings made the point, sometimes obliquely.

15-1.   *Censorship landmarks*, by Edward DeGrazia; Bowker, New York, 1969;
pp. 5-11. This is a highly useful compilation of major cases involving
censorship, especially obscenity, ranging from the judgement in the case
of Sir Charles Sedley to the trial of *I Am Curious—Yellow*, 1663-1968.
Queen vs. Hicklin, L.R. 3 Q.B. 360 (1968), is the legal citation. *Regina
vs. Hicklin*, as in the text, is the usual citation found in legal writing.
The quoted passage is on page 9 of De Grazia.

15-2.   *The end of obscenity; the trials of Lady Chatterley, Tropic of Cancer,
and Fanny Hill*, by Charles Rembar; Random House, New York, 1968.

16-1.   *Decision in Denmark; The legalizing of pornography*, comp. and ed.
by Lawrence S. Taylor; Academy Press, San Diego, 1970; 2 v. (Illustrated reprint of Danish legal documents; includes 'action photographs'
apparently reprinted from Danish periodicals.)

16-2.   De Grazia, 15-1., p. 96; *United States vs. One Book Called "Ulysses,"*
5 F Supp. 182 (1933).

17-1.   De Grazia, 15-1., pp. 97-101; *United States vs. One Book Entitled
"Ulysses,"* 72 F 2nd 705 (1934).

17-2.   *Lady Chatterley's lover*, by D. H. Lawrence; 3rd manuscript version
Grove Press, New York, 1959.

17-3.   *The memoirs of a woman of pleasure*, by John Cleland; Putnam, New
York, 1963.

17-4.   *Tropic of cancer*, by Henry Miller; Grove Press, New York.

17-5.   De Grazia, 15-1., pp. 290-300; *Roth vs. United States*, 354 U.S. 476
(1957).

18-1. *Report of the Commission on Obscenity and Pornography*; Bantam
       Books, New York, 1970; A *New York Times* Book. Also published
       by Random House, New York, 1970; pp. 26-32.
18-2. *Decision in Denmark*, 16-1., Appendix 7, "Letter of March 9, 1966,
       from Professor E. Tranekjaer Rasmussen," 2:374-383.
19-1. *Therese and Isabelle*, produced and directed by Radley Metzger, 1968.
19-2. The Pittsburgh *Post Gazette* contains full accounts of the various
       hearings and the trial of *Therese and Isabelle* in its issues of July and
       December, 1968. The transcript of the trial is in the Library of the
       Graduate School of Library and Information Sciences, University of
       Pittsburgh. *Pitt News* of July 26, 1968, included an article and an
       editorial entitled "Duggan?"
21-1. *I, a woman*, Nordisk Film, A.B. Europa, MacAhlberg, Director, 1966.
23-1. De Grazia, 15-1., pp. 637-642. *United States vs. A Motion Picture Film
       Entitled "I Am Curious–Yellow,"* 404 F. 2d 196 (1968).
24-1. *The fox*, Produced by Raymond Stross, 1968.
27-1. *Pornography and the law; The psychology of erotic realism and por-
       nography*, by Eberhard and Phyllis Kronhausen; rev. ed. Ballantine
       Books, New York, 1964.
27-2. *Leaves of grass*, by Walt Whitman; Thayer and Eldridge, Boston, 1860-
       61. Whitman was dismissed from his clerkship in the Indian Bureau
       because this was considered an immoral work. The postmaster of
       Boston tried to prevent use of the mails by the publisher.
28-1. *Moby Dick*, by Herman Melville; Modern Library, New York, 1926.
30-1. The case of *Therese and Isabelle* is *Commonwealth of Pennsylvania vs.
       Guild Theatre*, No. 888, October Term, Court of Common Pleas,
       Allegheny County, Pennsylvania.
31-1. *Without a stitch*, A-S Paladiam, Denmark, V.I.P. Distributors, 1968.
31-2. Reports of indictments and trials for perjury occupy space in issues of
       the *Pittsburgh Press* and Pittsburgh *Post Gazette* for 1970, 1971, and
       1972.
32-1. *Stanley vs. Georgia*, 89 S. Ct. 1234 (1969).

King Kong is a Faggot

34-1. *Decision in Denmark*, 16-1., "Letter of the Legal Medical Council of
       November 23, 1965." Appendix 5, 2:352-357.
35-1. President Nixon's statement rejecting the *Report of the Commission on
       Obscenity and Pornography, New York Times*. The published accept-
       ance speech omits the sentence boradcast over nation-wide television.
       President Nixon appointed Charles H. Keating to the Commission on
       Obscenity and Pornography. He refused to attend any meetings and

rejected the whole of the report without reading it. He is still Chairman
of Citizens for Decent Literature.

35-2.   *The satyricon*, by Lucius Petronius Arbiter; trans. with introd. by
William Arrowsmith; reprint of original University of Michigan Press
edition; New American Library, New York, 1959; MQ 1027.

35-3.   Huxley, 11-3.

36-1.   *Sexual behavior in the human male*, by Alfred C. Kinsey, Wardell B.
Pomeroy, and Clyde E. Martin; Saunders, Philadelphia, 1948.

37-1.   Rembar, 15-2., p. 492. The sentence containing the essence of the
misquotation reads: "Pornography, which is in the groin of the beholder, will lose its force—not, as Comstock hoped, by reason of the
scope and vigor of censorship laws, but by reason of the constitutional
restrictions put upon them."

40-1.   *Bible. N.T. Romans*; Rev. Standard version; 1:27-31.

Chapter II., The Horses of Instruction
Male Identity

43-1.   On October first, or thereabouts, when Johnny Carson celebrates the
anniversary of his first appearance as host of the *Tonight Show*, the
Ed Ames episode is one of the film clips shown. The golfer's wife can
be heard in a phonorecording: *The Bloopy Awards*; Kermit Schaefer
Productions; Kapp KS-3631; side 1, band 1.

44-1.   *Hitler, a study in tyranny*, by Alan Bullock; Harper & Row, New York,
1962 (rev. ed.). p. 392, asserts that Hitler was impotent, quoting Putzi
Hanfstaengl. *Eva Braun, Hitler's mistress*, by Nerin Gun; Meredith,
New York, 1968, hints openly at phimosis.

44-2.   *The biology of human starvation*, by Ancel Keys and others; University of Minnesota Press, Minneapolis, 1950; 1:749-762, 2:823, 2:850.

46-1.   *Men in groups*, by Lionel Tiger; Random House, New York, 1969.
pp. 216-217.

47-1.   *Sexual self-stimulation*, ed. by R. E. L. Masters; Sherbourne Press,
Los Angeles, 1967; pp. 19-51.

47-2.   Ellis, 4-2., "Histories of sexual development," appendices in v. 1, part
two, and v. 2, part one. Also "Auto-eroticism." 1:161-283.

48-1.   *The art of love*, by W. F. Robie; Brown Books, Deer Park, N.Y.:
Paperback Library, New York, 1969.

48-2.   "Foreword," by Morris L. Ernst; in Ellis, 4-2., 1:v-viii.

48-3.   *The sex researchers*, by Edward M. Brecher; New American Library,
New York, 1971; pp. 40-45. The paperback edition contains material
not found in the original edition.

48-4.   *Boys and sex*, by Wardell B. Pomeroy; Dell, New York, 1971; pp. 37-
         38. Bound edition published by Delacorte, New York, 1968.
49-1.   *Light on dark corners*, by B. B. Jefferis and J. L. Nichols; reprint of last
         edition under this title; Grove Press, New York, 1967; pp. 149-155,
         208-220, 226-227. E. G. "From all I know about the way in which
         boys are thrown into the company of each other, I am sure that the
         enemy in disguise is the older boy or the chum of your own age who
         has the intention to teach you bad practices as he talks with you about
         matters of sex, excites your mind, and finally tries to get you into the
         practice of self-abuse." "Man to man from father to son on sexual
         problems of boyhood," by Ozora S. Davies; in Jefferis, pp. 207-231.
52-1.   Tiger, 46-1., Chapter Six, "Men court men: initiations and secret
         societies;" pp. 126-155.

Naked Manhood

53-1.   Large posters duplicating the picture in *Cosmopolitan*, April, 1972,
         have had extensive sale throughout the United States. Nude males are
         featured in *Playgirl*.
55-1.   *Nijinsky*, by Romola Nijinsky; Simon and Schuster, New York, 1934;
         pp. 119-120. "The small slip that male athletes and dancers wear had
         not been included by Benois . . ." who designed the costumes as well
         as the set. Whether it was the escort of the Grand Duchesses Olga and
         Tatiana or the Dowager Empress Maria Feodorovna has not been re-
         solved. In any case, some one in the Imperial Household protested to
         Nicholas II and Nijinsky was dismissed. Other dancers who formed the
         original Ballet Russe performed in Russia as well as in Europe.
57-1.   *The naked ape*, by Desmond Morris; reprint of original McGraw-Hill
         edition; Dell, New York, c1967, 1969; pp. 61-63.
59-1.   *Man's most dangerous myth: The fallacy of race*, by Ashley Montagu;
         4th ed. rev.; World, Cleveland, 1964.
59-2.   *Erotic art, a survey of erotic fact and fancy in the fine arts*, comp. by
         Phyllis and Eberhard Kronhausen; Grove Press, New York, 1968;
         "Japan," pp. 260-312.
60-1.   *Who's afraid of Virginia Woolf*, by Edward Albee; Atheneum, New
         York, 1962. This view was advanced to me verbally by a colleague.
         It is usually seen as a 'disguised homosexual' play. Cf. *Homosexual
         liberation, a personal view*, by John Murphey; Praeger, New York,
         1971; p. 64.
61-1.   *Oxford English dictionary* gives 1897 as first use in English. Havelock
         Ellis, 4-2., 2:2, 2-3, *Sexual inversion* identifies the first use in English

by J. A. Symond in a privately printed essay, *A problem in Greek ethics*, in 1883.

Crime Against Nature

61-2.   *Roderick Random*, by Tobias Smollet; New American Library, New York, 1972?

61-3.   *Sexuality and homosexuality, a new view*, by Arno Karlen; Norton, New York, 1971; p. 187.

61-4.   *Encyclopedia of psychoanalysis*, ed. by Ludwig Eidelberg; Free Press, New York, 1968; p. 462: "Uranism is a rarely used synonym for homosexuality, usually in the male; first employed by Karl Heinrich Ulrichs in 1862. The term is derived from the mythical figure of Aphrodite Urania, the source of heavenly love between males, in contrast to physical and earthly love . . .."

61-5.   *Psychopathia sexualis*, by Richard von Krafft-Ebing; 12th ed. rev. Physicians and Surgeons Book Co., Brooklyn, New York, 1904.

62-1.   *Bible. O.T. Leviticus*; Rev. Standard Version; 20:13, "If a man lies with a male as with a woman, both of them have committed an abomination; they shall be put to death, their blood is upon them."

62-2.   *Peccatum mutum, the secret sin*, by Friar Ludovico Maria Sinistrari; introd. by the Rev. Montague Summers; Collection 'Le Ballet de Muses' Paris, c158. A translation of a section of Sinistrari's *De Delictis et Poenis*, 1688. It was first published in Venice in 1700. It was placed on the *Index Librorum Prohibitorum* in 1709 where it remained, *donec corrigatur*, "until such time as it may be amended."

63-1.   *The boys of Boise; Furor, vice, and folly in an American city*, by John Gerassi; Macmillan, New York, 1966; 5-11.

63-2.   Karlen, 61-3. Also, *Homosexuality, an annotated bibliography*, ed. by Martin S. Weinberg and Alan Bell; Harper & Row (Harper Torcbook), New York, 1972; and *Homosexuality, a selective bibliography of over 3,000 items*, by William Parker, Scarecrow, New York, 1972.

64-1.   *On being different; What it means to be a homosexual*, by Merle Miller; *New York Times Magazine*, Jan. 17, 1971; pp. 9-11+.

64-2.   *Manual of psychiatry*, by Aaron Rosanoff; 7th ed.; John Wiley, New York, 1938; p. 557. Strictly interpreted, Rosanoff's experimentation was an effort to show that monozygotic twins reared separately became schizophrenic, a method that would seem to make hereditary what he called "chaotic sexuality." Rosanoff was developing a theory that schizophrenia arose from unacceptable homosexual impulse that caused conflict in the psyche. Early studies limited to homosexuality had been

previously made, though inconclusive. Cf. *Encyclopedia Sexualis*, ed. by
by Victor Robinson; Dingwell-Rock.

64-3.   *Homosexuality*, by Irving Bieber and others; Random House, New
        York, 1962. Karlen labels this "A must. The most important modern
        psychiatric study."
65-1.   Kinsey, 36-1., p. 638.
68-1.   *Maxims for revolutionists*, by George Bernard Shaw. Cf. *Familiar quo-
        tations*, by John Bartlett: "Marriage is popular because it combines the
        maximum of temptation with the maximum of opportunity." The mis-
        quotation is the common version, and an improvement, of the above.

Chapter III., The Tigers of Wrath
Burning Bright

70-1.   *Sex life of a cop*, by Oscar Peck. Saber Books, Los Angeles; 1967.
        Foreword signed Stanley Fleishman gives the history of the trial, sen-
        tence, and appeals up to the U.S. Supreme Court.
71-1.   De Grazia, 15-1., pp. 40-41; *Commonwealth of Massachusetts vs.
        Holmes*, 17 Mass. 336 (1821).
71-2.   De Grazia, 15-1., pp. 469-471; *Larkin vs. G. P. Putnam's Sons*, 243
        N.Y.S. 2d 145 (1963), New York City case; pp. 509-514; *G. P. Put-
        nam's Sons vs. Calissi*, 205 A. 2d 913 (1964), New Jersey case; pp. 518-
        521; *Attorney General vs. A Book Named "John Cleland's Memoirs of
        a Woman of Pleasure,"* 206 N.E. 2d 403 (1965), Massachusetts case.
71-3.   De Grazia, 15-1., pp. 521-535; *A Book Named "John Cleland's Mem-
        oirs of a Woman of Pleasure" vs. Attorney General*, 86 S. Ct. 975
        (1966); decision of U.S. Supreme Court.
72-1.   *The encyclopedia of erotic literature . . .*, by Pisanus Fraxi, Documen-
        tary Books, New York, 1962; *Catena Librorum Tacendorum*, 3:60-91.
        "It undoubtedly is, and will probably long remain, the best erotic
        novel in the English language." Ashbee's evaluation is accurate if
        durability is a test.
72-2.   *The memoirs of a woman of pleasure; Fanny Hill*, by John Cleland;
        complete uncensored edition; no imprint; pp. 189-191. The quotation
        is from the last page and may also be found in Pisanus Fraxi, 3:61.
73-1.   *Manual Enterprises vs. Day*; 82 S. Ct. 1462 (1966).
73-2.   De Grazia, 15-1., pp. 5-11. *Queen vs. Hicklin*, L.R. 3 Q.B. 360 (1868).
73-3.   Pisanus Fraxi, 72-1., *Centuria Librorum Absconditorum* 2:88-111. The
        tangled history begins with copies of a pamphlet sold by Strange in
        Paternoster Row. These were purchased and sent to members of the
        House of Commons. Later the Protestant Evangelical Mission and
        Electoral Union bought the stereo plates and printed the pamphlet with

a new cover. The "Watch Committee" obtained a warrant and searched the premises of H. Scott, the metal worker in Wolverhampton, on March 18, 1867. The magistrates ordered the books destroyed, but the Recorder, a man named Powell, quashed the verdict of the magistrates pending the decision of the Queen's Bench. The upshot of the trial was that the pamphlets were destroyed. New ones with revisions were printed, on which George Mackey delivered three of five lectures. He was arrested, tried, and imprisoned for fifteen months in Winchester Jail. A variety of authors have, understandably, become confused about who was tried, what happened, and who appealed. Specifically Scott appealed the judgement of the magistrates of Wolverhampton, one of whom was Benjamin Hicklin. The imprisonment of Mackey as a felon occurred after the revised edition, much toned down from the original, had been published. His was a case involving freedom of speech. It is fascinating that the members of the House of Commons did not protest when they received the pamphlet.

74-1. De Grazia, 15-1., pp. 35-40; *Commonwealth of Pennsylvania vs. Sharpless*, 2 Serg. & R. 91 (1815).

74-2. "A short view of immorality on the English stage . . . 1730," by Jeremy Collier; Reprint. Adler's Foreign Books, Inc., New York, 1972.

74-3. *My secret life*, 7-1., 2:1535-1536.

74-4. Numerous editions of these works are available. None seems worth identifying here.

75-1. Petronius, 35-2., pp. 27-28, 36-37, etc. Customarily such sections were left in the original (including Eumolpus story of his experiences as a tutor in Pergamum, pp. 90-92) until after the second World War.

75-2. Ellis, 4-2., "Histories of sexual development," appendices at the end of some volumes.

76-1. In New York City, the book was sold above and below the counter, depending on the state of the trial and the appeals. At the time, illicit volumes could be purchased in some stores and licit ones in others.

77-1. De Grazia, 15-1., pp. 477-493; *United States vs. Ginzburg*, 224 F. Supp. 129 (1963), criminal trial in Philadelphia before Judge Body; *United States vs. Ginzburg*, 338 F. 2d 12 (1964), his appeal, and *Ginzburg vs. United States*, 86 S. Ct. 942 (1966), the U.S. Supreme Court decision. Justices Douglas, Black, Harlan, and Stewart dissented. Five justices, however, decided to affirm the decision of the lower court. Ginzburg served only a few months nearly ten years after the original trial when the mild eroticism of *Eros* had been surpassed in candor by innumerable works.

78-1. Cf. *United States vs. Lethe*, 312 F Supp. 421 (1970). Justice MacBride granted a motion to dismiss portions of an indictment ruling on the basis of *Stanley vs. Georgia*. Robert Irvine Lethe published *An illus-trated history of pornography*, by Abe Richards and Rob't Irvine; Athena Books, Los Angeles? 1968. Advertising and mailing the book to those who requested it brought the postal authorities down on Lethe.

78-2.   "Infidel traps," in *Traps for the young*, by Anthony Comstock; reprint of original edition; Belknap press, Harvard University, Cambridge, Mass., 1967.

79-1.   De Grazia, 15-1., pp. 44-45; *In re Worthington Co.* 30 N.Y.S. 361 (1894), Justice O'Brien, p. 45, the complete quotation is: "There is no evil to be feared from the sale of these rare and costly books as the imagination of many even well-disposed people might apprehend. They rank with the higher literature, and would not be bought nor appre-ciated by the class of people from whom unclean publications ought to be withheld."

79-2.   *Pamela*, by Samuel Richardson; Dutton, New York, 1914. 2 v.

80-1.   *My secret life*, 7-1., 1:1036-1153.

80-2.   De Grazia, 15-1., pp. 71-74; *Halsey vs. The New York Society for the Suppression of Vice*, 234 N.Y. 1 (1922).

80-3.   De Grazia, 15-1., pp. 78-79; *People vs. Friede*, 233 N.Y.S. 565 (1929).

80-4.   De Grazia, 15-1., pp. 83-86; *United States vs. Dennett*, 39 F. 2d 564 (1930). A complete discussion of Mrs. Dennett's difficulties with the postal service is contained in her book, *Who's obscene?* by Mary Ware Dennett; Vanguard, New York, c1930.

80-5.   *Well of loneliness*, by Radcliffe Hall; commentary by Havelock Ellis; Sundial Press, Garden City, N.Y., 1928.

80-6.   De Grazia, 15-1., pp. 88-90; *United States vs. One Obscene Book Entitled "Married Love."* 48 F. 2d 821 (1931).

80-7.   De Grazia, 15-1., pp. 90-91; *United States vs. One Book Entitled "Contraception," by Marie C. Stopes*, 51 F. 2d 525 (1931).

81-1.   De Grazia, 15-1., pp. 103-105; *People on Complaint of Savery vs. Gotham Book Mart*, 285 N.Y.S. 563 (1936).

81-2.   *Corydon* by Andre Guide; Farrar, Strauss, New York, 1950. First published in 1911, the incomplete original edition of 12 copies was privately printed at the expense of the author.

81-3.   Code to Govern the Making of Talking, Sychronized and Silent Motion Pictures. Formulated by the Association of Motion Picture Producers, Inc., and the Motion Picture Producers and Distributors of America, Inc. Appendix E in *The Hays Office* by Raymond Moley; Bobbs-Merrill, Indianapolis, 1945, pp. 241-243. Reprinted by J. L. Ozer, New York, 1971.

82-1. *Little "dirty" comics*; editorial comment by R. G. Holt, an apprecia-
       tion by Robert Reitman; Socio Library, San Diego, Calif. 1971; pp. 11-
       37.

82-2. "After a book is published, its lot in the world is like that of anything
       else. It must conform to the law and, if it does not, must be subject to
       the penalties involved in its failure to do so. Laws which are thus dis-
       ciplinary of publications, whether involving exclusion from the mails
       or from this country, do not interfere with freedom of the press."
       De Grazia, 15-1., p. 88. Judge Woolsey made this point in ruling in
       favor of "Married Love," by Marie C. Stopes.

82-3. *The damned*, directed by Luchino Visconti, 1970.

82-4. De Grazia, 15-1.; 354. *The great dictator*, produced by Charles
       Chaplin, 1940, was also banned in Chicago.

82-5. *Human behavior in the concentration camp*, by Elie Cohen; Norton,
       New York, 1953.

83-1. *The nemesis of power*, by John W. Wheeler-Bennett; St. Martin, New
       York, 1956.

83-2. *Mary, Queen of Scots*, by Antonia Fraser; reprint of original Delacorte
       Press edition; Dell, New York, 1971; pp. 254-255.

83-3. *Edward second*, by Christopher Marlowe; edited, with introduction and
       notes by Roma Gill; London, Oxford, 1967.

83-4. "Calamus," in *Leaves of grass*, by Walt Whitman; New American
       Library, New York, 1955. pp. 112-127. Lines from "For You,
       O Democracy," p. 115.

83-5. *Oscar Wilde and the yellow nineties*, by Frances Winwar; Harper, New
       York, 1940.

84-1. Gerassi, 63-1., pp. 117-119.

85-1. *Report of the Commission on Obscenity and Pornography*, 18-1., 1970.

86-1. De Grazia, 15-1., pp. 46-47; *Swearingen vs. United States* 161 U.S. 446
       (1896).

86-2. The regulation was in effect during the presidential campaign of 1944.

86-3. De Grazia, 15-1., pp. 180-192; *Joseph Burstyn vs. Wilson*, 343 U.S. 495
       (1952).

86-4. *The ways of love*, produced by Roberto Rossellini, 1948.

87-1. De Grazia, 15-1., p. 184, the concurring opinion of Justice Frankfurter
       includes references to Piero Regnoli's two reviews in *L'Osservatore
       Romano*, August 25, 1948, p. 2, col. 1, and November 12, 1948, p. 2,
       cols. 3-4.

87-2. Cardinal Spellman's letter to parishes in his diocese is reprinted, in part,
       in *New York Times*, Jan. 8, 1951, p. 1, col. 2. Such letters are ordi-
       narily read aloud from the pulpit at each Sunday Mass.

87-3.   Senator McCarthy, Republican, of Wisconsin, made his charges on the floor of the Senate where he was immune to libel. Cf. *Senator Joe McCarthy*, by Richard H. Rovere; Harcourt, Brace and World, New York, 1959.

88-1.   De Grazia, 15-1., pp. 51-53; Walter Holcombe, in *Holcombe vs. State of Georgia*, 5 Ga. App. 47 (1908), was convicted of using obscene and vulgar language when he said, "You woman with the big fat rump pointed toward us, get out of the way," in an effort to clear the Tabernacle in Cartersville, Georgia, of women so that a lecture for men only could get underway.

88-2.   *The panther's feast*, by Robert B. Asprey; Putnam, New York, 1959. This is an excellent study not only of Alfred Redl but also of Imperial Austria, its army and intelligence apparatus. Along with valid, well-researched history is a very exciting story.

88-3.   De Grazia, 15-1., pp. 195-199; *Sunshine Book Co. vs. McCaffrey*, 112 N.Y.S. 2d 476 (1952); pp. 227-233, *New American Library of World Literature, Inc. vs. Allen*, 114 F. Supp. 823 (1953), etc. The cases probably stemmed from the investigation and reports of the Gathings Committee in the House of Representatives, 1952.

89-1.   *The Olympia reader*, ed. by Maurice Girodias. Grove, New York, 1965; "Introduction," pp. 11-29.

89-2.   *People on Complaint of Sumner vs. Dial Press*, 48 N.Y.S. 2d 480 (1944). De Grazia, 15-1., pp. 121-122; *Besig vs. United States*, 208 F. 2d 142 (1953). De Grazia, 15-1., pp. 233-235. Besig was trying to import, rather than publish, the two books by Henry Miller, but it is a safe assumption that having succeeded in importing them, his next step would have been to put them on sale, if not print them locally. While I spent a week in Beirut in 1953, the books were available to me along with other publications of the Olympia Press. Rather than run dangers with customs officials in further travels, I discarded them, much to the dismay of my associates in the United States who wished that I had taken the risk.

90-1.   De Grazia, 15-1., p. 96. Woolsey was referring to Mrs. Bloom's monologue in *Ulysses*.

90-2.   Kinsey, 36-1.; 1948.

91-1.   "My buddy," music by Walter Donaldson, words by Gus Kahn. New York, Jerome H. Remick & Co., 1922.

91-2.   De Grazia, 15-1., pp. 242-253; *Sunshine Book Company vs. Summerfield*, 128 F. Supp. 564 (1955), 249 F. 2d 114 (1957), 355 U.S. 372 (1958).

92-1.   De Grazia, 15-1., pp. 272-300; *United States vs. Roth*, 237 F. 2d 796 (1956); *Roth vs. United States*, 352 U.S. 476 (1957).

92-2. De Grazia, 15-1., p. 58; *United States vs. Kennerly*, 209 F. 119 (1913).

92-3. De Grazia, 15-1., pp. 326-333; *Kingsley International Pictures Corp. vs. Regents of the University of the State of New York*, 360 U.S. 684 (1959).

93-1. Sears, Roebuck Co., and Montgomery-Ward published catalogues. Some have been reprinted.

94-1. "Blackout fallout"; birth rate rise in New York City nine months after blackout. *Time*, 88:40-41, August 19, 1966.

95-1. Kinsey, 36-1., p. 12; attempts were made to censor the study before it could be published. The sample was established on the basis of the 1940 census. The history of the project is recorded in the biography of Alfred Kinsey by Paul Gebhard.

97-1. De Grazia, 15-1., pp. 360-375; *Manual Enterprises, Inc. vs. Day*, 289 F. 2d 455 (1961), 82 S. Ct. 1432 (1962).

99-1. De Grazia, 15-1., pp. 367-373.

100-1. De Grazia, 15-1., p. 375.

101-1. *The city and the pillar*, by Gore Vidal; Dutton, New York, 1948. *The city and the pillar*, revised, including an essay "Sex and the law" and an afterword, by Gore Vidal; reprint of original Dutton edition; New American Library, New York, c1965; Signet P2817.

101-2. *Two*, by Eric Jourdan; trans. from the French by Richard Howard; originally published as *Les mauvais anges* by Editions de la Pensee Moderne, 1955; Pyramid Books, New York, c1963; R-877.

101-3. *Naked lunch*, by William Burroughs; Grove Press, New York, 1959.

101-4. E. G. *Homo action, Manner klimaks*.

102-1. *Erotic fantasies; A study of the sexual imagination*, by Phyllis and Eberhard Kronhausen; Grove Press, New York, c1969; Introduction, pp. xi-xviii.

102-2. *The city of night*, by John Rechy; Grove Press, New York, 1963.

102-3. *Grecian Guild Pictorial*. "We are all Greeks. Our laws, our literature, our religion, our arts have their roots in Greece." Shelley in the Preface to *Hellas*. Each issue contained this statement, in italics.

104-1. "The Grecian Guild is a brotherhood of bodybuilders, artists, physique students and others dedicated to radiant health of body, mind, and spirit which frees man from the vulgar and base and inspires him to noble ideals and endeavors. It is pledged to the perfection of the body as the divinely created temple of the mind and spirit; to the appreciation of all beauty and worthy art; to the accomplishment of the best of which each man is capable; to the love of God, truth, honor, purity, friendship and native land.

"The Guild is universal in its precepts, embracing the best in all nations and cultures, but in its name it honors those high ideals and glorious achievements which characterized Grecian civilization during its Gold Age and which have since enriched the lives of all nations.

"Our goal is the development of a sound mind in a sound body that we may best serve our God, our fellow man and our country."

104-2.   E. G. "Adults are afriad to discuss sex," and "Be honest, be friendly, and enjoy life," in *Butch*, issue 5, (no date) 1966, pp. 4-7, 33-36. The quotation may be found on pages 9, 10, 11, 12, 13, 14, and 37.

106-1.   *The phallus, a picture study of the male penis*; Photographers' Guild, Los Angeles, c1969.

106-2.   *Modern penis enlargement techniques, a philosophic approach*, by J. W. Harris; Collectors Specialties, Hollywood, Calif., c1970.

107-1.   Sometimes the author is not identified, for instance *Comin' on campus*, which contains the story "Runaway sex." No publisher is identified, and the work is evidently not copyrighted. *Genitalia* is similar, except that even the story is untitled, without identification of author or publisher, and with no notice of copyright.

107-2.   De Grazia, 15-1.; *One, Inc. vs. Oleson, Postmaster of Los Angeles*; 355 U.S. 371 (1958).

108-1.   *Teen-age masturbation*, by Nicholas M. Dort; Spartan House, Los Angeles, c1968. The letter from Hackney appears on pp. 37-38. Cf. *Handbook of masturbation*, by J. C. Hackney; Spartan House, Los Angeles, c1971. Hackney's amazing first volume of a two volume work (the second was not examined) gives 89,301 different ways of masturbating. Many of these are combinations of other methods, each carefully numbered, although toward the end of the work many are summarized rather than explained in detail, for instance: "60029-61068. With your right hand, use any of the 10 bare-head grips No. 327-328, or 383-385. With your left hand, use any of the 104 inner-shaft and skin-of-the-bag methods as listed in No. 52370-53041."

The remarks about masturbation while driving are on page 17.

109-1.   *Auto-fellatio & masturbation, an autobiographical, scientific and photographic study*; Media Arts, New York, c1969.

109-2.   *Oral genital activity, a photo study of sexual activity between males*; text material by Larry Stevens; DSI, Burbank, Calif., c1970.

109-3.   *Stanley vs. Georgia*, 32-1.

110-1.   DSI has October sales, but in view of their cashing my check and not sending all the material, the firm could be judged as engaging in mail fraud.

110-2.   *L'Affaire*, Issue two; All Star Enterprises, Hollywood, Calif., c1969. This picture book contains some dubious verse and photographs of Ray Fuller with another model.

111-1.   *The picture of Dorian Gray*, by Oscar Wilde; Heritage Press, New York, 1957.

111-2.   *The asbestos diary*, by Casimir Dukahz; Oliver Layton Press, New York, 1966.

111-3.   *True confessions*; Parisian Press, San Francisco, no date. *Love machines*, volume one; no publisher, place or date. *Manly devotion*, vol. 1, no. 1.; editorial by Robert Skully; no publisher, place or date; *Muscle up*, vol. 1, no. 1, editorial by Jonathan Crooks; no publisher, place or date; *Up-close; The male as seen thru the close-up lens*, vol. 2; Press Arts, Canoga Park, Calif., c1969. *Genitalia*, no publisher, place, or date.

112-1.   Guild Press books are distributed by Potomac News Company, Washington, D.C.

112-2.   Kronhausen, 27-1., pp. 277-278.

112-3.   *Seven in a barn*; no publisher, place or date; 111 p.

112-4.   *Glory hole*, no publisher, place or date. Not examined. "Ardmore station," no publisher, place, or date, in the copy examined. Also published by Guild Press, as "East Ardmore."

114-1.   *First time round*; *My little brother*; *The gypsy's ball*; *Gay guide to cruising*; and *Seven in a barn*. Joe Markham is starred in the first picture, along with other names that meant nothing to me. In the more recent films, especially *First time round*, a kind of plot is developed, rather like *La Ronde* by Arthur Schnitzler. These are all sound movies shown in theatres in New York City. The clientele is very much like that of heterosexual pornographic films. All adult males, most of them well-dressed.

115-1.   *Gay sex guide*; no publisher, place or date. Issue examined is no. 2, subtitled "Sex techniques for the complete homosexual." It is labelled "educational material for adults only."

115-2.   *Homosexual boys, a study of today's sexual mores among teenage boys with homosexual tendencies*, researched by Dr. Albin Womac Ph.D. Homo-scientific publications, no place, no date. The quotation is from the middle. The further quotation is on the verso of the second leaf, excluding the cover.

117-1.   Ellis, 4-2.; *Sexual inversion*, 2:pt. 2, 291-299.

117-2.   Tom of Finland drawings are collected in several editions, as are Colt drawings. Quaintance seems to have been published only in such periodicals as *Fizeek Art Quarterly*.

118-1.   *Charley's aunt*, by Thomas Brandon; Heineman Educational, London, 1969. (The Hereford Plays).

118-2.   *Doctor in the house*, by Richard Gordon; (pseud. of Gordon Ostlere)
          M. Joseph, London, 1952.

118-3.   *Doctor at sea*, by Richard Gordon; (pseud. of Gordon Ostlere)
          M. Joseph, London, 1953.

119-1.   *My first time; Rick's tale of his discovery and breakthrough into sex*;
          DSI, Los Angeles? no date (1970?), unnumbered pages, the quoted
          passage is from the recto of the first leaf, marked "Forword." It is the
          last paragraph.

120-1.   *My first time . . . .* The book form was not examined. Advertising
          material from DSI is cited here.

120-2.   *Manly devotion*; no publisher, place or date.

120-3.   Advertising copy from DSI.

121-1.   *The complete poetry and selected prose of John Donne and the com-
          plete poetry of William Blake*; introd. by Robert Silliman Hillyer;
          Random House, New York, 1941. p. 653; The line is from "Proverbs
          of Hell."

122-1.   *The erotic experience*; DSI? no place, no date.

123-1.   *Ray Fuller album*, unnumbered pages, the sequence of pictures begins
          two leaves from the middle and continues to the end.

123-2.   De Grazia, 15-1., pp. 361-375.

Chapter IV., The Palace of Wisdom
The Cool Medium

125-1.   *Understanding media; The extensions of man*, by Marshall McLuhan;
          McGraw-Hill, New York, 1964.

126-1.   *Maurice, a novel*, by Paul Goodman; New American Library, New York,
          1971.

126-2.   *Making do*, by Paul Goodman; New American Library, New York,
          1964; Signet T2564; also Macmillan, 1963. Cf. pp. 70-82.

127-1.   *Seven in a barn*, *East Ardmore*, *Under the bridge*, *San Diego sailor*, *The
          team*, *A night in the hayloft*, *The boys of muscle beach*, *Bail out*, *Box-
          ing camp*, *The first job*, Guild Press, Washington, D.C., c1969; Black
          Knight Classics.
          Each is 4" by 6" and about 100 pages in length. There are no illustra-
          tions. Many have been reprinted in The Lancelot Series.

127-2.   *3 big underground classics in one book, One man's meat, plus The adve
          adventures of Buddy, & The adventures of Edward*; Guild Press,
          Washington, D.C., c1972.

128-1.   "Porthole buddies," p. 22.

128-2.   "Angelo," p. 45.

128-3.   "One man's meat," p. 23

128-4. "The adventures of Buddy," p. 129.

129-1. "The adventures of Buddy," p. 130.

129-2. "The adventures of Edward," pp. 133-180.

130-1. "A crack in the wall," p. 22; p. 68; p. 78; p. 93; p. 94.

131-1. "A crack in the wall," p. 85. The title of the film is usually given as *I am curious—yellow*. The blurb is on the back cover.

Paperback Genre

135-1. Rembar, 15-2.

135-2. De Grazia, 15-1., pp. 360-375.

136-1. *Teleny; or, The reverse of the medal*, attributed to Oscar Wilde, with an introd. by Jack Hirschman; Brandon House, North Hollywood, Calif., c1967.

136-2. Vidal, 101-1., p. 157.

137-1. Cf. *The occasional man*, by James Barr; Paperback Library, New York, 1966. Quatrefoil, by James Barr; Greenberg, New York, 1951.

137-2. *Maybe-Tomorrow*, by Jay Little; Pageant Press, New York, c1952; reprinted 1956, 1957, 1960, 1962; p. 227.

138-1. De Grazia, 15-1., pp. 581-585; *Attorney General vs. A Book Named "Naked Lunch,"* 218 N.E. 2d 571 (1966).

139-1. Banning of *Les Fleurs du Mal* of Baudelaire and *Madame Bovary* of Flaubert.

139-2. Jourdan, 101-2.

139-3. Rechy, 102-2.

141-1. De Grazia, 15-1., pp. 610-622; *Ginsberg vs. New York*, 390 U.S. 692 (1968); p. 617.

141-2. *They foresaw the future; The story of fulfilled prophecy*, by Justine Glass; Putnam, New York, 1965; pp. 169-172.

142-2. *A gift of prophecy; The phenomenal Jeane Dixon*, by Ruth Montgomery; William Morrow, New York, 1965; pp. 169-172.

143-1. Dennett, 80-4. *Who's obscene?* describes in detail Mrs. Dennett's problems with the United States Postal Service. Her pamphlet was printed in *Medical Review of Reviews*, February, 1918. It had been written for a contest held by Metropolitan Life Insurance company, but especially for the author's two sons to whom she gave the manuscript and then the pamphlet when it was printed. The pamphlet was declared unmailable in 1922. The post office created a fictitious character, Carl A. Miles, gave him a fictitious address, and then had his fictitious wife write to Mrs. Dennett requesting a copy of the pamphlet. C. E. Dunbar, the Post Office Inspector, admitted that the letter was a trap. The indictment was mailed on January 2, 1929. The trial dragged on and finally ended in Augustus Hand's decision.

The Raunchy Romances

144-1. *Anthology of gay stories*, by Alexander Goodman and J. J. Proferes; Guild Press, Washington, D.C., c1971. 2 vol.
144-2. Olympia Press mailed this statement to writers as well. It can be found somewhat abbreviated, in *Writers yearbook*, 1971. The series was a failure and its editor, Frances Green, is now associated with Renaissance House, a book club and publisher.
146-1. "Boxing camp," 127-1.
146-2. *Like father, like son*, by Dennis Drew; Publishers Export Company, San Diego, California, c1967.
147-1. Drew, 146-2., p. 104.
147-2. *Brothers*, by Jerry Evans; Taurus Publications, Wilmington, Del. 1970.
147-3. *Like father, like son*, by Jack Evans; Guild Press, Washington, D.C., c1971; Roadhouse Classics.
147-4. *Up daddy, a love story*, by Karl Flinders; The Traveller's Companion, New York, c1971; The Other Traveller Series.
147-5. *A father in the shadows*, by Douglas Dean; Greenleaf Classics, San Diego, Calif., c1971; A Pleasure Reader, PR 133.
148-1. Dean, 147-5., pp. 163, 168.
148-2. *Brothers in love*, by Don Holliday; Corinth Publications, San Diego, Calif., c1967. Leisure Book LB 1204.
148-3. *Gay brother*, by James Harper; Publishers Export Company, San Diego, Calif., c1970. p. 157; French Line Novel, FL-78.
149-1. *Man from C.A.M.P.*, by Don Holliday; Corinth Publications, San Diego, Calif., c1966; Leisure Book LB 1164. Cover title: *The man from C.A.M.P.*
149-2. *Gothic gaye*, by Don Holliday; Corinth Publications, San Diego, Calif., c1966; Leisure Book LB 1184.
149-3. *The son goes down*, by Don Holliday; Corinth Publications, San Diego, Calif., c1966; Leisure Book, LB 1177.
149-4. *Rally round the fag*, by Don Holliday; Greenleaf Classics, San Diego, Calif., c1967; Ember Library, EL367.
149-5. Holliday, 149-2., p. 160.
149-6. *Song of the loon, a gay pastoral in five books and an interlude*, by Richard Amory; Greenleaf Classics, San Diego, Calif., c1966; GC 213.
149-7. *Song of Aaron, book two, the Loon Songs Trilogy*, by Richard Amory; Greenleaf Classics, San Diego, Calif., c1967; GC 222.

149-8. *Listen, the loon sings, book three, of the Loon Songs Trilogy*, by
       Richard Amory; Greenleaf Classics, San Diego, Calif., c1968; GC 284.

151-1. *Frost*, by Richard Amory; Travellers Companion, New York, 1971; The
       Other Traveller, TC 510; p. 117.

152-1. *Windows and mirrors*, by Douglas Dean; Greenleaf Classics, San Diego,
       Calif., c1971; Pleasure Reader, PR 327, PR 328; 2 vol.

152-2. *All is well*, by Dirk Vanden; The Traveller's Companion, New York,
       c1971; The Other Traveller, TC 512; "Author's note," frontal matter.

153-1. *Clint wins his letter*, by Lance Lester; Phoenix Publishers, San Diego,
       Calif., c1970; Pleasure Reader PR 254.

153-2. *Clint scores big*, by Lance Lester; Greenleaf Classics, San Diego, Calif.,
       c1971; Pleasure Reader PR 336.

153-3. *Jet*, by Lance Lester; Phenix Publishers, San Diego, Calif., c1970;
       Pleasure Reader PR 257.

153-4. *Remake*, by Peter Tuesday Hughes; Greenleaf Classics, San Diego,
       Calif., c1971; Pleasure Reader PR 330.

153-5. *The scorpius equation*, by Larry Townsend; The Traveller's Companion,
       New York, c1971; The Other Traveller, TC 513.

153-6. *One for the money*, by Douglas Dean; Greenleaf Classics, San Diego,
       Calif., c1972; Pleasure Reader, PR 342.

153-7. *The casting couch*, by Carl Driver; Greenleaf Classics, San Diego, Calif.,
       c1972; Pleasure Reader PR 346.

153-8. *The mirror chronicles*, by Peter Tuesday Hughes; Eros Publishing,
       Wilmington, Del., c1971; Frenchy's Gay Line, FGL 22.

153-9. *Todd*, by James Colton; The Traveller's Companion, New York, c1971;
       The Other Traveller, TC 514.

153-10. *The Judas match*, by Frederick Raborg; Greenleaf Classics, San Diego,
       Calif., c1972; Pleasure Reader PR 354.

153-11. *Frontier boys*, by George Delacourt; Greenleaf Classics, San Diego,
       Calif., c1971; Pleasure Reader, PR 323.

153-12. *Climax at Bull Run*, by Billy Peale; Greenleaf Classics, San Diego, Calif.,
       c1971; Pleasure Reader PR 331.

153-13. *I am dying, Egypt*, by Peter Tuesday Hughes; Greenleaf Classics, San
       Diego, Calif., c1972; Pleasure Reader PR 355.

153-14. *Judas goat*, by Lance Lester; Greenleaf Classics, San Diego, Calif.,
       c1971; Pleasure Reader PR 321.

153-15. *The godfather*, by Mario Puzo; Fawcett World Library, New York,
       1970; TC 484.

153-16. *The gay haunt*, by Victor Jay; The Traveller's Companion, New York,
       c1970; TC 484.

153-17. *Say, mister*, by Greg Foster; Greenleaf Classics, San Diego, Calif.,
       c1972; Pleasure Reader PR 353.

153-18. *Lover's island*, by Frederick Raborg; Greenleaf Classics, San Diego, Calif., c1972.

153-19. *Tearoom castles*, by Dick Garfield; GX, Chatsworth, Calif., c1971; Trojan Classic, TC 202.

153-20. *He's gay and married*, by Dylan Danbury; Paramount Publishers, no place, c1971; Supreme Library SL 515.

154-1. *Whores, queers, and others*, by Philip Barrows; The Traveller's Companion, New York, c1967; TC 211.

154-2. Foster, 153-17.

154-3. Peale, 153-12.

154-4. *My brother, the hustler*, by Phil Andros; Gay Parisian Press, San Francisco?, c1970; GPP 101.

155-1. *Son of Adam*, by Llewellyn Hollingsworthy; Greenleaf Classics, San Diego, Calif., c1972; Pleasure Reader PR 356.

155-2. *Henry Esmond*, by William Thackeray; Dodd, Mead & Co., New York; Great Illustrated Classics.

155-3. *The other party*, by Peter Tuesday Hughes; Greenleaf Classics, San Diego, Calif., c1972; Pleasure Reader PR 352.

155-4. *Something in the blood*, by Peter Tuesday Hughes; Greenleaf Classics, San Diego, Calif., c1972; Pleasure Reader PR 352.

155-5. *Yours to keep*, by James Insley; Greenleaf Classics, San Diego, Calif., c1971; Pleasure Reader PR 317.

155-6. *The flesh mast*, by Rod Sawyers; Brandon House, North Hollywood, Calif., c1969; 3073.

156-1. Amory, 151-2.

156-2. *The gay force*, by Trock Bender; Central Sales, Baltimore, Maryland, c1969; Vibra Books V.B. 101.

156-3. *Buddy*, by Brad Powell; Greenleaf Classics, San Diego, Calif., c1969; GL 135.

156-4. *The second Tijuana Bible reader*; Greenleaf Classics, San Diego, Calif., c1969; GL 133.

156-5. *Staircase*, by Charles Dyer; Avon Books, New York, 1969; also Doubleday, c1969.

156-6. *Forbidden colors*, by Yukio Mishima; trans. from the Japanese by Alfred H. Marks; Avon Books, New York, 1968; also Knopf, c1968; original title, *Kinjiki*.

156-7. *Confessions of a mask*, by Yukio Mishima; trans. by Meredith Weatherby; Tuttle, Tokyo, Japan, c1958; also New Directions; original title, *Kamen no kokuhaku*.

156-8. *The temple of pederasty*, after Ihara Saikaku; trans. by Hideki Okada, illus. by Philip Core; Hanover House, North Hollywood, Calif., c1970; 5004.

157-1. *A sand fortress,* by John Coriolan; Award Books, New York, c1968; A363N.

157-2. *Gov't inspected meat and other fun summer things,* by Dotson Rader; Paperback Library, New York, 1972; also David McKay, c1971.

157-3. Dyer, 156-5.

157-4. *The boys in the band,* by Mart Crowley; Dell, New York, 1969; also Farrar, Straus, and Giroux, c1968.

157-5. *The Lord won't mind,* by Gordon Merrick; Avon Books, New York, 1971; also Bernard Geis, c1970.

158-1. *One for the gods,* a novel by Gordon Merrick; Bernard Beis, New York, c1971.

160-1. "Nebraska regent's blast at gays backfired," and "Homophile course may be revived;" *Advocate,* May 10, 1972; issue 85, p. 7.

160-2. *Homosexuality: disease or way of life,* by Edmund Bergler; Collier-Macmillan, New York, 1962.

160-3. *Prison sex,* by Ed Carpenter as told to Ted Baxter; M-T Publishers, Las Vegas, Nevada, c1969; Ram Classic RC 568.

161-1. *The gay insider, a hunter's guide to New York and a thesaurus of phallic lore,* by John Francis Hunter; The Traveller's Companion, New York, c1971; Other Traveller TC 504.

161-2. *International guild guide,* ed. varies; Guild Press, Washington, D.C., 1963-; Issues examined: 1964, 1972.

161-3. *The homosexual's handbook,* by Arco Arcangelo; Traveller's Companion, New York.

161-4. *American grotesque, an account of the Clay Shaw-Jim Garrison affair in the City of New Orleans,* by James Kirkwood; Simon and Schuster, New York, c1970.

161-5. *Male homosexual marriages,* by Leslie Lucas; photo-illustrated; Publishers Export Company, San Diego, Calif., c1970; Human Experience Series HES 110.

161-6. *Homosexuality then and now,* by Marvin Johnson; Eros Publishing, Wilmington, Del., c1971.

161-7. *The ways homosexuals make love, male-to-male sex techniques,* by Dodd V. Banson; Academy Press, San Diego, Calif., c1970. vol. 1.

162-1. *The gay militants,* by Donn Teale; Stein & Day, New York, 1971.

171-1. "Featherless biped with a backache." Attributed to Mark Twain.

171-2. *Gone with the wind,* by Margaret Mitchell; Macmillan, New York, 1936.

171-3. *Sex in history,* by George Rattray Taylor; Vanguard Press, New York, c1954.

173-1. *Banned books,* by Anne Lyon Haight; R. R. Bowker, New York, 1970. p. 53.

173-2. *My secret life*, 7-1.
173-3. *The lady with the swansdown seat*, by Cyril Pearl; Bobbs-Merrill, Indianaoplis, 1956.
174-1. *My secret life*, 7-1.
174-2. Richardson, 79-2.
174-3. *My secret life*, 7-1., "Publisher's preface," 1:xi-xviii.
174-4. Ellis, 4-2.
175-1. *My secret life*, 7-1., 1:26-37; 57-83; etc. The book is quite well indexed, and the style of indexing is at least additional evidence that Ashbee is the Walter of the story.
178-1. *My secret life*, 7-1., Introduction, 1:xvii-xviii.
179-1. *Nineteen eighty-four, a novel*, by George Orwell, Harcourt, Brace, New York, 1949.

Digression in Korea

180-1. This had generally been obscured in official histories of the period, but it was common discussion among my students when I taught English as a foreign language in Seoul in 1947-8.
180-2. *Future shock*, by Alvin Toffler; Random House, New York, 1970.
185-1. *Sexual relations of mankind*, by Paolo Mantegazza; trans. by Samuel Putnam; Eugenics Publishing Company, New York, 1937.
186-1. *Swingers life*, published by Swingers International, Inc. Enola, Pa.
186-2. *Swingers life*, 186-1., 6:issue 2, 20-27.
187-1. *Swingers life*, 186-1., p. 57.
191-1. *All in the family*, produced by Norman Lear, 1971.

Mother is a Lady

192-1. *Intimate behavior*, by Desmond Morris; Random House, New York, c1971.
193-1. "How different are they?" by Stanley F. Yolles; *New York Times Magazine*, pp. 64-65+, February 5, 1967.
193-2. *Rock-a-bye-baby*; Time-Life films, 1971.
196-1. "Laymen scold bishops' lobbying," *Pittsburgh Press*, January 11, 1972.
    "The report [of the National Association of Laity (NAL)] said the Pittsburgh Diocese, one of eight Catholic dioces in Pennsylvania, paid an annual 'assessment' of $78,611 to the Pennsylvania Catholic Conference, the lobby of the Cathblic bishops in the state legislature.
    "The Pennsylvania Catholic Conference successfully campaigned for the passage of the Pennsylvania Elementary and Secondary Education

Act, which until ruled unconstitutional by the Supreme Court, provided,for substantial payment to Catholic schools throughout the
state," the report said.

The Report of NAL was highly critical of the Catholic lobbying.

196-2. *The time has come: A Catholic doctor's proposals to end the battle
over birth control*, by John Charles Rock; Knopf, New York, 1963.

197-1. *Inherit the wind*, by Jerome Lawrence and Robert E. Lee; Random
House, New York, 1955.

199-1. Morris, 192-1., pp. 39-40.

201-1. Morris, 192-1., pp. 72-79.

201-2. *My secret life*, 7-1.

202-1. *The damned*, 82-3.

204-1. "What Nixon brings home from Moscow," *Time*, 99:13-18, June 5,
1972. It is briefly mentioned in this article that the wife of a Moscow
correspondent for the pro-Communist Italian newspaper *Paesa Sera*
shouted "Freedom to Vietnam!"

204-2. *Of the imitation of Christ*, by Thomas a Kempis; Burns, Oats and Wash-
bourne, London, 1952; pp. 134-135, 166, 203-208.

Chapter VI., Sensuous Education
Sex as a Home Study Course

207-1. Kinsey, 36-1., p. 226.

208-1. De Grazia, 15-1., pp. 83-86.

209-1. *New York Times*, July 21, 1971 (p. 70, column 1).
Contract of 52 year old New Jersey elementary school music teacher
who underwent sex change operation comes under review by local
school board; teacher who is currently Mrs. P. M. Grossman, underwent
operation from male to female during Easter recess and kept it secret
but has worn male clothing since; school board president says case is
complicated and without precedent.
New York Times, August 13, 1971 (p. 13, column 7).
Local board suspends and moves to dismiss Grossman; Grossman's
lawyer, H. Kestner, scores board's move; case reviewed.

210-1. *Light on dark corners*, 49-1.

210-2. *The gods, and other lectures*, by Robert Green Ingersoll; D. M. Bennett,
New York, 1876.

211-1. Ellis, 4-2., 4:430-433.

213-1. *Doctrine and discipline of divorce: restor'd to the good of both sexes,
from the bondage of canon law, and other mistakes, to Christian freedom, guided by the rule of charity. Wherein also many places of
scripture, have recover'd their long-lost meaning. Seasonable to be*

now thought on in the Reformation intended. London, Printed by
T. P. and M. S., 1643.

214-1. *The sensuous woman,* by "J;" Dell, New York, 1971; also Lyle Stuart, c1969.

214-2. *The sensuous man,* by "M;" Dell, New York, 1972; also Lyle Stuart, c1971.

215-1. *The sensuous couple,* by Robert Chartham; Ballantine Books, New York, c1971.

215-2. *Married love, a new contribution to the solution of sex difficulties,* by Marie Charlotte Carmichael Stopes; Eugenics Publishing Co., New York, 1931.

215-3. *The ideal marriage, its physiology and technique,* by Theodoor Hendrik van de Velde; trans. by Stella Browne; Random House, New York, c1965.

215-4. Brecher, 48-3., pp. 109-131.

216-1. *Everything you always wanted to know about sex but were afraid to ask,* by David Reuben; David MacKay, New York, c1970.

217-1. *Love and orgasm,* by Alexander Lowen; Macmillan, New York, c1965.

217-2. Chartham, 215-1.

218-1. "Invitation to a march," Play written and directed by Arthur Laurents, New York, 1960.

219-1. *Human sexual response,* by William H. Masters and Virginia E. Johnson; Little, Brown, Boston, c1966. *Human sexual inadequacy,* by William H. Masters and Virginia E. Johnson; Little, Brown, Boston, 1970.

219-2. *Sex without guilt,* by Albert Ellis; Lyle Stuart, New York, c1958, 1966.

219-3. *An ABZ of love,* by Inge and Sten Hegeler; trans. by David Hohnen, drawings by Eiler Krag; Medical Press of New York, 1963.

220-1. Reuben, 216-1.

220-2. *Light on dark corners,* 49-1.

220-3. Chartham, 215-1.

220-4. *Sensuous man,* 214-2.

220-5. *Sensuous woman,* 214-1.

Burning Sappho

221-1. *The lesbian in America,* by Donald Webster Cory; Tower Publications, New York, 1964; also Citadel Press; pp. 65-70.

221-2. Morris, 192-1., p. 49.

223-1. Cleland, 17-3.

223-2. Hall, 80-5.

223-3. *The fox,* 24-1.

223-4. *The killing of sister George,* directed by Robert Aldrich, 1968.

223-5.   Reuben, 216-1., p. 221.
223-6.   Kinsey, 36-1., pp. 193-217.
225-1.   Hall, 80-5.
225-2.   Cory, 221-1., pp. 111-123.
228-1.   *Venus in furs*, by Leopold ritter von Sacher-Masoch; John Amslow &
         Associates, Culver City, Calif., 1964.
228-2.   *Submit I must (the diary of a masochist)*, by Lana Johnson; pp. 9-190;
         Masochists are nice people, by Martine Horton; Bilife Publications,
         Wilmington, Del., c1968; Original Gilt Edge Publication GE 106.
229-1.   *Story of O*, by Pauline Reage; trans. from the French by Sabine
         d'Estree; Grove Press, New York, c1965.
229-2.   *Maude Cameron and her guardian*; Bilife Publications, Wilmington, Del.,
         c1968; Gilt Edge GE 103.   Reprint of a novel originally published
         about 1880 or 1890.

Prince of Hell

230-1.   Morris, 57-1.
230-2.   *African genesis; A personal investigation into the animal origins and
         nature of man*, by Robert Ardrey; Atheneum, New York, 1970.
         *The social contract; A personal inquiry into the evolutionary sources of
         order and disorder*, by Robert Ardrey; Atheneum, New York, 1970.
231-1.   "Chronology," in *The complete Justine, philosophy in the bedroom,
         and other writings*, by the Marquis de Sade; comp. and trans. by
         Richard Seaver and Austryn Wainhouse, with introd. by Jean Paulhan
         and Maurice Blanchot; Grove Press, New York, c1965; pp. 73-119.
233-1.   *Juliette*, by the Marquis de Sade; trans. by Austryn Wainhouse; Grove
         Press, New York, c1968; 6 vols, in one.
233-2.   *The 120 days of Sodom, and other writings*, by the Marquis de Sade;
         comp. and trans. by Austryn Wainhouse and Richard Seaver; introd. by
         Simone de Beauvoir and Pierre Klossowski; Grove Press, New York,
         c1966.
234-1.   *The ingenious gentleman Don Quixote de la Mancha*, by Miguel de
         Saavedra Cervantes; Complete in two parts.   A new translation from the
         Spanish, with a critical text based upon the first editions of 1605 and
         1615, and with variant readings, variorum notes and introd. by Samuel
         Putnam; Modern Library, New York, 1949.
234-2.   *The remembrance of things past*, by Marcel Proust; trans. by C. K.
         Scott Moncrieff, introd. by Joseph Wood Crutch; Random House,
         New York, 1934.
234-3.   de Sade, 233-2., p. 198
235-2.   de Sade, 233-2., p. 203.

235-3.   de Sade, 233-2., pp. 205-210.
236-1.   de Sade, 233-2., p. 205.
236-2.   de Sade, 233-2., p. 210.
236-3.   de Sade, 233-2., p. 216.
237-1.   de Sade, 233-2., pp. 241-249.
237-2.   de Sade, 233-2., pp. 250-252; the quoted section is on p. 252. He begins the speech with the words "Feeble, enfettered creatures destined solely for our pleasures," p. 250.

Chapter VII., To Turn a Trick
Erotica

245-1.   Georgia, 8-4.
246-1.   Ancell Keys, 44-2.
247-1.   *The other Victorians, a study of sexuality and pornography in mid-nineteenth-century England*, by Steven Marcus; Basic Books, New York, c1964-1966; pp. 1-33.
249-1.   *Irma La Douce*, directed by Billy Wilder, 1963.
250-1.   "Press lord without portfolio." *Time*, 97:71 (May 31, 1971).
251-2.   Puzo, 153-15.
251-3.   *Tricks of the trade; A hooker's handbook of sexual technique*, by John Warren; New American Library, New York, c1970; Signet T 4155.
252-1.   *Pleasure was my business*, by Madam Sherry as told to S. Robert Tralins; Paperback Library, New York, 1963; also Lyle Stuart, 1961. (Madam Sherry's name is Ruth Barnes.)
253-1.   *Couples*, by John Updike; Knopf, New York, 1968.
253-2.   *Myra Breckinridge*, by Gore Vidal; Little, Brown, Boston, c1968.
253-3.   *The love machine*, by Jacqueline Susann; Simon and Schuster, New York, 1969.

Pornography

254-1.   *Adam and Eve*, by Marcus Van Heller; Collectors Publications, Covina, Calif., 1967; p. 153.
255-1.   *Bishop's gambol*, by Roger Agile; The Traveller's Companion, New York, c1968.
256-1.   *Do it; Scenarios of the revolution*, by Jerry Rubin; introd. by Eldridge Cleaver; Simon and Schuster, New York, c1970.
257-1.   *Autobiography of a flea*; no publisher, place, or date.
257-2.   *A Catholic runs for president, the campaign of 1928*, by Edmund A. Moore; Ronald Press, New York, c1956.

(A chapter in the above title is devoted to anti-Catholicism during the campaign.)

258-1. *Censorship: the Irish experience*, by Michael William Adams; University of Alabama Press, University, Ala., 1968.

258-2. *Lolita*, by Vladimir Nobokov; G. P. Putnam, New York, 1955.

258-3. *The double-bellied companion*, by Akbar Del Piombo; 2 novellas; Traveller's Companion, 1967.

260-1. *The godfather*, directed by Francis Ford Coppola, 1972.

261-1. Merrick, 157-5.

261-2. Merrick, 158-1.

262-1. Cf. *Love's picture book; The history of pleasure and moral indignation*, by Ove Brusendorff and Poul Henningsen; trans. by H. B. Ward; Lyle Stuart, New York, c1960. 4 vols.

Obscenity

263-1. *Bible. O.T. Leviticus*, 15:16.

265-1. *Ball four; My life and hard times throwing the knuckleball in the big leagues*, by Jim Bouton; Dell, New York, c1970; also World Publishing.

265-2. *I'm glad you didn't take it personally*, by Jim Bouton; Dell, New York, c1971; also William Morrow.

267-1. Hayakawa, 3-1., p. 30.

268-1. *New York Times*, Feb. 28, 1963 (p. 1, col. 2) Madalyn Murray O'Hair's suit to ban prayer in public schools.
New York Times, June 18, 1963 (p. 1, col. 8) Report of Supreme Court's ruling on school prayer.
New York Times, April 7, 1964 (p. 9, col. 1) Murray demands Baltimore Education Board to delete reference to God in Pledge of Allegiance.
New York Times, July 2, 1964 (p. 17, col. 4) Maryland seeks to extradite Murray, her son, and mother from Hawaii for assaulting Baltimore policeman.
New York Times, July 23, 1964 (p. 56, col. 6) Murray gets 1 year jail term and $500 fine for contempt of court over son's marriage to Jewish girl.
New York Times, Aug. 19, 1964 (p. 26, col. 3) Hawaii Circuit Court denies Murray plea for habeas corpus writ, orders her and her son extradited to Baltimore, says order pending her appeal to Hawaii Supreme Court.
New York Times, Dec. 18, 1964 (p. 39, col. 4) Baltimore Judge Barnes dismisses suit by Murray and others against Maryland and Baltimore authorities for exempting church properties from taxes.

New York Times, Sept. 28, 1965 (p. 3, col. 7) Freed on bond, San Antonio, Texas, after arrest on Baltimore warrant for extradition on charges involving scuffle with police; says she will fight extradition.
New York Times, Oct. 13, 1965 (p. 61, col. 1) Gets 10 days to appeal Gov. Connally's extradition order.
New York Times, Nov. 6, 1965 (p. 13, col. 5) Maryland drops charges against her.
New York Times, Aug. 7, 1969 (p. 23, col. 7) Asks Federal Court, Austin, Texas, to bar U.S. astronauts from reading Bible in space.
New York Times, Aug. 16, 1969 (p. 10, col. 4) Federal Court grants her hearing on her suit to stop astronauts from conducting religious activities in space.
New York Times, Nov. 25, 1969 (p. 33, col. 3) Federal judges reject her motion that they disqualify themselves from hearing her suit against religious activities by astronauts in space because they were required to take oaths before they assumed office. She says she will appeal ruling to Supreme Court.
New York Times, May 5, 1970 (p. 1, col. 1) She backs suit by F. Waltz, who challenged New York State law exempting church property from taxation.
269-1.   *Unpopular essays*, by Bertrand Russell; Simon & Schuster, New York, 1951.

Chapter VII., Masquerade for Wolves
Political Orthodoxy

273-1.   *Confessions of a congressman*, by Jerry Voorhis; Garden City, New York, 1947.
273-2.   "Red smear in California," by Henry W. Flannery; *Commonweal*, 53:223-5, Dec. 8, 1950.
273-3.   *She*, directed by David Chantler, 1965.
274-1.   "The remarkable tornado," *Time*, 60:11-12, Sept. 29, 1952.
275-1.   Toffler, 180-2.
276-1.   "Vice is a monster of so frightful mien,
         "As to be hated needs but to be seen;
         "Yet seen too oft, familiar with her face,
         "We first endure, then pity, then embrace." Alexander Pope, *Essay on man*, Epistle II, lines 217-220.
277-1.   *Hitler was my friend*, by Heinrich Hoffmann; trans. by R. H. Stevens; Burke, London, 1955.
277-2.   *The great dictator*, directed by Charlie Chaplin, 1940.
277-3.   *Fact*, vol. 1, Sept., Oct., 1964.

278-1.   "Campaign teardrops," *Time*, 99:20+, March 13, 1972.

278-2.   Also attributed to Alice Roosevelt Longworth.

279-1.   *The essential Lenny Bruce*, compiled and ed. by John Cohen; Ballentine Books, New York, c1967.

279-2.   *American freedom and Catholic power*, by Paul Blanshard; Beacon Press, Boston, 1949.

280-1.   *Pentagon papers*, 3-5.

280-2.   "AAP files amicus brief for ex-CIA agent restrained from writing book on agency," *Publishers Weekly*, 201:113, June 5, 1972.

281-1.   *The FBI story; A report to the people*, by Don Whitehead; Random House, New York, 1956.

281-2.   *The FBI nobody knows*, by Fred J. Cook; Pyramid Books, New York, 1965; also Macmillan, c1964.

281-3.   *Hoover's FBI; The men and the myth*, by William W. Turner; Dell, New York, 1971; also Sherbourn Press, c1971.

281-4.   This information came from several different refugees who managed to escape from Burma and passed through Singapore while I was there. As friends of my brother-and sister-in-law, Mr. and Mrs. James Kyaw Hoe, the refugees had many stories to tell about life under Ne Win's dictatorship. They were on their way to Australia, on a Certificate of Identity, having been denied a passport or the privilege of returning to Burma.

282-1.   *Steal this book*, by Abbie Hoffman; Pirate Editions, New York, c1971; distributed by Grove Press.

283-1.   Rubin, 256-1.

283-2.   This information was given to me by my colleague, John Forsman.

283-3.   *Berkeley barb*, vol. 1, July 12, 1963–.

283-4.   *Screw*; subtitle varies; pub. by Milky Way Productions, 1969–.

Scientific Orthodoxy

285-1.   "Rise and fall of Lysenko," by E. W. Caspari and R. E. Marshak. *Science*, 149:275-278, July 16, 1965.

285-2.   "Immanuel Velikovsky–how much of yesterday's heresy is today's science?" special issue, *Pensee*, (pub. by Student Academic Freedom Forum with the assistance of Lewis and Clark College, Portland, Oregon) May, 1972; 2:no. 2.

285-3.   *Pensee*, 295-2., "A short biography," p. 5.

286-1.   "Day the sun stood still," by Eric Larrabee; *Harper's Magazine*, 200: 19-26, January, 1950. Discussion: *Harper's Magazine*, 200:18-19, March, 1950.

286-2. "Scientists in collision: Was Velikovsky right?" *Harper's Magazine*, 227:12+, Oct., 1963; 227:83-87, Dec., 1963.

287-1. "Theories denounced," *Science News Letter*, 57:119, Feb. 25, 1950.

287-2. "The day the earth stood still," (Review) by Cecilia Paine-Gaposchkin, *The Reporter*, 2:37-40 (March 14, 1950).

287-3. *Worlds in collision*, by Immanuel Velikovsky; Dell, New York, 1965; also Doubleday and Macmillan, c1950.

287-4. *Earth in upheaval*, by Immanuel Velikovsky, Doubleday, Garden City, New York, 1955.

288-1. *Pnesee*, 285-2.

288-2. Russell, 269-1.

289-1. "Minds in chaos," by Ralph E. Jeurgens, *American Behavioral Scientist*, 7:4-17 (Sept., 1963).

290-1. "Why do galaxies have a spiral form," by Cecilia Paine-Gaposchkin, *Scientific American*, 189:34, 89-99, Sept., 1953.

291-1. Velikovsky, 287-4.
      "Stellar populations and collisions of galaxies," by Lyman Spitzer and Walter Baade; *Astrophysical Journal*, 113:413-418, March, 1951.
      "Galaxies in collision," by Fritz Leiber; *Science Digest*, 29:69-72, Jan., 1951.

291-2. *On formally undecidable propositions of principia mathematica and related systems*, by Kurt Godel; Oliver & Boyd, Edinburgh, 1962.

291-3. *Dianetics; The modern science of mental health*, by La Fayette Ronald Hubbard; Hubbard, Auckland, New Zealand, 1959.

291-4. *Antioch Review*, 10:447-457, Dec., 1950.
      Nation, 171:131, Aug. 5, 1950.
      New Republic, 123:20, Aug. 14, 1950.
      New York Times, p. 9, July 2, 1950.
      Time, 56:64+, July 24, 1950.

291-5. *The humanoids*, ed. by Charles Bowen; Regnery, Chicago, 1970.
      Final report of the scientific study of unidentified flying objects, conducted by the University of Colorado under contract to the United States Air Force. University of Colorado; Dutton, New York, 1970.
      Chariots of the gods? Unsolved mysteries of the past, by Erich von Daniken; Putnam, New York, 1970.
      Flying saucers—here and now! by Frank Edwards; L. Stuart, Secaucus, N.J., 1968
      Flying saucers—serious business, by Frank Edwards; L. Stuart, Secaucus, N.J., 1966.
      The age of flying saucers; Notes on a projected history of unidentified flying objects, by Paris Flammonde; Hawthorne Books, New York, 1972.

Aliens in the skies; The scientific rebuttal to the Condon Committee Report, ed. by John G. Fuller; Putnam, New York, 1969.

The interrupted journey: Two hours "Aboard a flying saucer." by John G. Fuller; Dial Press, New York, 1967.

Incident at Exeter; The story of unidentified flying objects over America today, by John G. Fuller; Putnam, New York, 1966.

UFOs: Operation Trojan Horse, by John A. Keel, Putnam, New York, 1970.

Mysteries of the skies; UFOs in perspective, by Gordon I. R. Lore and Harold H. Deneault; Prentice-Hall, New York, 1969.

Uninvited visitors: A biologist looks at UFOs, by Ivan T. Sanderson; Cowles, Chicago, 1968.

Anatomy of a phenomenon; Unidentified objects in space— a scientific appraisal, by Jaques Vallee; Regnery, Chicago, 1966.

Passport to Magonia; From folklore to flying saucers, by Jaques Vallee; Regnery, Cahicgo, 1970.

Intercept—but don't shoot; The true story of flying saucers, by Renato Vesco; Grove, New York, 1971.

292-1.   "The problem of aerial navigation," by Simon Newcomb; *19th Century and After,* 64:430-432 (Sept., 1908).

292-2.   *New York Times,* Sept.,29, 1966 (p. 13, col. 1). "Dr. I. Velikovsky says mankind harbors in collective soul memory of cataclysmic events that shaped solar system, seeks to match them with development of weapons that can destroy earth, speech, Princeton University."

293-1.   *Nutrition against disease: Environmental protection,* by Roger J. Williams; Pitman, New York, c1971; pp. 229-301.

294-1.   "Moriturus," by Edna St. Vincent Millay; *Collected Lyrics*; Harder, New York, 1943; pp. 199-207.

295-1.   *Vitamin C and the common cold,* by Linus Carl Pauling; W. H. Freeman, San Francisco, 1970.

295-2.   *Selected writings, an introduction to orgonomy,* by Wilhelm Reich; Farrar, Straus, Cudahy, New York, 1960.

295-3.   *New York Times,* July 13, 1956 (p. 40, col. 7) "ACLU urges Food and Drug Administration not to destroy books by Dr. Reich; calls destruction censorship."

296-1.   *Microbiology and man,* by Jorgen Birkeland; Wilkins and Wilkins Company, Baltimore, 1942; p. 281.

297-1.   "Subject headings and the theory of classification," by Jay E. Daily; *American Documentation,* 8:269-274, Oct., 1957. The analogy was originally used in this article.

Orthodox History

297-2. *The analects of Confucius*, trans. and annotated by Arthur Waley;
        George Allen & Unwin, London, 1964.
298-1. *Frame-up; The Martin Luther King/James Earl Ray Case, containing
        suppressed evidence*, by Harold Weisberg with a postscript by James
        Earl Ray; Outerbridge and Dienstfrey, New York, c1969, 1971; dis-
        tributed by Dutton. Cf. *Whitewash; The report on the Warren Report*,
        by Harold Weisberg; published by the author, 1965. *Whitewash II; The
        FBI Secret Service cover-up*; published by the author, Hyattstown, Md.,
        c1966.
301-1. Weisberg, *Frame-up*, 298-1., pp. 312-431.
302-1. Turner, *Hoover's FBI*, 281-3., pp. 3-60.
302-2. Weisberg, *Frame-up*, 298-1., pp. 400, 424.
303-1. Kirkwood, 161-4., pp. 405-410.
304-1. Orwell, 179-1., p. 302.
305-1. *Edgar Cayce on Atlantis*, by Edgar Evans Cayce; Paperback Library,
        New York, c1968; pp. 54-656.
306-1. *The documents of Vatican II*. Vatican Council. 2d, 1962-1965. Guild
        Press, New York, c1966.
306-2. *A new catechism, the Catholic faith for adults*, by Higher Catechetical
        Institute, Nijmegen; Herder, New York, 1966; pp. 384-385.
307-1. Others calculated the period from the birth of Adam to the year
        A.D. 1 as 4,129 years, rather than 4,005 years in Usher's calculations.
        Radio-carbon dating have made this engaging exercise impractical.
        James Usher, or Ussher, 1581-1656, was an archbishop and chancellor
        of St. Patrick's Cathedral, Dublin.
307-2. *Beyond freedom and dignity*, by B. F. Skinner; Knopf, New York,
        1971.
308-1. Cf. *There is a river*, by Thomas Sugrue; Henry Holt, New York, c1942,
        1945. Also published as *The story of Edgar Cayce*, by Thomas Sugrue,
        Dell, New York, c1945; pp. 9-33, 135-161, 147, 150, 236, 290. *Edgar
        Cayce–the sleeping prophet*, by Jess Stearn; Bantam Books, New York,
        1968; also Doubleday, 1967; pp. 99-119.
310-1. "The road to Mandalay," by Rudyard Kipling.

Chapter IX., Intellectual Freedom and the World Community
Beyond Good and Evil

315-1. Rembar, 15-1.
316-1. *Stanley vs. Georgia*, 15-2.

316-2. *Out of the blue*, produced by Kermit Schaefer, 1971.
320-1. *Gay vigilante*, by Frederick Raborg; Greenleaf Classics, San Diego, Calif., c1972; Pleasure Reader, PR 357.
321-1. *Bible. O.T. Exodus*; 22:18.

The Information Avalanche

322-1. *Asimov's biographical encyclopedia of science and technology*, by Isaac Asimov; New Revised ed., Doubleday, Garden City, N.Y., 1972; pp. 366-368.
322-2. Weisberg, 298-1., *Whitewash*; pp. v-viii, pp. 188-212; *Whitewash II*; pp. 230-250.
326-1. *The murder of Christ* (Vol. 2 of *The emotional plague of mankind*), by Wilhelm Reich; Orgone Institute Press, Rangeley, Maine, 1953.
328-1. *La vie et l'oeuvre du Docteur W. Reich*, by Michel Cattier; L'Age de L'Homme. Lausanne, 10 Metropolis, Editions l'age d'homme—LA Cite, 1969.
328-2. *The mass psychology of fascism*, by Wilhelm Reich; newly trans. from the German by Vincent R. Carfagno; Farrar, Straus and Giroux, New York, 1970.
328-3. *The sexual revolution; Toward a self-governing character structure*, by Wilhelm Reich; trans. by Theodore P. Wolfe; Orgone Institute Press, New York, 1945.
328-4. *Character analysis; Principles and technique for psychoanalysts in practice and in training*, by Wilhelm Reich; trans. by Theodore P. Wolfe; Orgone Institute Press, New York, 1949.
328-5. *The function of the orgasm, sex-economic problems of biological energy*, by Wilhelm Reich; Noonday Press, New York, c1961.
328-6. *The invasion of compulsory sex-morality*, by Wilhelm Reich; Farrar, Straus and Giroux, New York, 1971.
329-1. *The Harrad experiment*, a novel by Robert Rimmer; Bantam Books, New York, 1967; also Sherbourn Press, c1966.
329-2. *WR; mysteries of the orgasm*, produced by Dusan Makavejev, 1971.
330-1. *Me and the orgone*, by Orson Bean; introd. by A. S. Neill; Fawcett Publications, Greenwich, Conn., 1972; reprint of St. Martin's Press edition, c1971.
332-1. *Congressional Digest*, 13:65-83.
334-1. Reich, 328-6.
335-1. *The true believer; thoughts on the nature of mass movements*, by Eric Hoffer; Harper, New York, 1951.

Toward a World of Peace

337-1. *The process of education*, by Jerome Bruner; Harvard University Press, Cambridge, Mass., 1960.
337-2. Multi-national Conference, Graduate School of Library and Information Sciences, University of Pittsburgh, 1970.
340-1. *U.S. Declaration of Independence*.
341-1. *Critique of the Gotha Program*, by Karl Marx; with Appendices by F. Engles and V. I. Lenin; International Publishers, New York, 1933.
342-1. "Thou has made me . . ." Holy Sonnets, I, lines 3 and 4 in Donne, 121-1.
343-1. "The American family: future uncertain." *Time*, 96:34-39, Dec. 28, 1970.
345-1. *Out of the blue*, 316-2.
345-2. EG, *Bible. N.T. St. John*, 8:11 ". . . And Jesus said unto her [the woman taken in adultery], Neither do I condemn thee; go, and sin no more.

INDEX